REALISM AND TRUTH

D1104429

B

Realism and Truth

Second Edition

MICHAEL DEVITT

BLACKWELL
Oxford UK & Cambridge USA

First published 1984, Second Edition 1991

Basil Blackwell, Inc.
3 Cambridge Center
Cambridge, Massachusetts 02142, USA

Basil Blackwell Ltd
108 Cowley Road, Oxford, OX4 1JF, UK

Library of Congress Cataloging in Publication Data

Devitt, Michael, 1938–
    Realism and truth/Michael Devitt.—2nd ed.
       p.   cm.
    Includes bibliographical references and index.
    ISBN 0-631-17551-2
    1. Realism.   2. Truth.   3. Science—Philosophy.   I. Title.
B835.D48   1991
149′.2—dc20   91-3062
                                                                    CIP

British Library Cataloguing in Publication Data

A CIP catalogue record for this book is available from
the British Library.

Typeset in 10½ on 12pt Baskerville
by Best-Set Typesetter Ltd.
Printed in Great Britain by
T.J. Press (Padstow) Ltd, Padstow, Cornwall.

This book is printed on acid-free paper.

Contents

Preface to the Second Edition

I am always trying to kick the habit of the realism issue. There is something a little shameful about spending one's time defending something so apparently humdrum as the independent existence of the familiar world. But the provocations are so great, and my flesh is too weak. The chaos of the realism debate has deepened since I wrote the first edition. Dozens of different metaphysical, semantic, and epistemological theses jostle for the name 'realism' (e.g. see the nine senses of 'realism' in Haack 1987). The British School continues to write as if *the* realism issue were all a matter of what a speaker can or cannot 'manifest'. There is no sign that the 'sociologists of knowledge' are anywhere near distinguishing epistemology from metaphysics. Hilary Putnam ingeniously derives anti-realism from just about everything. And so on, and on and on. As John Heil remarks in a survey, 'anti-realist tracts overwhelm both in number and in sheer density a steady but comparatively modest realist output' (1989: 65). Why is it so? Why is anti-realism an occupational hazard of philosophy? My former colleague David Stove has some witty and unflattering answers in his recent book (1991).

Though anti-realism may seem to be everywhere, Heil points out that 'Australia, isolated and out of the loop evolutionarily, continues as stronghold of realists and marsupials' (p. 65). I remarked on this in the preface to the first edition. Barry Taylor protested (1987: 45), and rightly so: there is indeed a small anti-realist enclave in Melbourne where the sun does not shine so much.

Aside from the provocations, my habit has been sustained by several agreeable invitations to give talks or write papers on realism. These have led to the following publications: a review of Passmore 1985 (1986); 'Realism without Truth: A Response to Bertolet' (1988a); 'Rorty's Mirrorless World' (1988b); 'Aberrations of the Realism Debate' (1991a); 'Realism without Representation: A

viii   *Preface to the Second Edition*

Response to Appiah' (1991c). Finally, the habit was sustained by
Stephan Chambers' request that I undertake this new edition for
Basil Blackwell.

Most of the contents of the above publications have been incor-
porated into this edition. A lot of other new material has been added
as well. The book has been revised throughout to take account of
recent literature and some changes in my views. In making these
revisions, I have tried to respect the integrity of the original. All in
all, something like half this edition was not in the first.

The Rorty paper yielded the new chapter 11, which removes an
obvious deficiency in the first edition. I argue that, contrary to
common opinion, Rorty is not anti-realist. My disagreements with
him are over truth, reference, and the future of philosophy. These
disagreements led me to add a maxim to the four already urged in
the book: distinguish the issue of correspondence truth from any
epistemic issue.

A central thesis of the first edition was that the metaphysical issue
of realism has almost nothing to do with semantic issues about
correspondence truth and reference. This thesis is vital to the defence
of realism, for it is much easier to argue for realism than for any
semantic doctrine. I think that my separation of realism and truth
is the most distinctive thing about my book. It does not seem to
have won many converts, however. In this edition, I have argued for
the thesis more thoroughly and, I think, much better (chapter 4).
Related to this, I have greatly improved my discussion of deflationary truth (section 3.4).

I do not distinguish correspondence truth from realism in order to
drop it. A full defence of correspondence truth would show why we
are *entitled* to it. That is too big a task for a book like this. However,
in the first edition, I did attempt to say why we *needed* correspondence truth. Not surprisingly, staunchly realist reviewers like Frank
Jackson tended to focus on this chapter. Jackson remarked that it
was 'uncharacteristically tentative' (1986: 536). Just as well. I had
barely sent the book off before I started having second thoughts. The
discussion in this edition is mostly new (chapter 6).

My views on realism have not changed. They arise from naturalism and physicalism. The latter doctrines are what Putnam is rejecting in saying that 'scientism is . . . one of the most dangerous
contemporary intellectual tendencies' (1983: 211). How far he has
travelled since he influenced so many of us in the 1960s! I have a
candidate for *the* most dangerous contemporary intellectual tendency.
Sadly, it is a doctrine that Putnam himself embraces: construc-

tivism. Constructivism is a combination of two Kantian ideas with twentieth-century relativism. The two Kantian ideas are, first, that we make the known world by imposing concepts, and, second, that the independent world is (at most) a mere 'thing-in-itself' for ever beyond our ken. Putnam's relativism is conservative, and so constructivism may seem rather benign in his hands. It may even seem so in Nelson Goodman's. But consider its role in France, in the social sciences, in literature departments, and in some largely well-meaning, but confused, political movements. Constructivism has led to a veritable epidemic of 'worldmaking'. It attacks the immune system that saves us from silliness.

The first edition did not have a unified or thorough discussion of constructivism and worldmaking. This edition does: chapter 13. Trying to make sense of constructivism leads to a discussion of artifacts, tools, social entities, and secondary qualities, as well as further reflection on the type of independence that realism requires of its entities.

Since the first edition, Bas van Fraassen has replied to his critics (1985). I have expanded my discussion of his views to take account of these replies (sections 8.5–8.7).

Donald Davidson is an elusive figure. I had him wrong in two ways: first, I made what I know see to have been a straightforward error in concluding that he was anti-realist; second, I did not see that the Davidsonian view of reference that I was criticizing arose from a perspective on the semantic task that was radically different from mine. His perspective has since become much clearer to me, partly as a result of an interesting and forthright paper, 'The Structure and Content of Truth' (1990). I have rewritten chapter 10 to correct these two errors.

My discussion of Michael Dummett and the British School remains largely unchanged (chapter 14). In so far as I know of responses to criticisms like mine, I have taken account of them. However, the School seems fairly indifferent to the outside world.

Finally, I have added sections on three matters: Simon Blackburn's idea of 'quasi-realism' (4.8); inference to the best explanation, or 'abduction' (7.2); and the classical empiricist argument against scientific realism arising from the alleged underdetermination of theories by evidence (7.4).

Michael Devitt
January 1991

Preface to the First Edition

I have always been a realist about the external world. Such realism is common in Australia. Some say that Australian philosophers are born realists. I prefer to attribute our realism to nurture rather than nature. David Armstrong has suggested (lightly) that the strong sunlight and harsh brown landscape of Australia force reality upon us. In contrast, the mists and gentle green landscape of Europe weaken the grip on reality.

Realism was confirmed in me by my early teachers: Graham Nerlich, David Armstrong, and Charlie Martin. The first major influence on the present shape of my realism was Hilary Putnam, in lectures at Harvard in the late sixties. The second, at the same time, was the writings of W. V. Quine. From Putnam and Quine I derived, *inter alia*, my view of philosophy and of the place of epistemology in it.

The third major influence was Hartry Field. The influence of his published work on my thought is obvious. Aside from that, we began talking at Harvard and have been talking and corresponding on and off ever since. The help and encouragement I have got from this have been enormous. My thinking has meshed with his so often that it is now impossible for me to identify many of my debts. One that is vital to the present work can, however, be identified. His doubts about truth in discussions in 1978 set me firmly on the path to disentangling the semantic issue of truth from the metaphysical issue of realism.

Shortly after those discussions I read an article by Stephen Leeds, 'Theories of Reference and Truth' (1978), which took me further down that path. Leeds' paper was the fourth and final major influence on the shape of my realism.

Though I wish to separate truth from realism, I want to defend both. And the notion of truth I want to defend is a robust 'correspondence' notion explained in terms of reference. Some of that defence is to be found in my previous book, *Designation* (1981a), which offers a 'causal' theory of reference. However, when I wrote that book, I had not clearly separated truth from realism or clearly grasped the very difficult problem of saying why we need truth.

My enthusiasm for truth is at odds with Quine's scepticism about semantics and the mind. Though I have often been bothered by Quine's arguments for indeterminacy of translation and inscrutability of reference, I have never been convinced by them (and even less by those for the apparently anti-realist position of 'ontological relativity'). Sometimes these arguments seem to rest on an implausible verificationism and behaviourism. However, one powerful Quinean argument rests only on physicalism, as Leeds shows in the aforementioned article. A major concern of this book is to argue that a physicalist needs, and is entitled to, truth.

Work on this book began, in effect, in 1974, when I delivered the first version of the paper 'Against Incommensurability' (1979). That paper was prompted by discussions with several Sydney philosophers of the views of Thomas Kuhn, Paul Feyerabend, and Louis Althusser. These views are 'soft' on truth and realism, and yet they have many attractive features.

The next stimulus to the book was provided by comments on the first draft of *Designation*. These led me in 1978 into a thorough examination of various popular views in the philosophy of language. This led in turn to Part II of the final version of *Designation* and to the awareness that my disagreement with those views, particularly those of Donald Davidson and Michael Dummett, required further discussion. My paper 'Dummett's Anti-Realism' (1983a) was one result of this awareness.

Finally I was prompted to action by Putnam's book *Meaning and the Moral Sciences* (1978). The prompt came first from the shock of discovering that Putnam too had joined the opposition. Secondly it came from the baffling nature of the book. What, according to Putnam, was realism? What had it to do with truth? What had it to do with convergence? What had reference to do with truth? I found no clear answers in the book; but struggling with the questions forced me to be much clearer in my own mind. The struggle also led to a critical notice (1980a) and a critical study (1983b).

Once started on the book, I received stimulus from discussions and seminars at the universities of Sydney, Southern California, and Michigan, and from other recent books. I have written reviews of van Fraassen 1980 (1982) and Putnam 1981 (1984b) and a critical study of French, Uehling, and Wettstein 1980 (1983c). I delivered a paper, 'Does Realism Explain Success?' at the annual conference of the Australasian Association of Philosophers in Adelaide in August 1983.

I have included modified and edited versions of these earlier works (except *Designation*) in the present work. They constitute about one quarter of the total.

It once seemed to me that everyone now writing about realism (though not, I thought, the silent majority of philosophers) was approaching the issue in the wrong way and that, as a result, anti-realism was rampant. As I wrote the book, I discovered that this was not the case: other voices were crying in the wilderness. Some with whom I am in varying degrees sympathetic are William Alston (1979), Alan Goldman (1979), Paul Horwich (1982), Michael Levin (1984), and Roger Trigg (1980).

I think I have discussed most of the influential contemporary forms of anti-realism. However, for a variety of reasons, some such forms are discussed only briefly or in passing. In particular this is true of the views of Nelson Goodman, Richard Rorty, and some contemporary Marxists. I mean no disrespect by this slight treatment.

Further acknowledgements are appropriate. Some of these were made in the aforementioned publications which were the basis for part of this work, and have not been repeated. Some have been made in the notes. Some, I'm afraid, have been forgotten. Aside from those, I am grateful first to the following for comments on early drafts of parts of this book: David Armstrong, Hartry Field, Peter Forrest, David Lewis, William Lycan, J. J. C. Smart, and David Stove. Second, I am grateful to the following for commenting on the penultimate draft: John Bigelow, Keith Campbell, Gregory Currie, Gilbert Harman, and Kim Sterelny. Perhaps I would have been wiser to have taken their advice more often that I have. Finally, I am grateful to Anthea Bankoff for her enthusiasm, good humour, and efficiency in typing the drafts.

Part I
Introduction

1

Introduction

1.1 MAXIMS

What *is* realism about the external world? One of the most striking aspects of the current debate is that no clear, let alone single, answer to this question shines through. In particular it is often hard to see what is supposed to *be* realism and what is supposed to be *an argument for* it, especially when the subject is scientific realism. I think that a successful defence of realism depends on being very clear about the difference between the constitutive and the evidential issues. Accordingly I urge:

> *Maxim 1* In considering realism, distinguish the constitutive and evidential issues.

This book is concerned not only with the metaphysical – in particular, ontological – issue of realism, but also with the semantic issue of truth. In recent times it has become common to identify these issues or to approach the former from a perspective on the latter. I think this is a mistake. The metaphysical issue of realism is the fundamental one in our theory of the largely impersonal world. Semantic issues arise only in our theory of people (and their like) in their relations to that world. Accordingly I urge:

> *Maxim 2* Distinguish the metaphysical (ontological) issue of realism from any semantic issue.

The main traditional arguments against realism about the commonsense world have come from an *a priori* epistemology, though it has often been possible to see semantics (the theory of meaning) lurking in the background. From the epistemic perspective for which I shall argue – naturalized epistemology – these arguments put the epistemic cart before the realist horse.

The main contemporary arguments against realism have come from an *a priori* semantics, though it has usually been possible to see epistemology lurking in the background. From the semantic perspective for which I shall argue – naturalized semantics – these arguments put the semantic cart before the realist horse.

Accordingly, I urge:

> *Maxim 3* Settle the realism issue before any epistemic or semantic issue.

(This maxim is oversimplified because realism, though largely metaphysical, *is* a little bit epistemic and semantic: the world must be independent of our knowledge of it and of our capacity to refer to it. So at least that much epistemology and semantics must be settled to settle realism.)

Once these carts have been restored to their rightful places, realism becomes, I think, a somewhat boring doctrine, perhaps even a little vulgar. I am not bothered by this, or even by comparisons with 'village atheism' (Putnam 1978: 20). I think that a certain amount of vulgarity is appropriate in approaching the realism issue (and the religion issue too, for that matter).

The distinct issue of truth is far from boring. Do we need, and are we entitled to, a correspondence notion of truth? What does such a notion explain? These are very difficult question. Accordingly I urge:

> *Maxim 4* In considering the semantic issue, don't take truth for granted.

The claim that a sentence is correspondence-true is often taken to entail something about whether or how we can *tell* if it is true. In particular, the claim is often thought to conflict with the view that our judgements of truth are theory-laden. I shall argue that this is not so. Accordingly, I urge:

> *Maxim 5* Distinguish the issue of correspondence truth from any epistemic issue.

1.2 SUMMARY

Part II of the book is constructive: I argue for the main theses I propose. In Part III, using this background, I adopt a critical stance toward the views of many contemporary philosophers. This will lead to further development of, and argument for, the theses of Part II. In Part IV I state conclusions.

In chapter 2 I describe the doctrine of realism that I aim to defend. It has two dimensions: (1) a view of what exists – the physical entities of common sense and science; (2) a view of their nature – independence from the mental. I distinguish realism from physicalism.

In chapter 3 I describe the notion of truth that I aim to defend. It is a 'correspondence' notion which is stronger than a mere 'deflationary' notion. It is an explanatory notion which is itself explained in terms of genuine referential relations between words and the world. These relations must be explained in turn. The only hope, ultimately, is for causal theories of reference. I distinguish the correspondence notion of truth from epistemic notions like warranted assertability (Maxim 5).

In chapter 4 I argue that doctrines of truth have little to do with realism. No doctrine of truth is constitutive of realism: there is no entailment from the one doctrine to the other (Maxim 2). Further, I argue for a view of ontological commitment which shows that it is a mistake to think that the issue of realism can be stated clearly only as an issue of interpretation. The possibility of quasi-realism should not change this conclusion.

In chapter 5 I argue for common-sense realism. I set out Cartesian scepticism, claiming that it leads to a world no richer than that of 'instantaneous solipsism'. I reject all foundationalist attempts to defeat scepticism, and hence all arguments for or against realism from the foundationalist perspective. I describe Kantian anti-realism, postponing major discussion until chapter 13. I argue for realism by rejecting *a priori* epistemology. Epistemology is made subsidiary to science and metaphysics (Maxim 3): it is naturalized. From this perspective the case for realism is very strong. Scepticism is seen, in the final analysis, as unanswerable, but uninteresting. I finish by arguing that scientific realism does not undermine common-sense realism.

In chapter 6 I consider the deep and difficult question of truth. Why do we need truth, and what entitles us to have it? *Entitlement* to a correspondence notion of truth must come from the above-mentioned explanations of reference. Though it may seem obvious that we *need* an explanatory notion of truth, it is hard to see why we need it. Much of truth's role can be accounted for by taking it not as explanatory but as deflationary. Further, drawing on Quine's semantic scepticism, Stephen Leeds has described a realist world-view that is austerely physicalist and has no place for an explanatory notion of truth (Maxim 4). What is it that we might require truth to explain? It must be something about people (and other believer-desirers) and their language. Yet it seems that we do not need truth to explain either behaviour or the success of behaviour. What we need it for, I suggest, is to describe and explain the properties of *symbols* that enable them to play a variety of social roles.

In chapter 7 I argue for scientific realism. We need to posit the unobservables of scientific realism in order to explain the behaviour and characteristics of observed entities. The earlier arguments about the need for, and entitlement to, truth can then be extended to scientific statements. Putnam has made popular the idea that the main argument for realism is that it explains the success of theories at the observational level. (This success is very different from the above behavioural success). There is some truth in this idea, but what scientific realism primarily explains is the observed world, rather than observational success. Putnam has also linked convergence to realism (and some have identified the two; cf. Maxim 1). The links are weak, I argue, except in one respect to be considered later. I reject a classical empiricist argument against scientific realism arising from the alleged underdetermination of theories by evidence. I briefly discuss operationism and instrumentalism, and conclude by indicating the variety of epistemic attitudes to theories that the realist encourages.

Chapters 4–7 exemplify, and to a degree argue for, commitment to Maxim 3: settle the realism issue before any epistemic or semantic issue. Exemplification and argument continue throughout the polemics of Part III.

Bas van Fraassen (1980) is a common-sense realist, but an anti-scientific-realist. Yet he rejects both positivistic epistemology and semantics, leaving the motivation for his anti-realism unclear. I argue, in chapter 8, part I, that this anti-realism requires observation to have an epistemic significance it cannot have. We can learn about objects that affect us indirectly, just as we can learn about objects that affect us directly in the way we call observation. This is particularly obvious when we consider senses other than that of sight. In part II, I consider van Fraassen's response to his critics (1985). I argue that his response exemplifies an unjustified selective scepticism against unobservables.

Thomas Kuhn, Paul Feyerabend, and other radical philosophers of science are obviously opposed to a correspondence notion of truth, but their position on realism is less clear. In chapter 9 I argue that they are implicitly committed to 'constructivism', a relativistic Kantian anti-realism. Any plausibility that this position has must come from the difficulties their argument raises for realism. These difficulties stem from a certain meta-induction: from our present perspective, the entities posited in the past can be seen not to exist; so it is likely that, from some future perspective, the entities now posited will be seen not to exist. I claim that this argument has no force against common-sense realism. Though it is a powerful argument against scientific realism, I claim that the realist has several defences against it. The radicals' opposition to truth stems from their incommensurability thesis. I argue against this thesis from the already established realist perspective. I return to the issue of convergence. Finally I consider several radical objections to my views.

Donald Davidson and John McDowell make use of an explanatory notion of truth, but argue against Hartry Field that truth itself does not need to be explained in terms of reference, and hence that reference does not need to be explained (e.g. causally). In chapter 10 I argue first that, from a perspective that takes semantics to be concerned with a factual realm open to ordinary scientific investigation, their position is an implausible combination of 'semanticalism' about truth and instrumentalism about reference. However, the Davidsonians seem to have a different, 'interpretative' perspective on semantics. I argue that this perspective is mistaken in its view of the semantic task and in its commitment to principles of charity and rationality. I conclude by pointing out that, despite this commitment, Davidson is a realist.

In chapter 11 I consider Rorty. I have two objections to his position and one worry about it. Objection 1: freeing ourselves from the sceptical problematic does not require abandoning a strong correspondence theory of truth in favour of Davidsonian semantics (Maxim 5); the correspondence theory is part of an empirical theory of language. Objection 2: philosophy should not become hermeneutics; philosophy has a systematic and constructive task in theorizing about mind, language, and other matters. Worry: there is an aura of anti-realism about Rorty's discussion. However, once realism is sharply distinguished from semantics, this aura is seen to be misleading: Rorty is a realist.

In chapter 12 I start by rejecting Hilary Putnam's argument against reference from the interest-relativity of explanation. However, my main concern is with the view of realism that Putnam has developed in recent years. I reject his model-theoretic argument against realism, pointing out that it begs the question. I begin the criticism of Putnam's new anti-realism, which is a form of constructivism. I conclude by responding to a common idea, urged by Putnam, that realism requires a 'God's Eye View'. This mistaken idea explains the above question-begging.

Chapter 13 is primarily concerned with constructivism, which is the metaphysics of the radical philosophers of science, Putnam, Goodman, and many many others. Taken literally, constructivist talk of our making worlds by imposing concepts is absurd; but a metaphorical interpretation proves impossible to sustain. Constructivists blur the crucial distinction between theories and the world. I offer a tentative diagnosis. I go on to examine entities that, in interesting respects, we do 'make': tools and entities classified by their social and secondary properties. This throws more light on the independence dimension of realism. It is also relevant to an interesting route to constructivism proposed by Putnam: generalize a Lockean account of secondary properties to all properties. This route does not make constructivism plausible, but it comes closer than any other to making it seem rational.

Perhaps the most influential contemporary argument against realism is that of Michael Dummett. In chapter 14 I claim that this argument has three premises:

> A   The realism dispute is the dispute about whether statements have realist (evidence-transcendent) or only verificationist truth conditions.

This premise is opposed to Maxim 2 and is, in effect, argued against in chapter 4. Dummett's argument for it is minimal.

> B   The dispute about truth conditions is the dispute about whether the competent speaker's understanding is realist (evidence-transcendent) or only verificationist.
>
> C   The competent speaker's understanding is only verificationist.

I distinguish two versions of B, and hence two of C, which Dummett conflates. B_1 and C_1 are based on the assumption that linguistic competence involves propositional knowledge of truth conditions. B_2 and C_2 see competence as merely a practical ability. I argue that Dummett gives the 'propositional assumption' about competence no adequate support and that it is false. So B_1 and C_1 are false. Verificationist arguments to show that speakers do not *know* realist truth conditions are irrelevant to realist truth. I go on to consider competence as a practical ability. Interest then centres on C_2, the view that the sentences understood by the competent speaker *have* only verificationist truth conditions. I set out Dummett's argument for this, and reject it. I argue that, in any case, verificationism has little bearing on realism. Theories of language and understanding should not determine theories of the world.

In chapter 15, the only chapter of Part IV, I state conclusions, concentrating on giving the inferences to best explanation ('abductions') that I think are good.

Part II
Proposals

2

What is Realism?

2.1 INTRODUCTION

My concern in this chapter is to describe the traditional doctrine of
realism about the external world, a doctrine that has always seemed
so plausible to reflective common sense. I am not concerned with
other realisms. In particular, I am not concerned with realism about
abstract entities such as properties, types, or numbers.

There is not, or course, just one traditional doctrine of realism
about the external world: there is a range of related doctrines. My
aim is not to settle on one of these, but rather to settle on a description, actually two descriptions, that are loose enough to cover at least
the important part of the range. I shall not be bothered that my use
of 'realism' will remain a bit vague, provided the limits of vagueness
have been roughly marked out and provided the doctrines described
are clearly distinct from various other doctrines, to be introduced
later, that might be regarded as *reasons for* believing the realist doctrines (Maxim 1).

R. J. Hirst has given the following account of the traditional
doctrine in *The Encyclopedia of Philosophy*:

The view that material objects exist externally to us and independently of
our sense experience. Realism is thus opposed to idealism, which holds that
no such material objects or external realities exist apart from our knowledge
or consciousness of them, the whole universe thus being dependent on the
mind or in some sense mental. (Hirst 1967: 77)

My characterization of realism will be along these lines.

Various influences, including those of the positivists and Michael
Dummett, lead many contemporary philosophers to regard this way
of approaching realism as old-fashioned. The realism dispute, it is
thought, must be approached from within a theory of language or
meaning. It is important to distinguish two different responses here.

Some philosophers respond to a statement like Hirst's with a yawn. They think that nobody – at least, nobody sophisticated – denies realism in that sense. The interesting question about realism is a different one, a question about meaning and truth conditions. So, according to this response, the traditional doctrine called 'realism' is true but boring, and is not to be confused with a quite different but interesting doctrine now called 'realism'.

I have two comments on this response. First, it is certainly the case that some philosophers have denied realism in Hirst's sense: the idealists did. More to the point, I think that Dummett denies it, as I shall argue (in sections 14.2 and 14.3). And it is largely because he is thought to deny it that his philosophy has attracted so much attention. Second, we must never forget what is conceded in this first response as we consider arguments to establish doctrines that it is now thought are appropriately called 'anti-realism'. In my view, the boring truth that is here conceded can be used to undermine these arguments (Maxim 3).

Some philosophers respond differently to a statement like Hirst's. They think that it may do for a start, but that it is little more than a metaphor. Progress requires that we see the traditional dispute over realism in a quite different light: the way to understand it is as a dispute about meaning and truth conditions. From this perspective the traditional doctrine of realism does not seem boring and true but, rather, controversial and very likely false. I take this to be Dummett's view. It is a central thesis of this book (Maxim 2; chapters 4 and 14) that realism is quite distinct from any semantic doctrine. So in this chapter I shall follow Hirst in ignoring truth in characterizing realism.

Finally, some philosophers seem tempted to try to have it both ways: on the one hand, to say that the traditional doctrine of realism is distinct from a doctrine about meaning and truth; on the other, that it is a metaphorical version of it (e.g. Genova 1988).

Hirst brings out well the two dimensions of realism: a claim about what entities exist and a claim about their independent nature. I shall consider each dimension in turn, starting with the latter.

2.2 THE INDEPENDENCE DIMENSION

Key terms that feature in statements of this dimension of realism are 'independent', 'external', and 'objective'. Hirst uses the first two, and when he says that material objects exist 'apart from our

knowledge . . . of them', he might just as well have used the third. For
an object has objective existence, in some sense, if it exists and has its
nature whatever we believe, think, or can discover: it is independent
of the cognitive activities of the mind.

To say that an object has objective existence is not to say that it is
unknowable. It is to say that it is not *constituted by* our knowledge,
by our epistemic values, by our capacity to refer to it, by the syn-
thesizing power of the mind, by our imposition of concepts, theories,
or languages. Many worlds lack this sort of objectivity: Kant's
'phenomenal' world (5.6), Dummett's verifiable world (14.2), the
stars made by a Goodman 'version' (13.3), the constructed world
of Putnam's 'internal realism' (12.5), Kuhn's world of theoretical
ontologies (9.2), and the many worlds created by the 'discourses' of
structuralists and post-structuralists.

The extent to which and the manner in which we can come to
know about an object are, for the realist, epistemic issues which are
quite distinct from ontological questions about the object.

Would it be sufficient, then, to characterize the required independent existence of entities as objective existence? It would not, because
on some views mental entities have such existence. It seems, for
example, as if the unsensed sense data of some empiricists, and
Kant's pre-conceptualized intuitions, have objective existence in the
above sense (Ruben 1977: 20). Further, some contemporary physicalists think that any mental entities there may be have this existence.
They reject both the 'incorrigibility thesis' and the 'self-intimation
thesis' about the mental. According to the first thesis, a person
cannot be wrong about his mental states; according to the second, he
cannot be ignorant of them (Armstrong 1968a: 101). A person who
rejects these theses – and in my view recent work in the philosophy of
mind suggests that they should be rejected – thinks that whether or
not a mental entity exists is an altogether separate question from
whether or not anyone believes it exists: it is an objective question. In
the light of this, if a person is to be able to state her commitment
to a *non-mental* external world, she must talk of more than objective
existence. Otherwise her position is indistinguishable from a form of
idealism: the doctrine that the only reality is an objectively existing
mental one.

For the realist, the material or physical world he believes in must
exist not only objectively, but non-mentally. We can roughly distinguish two aspects of this: (1) the world does not consist in mental
objects of experience, either in 'ideas', as idealists like Berkeley
thought, or in 'sense data', as many phenomenalists thought; (2) the

world is not made up of minds, as Leibniz thought, or of something ultimately spiritual, as the absolute idealists thought. Both (1) and (2) are well enough covered by saying that, for the realist, the world exists *independently of the mental*.[1]

There is a minor problem about this characterization of independence. Part of the independent world that the realist believes in is made up of higher animals like people. It may be that the realist will think that an object would not be a person if it lacked a mind. That is the likely view of two common sorts of realist: non-eliminative physicalists and dualists. For such a realist, a person does not exist independently of the mental. The problem is only minor, because the defence of a realism that did not cover the higher animals would be sufficient for our purposes. The belief in those animals would then be something additional to realism. I shall not complicate the characterization to take account of the problem. Rather, I shall ignore the problem, assuming that realism does cover these animals.

If an object exists independently of the mental, then it can exist unobserved. The realist rejects *esse est percipi* for the objects he believes in. No object that is tied to perception for its very existence has the required independence.

We have seen that mere talk of objective existence does not give the required independence from the mental in the characterization of realism. Does talk of independence give the required objectivity? It seems not. Kant's phenomenal world and Dummett's verifiable world lack objectivity, but may satisfy the requirement of independence described in (1) and (2). So, at the insignificant risk of overkill, it seems best to talk of both objectivity and independence in characterizing realism.

I have written as if all dependencies of reality on mind and opinion alleged by anti-realists were intelligible. In fact, I doubt this. However, I want to rest nothing on the claim that an anti-realist dependency claim is unintelligible. In so far as it is intelligible, I argue that it is false. In so far as it is unintelligible, the realist needs no argument to dismiss it.

Finally, in asserting the independence and objectivity of the world, the realist does not mean to deny certain familiar causal relations involving minds. Beliefs, desires, sensations, and so forth cause behaviour which affects external reality, even creating some items (offspring). And reality acts on minds, causing beliefs, desires, sensations, and so on. These relations, long noted by folk theory and studied by science, pose no threat to realism.

I shall return to the discussion of the independence dimension in chapter 13.

In the next section I shall consider the further dimension of realism: what entities the realist claims exist. In the section after that I shall bring together the two dimensions, and attempt a statement of realism.

2.3 THE EXISTENCE DIMENSION

The very weakest form of realism is completely unspecific about what exists; it requires only that *something* does. When the independence dimension is added, this 'weak realism' amounts simply to the claim that something objectively exists independently of the mental. This commits realism only to an undifferentiated, uncategorized, external world, a Kantian 'thing-in-itself'. The position is of contemporary interest, because many philosophers who call themselves realists, particularly those impressed by the 'radical' philosophy of science, are committed to nothing stronger than this. (9.2).

The weak realist's world is one that perhaps even Nelson Goodman would allow, a world 'without kinds or order or motion or rest or pattern'. As Goodman points out, this world 'is not worth fighting for' (1978: 20). What difference does believing in it make? It is a world we cannot know about or talk about. It cannot play a role in explaining any phenomenon. It is an idle addition to idealism: anti-realism with a fig-leaf.

A tiny move in the right direction is to say that the world consists not just of something, but of a structured set of entities. This yields a realism that is still to weak, for it does not require the existence of any familiar objects, but simply a Kantian noumenal world of 'things-in-themselves'.

A significant move in the right direction comes with the description of the world to which the realist is committed as that of common-sense physical or material objects; for example, stones, trees, and cats. We would also want realism to cover common-sense stuff like water. Let us use the word 'entity' to cover objects and stuff. And let us use 'physical' to cover physical and material entities (between which there may well be no difference). Then we make realism much more specific by committing it to the existence of common-sense physical entities.

Should artifacts and tools – hammers, pencils, chairs, and the like – be included in the entities that realism is committed to? These entities raise interesting issues about independence which will be taken up later (13.5). Meanwhile, realism should not be taken as applying to these entities.

With the advance of science, realists have committed themselves to further entities, those apparently posited by our scientific theories. These are of two sorts. One sort is like common-sense physical entities in being *observable*, but unlike them in being remote from everyday life – for example, rare molluscs and the moons of Jupiter. These scientific entities have not been thought to pose any problem for realism beyond that posed by the common-sense ones. By contrast, entities of the other sort, *unobservable* entities, have been thought to pose special problems. Examples are such scientific posits as electrons, muons, and curved space-time. Instrumentalists and operationists are realist about observable entities, but anti-realist about unobservable ones; they are against 'scientific realism' (7.7 and 7.8). (Instrumentalism and operationism both consist also of semantic doctrines. Partly as a result of this, the term 'scientific realism' is often used, misleadingly in my view, for positions opposed to those semantic doctrines; see 4.1.)

I shall write as if the distinction between observable and unobservable entities were clear and useful, though I think there are reasons for doubting this (8.4). The distinction does not matter to me, for I attach no epistemic significance to it. I think we should be realist about the observable and the unobservable alike.

We have gone far enough along the road to making realism specific about its entities. In doing so, we have raised another problem. What quantifier should we use to state realism? We certainly do not want to say that *all* common-sense and scientific physical entities exist. Examples like flying saucers and phlogiston show that such a doctrine would certainly be false. Not only would it be false; it would be unnecessary. It is no skin off the nose of the realist that we occasionally make mistaken posits. We need to be more cautious. However, it is not enough to say that only *some* common-sense and scientific physical entities exist. The realism that is worth fighting for holds that we are *more or less right* in the physical entities we posit. It is committed to the existence of *most* of those entities.

This seems to adopt too uncritical an attitude to the posits of common-sense and scientific theories. Indeed, two sorts of criticism are appropriate. The first is a particularly philosophical one. Apparent posits may not be real posits, or they may not be necessary. We consider how the entity apparently posited would fit into *the landscape as a whole* (Sellars 1963: 4). We consider whether the purposes of the theorist could be served well enough without that entity. For, in ontology, the less the better.

Hartry Field has provided an example of such a critical approach.

He argues that though science apparently posits numbers, it need not posit them: its purposes could be served just as well without them (1980, 1989). (If he is wrong, and I hope he isn't, then numbers presumably count as physical entities, for they are apparently posited by physics. In which case they would be abstract physical entities, which are not the concern of my realism: see (2.1.)

The second sort of criticism is epistemic. Scientists do not take the same epistemic attitude to all theories, even to the ones they 'accept'. Attitudes range from strong belief, through mild belief and agnosticism, to outright disbelief. The realist can go along with this. He even sees an instrumentalist aspect to science; the ostensible subject-matters of some theories are 'mere models' (7.9). However, he thinks that what science aims for is theories to believe. It is the entities posited by the theories we believe that the realist is interested in. He is committed to the existence of most of these *confident* posits.[2]

This may seem to saddle the realist with an overly conservative view of science: he seems to be overlooking scientific *change* and committing himself heavily to current science.

I do not think the realist can accept the view of scientific change suggested by Kuhn and Feyerabend. (I shall argue against it in chapter 9.) According to this view, with each radical theory change goes a change in ontology. As a result, from the perspective of the new theory, the entities of its predecessor do not exist. Suppose this were so. A certain 'meta-induction' (Putnam 1978: 25) would become compelling: the entities of present theories do not exist from the perspective of some theory we shall adopt in the future. So we have no reason to suppose these entities exist. Anti-realism would be more plausible than realism.

This line of thought prevents any realist retreat from the apparently conservative commitment to the entities of current science to, say, commitment to the entities of an ideal future science. In so far as we have reason for supposing that the entities of an ideal future science will not include those of current science, that reason comes from the above meta-induction. If we accept that meta-induction, then we should be altogether anti-realist about actual science. Furthermore, in so far as future entities are not the present ones, it is *idle* for us now to be realist about them. Such entities are, for us, mere Kantian things-in-themselves which play no explanatory role.

The realist should not commit himself to future entities. It would be absurd to commit himself to past ones unless they are also present ones. So he must commit himself to present ones.

If this seems objectionable, the following considerations may

improve matters. What I am really *defining* is realism(t) for any time
t. What I think the present-day realist should defend is realism-
(now). Because of the meta-induction, he faces a problem if, looking
back, he finds, say, realism(1066), realism(1500), realism(1700), and
realism(1990) all false (but see 9.4). However, he could, without
fear, find realism(t) for some t false. And he could allow – indeed, he
should allow – that our current science *might be* massively wrong in
its ontology, so that realism(now) would be false (as Hartry Field
pointed out to me).   .

What then is it to be a 'realist' at time t? A simple answer to this is
implied by the above discussion: a realist at time t believes realism-
(t). Some will find this too demanding. Couldn't someone be a realist
in an interesting sense and yet be sceptical of the contemporary
science on which realism, as I am defining it, is based? Don't we
need a less demanding account to capture a realistic attitude to
science *in general* that is not committed to science *at a particular time?*
Perhaps. If so, we should define a realist as someone who at any time
t *tends to* believe realism(t); or, even weaker, someone who expects to
find theories which he would take as the basis for believing realism(t)
for some time t. I have no serious objections to these weaker definitions, but I shall rest with my stronger one. As far as I know, nothing
significant to the argument of this book hinges on these differences.[3]

My interest is in realism(now). I shall continue simply to call this
'realism'.

Realism might be wrong: it is an overarching empirical hypothesis
in science. The dimension that I am now describing takes at face
value, and seriously, each of the apparent commitments of common-
sense and scientific theories that withstands the aforementioned
criticisms. We have good reason to believe in *each* such posit. However, it does not follow that we have good reason to believe in *all*
these posits. Realism is more cautious: it holds that most of those
posits exist.

My discussion so far has had a common token/type ambiguity. Is
the realism I am concerned with committed to tokens or to types?
The ambiguity arises because each token is, of course, of some type,
and because realism is mostly not concerned with the existence of
any particular token: it does not matter to realism whether or not this
stone or that tree exists. However, I take it that it is tokens that our
sort of realism is committed to. On the question of the existence of
types, the other question traditionally known as 'realism', I want to
remain neutral. But, interestingly enough, it seems difficult to state
realism in the specific form that I seek, without quantifying over

types. For the natural statement of existence for my realism, sensitive to the token/type distinction, runs as follows: tokens of most common-sense and scientific physical types exist. However, the apparent commitment to types is not necessary, only convenient.

We could make a *list* of all the existential statements that concern us: 'Stones exist'; 'Trees exist'; 'Cats exist';...; 'Electrons exist'; 'Muons exist'; 'Curved space-time exists';.... Each of these statements, drawn from common sense and science, is committed only to tokens. If we were to conjoin all these statements, we would have a foolhardy realism. We want to capture the more cautious view that tokens of *most* types exist. This we can do by constructing a certain disjunction of conjunctions. Each conjunction is made up from just over half the listed statements. All possible conjunctions meeting this condition are included in the disjunction.

Commitment to types is therefore unnecessary in our definition. So also is the reference to contemporary common sense and science (and to common sense and science at *t* in the definition of realism(*t*)). However, it would be extremely arduous and inelegant to remove the apparent commitment. So I shall continue with it. The definition should be regarded as shorthand for the appropriate lengthy disjunction of conjunctions. (In section 4.2 I propose another shorthand, using deflationary truth.)

Next, we need to consider the objection that our realism is not specific enough, because it does not say enough about what the entities to which realism is committed must be like. We have said that the entities must be of common-sense and scientific types; but perhaps we ought to say also that they must have some of the properties which tokens of that type are believed to have. Or perhaps we ought to say that the entities must have properties of some kind, even if not the ones we believe them to have (cf. Goldman 1979: 175).

One sort of essentialism would make the first proposal partly otiose. This is an *a priori* essentialism associated with description theories of reference. It is thought, for example, that the meaning of 'tiger' is given by 'large black-and-yellow-striped feline, etc.' and that, as a result, our understanding of that meaning yields the knowledge that something would not be a tiger unless it were a large black-and-yellow-striped feline, etc. So commitment to the existence of tigers would be commitment to things having those properties. So, to that extent, requiring that tigers have the properties they are believed to have would add nothing to the characterization of realism.

I think that this form of essentialism is false, at least for the types of entities that concern realism. I favour a form of *a posteriori* essentialism for these types (though my defence of realism in no way depends on this). According to this view, there are certain essential properties of being a tiger, determined by the genetic structure of tigers, and it is a task of science to discover which these properties are. We could be wrong about the essential properties of tigers, just as we could about any others. So committing realism about tigers to any of the properties that tigers are believed to have, except being tigers, would be a clear strengthening of the doctrine. I think that a stronger doctrine is correct but that, nevertheless, it would be tactically unwise to commit realism to more than the existence of entities of certain kinds (but see 7.1). The stronger the doctrine, the harder it is to defend.

The second proposal, that realism ought to require that the entities it is committed to have properties, even if not the ones we believe them to have, is redundant as it stands. *Of course* an entity will have properties (setting aside nominalist scruples). Why do we need to say anything so obvious? One reason, perhaps, is the fear that if we don't say this, then our realism is committed only to the propertyless 'substrata' of the old-time metaphysics. But, to the modern mind, the idea of such a substratum is unintelligible. It arises, one supposes, from the pseudo-problem of the 'one over many' (*pace* David Armstrong; cf. Devitt 1980b).

Finally, contemporary worries about vagueness and bivalence may underlie an interest in the second proposal. There are some objects for which it is not a determinate matter of fact whether they are bald or not bald. Similarly, if evolution is to be believed, it is likely that there were once objects for which it was not a determinate matter of fact whether they were tigers or were not tigers. This indeterminacy seems irrelevant to realism. Realism is committed to the existence of tokens of most common-sense and scientific types. This requires that there be tokens that are determinately of one of those types. It does not require that each token be determinately of one of those types. If there are independently existing entities that are determinately tigers, then that fact confirms realism. If there are independently existing freaks which are not determinately tigers or not tigers, then that fact is neutral to realism as I have characterized it. It simply shows that the external world is richer than my sort of realism requires. The realist should be all in favour of these added riches (13.4). However, the difficulty of being specific about their nature makes it inadvisable to attempt to include them in the world he is fighting for.

2.4 FORMULATIONS OF REALISM

It is clear from this discussion that there is a range of doctrines that might appropriately be called 'realism'. In this section I shall draw on the conclusions of the discussion to formulate and name several such doctrines.

I start with a minimal doctrine:

> *Weak, or Fig-Leaf, Realism* Something objectively exists independently of the mental.

This doctrine is so weak as to be uninteresting; but it is worth stating, because it is all that many so-called realists are committed to.

Interest comes when we take account of our recent attempt to specify the nature of the entities that the realist is committed to.

> *Realism* Tokens of most current common-sense and scientific physical types objectively exist independently of the mental.

Though this statement quantifies over types, it will be remembered that this is only a convenience (2.3). The statement is shorthand for a certain disjunction of conjunctions, a typical conjunct of which would be: 'Trees objectively exist independently of the mental.' This disjunction quantifies over tokens. It will be remembered further that it is only the confident and necessary posits of common sense and science that concern the realist.

When I use the term 'Realism', it will be this doctrine that I am referring to; analogously, 'Realist'. When I wish to be less particular about the form of realism in question, I shall use 'realism'; analogously, 'realist'.

Among the opponents of Realism are some, including operationists (7.7), instrumentalists (7.8), and van Fraassen (8.1), who accept the existence of observable entities but are dubious about the existence of unobservable ones. And there are some who are realists about the unobservables of science but deny the existence of the common-sense world. So, for the purposes of argument, we need to divide Realism in two. Call a type 'observable' if any token of it would be observable; similarly 'unobservable'. We shall remain fairly close to normal usage if we call the doctrine about observable entities 'Common-Sense Realism' (even though some of the entities it is committed to are not common-sense ones) and that about unobservable entities 'Scientific Realism'.

Common-Sense Realism Tokens of most current observable common-sense and scientific physical types objectively exist independently of the mental.

Scientific Realism Tokens of most current unobservable scientific physical types objectively exist independently of the mental.

(The expression 'physical' is necessary in the statement of Common-Sense Realism so as to exclude some of the more bizarre posits of folk theory; but it is doubtless unnecessary in the statement of Scientific Realism).

Where it is clear from the context that Common-Sense Realism is under discussion, I shall mostly abbreviate its name to 'Realism'; similarly, Scientific Realism.

In my view a doctrine at least as strong as Realism is worth fighting for. Further, that doctrine is sufficient to justify generally realist intuitions in theorizing about the world. Once it is established, the battle against anti-realism is won: all that remain are skirmishes. So it is tactically unwise to fight for more. However, I think that stronger doctrines are defensible. I think that we *are* mostly right about the properties of the objects we believe in, even though Realism does not require this. And I think that a doctrine which requires the existence of tokens of *the great majority* of physical types, and not merely of the most required by Realism, is also true.

The discussion leaves the nature of Realism a little vague, but not objectionably so, in my view: for nothing in what follows seems to trade on that vagueness.

2.5   REALISM AND PHYSICALISM

Physicalism is usually taken to be the doctrine that physics is basic in two respects:

(1)   the only entities that exist are physical entities (or those composed only of physical entities);
(2)   ultimately, physical laws explain everything (in some sense).

The major vagueness of this doctrine resides, of course, in (2). I shall have more to say about this as I attempt to say why we need truth (chapter 6); for I hold to physicalism as well as Realism. Consider now the difference between physicalism and Realism.

(1) obviously has some relation to Realism. At first sight it may seem as if (1) entails Realism. However, it is not clear whether (1)

requires the existence of many of the familar objects of Realism, or indeed of any of them. Perhaps it could be true if the only entities were those not of current physics but of some future physics. Certainly Realism does not entail (1), because Realism is compatible with dualism. Realism is not a reductive doctrine.

Realism and (2) are indifferent to one another. One could hold to (2) and yet be an idealist: physical laws explain everything, but physical entities are nothing but sense data. On the other hand, a non-reductive Realist (e.g. a dualist) would reject (2).

Physicalism and Realism have been confused by some philosophers (e.g. Lenin 1927), but they are in fact quite distinct doctrines.

NOTES

1 I am not claiming that this must be part of any appropriate characterization of realism about the external world. For example, a comparison of that realism with realism about the mental would be aided by modifying the requirement of non-mentality. And Keith Campbell has urged me to modify the characterization so as to place Leibniz among the realists. I have not made these modifications, but I have nothing against them. My characterization is, I hope, adequate for my purposes.

2 I am not impressed by the Popperian view that science gives no ground for confidence in any theory.

3 Thanks to Gregory Currie for comments that have led to this paragraph.

3
What is Truth?

3.1 INTRODUCTION

The question 'What is truth?' might be taken to be a question about our ordinary notion of truth; or if, as seems likely, there are several such notions, the question might be taken in the present context to be about one of those notions, the semantic notion. But what is the interest of this ordinary notion? Why should we bother with it? We should bother with it only if it plays a role in our best theory of the world. To say that a notion is ordinary is just to say that it occurs in folk theory. Clearly, not all the notions of folk theory deserve a place in our best theory. In chapter 6 I shall argue that the ordinary semantic notion of truth is one that does. In this chapter I shall simply assume that we need this notion of truth, and will say something about its explanation.

In my view, the ordinary (semantic) notion of truth is a 'correspondence' notion. Other notions of truth have been proposed. I take it that a minimum requirement for something being a notion of truth is that the 'equivalence thesis' (Dummett 1978: xx) holds for it: each instance of 'Schema T',

   s is true if and only if p,

obtained by substituting for 'p' a sentence which is a translation of the sentence referred to by the term substituted for 's', must come out true.[1] This thesis is the basis for Tarski's famous Convention T. If the equivalence thesis does not hold for a notion, there seems no good reason for calling it 'truth'. Of course, if I am right in thinking that the ordinary notion is a correspondence one, then it is arguable that any other notion is not truth even if the equivalence thesis does hold for it. In any case, it is the correspondence notion that I shall be concerned with. I shall consider other possible notions only to be extent that doing so helps to clarify the correspondence notion.

I shall not assume Realism here. The application of any correspondence notion of truth typically presupposes the existence of some form of objective reality, but it need not be the form required by Realism. In the next chapter I shall discuss the relationship between Realism and truth.

3.2   THE CLASSICAL CORRESPONDENCE NOTION

The basic idea of a correspondence notion of truth is familiar: a sentence is true if and only if it corresponds to the facts (or to reality). It is plausible to see signs of this in Aristotle: 'To say of what is that it is not, or of what is not that it is, is false, while to say of what is that it is, or what is not that it is not is true' (*Metaphysics*, Γ, 7, 27). However, it would be more cautious to see this as simply an expression of the equivalence thesis.[2]

Classical attempts to explain the correspondence notion of truth quickly ran into insurmountable difficulties. If truth holds of a sentence in virtue of its corresponding to a fact, then we need an explanation of this 'correspondence' and of these 'facts'. Attempts to explain correspondence sank quickly into metaphors: sentences 'mirrored' or 'pictured' facts. And facts were mysterious entities with uncertain identity conditions. They were particularly repugnant to those with a taste for desert landscapes. Some correspondence theorists created a further problem: they held that it was not sentences but the 'propositions' that sentences express which were the true bearers of truth values. This introduced another mysterious entity to be explained.

Despite these difficulties, we can abstract from these classical discussions the following features of the correspondence notion of truth. (1) It holds of a sentence (or proposition; I shall overlook this alternative in future) partly in virtue of the structure of the sentence. (2) It holds of a sentence partly in virtue of the relation the sentence has to reality. (3) It holds of a sentence partly in virtue of the objective, mind-independent nature of reality. This last feature is intended to capture the typical view of correspondence theorists, that a sentence is 'made true by independent reality'.

3.3 A CONTEMPORARY CORRESPONDENCE NOTION

Consider a true sentence with a very simple structure: the predication '*a* is *F*'. This sentence is true in virtue of the fact that there exists an object which '*a*' designates and which is among the objects '*F*' applies to. So this sentence is true because it has a predicational structure containing words standing in certain referential relations to parts of reality and because of the way that reality is. Provided that the reality is objective and mind-independent, then the sentence is *correspondence*-true: its truth has all the features that we have just abstracted from classical discussions. Yet this truth does not require any of the mysterious entities and relations of those discussions. The only entities we need are the familiar ones we already have, objects of one sort or another; and the only relations we need are ones of reference between the parts of the sentence and the objects. If we could generalize this approach to cover the many structures of natural language and explain the appropriate reference relations, then we would be well on the way, at least, to explaining the correspondence notion of truth.

The first major step in making generalization possible was taken by Alfred Tarski in 'The Concept of Truth in Formalized Languages' (in Tarski 1956: 152–278). He showed how to explain truth in terms of reference for various formal languages containing sentences with structures of central importance to natural languages: truth-functional, predicational, and quantificational structures. He was pessimistic about extending his approach to natural languages because of their complexity and the semantic paradoxes. Donald Davidson (1984) was the first to take an optimistic view of these difficulties. He pointed out the importance of work in modern linguistics in reducing the complexities of natural language to structures more open to Tarski's approach.

Should we be able to explain truth in terms of reference along these lines, it would still remain to explain structure and reference. Description theories have been popular for the explanation of reference. Such theories explain the reference of a word in terms of the reference of other words with which speakers associate it. But however appropriate these theories are for some words, they could not be appropriate for all words, for they simply pass the referential buck to the associated words. If the buck is to stop, the reference of all the associated words must be explained. Ultimately this requires a different sort of explanation, one not in terms of the reference of other words, but in terms of direct links to reality.

The naturalistically inclined must hope for causal theories of some sort to explain these direct links. Three basic ideas have emerged: explanation in terms of the *historical* cause, first suggested by Saul Kripke (1972), Keith Donnellan (1972), and Hilary Putnam (1975b); explanation in terms of the *reliable* cause, first suggested by Dennis Stampe (1979) and Fred Dretske (1981); and explanation in terms of a *teleofunction*, explained along Darwinian lines, first suggested by David Papineau (1984, 1987) and Ruth Millikan (1984). Unfortunately, each of these ideas faces difficulties which we cannot go into here.[3] However, I remain optimistic that a naturalistic account of reference can be found.

The features that a contemporary theory of truth along these lines shares with the classical theory are brought out in the following doctrine, 'Correspondence Truth (*x*)':

> Sentences of type *x* are true or false in virtue of: (1) their structure; (2) the referential relations between their parts and reality; (3) the objective and mind-independent nature of that reality.

The need to make the doctrine relative to a type of sentence is clear once it is realized that Correspondence Truth can hold for some sentences and not for others. Thus it is common to subscribe to Correspondence Truth (physical) while rejecting Correspondence Truth (ethical); see the later discussion of quasi-realism (4.8). (Where the context makes it obvious that sentences of type *x* are under discussion, I shall often abbreviate 'Correspondence Truth (*x*)' to 'Correspondence Truth'.)

Some might call Correspondence Truth (part of) 'semantic realism', but I shall not do so. As far as is convenient, I intend to use the term 'realism' only for entirely non-semantic doctrines. This should help to avoid many of the confusions in the current debate about Realism (Maxim 2).

Tarski (1949: 52–4, 69–70), Davidson (1984: 37–54), and Putnam (1975b: 70–84) also think that we are on the way to explaining a correspondence notion of truth.[4] However, their views of their own contributions to that explanation differ from mine. My view draws on Hartry Field's criticism (1972) of Tarski's list-like definitions of reference. Field argues that these are inadequate and that Tarski's theory needs to be supplemented by theories of reference. Davidson (1984: 215–25) and Putnam (1978: part I) have since argued that Tarski's definitions are sufficient for our purposes. Further, Putnam (1978: 57–8) does not see his work on causal theories of reference as being a theory of reference in the sense that Field requires. I shall say nothing on this latter point here (but see my 1980a: 401–2). To prepare for a discussion of the former point and of the relation of truth to Realism, we need to distinguish my correspondence notion of truth from a 'deflationary' notion. With this distinction, the difficulties of theorizing about truth begin to appear.

3.4 DEFLATIONARY NOTIONS

The basic idea for deflationary theories of truth is to be found in the famous 'redundancy' theory of F. P. Ramsey in 'Facts and Propositions' (in Ramsey 1931).[5] The idea is roughly that *there is no more to truth than the equivalence thesis*. There have been several subtle and important developments of this idea in recent years. Some of these are, briefly, as follows. (1) Stephen Leeds (1978) proposed a 'disquotational' theory, developing some remarks of Quine (1970b: 10–13): truth is captured by the fact that the sentence formed by placing any given sentence between quotation marks and following it by 'is true' is equivalent to the given sentence. (2) Dorothy Grover, Joseph Camp, and Nuel Belnap (1975) proposed a 'prosentential' theory, which is the most detailed development of the deflationary idea. The focus of this theory is on the sentences 'That is true' and 'It is true.' These sentences are not predications, but 'prosentences', which are the sentential analogues of pronouns. Like pronouns, prosentences have a dual anaphoric function: they can be prosentences of laziness, illustrated by 'That is true' referring anaphorically to an antecedent 'Chairman Mao is dead'; or they can be variables, illustrated by 'Everything Chairman Mao said was true', which is understood as 'For anything Mao says, it is true.' The latter function is very important, for it enables generalizations with respect to sentences. The prosentential theory can also explain such 'pragmatic' features as the use of 'That is true' to avoid plagiarism. (3) Robert Brandom (1988) has proposed an interesting modification of the prosentential theory, which treats ' . . . is true' not as a mere syncategorematic part of a prosentence, but rather as a prosentence-forming operator. (4) Most recently, Paul Horwich (1990) has offered a sustained defence of a 'minimalist' theory, which is like the disquotational one except that it takes propositions as the primary vehicles of truth.

For the purpose of distinguishing deflationary truth from correspondence truth, we need not be concerned with the details of, and differences between, these theories; nor need we take a stand on which is best.[6] The theories all bring out two related ways in which deflationary truth and correspondence truth differ: in their natures and their purposes. These ways are difficult to grasp.

Correspondence truth is a property which sentences have in virtue of their relations to reality. Correspondence truth has a nature which, I have just claimed, demands an explanation. In virtue of this nature, correspondence truth can be, and typically is, an explanatory notion in a theory of mind or language. The explanation of the meaning and role of a sentence or thought may be that it has the property of having a certain truth condition.

By contrast, on the deflationary view, whether or not we think of truth as a property, we should certainly not think of it as a property having some nature in need of scientific explanation. As Horwich nicely puts it, truth has no 'hidden structure awaiting our discovery' (Horwich 1990: 2). We should attend not to TRUTH, but to truth terms. A truth term is important to the *expressibility* of language. On many occasions it allows abbreviation: instead of repeating a person's statement 'Chairman Mao is dead,' I can say 'That is true.' Sometimes the abbreviation is very convenient: rather than repeat the contents of a whole article, I can say, 'Everything that article claims is true.' Sometimes the truth term is not just convenient, but essential: a person who has forgotten Goldbach's Conjecture can nevertheless agree with it by saying 'Goldbach's Conjecture is true'; a person who has lost track of all the utterances of the Great Helmsman can nevertheless express his commitment, 'Everything Chairman Mao said was true.' Without the truth term, these latter two assertions would require infinite conjunctions. The truth term is a very useful linguistic device for 'semantic ascent', for talking about non-linguistic reality by referring to sentences or thoughts. Setting aside some problems with indexicals, *to refer to a sentence and say that it is true is just to assert the sentence, while acknowledging one's lack of originality.*

The prosentential theory brings out vividly the contrast between deflationary and correspondence truth. On this theory, the truth term *is not really a predicate, and does not describe or say anything about a sentence* any more than anaphoric reference using 'it' describes or says anything about its antecedent singular term. 'Is true' is a syncategorematic part of a prosentence, an 'incomplete symbol'. Though '*s* is true' is superficially like '*s* is loud,' it is semantically quite different.

Since deflationary truth is not a natural property of a sentence or thought, it cannot be used to *explain* anything about the sentence or thought. Its purpose is simply to *facilitate expression*. It can fulfil this purpose in a theory of mind or language, as in any other theory; but it cannot play an explanatory role in such a theory. There is, therefore, a big price to pay for the view that truth is deflationary: the abandonment of truth-conditional semantics. But if that semantics is abandoned, we need a replacement: a semantics that explains meaning without any appeal to truth.

Correspondence truth can be explanatory, but perhaps it need not be: it might be, as Georges Rey nicely put it to me, epiphenomenal. In any case, the correspondence notion that is worth defending is one that plays an explanatory role in a theory of mind or language. So it is a presupposition of my doctrine Correspondence Truth that truth is explanatory. I shall argue for this presupposition in chapter 6.

The equivalence thesis (3.1) holds for a deflationary notion of truth, just as much as for a correspondence notion (or any other robust notion). Therein lies a source of the difficulty in distinguishing the two notions. For the equivalence thesis alone seems to pair a sentence with 'a worldly situation', its 'truth condition'; for example, the biconditional

' "Snow is white" is true if and only if snow is white,'

seems to pair the sentence 'Snow is white' with the situation of snow being white. So even deflationary truth seems to involve a 'correspondence' provided by this pairing. Indeed, on the strength of the equivalence thesis alone, many are prepared to *call* what is really a deflationary notion 'correspondence truth'. I do not follow that usage; but my concern is not this verbal one. It is to distinguish the robust notion form the deflationary one, whatever the two notions are called.

The distinction comes out in the explanation of *why* the equivalence thesis holds. According to the correspondence theory, the equivalence thesis holds because of relations sentences have to the world that are determined by facts about language-users and the environment. These facts yield a genuine pairing of sentences with situations. The classical theory tried to capture this relation with its talk of 'mirroring' or 'picturing'. But this talk is little more than metaphor. What the correspondence theory needs is some explanation of the relation. The explanation in section 3.3 is an example of what is required; a sentence has its truth conditions *in virtue of* its structure and the reference of its parts. It is a sure sign that a person is not taking a notion of truth to be deflationary if she sees it as depending on a correspondence to the world that requires this sort of 'reductive' explanation.

(This sign must be missing in a 'semanticalist', who is the analogue in semantics of a dualist about the mind or a vitalist about life (Field 1972: 92). The semanticalist believes in a robust notion of truth, but offers no reductive explanation of it. So she is harder to distinguish from a deflationist.)

According to deflationary theories, by contrast, the equivalence thesis does not hold in virtue of any pairing of sentences with situations. On the disquotational theory, it holds, first, because of the role of 'true': if the sentence of which 'true' is predicated on the left hand side of a biconditional is synonymous with the sentence used on the right hand side, then the two sides express the same thing. It holds, second, because of the empirical fact that the sentences of which 'true' is predicated on the left are indeed synonymous with the sentences used on the right. It holds, third, because of a truism of the form, '*p* if and only if *p*'. The disquotational role of 'true' together with the synonymies reduce the equivalence thesis to a set of truisms.

Once again, the prosentential theory brings out vividly the contrast with correspondence truth. On this theory, the equivalence thesis does not, despite appearances, pair each sentence with a certain situation. In order for the thesis to make such a pairing, it would have to be the case that the left-hand side of the above biconditional described the sentence 'Snow is white.' That is just what the prosententialist denies. The left-hand side is a prosentence anaphorically referring to an antecedent sentence (in this case the sentence 'Snow is white' that it contains). The left-hand side is analogous to the pronoun in 'It is white,' which anaphorically refers to an antecedent use of 'snow'. In both cases, the result of the anaphora is a description of snow, not of a linguistic expression. Since the equivalence thesis does not pair sentences with situations, it could not be in virtue of such pairings that the thesis holds.

Field's criticism of Tarski depends on taking truth to be correspondence. He points out that Tarski's list-like definitions of reference, along the following lines, are not explanatory but trivial:

n designates *a* = df *a* is France and *n* is 'France', or . . . , or *a* is Germany and *n* is 'Germany'.

Such a definition is not an adequate explanation of a robust notion of reference, of reference as a genuine relation in nature between words and the world. The explanation of correspondence truth requires robust reference. So, if Tarski is taken to be explaining *that* truth, his account needs to be supplemented by theories of reference. However, if he is taken to be defining a deflationary notion, his treatment of reference is satisfactory, for deflationary truth does not depend on robust reference.[7]

The possibility of deflationary truth raises doubts about my claim that the ordinary notion is a correspondence one. At least, the discussion has made it very plausible that the ordinary notion plays the expressive role of deflationary truth. Yet, perhaps a correspondence notion could play that role. The role seems to require only that the equivalence thesis holds, and that thesis must hold for any notion worthy of the name 'truth' (3.1). (And this makes it implausible that there are *two* ordinary notions, one robust and one deflationary. If an ordinary notion is robust it could play the expressive role and so there would be no need for a deflationary notion.) The more serious threat to correspondence truth comes from the deflationist claim that truth plays only the expressive role and that attempts by philosophers to make it explanatory in theories of meaning are misconceived.

Support for the view that the ordinary notion of truth is robust may seem to come from the ordinary notions of reference. For these seem to be robust; for example, designation seems to be a relation in nature that pairs 'France' with France, 'Germany' with Germany, and so on. If the ordinary notion of truth is explicable in terms of robust reference along the lines I suggested (following Tarski and Field), then that notion of truth is robust. However, it is not obvious that the ordinary notions of reference are robust. Indeed, Brandom (1984) has offered a deflationary account of them analogous to the prosentential theory of truth. On this view, 'refers' is a complex anaphoric pronoun-forming operator, and there is no natural relation of reference between expressions and objects.

I have pointed out that deflationary truth cannot be explanatory in a theory of meaning. This is not to say that it can play no role in *interpretation* (a point that has significance for the later discussion of Davidson; 10.4).

> An appropriate instance of Schema T,
> s is true if and only if p,

is one obtained by substituting for 'p' a sentence which means the same as the sentence referred to by the term substituted for 's'. (I ignore certain complications arising from indexicals.) Note, first, that in the following circumstances it is trivial for an English-speaker who has caught on to deflationary truth to know one of these instances:

she knows which sentence is referred to by the substituend for '*s*' *and can understand it*. Consider, for example, the instance

Harry is true if and only if snow is white.

'Harry' names the sentence 'Snow is white.' The person knows this, and understands that sentence. So, given her grasp of deflationary truth, knowledge of the instance is trivial.

Now suppose that she is confronted with an instance of Schema T, but not necessarily an appropriate instance, *which refers to a sentence she does not understand*. Suppose, further, that she has evidence for the truth of the instance. This can aid her in interpreting the sentence she does not understand. For, what would explain the truth of the instance? A good explanation would be that the sentence referred to means what is expressed on the right-hand side of the instance. That is to say, a good explanation of the truth of the instance is that it is an appropriate instance of Schema T. Thus, suppose that 'Harry' above named the German sentence 'Schnee ist weiss.' The person knows this, but does not understand German. Evidence for the truth of the instance is evidence that the sentence means that snow is white. Of course, the instance could be true even if the sentence did not mean that. Nevertheless, the truth of the instance is good evidence of what the sentence means. And if the truth were law-like, it would be very good evidence.

Return now to my differences with Davidson and Putnam. Davidson not only sees his notion of truth as a correspondence one, but also gives it a central role in his explanation of people and their language. If it is explanatory, then anyone who is physicalistically, or even scientifically, inclined should think it needs an explanation itself. Yet Davidson denies the need for an explanation in terms of reference, and seems to offer no other explanation. I shall criticize his position in chapter 10.

Putnam (1978: part I) has sided with Davidson against Field on the issue of reference. I have argued elsewhere (1980a) that he has given no good reason for doing so (see also 11.2 below).

3.5 EPISTEMIC NOTIONS

It follows from my explanation of correspondence truth that the notion is in no way epistemic. In this it differs from notions like *warranted assertability, verifiable, knowable,* and *rationally acceptable in the ideal limit of theorizing*.[8] Some philosophers have wanted to *identify* truth with some such epistemic notion. For the identification to have any support, it is necessary, in my view, that the equivalence thesis holds for the notion (3.1). If the notion does not satisfy this minimum requirement, then a more appropriate description of what the philosophers want would be the *elimination* of truth. However, this issue of elimination *vs* identification is beside my main point. I claim that truth is neither to be identified with nor to be eliminated in favour of any epistemic notion. Truth is one thing, evidence for it quite another (Maxim 5).

Despite this, a supporter of Correspondence Truth need not be committed to the strong thesis that a sentence might be false even though all possible evidence counted for its truth. He should regard this thesis as an epistemic one, logically distinct from his view of truth, to be settled in the light of his epistemology and the interpretation of 'possible evidence'.

The problem of interpretation concerns the constraints, if any, on what counts as possible evidence. Clearly, possible evidence covers more than the evidence actually gathered so far; but how much more? First, who is doing the further gathering? The perfect observer (God)? The ideal human observer (with good sense organs and a tertiary education in science) when awake, sober, and so on? The average human observer when awake, sober, and so forth? Second, whoever he is, where is he doing the observing? 'Anywhere that he might have been' in what sense? Logical possibility, empirical possibility, or technical possibility? In its early days the earth was too hot for humans. Later, when it was not so hot, we had not yet evolved. Until recently, it was not technically possible to make certain observations of Saturn. Third, are the observations 'with the naked eye' or instrument-assisted? Fourth, if the latter, what instruments can do the assisting? Those actually invented by humans at that point? Those that will actually be invented by humans in the long run? Those that might have been invented by humans? Those that might have been invented by anything? Fifth, does the observer note only what actually goes on or what might have gone on? Sixth, if the latter, in what ways may the observer interfere with nature? What experiments can he perform which were not performed? Those that were invented at that point? Those that will be invented in the long run? Those that might have been invented? Using what instruments? And so on.

The vagueness in the notion of *possible evidence* indicated by this brief discussion carries over to other modal epistemic notions such as *verifiable* and *knowable*. Before a Correspondence Theorist commits himself to any view on the relation between truth and one of these epistemic notions, he needs to have this vagueness removed. Then he can apply his epistemology to yield a view.

In sum, to hold to Correspondence Truth is to believe in a notion of truth that is not explained in terms of evidence. Questions of evidence are epistemic ones quite distinct from the constitutive question of the nature of truth. Doubtless, when the correspondence theorist confronts the epistemic questions, then for most interpretations of 'possible evidence', he will accept that a sentence might be false even though all possible evidence counted for its truth. However, on the most liberal interpretations – those not tied to human capacities – he might well reject it.

The interpretation of 'possible evidence' is relevant to several issues yet to be discussed: the relation between anti-realism and epistemic notions of truth (4.3), the underdetermination thesis that is the basis for an empiricist argument against Scientific Realism (7.4), and Putnam's argument against the intelligibility of 'metaphysical realism' arising from his view that truth is what is rationally acceptable in the ideal limit of theorizing (12.3). This latter view of truth is essentially Peirce's. It takes truth as compatibility with all possible evidence in a fairly liberal sense, but not in the *most* liberal, because, it seems, the possible evidence is restricted to what humans could discover.

NOTES

1 This is rough: we need to guard against the semantic paradoxes and allow for ambiguity, for indexicals, and for sentences that are, for reasons such as vagueness, neither true nor false. I shall let it stand because, as far as I can see, nothing hinges on these complications.
2 Jim Franklin tells me that Aristotle's followers commonly interpret passages in *De Anima* 430–1b as showing Aristotle's commitment to a correspondence theory of knowledge.
3 I have explored these difficulties elsewhere (1991b). My 1981a and b and Devitt and Sterelny 1987, chs 4–5, are developments of the historical idea.
4 Davidson has recently concluded that he was mistaken in describing his notion of truth as a correspondence notion, on the ground that 'there is nothing interesting or instructive to which true sentences might correspond' (1990: 303); there are no *facts*, for example. I agree with the ground, but think it insufficient. The issue is largely verbal; so I will continue to describe Davidson as a correspondence theorist.

5   The interpretation of Ramsey as a redundancy theorist is not as straightforward as it might appear; see Loar 1980 and Field 1986: 55–60
6   Soames (1984) and Williams (1986) also take a deflationary view of
truth. See Field 1986, Brandom 1988, Davidson 1990, and Grover 1990
for discussions of the relations between various deflationary notions.
7   Because of this, I agree with Putnam that Tarski's article should have
been called 'The *Non*semantic Conception of Truth' (1985: 63).
8   This section draws on my 1983b, sect. 5.

4

What has Truth to do with Realism?

Truth, like Mae West's goodness, has nothing to do with it.
Levin 1984: 124

4.1 INTRODUCTION

In section 2.4 I defined Realism thus:

Tokens of most current common-sense and scientific physical types objectively exist independently of the mental.

What has truth to do with Realism? On the face of it, nothing at all. Indeed, *Realism says nothing semantic at all* beyond, in its use of 'objective', making the negative point that our semantic capacities do *not* constitute the world.

It has recently become common to use the term 'realism' to refer to doctrines that are represented as, and/or seem to be, at least partly semantic. This is particularly the case when the term is preceded by 'scientific'. Thus, Jarrett Leplin's editorial introduction to a collection of papers on scientific realism lists ten 'characteristic realist claims' that are nearly all about the truth and reference of theories (1984a: 1–2).[1] Not one is straightforwardly metaphysical. Here are some other typical accounts of realism:

Formally, Scientific Realism is a semantical thesis, it is the view that the intended and proper sense of the theories of science is as literal descriptions of the physical world, as saying what there is and how it behaves. It is the view that if a scientific theory is in fact true then there is in the world exactly those entities which the theory says there is, having exactly those characteristics which the terms of the theory describe them as having. (Hooker 1974: 409)

I shall apply the term scientific *realism* to non-scepticism about semantico-ontological objectivity for scientific theories, to the view that scientific theories are answerable to an independent reality . . . there is a question for them to be more or less right (or wrong) about. (Papineau 1979: 126)

I understand scientific realism to be the view that the theoretical statements of science are, or purport to be, true generalized descriptions of reality. (Ellis 1979: 28)

Realism is a generic term for a number of views, all holding that theories consist of true or false statements referring to 'real' or 'existing' entities. (Hesse 1967: 407)

Despite the talk of meaning and truth in describing realism, it is usually possible – and is, for example, with the above authors - to discern a metaphysical (ontological) thesis behind the description. Indeed, given the possibility that the use of 'true' may be deflationary (3.4), it may be the case that its use in such descriptions is unnecessary: perhaps the thesis intended is really metaphysical.

The doctrine I have call 'Realism' is a *metaphysical* doctrine (though a little bit epistemological and semantic in its insistence on the objectivity of the world). I shall argue that this doctrine is quite distinct from any substantive semantic doctrine. My interest in the purely verbal question of which use of 'realism' is 'right' is only small. Nevertheless, I do think that uses of the term for doctrines that are partly semantic are unfortunate.

First, those uses encourage the conflation of semantic doctrines with the metaphysical ones, a conflation that has led to anti-Realism in the writings of many, including, for example, Dummett (considered in chapter 14). Second, if 'realism' is so used, what are we to call the metaphysical part of its referent, which is what most of the argument is about? We are forced, quite unnecessarily, to coin another term.[2] Third, I think that there is little historical basis for this usage. I have already quoted *The Encyclopedia of Philosophy* (2.1). See also John Passmore's *A Hundred Years of Philosophy* (1966). The *distinctive* thing about what has been called 'realism' until recently has been a view about the nature of the world, not about the nature of language or thought.

However, my main point is not verbal at all. I am insisting on a distinction between a certain metaphysical doctrine, whatever it is called, and anything significantly semantic. I am insisting on carving theory at reality's joints.

4.2 THE INDEPENDENCE OF REALISM AND TRUTH

Realism does not strictly entail any doctrine of truth at all.[3] It follows that a person could, without inconsistency, be a Realist without having any notion of truth in his theory. Nor is there an obviously true proposition which, together with Realism, entails any explanatory – hence non-deflationary – doctrine of truth. A Realist may take a thoroughly sceptical view of the need for explanatory truth. I take it that such a view is a central part of Quine's semantic eliminativism. It is very difficult for a physicalistically minded Realist to undermine this scepticism, as Stephen Leeds has pointed out (1978). Truth should not be taken for granted (Maxim 4). In chapter 6 I shall argue against eliminativism.

So much for the entailment from Realism to a doctrine of truth. What about the reverse entailment? Suppose that a person does have an explanatory notion of truth in his theory. Does that commit him to Realism? Clearly not, for two reasons. First, he may not apply his notion to the right statements; he may not apply it to the physical statements of common sense (which contain words like 'tree') and of science (which contain words like 'electron'). Second, his notion may be an epistemic one like *warranted assertability* (3.5), which involves no commitment to an objective independent reality.

It is common to link the *correspondence* notion of truth to realism: 'most scientific realists . . . see acceptance of a correspondence theory of truth as being essential to their position' (Ellis 1985: 50–1). Before assessing this, it is helpful to note a role that *deflationary* truth can play.

Suppose that one has in mind the metaphysical doctrine, Realism. The statement of this doctrine that began the chapter has an apparent commitment to types that can be paraphrased away only at great cost in convenience and elegance, as we have noted (2.3 and 2.4). However, there is a natural way to state the doctrine using deflationary truth that is convenient, elegant, and involves no commitment to types:

> *Realism** Most current common-sense and scientific physical existence statements are objectively and mind-independently (deflationary) true.

This is an illustration of the sort of 'semantic ascent' that deflationary truth makes possibly, and often convenient, *whatever the subject-matter.* Such ascent does not make a doctrine semantic, in the sense of being part of a theory of meaning; it does not change the subject-matter at all. Indeed, if it did, *any* doctrine about *anything* would become part of the theory of meaning.

Now consider correspondence truth. I have characterized the doctrine that this notion applies to sentences of type x, Correspondence Truth (x), as follows:

> Sentences of type x are true or false in virtue of: (1) their structure; (2) the referential relations between their parts and reality; (3) the objective and mind-independent nature of that reality.

Does Correspondence Truth (physical) entail Realism? It does not. It does require that whatever reality makes physical statements true or false must be objective and mind-independent. Thus it entails the independence dimension of Realism (2.2). However, it is still distant from Realism, because it is silent on the existence dimension (2.3). It tells us what it is for a sentence to be true or false, but it does not tell us which ones *are* true, and so *could* not tell us which particular entities exist. Of course, we might add the following claim to Correspondence Truth to deal with this: most current common-sense and scientific physical existence statements *are* true. This addition to a semantic theory is totally gratuitous. Furthermore, if its talk of truth is *minimally* interpreted as merely deflationary, it is simply *a statement of* the existence dimension. We have derived Realism from Correspondence Truth by adding half of it to Correspondence Truth![4]

This point can be strengthened. Correspondence Truth requires that the reality that makes sentences true or false be 'objective and mind-independent'. In formulating the doctrine of correspondence truth in this way, I am going along with what appears to be the traditional assumption of correspondence theorists. Yet this addition of Realism's independence dimension seems like a gratuitous intrusion of metaphysics into a semantic doctrine. If we dropped the addition, we would still be left with (1), (2), and a modified (3), which capture *all the strictly semantic import* of Correspondence Truth. And this modified semantic doctrine is *compatible with absolutely any metaphysics at all*. (Putnam allows that Kant could accept correspondence truth (1981: 63)). In adding the independence dimension to the semantic doctrine, we took one of the two steps required for Realism. If we were now to add the existence dimension, as contemplated in the last paragraph, we would have taken the other step. These two additions, with 'true' interpreted minimally as deflationary, simply *are* Realism*; that is, they *are* Realism. It is hardly surprising, then, that with the help of these additions we could derive Realism from a correspondence theory! The strictly semantic parts of the theory are entirely irrelevant to the derivation.

I claimed earlier that Realism does not entail any doctrine of truth. I now claim that no doctrine of truth entails Realism. I conclude that no doctrine of truth is in any way constitutive of Realism (Maxim 2).

Realism is about the nature of reality in general, about what there is and what it is like; it is about the largely inanimate impersonal world. If correspondence truth has a place, it is in our theory of only a small part of that reality: it is in our theory of people and their language.

Against this background, we can highlight some of the difficulties facing someone attempting to capture in terms of truth – as I think many do – the ontological intuitions that underlie the doctrine I call 'Realism'. These difficulties are partly illustrated by the examples in section 4.1. Consider to start with the simple, but obviously hopeless, 'All statements of our theories are true' (or even '*literally* true'). It is too weak in that it misses the independence dimension of Realism (2.2). This could easily be remedied (though it is noteworthy how often it is not: see Hooker, Ellis, and Hesse above). More seriously, it is also far too strong, even if we take 'theories' not to cover the more bizarre folk theories. It is foolhardy to be committed to the truth of even the best scientific theories, as the history of science shows. Faced with this problem, there are various temptations. One is to talk of the statements' being true *or false* (e.g. Papineau, Hesse). If the notion of truth in question is deflationary, this makes realism completely trivial. If the notion is not deflationary but, rather, is explained in terms of reference, then the truth or falsity of the statements is irrelevant to realism: what counts is the reference of terms. In so far as talk of reference here is really a disguised way of talking of the entities referred to (Hesse?), we would do better to drop the disguise. In so far as it is not, the talk is purely semantic, and is irrelevent to the ontological concerns of Realism.

A second temptation is to say that if the statements *were* true, then there *would be* certain entities (Hooker). But unless the statements *are* true, this would not amount to any ontological commitment at all. A third temptation is to say that the statements *purport*, or *are intended*, to be true (Hooker, Ellis). But what has a doctrine about intentions got to do with Realism? Perhaps all these good intentions come to nought, and the world is void! A fourth temptation is to say that the statements are *approximately* true (Putnam 1978: 20). Talk of approximate truth causes consternation (7.6). What is it? Aside from that, the talk is on the wrong track if we wish to capture the ontological intuitions of Realism. These do not require us to be committed to even the approximate truth of statements other than existence statements, and do require us to be committed to the *full* deflationary truth of *most* of the existence statements.

4.3 THE LINKS BETWEEN REALISM AND TRUTH

The discussion of deflationary truth has brought out some insignificant links between Realism and truth. There are also other, more significant ones.

First, I think it plausible to suppose that Leeds–Quine eliminativism can be undermined (though I am far from confident that I have done so in chapter 6), by showing that, from a Realist perspective, we need truth to explain the properties of symbols that enable them to play their wide variety of social roles. If we can show this, then we have an 'inference to the best explanation' (Harman 1965), or 'abduction', from Realism, together with some observations about the properties and relations of the objects the Realist believes in, to a comprehensive theory including Correspondence Truth (physical) as a part. We might represent this abduction:

Realism → Correspondence Truth.

Second, consider the relation between *anti*-Realism and epistemic (verificationist) doctrines of truth. It is already clear that anti-Realism does not entail an epistemic doctrine of truth: an idealist might even have a correspondence doctrine, provided it was stripped of any commitment to an objective and mind-independent world. I shall not consider what an abduction from anti-Realism might yield. Inferences from an epistemic doctrine of truth are more topical.

Let 'T_E' express the epistemic notion of truth in question. Then, given the equivalence thesis (3.1), the epistemic doctrine requires that the appropriate instances of

s is T_E if and only if p

hold. So, for example,

'Caesar had five moles' is T_E if and only if Caesar had five, moles.

Claims like this capture the closest link we can obtain between the epistemic doctrine and views of reality. These claims have no *immediate* bearing on Realism. They are brought to bear only when we seek an explanation of why they hold. And we should not assume in advance that the best explanation will be anti-Realist.

Consider, for example, the analogous claim that follows from a really bizarre theory of truth:

> 'Caesar had five moles' is affirmed by the Pope if and only if Caesar had five moles.

On its own, this shows nothing about Realism. When we supplement it with an explanation, we might prefer an anti-Realist one that has the Pope creating the world or a Realist one that ascribes to the Pope divine insight into reality. *An argument is needed to get from a theory of truth to anti-Realism.*

The explanation of the claims involving T_E requires an epistemology. The problem which the epistemic doctrine poses for the Realist is that it is hard to find a plausible Realist epistemology to do the explanatory job for most, if not all, the likely candidates to be T_E. Thus epistemic truth threatens Realism.

Suppose, for example, that T_E were *warranted assertability*. How could the Realist explain such a close link between a state of the world, Caesar having five moles, and our being warranted in asserting 'Caesar had five moles'? If there really were such a link (which I am quite sure there isn't), the best explanation of it might be that the world is in some way mind-dependent. Similarly, if T_E were the Dummettian notion, *discoverable by us to be warrantedly assertable*, the best explanation of the link might be some sort of anti-Realism. Perhaps if T_E were a Peircean notion, *rational acceptability in the ideal limit of theorizing*, the Realist could explain the link; though even this seems unlikely (3.5). However, in general, epistemic truth is likely to lead by abduction to anti-Realism:

> Epistemic truth → anti-Realism.[5]

We have seen earlier that no doctrine of truth is constitutive of realism. This abduction is the only significant respect in which a doctrine of truth is relevant even to the *assessment* of Realism.[6]

Whatever inference we can make to anti-Realism from an epistemic doctrine of truth does nothing to undermine the earlier inference from Realism to Correspondence Truth. Our choice between the two abductions should be guided by our view of which starting assumption is the stronger. I shall be arguing (see particularly 14.9) that we should prefer the inference that starts from Realism. The semantic cart should not be put before the metaphysical horse (Maxim 3).

Since epistemic truth has consequences for Realism, so too does any theory of meaning that involves that notion. This is *not* to say that an epistemic theory of meaning without the notion has such consequences. The consequences come via the equivalence thesis. Epistemic meaning without epistemic truth does not provide that route, and seems indifferent to Realism. For example, a theory of meaning based on the notion *discoverable by us to be warrantedly assertable* seems to have consequences for Realism only if that notion is identified with truth, thus bringing the equivalence thesis into play. Richard Kirkham has pointed out that Dummett himself might naturally – though wrongly – be taken to accept non-epistemic truth while arguing that such a notion can have no place in a theory of meaning because meaning must be epistemic (1989: 208).

Finally, there is one straightforward link between Realism and truth. Whether truth is deflationary, correspondence, or epistemic, Realism requires that it be '*absolute*'. If truth were only relative, then we could use the equivalence thesis to derive relativistic anti-Realism: *s* is not true absolutely, but only relative to *x*; so it is not the case that *p* absolutely, but only *p* relative to *x*.

Though this link between Realism and truth is close, it is not very significant. It shows that a reason for relativism about truth is a reason for relativism about reality. But what really matters to the debate, whether about truth or about reality, is the reason, not the link (13.1).

4.4 CONTEMPORARY REALISM

My view that realism does not involve correspondence truth flies so much in the face of entrenched opinion and has received so little support that I shall labour the point. I shall do so in the context of the contemporary debate over scientific realism. My doctrine, Scientific Realism, is an example of what is sometimes called 'entity realism'. For tactical reasons (2.3), I have chosen to defend this, rather than 'theory realism', a stronger metaphysical doctrine that usually underlies the debate. According to this stronger doctrine, science is mostly right, not only about which unobservables exist, *but also about their properties*. The following is a fairly typical example of a semantic version of this stronger doctrine:

> *Contemporary Realism* Most scientific statements about unobservables are (approximately) correspondence-true.

Why would people believe this? I suggest that it is only because they believe two other doctrines: first, something like

Strong Scientific Realism Tokens of most unobservable scientific types objectively exist independently of the mental, and (approximately) obey the laws of science;

and second, Correspondence Truth (physical). These two doctrines, together with the equivalence thesis, imply Contemporary Realism. Yet the two doctrines have almost nothing to do with each other. Contemporary Realism is an unfortunate hybrid.

Strong Scientific Realism is a metaphysical doctrine about the underlying nature of the world in general. To accept this doctrine, we have to be confident that science is discovering things about the unobservable world. Does the success of science show that we can be confident about this? Is abduction appropriate here? Should we take sceptical worries seriously? These are just the sort of epistemological questions that have been – and still largely are – at the centre of the realism debate (and will be the concern of chapters 7 and 8). *Their home is with Strong Scientific Realism, not Correspondence Truth.*

Correspondence Truth is a semantic doctrine about the pretensions of one small part of the world to represent the rest. The doctrine is the subject of lively debate in the philosophy of language, the philosophy of mind, and cognitive science. Do we need to ascribe truth conditions to sentences and thoughts to explain language or mind? Do we need reference to explain truth conditions? Should we prefer a conceptual-role semantics? Or should we, perhaps, near enough eliminate meaning altogether? These are interesting and difficult questions (which will be the concern of chapter 6); but they have no immediate bearing on scientific realism.

Semantic questions are not particularly concerned with the language of science. Even less are they particularly concerned with 'theoretical' language 'about unobservables'. In so far as the questions are concerned with scientific language, they have no direct relevance to the metaphysical concerns of Strong Scientific Realism. They bear directly on the sciences of language and mind and, via them, on the other human sciences. They do not bear directly on science in general. Many philosophers concerned with semantics and not in any way tainted by anti-realism are dubious of the need for a correspondence notion of truth.[7]

Are there atoms? Are there molecules? If there are, what are they like? How are they related to each other? Strong Scientific Realism says that we should take science's answers pretty much at face value. So there really are atoms, and they really do make up molecules. That is one issue. Another issue altogether concerns meaning. Do

statements have correspondence-truth conditions? Correspondence
Truth says that they do. This applies as much to 'Cats make up
atoms' as to 'Atoms make up molecules'. Indeed, it applies as much
to 'The moon is made of green cheese.' Put the first issue together
with the second, and we get a third: is 'Atoms make up molecules'
correspondence-true? My point is that this issue is completely derivative from the other two. It arises only if we are wondering about,
first, the meanings of sentences ranging from the scientific to the silly;
and second, the nature of the unobservable world.

Suppose we had established that Correspondence Truth was right
for familiar, everyday language. Suppose further that we believe that
atoms do make up molecules, and the like. Then, *of course*, we would
conclude that Correspondence Truth applies to 'Atoms make up
molecules' and the like, and so conclude that such sentences are
correspondence-true. What possible motive could there be for not
concluding this? Scientific theories raise special metaphysical questions, not semantic ones.

Strong Scientific Realism and Correspondence Truth have very
different subject–matters, and should be supported by very different
evidence. Underlying Contemporary Realism is a conflation of these
two doctrines that has been detrimental to both.

4.5   DIAGNOSING THE CONFLATION

Why has the metaphysical issue of realism been conflated with
semantic issues? I offer some tentative suggestions.

(a)   I suspect that the conflation is very much part of the 'linguistic
turn' in philosophy which the positivists did so much to popularize
(see, e.g., Schlick 1932–3). At its most extreme, this turn treats all
philosophical issues as about language.

(b)   There seems to be a special reason for the role given to correspondence truth. Using Realism* as an example, I have pointed
out that we can use the deflationary notion of truth to state a
metaphysical view (4.2). If the distinction between deflationary and
correspondence truth is overlooked, then a doctrine like Realism*
may seem to be making the partly semantic claim that certain statements are correspondence-true, that they 'picture' reality. And it
seems that the distinction is an easy one to overlook.[8]

(c)   Though doctrines of truth are not in any way essential to Realism, they have traditionally played a very significant role in *the way the issue has been argued* and the degree to which it seems interesting and controversial. But, of course, arguments are one thing, their conclusions another (Maxim 1).

The typical argument against realism has been along the following lines:

(1)   If the realist's independent reality exists, then our thoughts/ theories must mirror, picture, or represent that reality.

(2)   Our thoughts/theories cannot mirror, picture, or represent the realist's independent reality.

(3)   So the realist's independent reality does not exist.

The centre of the debate about this argument has been (2); that is to say, it has focused on the correspondence of our ideas or language to independent reality. Traditionally, the problem has come up in epistemology: 'How could we know about such a reality?' But more recently, the problem has come up in the theory of reference or intentionality: 'How could our language or thought refer to such a reality?'

These questions have seemed important metaphysically only because (1) has been assumed, mostly without argument. Indeed (1) has seemed so irresistible that to deny a correspondence theory has often been seen as tantamount to denying realism. Consider, for example, this statement by Putnam:

whatever authority [ontology and epistemology] had depended entirely on our conceiving of reality and sensations as, respectively, the makers-true and the makers-justified of the sentences we produce – not the makers-true and the makers-justified from within the story, but the things outside the story that hook language onto something outside itself. (1985: 78; see also, Putnam 1987: 15–16)[9]

Irresistible or not, (1) is false: 'to question whether our theories aim at "picturing" the world' is not 'to question whether electrons "really" exist' (Leeds 1978: 119). Realism may make the rejection of Correspondence Truth implausible, but it does not make it paradoxical or incoherent.

(d)   One historically important account of realism did involve correspondence truth, and hence may bear some distant responsibility for the contemporary confusion. Descartes and the British empiricists assume that what we immediately perceive are ideas in the mind. For them, realism is the view that there are objects outside the mind that cause and *resemble* these ideas. So the only account of the objects to which realism is committed is one in terms of their correspondence to ideas; commitment to cats comes from commitment to things resembling cat ideas. From this perspective, of course, realism seems very dubious. Descartes' case for it required the help of a Very Powerful Friend; and Berkeley demonstrated the desperate thinness of Locke's case. However, what needs stressing is that this way of identifying the realist world is not necessary: you can commit yourself to cats by committing yourself to cats. And the crude notion of resemblance (or mirroring) has no place in contemporary correspondence theories (3.3).

The view that we need to appeal to ideas to identify the realist world did not survive the impact of Kant on the debate. However, a shadow of it is to be found in the contemporary insistence on the importance of *interpretation* in characterizing realism. I shall now consider this.

4.6 ONTOLOGICAL COMMITMENT AND INTERPRETATION

In response to my sharp distinction between Realism and semantics, a certain line of objection can be expected. It will be claimed[10] that my doctrine of Realism is clearly realistic about entities only if it is interpreted in a certain way.[11] Merely stating, for example, 'Common-sense entities exist' does not ontologically commit you to those entities. Commitment depends on the truth conditions of the statements we accept; we are committed only to the entities which must exist for our statements to be true. The ontological question becomes clear only when we move into the metalanguage and consider this semantic question. The disagreement between the realist and the anti-realist is not over statements like the one above, but over how such statements are to be understood. So the disagreement is a semantic one.

My position on ontological commitment is as follows. We do not need to move into a metalanguage discussion of our object-language claims to establish ontological commitment. Indeed, if commitment could never be established at the level of the object language, it could never be established at all. I am not claiming that there is no problem in establishing a commitment, but simply that whatever problem there is arises as much at the level of the metalanguage as at the level of the object language. The idea that talk about the world is unclear and in need of interpretation, yet that talk about language and its relation to the world is straightforward on the face of it, reflects the damage of years of living under the linguistic turn.

In what circumstances is a person ontologically committed to *a*, or an *F*, in uttering assertively a sentence token *S*?[12] The criterion suggested by the above objection is as follows: a person is so committed if *a*, or an *F*, must exist for *S* to be true. This popular semantic criterion has general applicability, and is, I think, correct. However, my discussion of Realism presupposes another, more obvious criterion that seems sometimes to be strangely overlooked: a person is so committed if, in asserting *S*, he says that *a* exists or that there exists an *F*. My claim is that this criterion is more basic than the semantic one, though not as generally applicable.

To discover a person's ontological commitment using the first criterion, it is thought, we need a semantic theory for *S*. For it is only by applying a semantic theory that we can tell what must exist for a sentence to be true. To discover a person's commitment using the second criterion, we need only to understand *S*. This, of course, requires that we interpret *S* in some sense (and that is the truth behind the objection); but it does not require that we interpret *S* in the sense of applying a semantic theory to *S*. Our ordinary understanding of a language is a skill quite unlike any theoretical knowledge of the language (14.5 and 14.6).

The second, non-semantic criterion is more basic, because the first, semantic criterion depends on it: to apply the semantic criterion, we must rely on our ordinary understanding of existential statements.

Consider Tom's assertion

    (1)   Lulu is a cat.

Applying the semantic criterion, we see this assertion as ontologically committing Tom to Lulu and cats, because, first,

    (a)   (1) is true if and only if there exists something such that 'Lulu' designates it and 'cat' applies to it;

and second,

    (b)   If 'Lulu' designates, it designates Lulu;

    (c)   If 'cat' applies, it applies to cats.

What is it about (a), (b), and (c) that shows that Tom is ontologically committed to Lulu and cats in asserting (1)? Clearly it is our talk of existence. Tom is ontologically committed to cats if we are right in saying, as a consequence of (a) and (c), that cats must exist for (1) to be true. But if our rightly saying this can establish Tom's commitment, then he must be able to establish it simply by asserting

(2)   Cats exist.

The word 'exists' is not confined to semantics, and it is implausible (to put it mildly) that it is only in semantics that it really means existence, that it is genuinely ontological. Indeed, it is implausible to suppose that its meaning in semantics is any different from its meaning in other sciences and in folk theory.

Suppose Tom himself were the theorist, reflecting on his own utterance of (1). So Tom asserted (a), (b), and (c). It would be strange indeed to say that in so doing he shows he is committed to the existence of cats, but that in asserting (2) he does not show this.

Note that for the correct assertion of (a) and (c) to commit Tom to the existence of cats, we must understand them as saying that (1) is true only if cats exist. So in concluding that there is a commitment as a result of applying the semantic criterion, we have to rely on our ordinary understanding of existential statements. If we can rely on this understanding at that point, we can rely on it when Tom asserts (2). And if words were opaque when in the object language, they would hardly become transparent all of a sudden when in the metalanguage.

Statements like (2) are central to my account of Realism. If worries persist about what, in the absence of a semantic theory, these state-ments mean, we can respond with a dilemma. Either 'exists' in the metalanguage used to state the semantic theory and establish onto-logical commitment means the same as in (2), or it does not. If it does, then any worries we have at the object-language level of (2) recur at the level of the metalanguage. And clearly we are not going to resolve them by moving to a meta-metalanguage. So if (2) does not establish ontological commitment, then nothing does. If, on the other hand, 'exists' means something different in the metalanguage and it is there that it is ontologically committing, then we can decide to use it with that meaning in the object language. Let 'exists$_o$' express this meaning. Instead of (2) with its allegedly non-committal 'exists', we can capture our commitment to cats with

(2)*   Cats exists$_o$.

We still have ontological commitment without any recourse to a semantic theory.

It is a truism that a theory must be presented to us in language. So to draw any conclusions at all from the theory, whether about ontological commitment or about the price of eggs, we must understand the language in which it is presented. But this mundane fact supplies no reason for supposing that we must move to a semantic theory to determine the ontological commitment of our object theory, because the fact covers the semantic theory too: even semantics requires language. A semantic theory of a sentence could clearly help us to understand that sentence, but the theory is not necessary for the understanding (or we would understand very little). And, equally clearly, even when the theory does help, it does not make the issue that concerns the sentence semantic.

In sum, a person can be implicitly committed to the existence of something by the semantic criterion only because he can be explicitly committed to its existence by the non-semantic criterion.

Why do we need the semantic criterion at all? Clearly we would need it if we were considering the commitments of a person (or theory) whose language contained no notion of existence. However, that is a situation we are seldom, if ever, in. What we do often find is that a person does not make his implicit commitments explicit. Worse, he may explicitly deny what he is implicitly committed to (e.g.) – by denying (2) while asserting (1). For these cases we may need the semantic criterion.

What I have been concerned with in this section is the nature of *commitment* to existence, not the nature of existence itself. In my view, nothing informative can be said on the latter question. Existence is a fundamental and intuitively clear notion that stands in no need of explanation. Attempts to offer an explanation have either lapsed into triviality or changed the question to an epistemic one (about how we *tell* what exists) without noticing (7.8).

4.7   ONTOLOGICAL COMMITMENT AND PARAPHRASE

A problem I have ignored so far is that a person may not be ontologically committed, explicitly or implictly, to what he appears to be committed to. He may have been speaking carelessly or frivolously; what he said may have been a mere manner of speaking. It is here that the opportunity to paraphrase is important. It gives a person an opportunity to replace a sentence that he thinks literally false with one that he thinks literally true. His commitment depends on what he says after being given this opportunity.

I have claimed that Realism is an overarching empirical hypothesis. In folk theory and scientific theory, we are apparently committed to the existence of a range of physical entities. Some of these apparent commitments may be paraphrased away as not real or not necessary. However, by and large, Realism takes these commitments at face value. In this respect, Realism is science's philosophy of science and common sense's philosophy of common sense. Of course Realism is more cautious than the totality of theories we take at face value: it is concerned only with the theories of which we are confident and, in its use of the quantifier 'most', it allows for some errors even in our confident posits (2.3).

The provision for paraphrase seems plausible enough, but there is a difficulty (brought home to me by Jackson 1980). (i) Suppose a person asserts, as many would be prepared to,

(3)   There exists a good chance that she will come,

with as much seriousness as you like. He declines the opportunity to paraphrase. (ii) Alternatively, he accepts the paraphrase

(4)   She will probably come,

not because he thinks that (3) is literally false, but because he thinks that (4) is more or less equivalent to (3). What we have to say here, it seems, is that (3) is not equivalent to (4) and is false, and that in accepting (3), this person is explicitly committed to the existence of chances.

This is not appealing, because an ontology of chances is *prima facie* odd. Nevertheless, I think we must say that he has that ontology because the alternative is even less appealing. It is to say that (3) and (4) are equivalent, and yet that (3) exemplifies a non-ontological sense of 'exists'. But the positing of such a special sense of 'exists' seems *ad hoc*. And what is the sense? What are the truth conditions of sentences containing 'exists' in that sense? In virtue of what is that sense, rather than the ontological sense, exemplified in (3)? It seems preferable to see the person in case (i) as ignorant of the possibility of paraphrasing away the commitment to chances (as we nearly all are of the possibility of paraphrasing away the commitment to numbers if Field 1980 is right); and the person in case (ii) as insensitive to the significance of ontological questions, particularly those concerning abstract entities like chances, perhaps.

Whatever we make of this problem of paraphrase and of the difference between apparent and real commitment, it gives no support to the objection that was the main concern of the last section. The problem of paraphrase comes up in exactly the same way in the metalanguage as in the object language: a semantic remark can be paraphrased away, because it is a mere manner of speaking or lacks seriousness, just as any other sort of remark can. And if we should conclude (against my advice) that 'exists' is ambiguous, then it will be ambiguous in semantics as much as anywhere else.

The possibility of paraphrase enables me to turn the tables on the objector. Suppose the semantic criterion shows that, despite a person's apparent explicit commitment to the existence of x's in the sentences he asserts, he is really committed only to the existence of y's (because only y's need exist for the sentences to be true; e.g. he seems to be explicity committed to physical objects, but his sentences are made true by sense data). This shows that the person could have paraphrased away his apparent commitment to x's in the first place: he could have talked only of y's (given an adequate vocabulary). There is no ontological clarity to be gained at the level of the metalanguage that cannot also be obtained at the level of the object language. Anything that is implicit can be made explicit.

4.8 QUASI-REALISM

Stimulated by Hume's view of causality and by what he argues to be the intuitive plausibility of emotivism in ethics, Simon Blackburn (1984) has come up with an ingenious idea that may seem to threaten my line on ontological commitment. This is the idea of 'quasi-realism'. Blackburn claims that a person can be committed to some area of discourse, just like the realist, yet not be a realist; for example, she can engage in the full range of moral thought and talk, yet be a moral anti-realist. Such a person is a quasi-realist. Blackburn hopes to make quasi-realism possible by interpreting the discourse not as stating facts but, rather, as expressing attitudes; it has, we might say, an 'expressive semantics', not a 'factual semantics' (the favourite example of which is, of course, truth-conditional semantics). The surface form of its sentences misleads as to their logical form.

The point of this exercise is to make 'projectivist' anti-realisms (like emotivism) more plausible by showing that they do *not* require that the folk are *mistaken* in their commitments. The folk are committed to attitudes, not 'facts', and so are not mistaken about the facts.

It is important to see that quasi-realism is *a way of being anti-realist*. It starts from a straightforwardly metaphysical rejection of some reality – like causality or morality – and then goes on to show how, nevertheless, we can see language that seems to be a mistaken commitment to that reality – like '*x* caused *y*' or '*x* is good' – as really being a commitment to an attitude. It is a presupposition of this view that there is a way of rejecting the reality that is *not* covered by this expressive semantics. Perhaps, 'There is no causal relation' will do for causal anti-realism, and 'There are no moral properties' for moral anti-realism. Some such utterances are covered by factual semantics, and do not merely express attitudes. Moreover, if this were not so, quasi-realism would not be a way of being anti-realist, because there would be no way of stating its anti-realism. If *everything* one could say that was intuitively 'about morality' were simply expressive, there would no way to be a moral realist or a moral anti-realist.

Some people doubt that quasi-realism can work (e.g. Wright 1988: 30–5). But even if it does work, it does not show that realism can be stated only by moving into a metalanguage and doing semantics. On the contrary, it presupposes the opposite. It is a way of increasing the plausibility of an object-language statement of anti-realism in a certain area by proposing an expressive semantics for the apparently realist discourse in that area.

In an earlier paper (1980) Blackburn entertained (at least) a more radical thesis: that quasi-realism undermines debates between realism and anti-realism altogether. It would do this if we could not find 'a [realist] practice that a quasi-realist cannot imitate'. This would leave realism as 'images and perhaps attitudes to our discourse . . . not so much subjects for decision as for nostalgia (p. 353). Now to suppose that we cannot find a distinctly realist practice is to suppose, contrary to what I have just claimed, that the quasi-realist's expressive semantics infects *every* attempt to state a realist doctrine itself. Thus there will be no sentence like 'There are moral properties' that is covered by factual semantics. For if there were, we would have identified one practice that the quasi-realist cannot imitate: the practice of asserting that sentence.[13]

What are we to make of this radical thesis? It cannot rest on the suggestion that *all* discourse – even the metalinguistic semantic discourse! – is covered by expressive semantics. That suggestion is not only wildly implausible, it is destructive of the enterprise of quasi-realism. The enterprise depends on explaining a distinction within the class of apparently factual sentences between those that are really factual and those that are expressive. If all sentences were covered by expressive semantics, then that semantics would be of no help in explaining that distinction. It would be useless in showing that, for example, moral discourse is not factual as it appears to be. The moral realism debate would remain at the object-language level over, say, 'There are moral properties'; and expressive semantics would provide no support for the view that the anti-realist could mimic the realist. The excursion into semantics would be totally irrelevant to the debate.

If quasi-realism is to be possible, some language must have a factual semantics. Against this background of factual language, the quasi-realist is claiming that other language, apparently of the same sort, has an expressive semantics. The radical thesis then rests on the claim that *all* apparently factual *realist* claims can plausibly be seen as expressive. But why should we believe that? Why are such statements as 'There are moral properties' not paradigms of the factual? Blackburn himself, in his later work, makes several anti-realist statements about causality and morality, apparently taking them at face value (1984: 169, 180, 211–12). Semantic statements in the meta-language are not suspected of non-factuality *by anyone*. There is no more reason for suspecting philosophical statements of realism in the object language. Language does not suddenly become kosher when you start doing semantics.

The possibility of quasi-realism does not undermine the view that the various realisms are metaphysical, not semantic, doctrines. Nevertheless, it does add to the plausibility of some anti-realisms; for example, moral and causal anti-realism. Perhaps it does so also for anti-Scientific Realism; for instrumentalism is a sort of quasi-realism (7.8). Quasi-realism has no such role with the anti-realism that mostly concerns us: anti-Common-Sense Realism. If any language is to be factual, our discourse about the ordinary physical world must be.

4.9 ONTOLOGY AND SEMANTICS

Finally, the idea that the semantic criterion is the only criterion of ontological commitment presupposes that what must exist for a sentence to be true can be settled independently of other ontological considerations.[14] This presupposition is false. Furthermore, onto-logical views guide views on such semantic questions much more than vice versa (Maxim 3).

Consider my earlier application of the semantic criterion to (1). The first step was

(a)   (1) is true if and only if there exists something such that
      'Lulu' designates it and 'cat' applies to it.

This view of how the truth of a predication depends on the reference
of its parts reflects my nominalist liking for the ontological category
of *objects*. But suppose someone was a 'universalist', believing in
universals but not objects. He would think the first step should be

(a′) (1) is true if and only if there exists something such that
      'cat' specifies it and 'Lulu' picks-our-an-instance-of it.

There can be no *purely semantic* reason for preferring (a) to (a′); yet
(a′) yields a completely different view of what must exist for (1) to be
true. My preference for (a) over (a′) was determined by ontological
considerations that have nothing to do with semantics.

    We can see then that each science raises ontological questions
quite explicitly. The best ontology will be that of the best unified
science. With an eye to this unification, each science should take
account of the others in its positings. However, no science – least of
all semantics – simply dictates to the others. Even physics, which is
in the strongest position, cannot do that: physicalism is an empirical
hypothesis.

NOTES

1   See also, e.g., Boyd 1984: 41–2; Fales 1988: 253–4; Jennings 1989: 240;
    Matheson 1989.
2   On a charitable reading, that is what Arthur Fine has done in intro-
    ducing 'the Natural Ontological Attitude' (1986a, 1986b). However,
    some passages make it hard to take Fine as a Realist (1986b: 163–5);
    his rhetoric is, as Ernan McMullin remarks, 'anti-realist in tone' (1984:
    26). And van Fraassen's claim that Fine's view would be compatible
    with his 'with minor modifications' (1985: 246) should give the Realist
    pause. I agree with McMullin that Fine is trying to have 'the best of
    both worlds' (1984: 26).
3   The next four sections draw on parts of my 1983a, 1983b, 1988a, 1988b,
    and 1991a.
4   This paragraph represents a change from the analogous paragraph in
    the first edition (1984a: 36–7), partly in response to George 1984: 517.
5   Brian Ellis (1985) subscribes to a Peircean notion of truth, and yet
    seems to agree with much of Realism. However, at bottom, his position
    is anti-realist: 'there is no way that the world is absolutely, only ways in
    which it is relative to various kinds of beings' (p. 71). How does he

arrive at this view? He believes that choice of the ideal theory, hence truth, is not determined entirely by empirical evidence, but partly by 'pragmatic' considerations which are *our* 'epistemic values' (p. 68). So, he concludes, the world is dependent on those values. I assume that the intermediate step here involves the equivalence thesis in the way I illustrate.

6 Anthony Appiah (1991) and Michael Luntley (1991) both wrongly attribute to me the view that semantics is irrelevant to Realism.

7 See, e.g., Field 1978, Churchland 1979, Stich 1983.

8 Is Barry Taylor's determination to make realism semantic, against all the evidence of his own discussion (1987), to be explained in this way? There is a similar difficulty in distinguishing substantive from merely deflationary reference; see Appiah 1991 and my response, 1991c.

9 A similar view may lie behind Kim 1980: 596–7. See also Wright 1986: 1–2.

10 This section has been stimulated partly by arguments with Ken Gemes.

11 See, e.g., Fine 1986a: 138–9.

12 Though my answer to this question is not, I think, Quine's, his in-fluence on my answer is obvious; see particularly 'On What There Is' (Quine 1953: 1–19).

13 Blackburn is attracted to the radical thesis because he finds wanting four complicated practices that he thinks might distinguish the realist from the quasi-realist. These four are largely drawn from the works of Dummett and Putnam (see chs. 12 and 14 below). He does not consider practices, like the one I propose, of *simply stating realism* in the object language. I have criticized Blackburn's paper elsewhere (1983c; 669–74).

14 This section has been stimulated partly by correspondence with Frank Jackson about my 1980b.

5

Why be a Common-Sense Realist?

Dare I suggest at last that a kind of highmindedness and sportsmanship have conspired against the vulgar plethora of he evidence for realism to protect from bathos the 'persistent problems' and the laborious ritual of our profession? To bring such gross implements as Mill's methods to the limpid regions of philosophic discourse is like dynamiting a trout stream. It gets the fish, but it misses all the exquisite impractical pleasure of angling with the thin line of dialectic. Besides, it depletes the game supply. These punctilios may, of course, mean simply a resolve that philosophy must be critical of the most obvious of mundane opinions and methods. But in so far as they are a mood of gratuitous superiority, the philosopher who does not think of philosophy as mere courtly pastime like parchesi will abandon them. The disclaimer of the earthier sorts of knowledge has isolated philosophy, made it a mystery or a jest, an escape from reality or a visionary interpretation. Philosophy is not higher and suprascientific. It is the lowest and grubbiest inquiry round the roots of things, and when it answers real questions about the world, it is and can only be an inductive science.
(Williams 1966: 146–7)

5.1 INTRODUCTION

Realism about the oridinary observable physical world is a compelling doctrine. It is almost universally held outside philosophical circles. From an early age, we come to believe that such objects as stones, trees, and cats exist. Further, we believe that these objects exist even when we are not perceiving them, and that they do not depend for their existence on our opinions or on anything mental. These beliefs about ordinary objects are central to our whole way of viewing the world, to our conceptual scheme. The doctrine I have defined to capture these beliefs (2.4) is aptly named 'Common-Sense Realism', because it is in fact the core of common sense.

It does not follow from this that Common-Sense Realism, which I shall often in this chapter simply call 'Realism', should be accepted uncritically. However, it does follow that we should give it up only in the face of very convincing arguments against it and for an alternative. So the main argument for Realism will be that the arguments against it and for alternatives fail (5.2–5.6). I think that Popper is not far wrong in claiming that 'no sensible alternative has ever been offered' (1972: 42). I do offer a positive argument for Realism (5.7). It requires that epistemology be naturalized (5.8 and 5.9). Finally, I shall reject the view that Scientific Realism undermines Common-Sense Realism (5.10).

The elements in my argument are mostly not novel, though there is perhaps some novelty in the way in which they are arranged. It seems necessary to rehearse the familiar strengths of Realism in order to make the rejection of contemporary anti-Realist tendencies in part III persuasive.

In chapter 6 I shall argue for Correspondence Truth (physical) from a Realist perspective. If that argument is good, it provides further support for Realism, for its shows how Realism is part of a plausible explanation of people and their language.

In chapter 7 I shall argue for Scientific Realism.

5.2 CARTESIAN SCEPTICISM

Perhaps the most famous argument against Realism is that advanced by Descartes in the First Meditation. It is tempting to construe such Cartesian scepticism in ways that make it easy to dismiss. (1) The sceptic is seen as requiring absolute certainty – the absence of any possibility of error – before we can be said to have knowledge. Such a standard for knowledge seems unreasonably high. (2) The sceptic is seen as offering reasons for doubting that we know anything. But if these reasons are to carry any weight, they must be propositions we claim to know. So scepticism is self-defeating. These temptations should be resisted, because they seriously underestimate the power of the sceptical argument.

Concerning (1), the sceptic does not have to tie knowledge to absolute certainty. Indeed, he does not have to talk of knowledge at all: he can make his case by talking only of justified, or rational, belief. Concerning (2), the sceptic need not make any knowledge (or belief) claims. He asks the Realist to justify his position and uses assumptions that *the Realist* seems in no position to deny to show that these attempted justifications fail. The sceptic is himself dubious about these assumptions, as of almost everything else. The argument, therefore, is something of a *reductio* of Realism: the Realist perspective itself shows Realism to be unjustified.

The sceptical strategy is to insist that the Realist is justified in his belief only if he can give good reasons for eliminating alternative hypotheses to Realism. Yet, the sceptic argues, the Realist is unable to give such reasons, as he (the Realist) should be able to see. Realism collapses from within.

If we have knowledge, or justified belief, of the external world it is obvious that we acquire that knowledge or belief through our sensory experiences. Yet, how can we rely on these, Descartes asks? First, the Realist must allow that our senses sometimes deceive us: there are the familiar examples of illusion and hallucination. How, then, can we ever be justified in relying on our senses. Second, how can we be sure that we are not dreaming? Though we think we are perceiving the external world, perhaps we are only dreaming that we are. Finally, perhaps there is a 'Deceitful Demon' causing us to have sensory experiences *as if* of an external world, when in fact there is no such world. If we do not know that this is not the case, how can we know that Realism is correct? How can it even be rational to believe Realism?

This Cartesian doubt reflects the truth of 'underdetermination'. The evidence of our senses underdetermines our views of the world: other opinions are compatible with the evidence. This truth is supported by our best modern science.

Consider our scientific account of the mechanics of perception. According to this account, when a person sees an object, roughly the following occurs. Light waves reflected from the object are focused onto the retina in each of the person's eyes. These cause chemical changes, which in turn cause electrical impulses to pass along nerve fibres to the visual areas of the brain. As a result, the person may come to believe that the object is before him. Precisely which series of nerves 'fire' and precisely what belief is formed depend not only on the nature of the stimulation, but also on various aspects of the person's physiological and psychological state, including his expectations. These expectations depend on the theories of the world he has built up over many years, as a result of many earlier experiences. What we see and what we come to believe, following stimulation, are partly a result of (largely unconscious) processing; *to a degree*, we impose a view, perceiving what we expert to perceive.

The mere fact that a person, as a result of a perceptual experience, comes to believe that a certain object is in front of him does not establish that it is in front of him. It is compatible with our theory of perception that he should come to this belief and yet that there be no such object in front of him. It is compatible with that theory that he should come to beliefs about the external world as a result of perceptual experiences and yet that there be no such world at all.

First, the stimulation that the person received is not necessary for him to come to have the belief: other stimulations, perhaps having nothing to do with the object in question, could bring about a similar series of nerve firings and the same belief; he could impose the same view on the consequences of different stimulations. Second, the existence of the object is not necessary for the particular stimulation that led to the belief. The stimulation consisted in a certain pattern of light falling on his retinas. *Anything* that produces that particular pattern would do as well. The object is only one of many things that could do so.

The position can be put in more extreme form. Were the Realist now a brain in a vat appropriately stimulated for years on end by the modern equivalent of Descartes' Deceitful Demon, Superscientist, he would have the same view of the world that he now has. He would find the idea that he was a brain in a vat just as fantastic and impossible to imagine as he now finds it. On what ground does the Realist rule this possibility out? As a result of an enormously complicated series of happenings in his nervous system, he comes to have a certain view of the world. But these happenings are compatible with other hypotheses. On what grounds do we rule out these hypotheses? It seems that the Realist cannot know that there is an external world. And the problem is not merely that he lacks certainty about it: it seems that his belief in it is unjustified.

A Realist is in no position to deny the findings of our best science. Indeed, it is largely the explanatory success of this science that gives him his great confidence in Realism. Yet this Realist science includes a theory of perception that seems to show that Realism is unjustified; for it shows that we have no evidence favouring Realism over other hypotheses. Part of our Realist world-view shows that Realism is unjustified.

There are four basic ways of reacting to this:

(1) The traditional way, adopted by Descartes himself, accepts the 'sceptical problematic', but seeks an area of knowledge which is not open to sceptical doubt and which can serve as a 'foundation' for all or most claims to knowledge. Since even the most basic common-sense knowledge – that of the existence of the external world – is open to doubt, as we have seen, this search is for a special philosophical realm of knowledge. This has been found in knowledge of

'ideas' or 'sense data'. I shall consider these foundations in section
5.3. Some philosophers have attempted to build a Realist position on
these foundations. I shall consider such attempts in section 5.4.
However, it has seemed to most foundationalists that the way to save
our knowledge was to give up the Realist ontology. I shall consider
anti-Realist foundationalism in section 5.5.

(2) The Kantian reaction might be regarded as some sort of
foundationalism. However, it is very different from (1), and so I shall
treat it separately. It takes scepticism very seriously, but it does not
find an answer in knowledge of sense data. It claims that the familiar
external world is partly constituted by us, and so is knowable. I
consider it first in section 5.6, returning to it in chapter 13.

(3) Another way of reacting would be to accept the argument and
adopt scepticism. The problem with this reaction is that it leaves us
so little. If Cartesian doubt undermines knowledge (justified belief)
claims anywhere, it will undermine them *almost everywhere*. Scepticism
that starts with physical objects soon spreads to other minds, and
then to one's own mind at other times. A person is left, at most, with
the belief that he is now experiencing. He can believe only in a world
of drastic simplicity, that of 'solipsism of the moment' (Russell 1948:
196) or 'instantaneous solipsism' (Williams 1966: 124).[1] A story of
Russell's brings out the fact that solipsism is literally incredible: 'I
once received a letter from an eminent logician, Mrs Christine Ladd
Franklin, saying that she was a solipsist, and was surprised that there
were not others' (1948: 196).

(4) Finally there is a way of reacting to the problem that reflects
the influence of W. V. Quine. It rejects the sceptical problematic and
the *a priori* epistemology of the foundationalist and Kant altogether.
It does not drop the claims of folk theory and science in the face of a
sceptical epistemology. Rather, it starts from those claims, including
the posits on which Realism is based, and seeks an epistemology
from within science. This leads to a less demanding sort of justification than that required by the sceptic. It leads to a 'naturalized
epistemology'.

From this perspective, scepticism is seen as a consistent position
which is, ultimately, unanswerable.[2] Our beliefs are underdetermined
by the evidence. We could be wrong about anything. Yet we hold to
our beliefs, rejecting other hypotheses against which we have no
evidence. We are confident that the sceptic who refuses to follow us
in this will have a short life; but in the end, we find ourselves with no
argument to convince him. Extreme scepticism is simply *uninteresting*.
Instantaneous solipsism, the brain-in-the-vat hypothesis, and other
such fantasies are too implausible to take seriously.

This reaction is in accord with Maxim 3, and is the one I favour in sections 5.7–5.9.

5.3 'IDEAS' AND 'SENSE DATA'

The foundationalist accepts the rigorous sceptical standard for knowledge, but claims that all or most of our beliefs, properly construed, meet that standard. He attempts to defeat the sceptic on the sceptic's own terms. I shall argue that the attempt fails: sceptical standards lead inexorably to acceptance of only the impoverished world of instantaneous solipsism. If we want to accept more, the standards must be abandoned.

The foundationalist seeks a realm of knowledge that cannot be doubted, which can form the foundation for his beliefs. He has always found it in the same place. 'In the search for certainty, it is natural to begin with our present experiences' (Russell 1912: 1). This natural beginning led traditionally to the view that we could not be mistaken about entities called 'ideas'. More recently, it has led to the similar view that we could not be mistaken about entities called 'sense data'. These entities are 'the given'. I shall talk of 'sense data'. But why suppose that there *are* any sense data?

Arguments for sense data stem from three facts: first, when we think we see a physical object, we do not see all parts of it at once; second, in some sense a physical object 'looks different' from different perspectives and in different circumstances; third, on occasions we experience illusions and hallucinations. Perhaps the most famous argument stems from the third fact: the Argument from Illusion. It is the argument I shall consider. It is easy enough to see how my discussion could be adapted to arguments based on the first and second facts.

The Argument from Illusion runs as follows:

(1) Illusions and hallucinations occur, leading to mistaken observation statements; e.g. a person says, 'That stick is bent,' when it is in fact a straight stick half of which is in water.

(2) A person suffering from an illusion or hallucination nevertheless does perceive something with the property in question. That something is a sense datum. Thus the person in the example perceives a bent sense datum.

(3) Veridical perceptions are indistinguishable from illusions and hallucinations.

∴ (4) What people perceive are sense data.

The key step in this argument is (2). Why should the sceptic accept that? Cartesian doubt may allow that in the case of illusory perception the person is experiencing; but why should he grant that there exists some object which the person is having experience of and hence has knowledge of? How can we know that there is such an object? The traditional response is that we *just do* have indubitable knowledge that there is such an object with certain properties – in our example, that there is a sense datum that is bent. This response is mere dogma. It exemplifies the fatal flaw in foundationalism. The foundationalist goes along with the application of the sceptical standard to most areas of knowledge, but refuses, for no apparent reason, to apply it to areas he cherishes. Sense data are as open to doubt as material objects.

The plausibility of (2) comes from overlooking Moore's distinction between an *act* of perceiving and an *object* perceived (1922: 17–20). Whereas it may be undeniable that the person in question is perceiving, the sceptic sees no reason for positing an object which he is perceiving. Indeed, *I* see no ground for positing a bent object.

The foundationalist's illegitimate slide away from scepticism is encouraged, of course, by our ordinary way of talking. Whenever we are prepared to say that a person is perceiving (experiencing, etc.), we are prepared to say that he is perceiving something. But this no more establishes the existence of sense data than our similar practice with the verb 'worship' establishes the existence of God. Verbs like 'perceive' are 'intentional' (Anscombe 1965) or 'opaque' (Quine 1960: §32).

The foundationalist might at this point abandon all claims to sense data (as objects) and take an 'adverbial' or 'as-if' approach to experiential statements. 'At least, in the case of illusion, the person knows that he is perceiving bent-stickishly; or at least he knows that it is *as if* he is perceiving a bent stick. Here is a foundation that does not posit objectionable entities.'

The sceptic should not allow even that foundation. Perhaps he should concede that the person is perceiving; but how does the person know that he is perceiving bent-stickishly rather than round-stonishly? What is the justification for any particular characterization of the experience? The characterization must depend on a comparison with remembered experiences. Yet memory is fallible. At most, the person can be confident of his own currently experiencing ego.

In sum, if the sceptical ground rules are taken seriously, they give the would-be foundationalist no place to build his foundations.

5.4 FOUNDATIONALISM AND REALISM

In this section I will set aside the failure of the foundationalist to establish his foundations against the sceptic, and consider the attempt to build Realism on those foundations. In the next, I shall do likewise for the attempt to build (non-sceptical) anti-Realism on those foundations.

The most appealing from of foundationalist Realism is 'representative' Realism, the *locus classicus* for which is Locke's *Essay Concerning Human Understanding*. From our perceptual knowledge of sense data, we *infer* the existence of physical objects that *resemble* and *cause* the sense data. Berkeley made what seemed to be a crushing objection to representative Realism: there is no basis for the inference. It is obviously not deductively valid, and it cannot be based on experience, since, according to the view in question, all we experience are our own sense data. Certainly there is no reason why the sceptic should accept the inference.

The failure of representative Realism is particularly vivid in Locke. His basic position is that knowledge is 'nothing but *the perception of the connexion of and agreement, or disagreement and repugnancy of any of our ideas*' (bk IV, ch. I, sect. 2). For in our thinking we are confined to our ideas. This position indicates how seriously Locke takes the sceptic *in general*. It leaves no room for knowledge of connections between ideas and *non*-ideas, which is what representative Realism requires. When faced with this problem, Locke partly begs the question against the sceptic and partly makes appeals to common sense (bk IV, ch. XI). But, of course, if we are prepared to rest on common sense, we can ignore the sceptic in the first place. Locke's discussion is another illustration of foundationalism's fatal flaw (5.3).

We can capture the way in which the sceptical problematic presents itself to the representative Realist with the following 'picture'. Sense data are a series of images playing on a screen in the inner theatre of the mind. He (a homunculus) sits watching this movie and asks himself: (1) Is there anything outside causing the show? (2) If so, is it anything like the images on the screen? The sceptic remains steadfastly sceptical about any answers.

In the last section I mentioned the possibility of a foundationalism not resting on entities but of an 'adverbial' or 'as-if' sort. Can this save representative Realism? Clearly the sceptic will not think so. The inference from these foundations to the external world is no better than the classical one we have just dismissed.

Representative Realism fails as an answer to scepticism, yet it remains appealing. A great part of its appeal comes from its evident agreement with the simple facts of perception. Assume Realism. How then do we humans learn about the Realist world? The answer is obvious: as a result of the causal action of that world on our sense organs. Representative Realism has got that right. Furthermore, once we set scepticism aside and seek a positive argument for Realism (5.7), we find that the best we can do is along the lines of representative Realism: an inference to the best explanation from experiential facts of the 'as-if' sort.

The problem for representative Realism in answering the sceptic is 'the gap' between the mental sense data and the represented reality about which it is claimed that we have knowledge. Some twentieth-century foundationalists have attempted to close this gap by moving sense data outside the mind (e.g. Russell 1912: 21; Ayer 1940: 75–8). The Realist aim would then be to move these non-mental sense data sufficiently close to physical objects to show that the objects are, in some sense, constructed out of the sense data. (The 'adverbial' or 'as-if' approaches, which do not posit sense data, would of course be useless for this strategy.)

We are setting aside sceptical objections to the positing of sense data. Nevertheless, it is worth noting that these non-mental sense data were obscure entities. They tended to lead an uncertain existence, in limbo between mind and physical object.

This reductionist Realism has an insuperable problem. How is the physical object to be constructed? A straightforward way would be to constitute it, literally, out of sense data: a physical object is nothing but a bundle of sense data (cf. the Realist view that an object is nothing but a bundle of atoms). But how, then, can we explain the fact that the object can exist unobserved? The obvious answer is that *sense data* can exist unobserved. The assumption that such unobserved entities exist is, of course, quite gratuitous from the sceptical viewpoint (foundationalism's fatal flaw again). How can we know of these entities, and hence how can we know of the physical entities partly made up of them?

The phenomenalist programme attempted a different sort of construction: 'logical construction'. Each sentence about a physical object was to be translated, in some loose sense, into sentences about sense data. I shall consider the failure of this programme in the next section. However, even if it had succeeded, it would not have saved Realism; for it is a programme to *paraphrase away* apparent commitment to physical objects: when the chips are down, we talk only of sense data. Or, putting the point in another way, the programme would show how the truth of a physical-object sentence depended not on the existence of physical objects but only on that of sense data (4.6 and 4.7). Though we may regard the programme as one of linguistic reduction, it is in fact one of ontological elimination.

The fundamentally anti-Realist nature of the phenomenalist's position was often obscured by the positivists. Their interest in eliminating metaphysics led to a linguistic turn that *mystified* metaphysics (cf. Maxim 2). Thus Ayer (1940) does not represent himself as denying that material things exist. He regards the choice of a phenomenalist's sense-datum language over a material-thing language as a mere matter of convenience: it is pragmatic, not factual. What then *is* factual? What is the reality that constrains us and prevents us saying absolutely anything? It is the realm of 'empirical facts', or 'evidence', against which all statements are tested. It is in these facts alone that we must find Ayer's ontology. In talking of them, Ayer is not talking of language; he is doing metaphysics, despite the disclaimers (likewise Schlick in talking of 'the given': 1932–3). What does Ayer tell us about these facts? Directly, almost nothing. His discussion is devoted to the sense-datum language which is to be an instrument for capturing these facts; the metaphysics is concealed. Nevertheless, we get some clues: the facts are 'sense-experiences' having 'contents' (p. 26). If we do not take these facts as experiences of sense data, thereby making the choice of the phenomenalist's language *not* a matter of convenience, we have no idea what they are. Certainly, the facts do not include material things, and so Ayer's implicit ontology is anti-Realist. (See the discussion of instrumentalism in section 7.8 for a similar criticism of the positivists.)

I conclude that the foundationalist has no answer to the sceptical argument against Realism.

5.5 FOUNDATIONALISM AND ANTI-REALISM

Saving Realism is a very tall order for foundationalism. Typically, foundationalism has led to anti-Realism by an argument along the following lines:

(1) We have non-inferential (immediate, direct) knowledge only of the existence of sense data.
(2) We cannot gain inferential knowledge of the existence of a reality beyond sense data from knowledge of the existence of sense data.

∴   (3)   We do not know of the existence of a reality beyond sense
           data.

If sense data are taken to be mental entities of some sort, the
argument leads to idealism (e.g. in Berkeley). If they are taken to be
non-mental, it leads to some other form of anti-Realism. Thus the
price for knowledge turns out to be the abandonment of familiar
reality. Epistemology determines metaphysics (cf. Maxim 3).

Foundationalist anti-Realism is intended to save our knowledge
from scepticism, starting with our singular knowledge of physical
objects. How can it do that? The two strategies of the failed attempt
to save Realism (5.4) occur again.

First, were a physical object nothing but a bundle of sense data, we
might hope to derive knowledge of the object from knowledge of its
sense data. However, the problem of the unobserved object makes
this hope vain. The sceptic will see no basis for an inference to the
existence of unobserved sense data that must, on this view, partly
constitute the object.

Second, the phenomenalist programme attempted to translate all
physical-object statements into sense-datum statements. Since the
latter statements are of the sort that the foundationalist thinks we
know, it was hoped in this way to save our knowledge, albeit in a
new form. However, the total failure of all attempts to fulfil this
programme over many years of trying is so impressive as to make
it 'overwhelmingly likely' that the programme *cannot* be fulfilled
(Putnam 1975b: 20).

From a Realist perspective, it is easy to see the problem for
phenomenalism: there is a loose link between a physical object and
any set of experiences we might have of it. As a result, no finite
set of sense-datum statements is either necessary or sufficient for a
physical-object statement (as Ayer himself points out: 1940: 238–40).
The problem is too familiar to need further illustration (see e.g.
Smart 1963: 20).

Aside from this problem in practice, the phenomenalist programme has a problem in principle, which is also familiar. The
sense-datum statements which are to do the job are not reports of
actual sense data; they are subjunctive conditionals: 'If x were to
do such and such, then he would experience so and so.' These
conditionals need bases; they need something that makes them true:
they do not express 'brute facts'. What could their bases be? The
obvious answer is not available to the phenomenalist, for it involves
talk of the external world, a world independent of sense data. An

answer in terms of non-actual, but possible, sense data is, in my view, completely unacceptable. The phenomenalist can give no answer. (A dramatic illustration of the problem is that the phenomenalist can make no sense of the idea of a lifeless universe: Armstrong 1961: 56–7.)

The phenomenalists seemed to posit sense data. In any case, it is obvious that the 'adverbial' or 'as if' approach would do nothing to save the phenomenalist translation programme.

The foundationalist anti-Realist cannot save physical objects. He cannot save our singular knowledge of physical objects by reconstruing it as knowledge of sense data. Perhaps he could, like Hume, build *something* (to sceptical standards) on the foundations which, for the sake of argument, we are allowing him. However, the world-view he could offer would not be much more palatable than instantaneous solipsism. It is no accident that anti-Realists have typically been, like Berkeley, conservative, accepting the existence dimension of Realism. A doctrine that seems to allow us our familiar objects and beliefs, even if it says some rather surprising things about their dependence on us, has some initial plausibility. A radical doctrine that does not do this is very hard to swallow, as Hume himself found, once he left his study.

The foundationalist is not entitled to his foundations. Setting that aside, Realism cannot be built to sceptical standards on those foundations. Further, anti-Realism cannot meet those standards even for singular knowledge about the physical world. The sceptical problematic leaves the knowledge-seeker no place to stand and no way to move. The foundationalist programme is hopeless.

5.6 KANT

If Kant is regarded as a foundationalist, this conclusion may seem too hasty. Certainly Kant took scepticism, particularly that of Hume, seriously: he regarded it as a scandal, and set out to save knowledge. His approach is very different from the classical foundationalism of, for example, Berkeley. It is deep, dark, and difficult.

He raises the question 'How is knowledge possible?' His answer involves a distinction between an *appearance*, which is part of the phenomenal world, and a *thing-in-itself*, which is part of the noumenal world. It is tempting to equate an appearance with the foundationalist's sense datum, taking the thing-in-itself as the unknowable external cause of this mental entity. Kant's writing often encourages this temptation. Nevertheless, scholars seem generally agreed – and have convinced me – that this two-worlds interpretation is wrong. What Kant intends is the following very influential one-world view.

An appearance is not a mental sense datum, but an external object *as we know it*. By contrast, the thing-in-itself is the object *independent of our knowledge of it*; it is not a second object and does not – indeed, could not – cause an appearance, for causation has its place only in the phenomenal world. Appearances are familiar objects like stones, trees, and cats. Our knowledge of these objects has two elements, both of which are essential: a perceptual, or experiential, element and a conceptual element. The conceptual element consists in the mind's imposition of *a priori* concepts (e.g. causality) and a spatio-temporal setting on objects.

Kant is a Weak Realist (2.4). External objects exist objectively (in my sense: 2.2) only as things-in-themselves. As we know them – that is as familiar objects – they exist partly in virtue of our imposition of concepts and a spatio-temporal setting. To a degree, we *create* the world we live in.

Kant is concerned to bridge the gap left by Locke between the knower and the object of knowledge, a gap that was thought to lead to scepticism. Berkeley's solution was to be bring the object into the mind. Kant thinks of himself as rejecting this view: the object is external to the mind – 'out there' – but is partly constituted by us. His key step is that from

> Certain conditions must hold if we are to know objects

to

> Objects known must be constituted, in part, by those conditions.

Once again we see epistemology determining metaphysics (cf. Maxim 3).

Does Kant answer the sceptic? Strictly not, because he *assumes* that knowledge is possible and sets out to show how it is. If his argument is right, then without our imposition there would be no order to experience at all; there would be phenomenal chaos. I take it that even instantaneous solipsism is a step beyond this chaos. What could he say to the sceptic who replied 'Perhaps there is just chaos?' So far as I can see, nothing. But, if his argument is right, he has raised the stakes of scepticism.

Kant's metaphysics is often explained with the help of the cookie-cutter metaphor. The dough (things-in-themselves) is independent of the cook (us). The cook imposes cookie cutters (concepts) on the dough in order to create cookies (appearances).

This deeply mysterious metaphysics has fascinated philosophers for two centuries. Reality as it is in itself is mysterious in being for ever inaccessible. Reality as we know it is mysterious in being somehow the result of our own handiwork. How could the cookie cutters in our head reach out, literally, and make the stars?

Many contemporary anti-Realisms combine Kantianism with relativism. We shall come across some examples later: Kuhn, Feyerabend, and the radical philosophers of science (9.2); Putnam (12.5). I shall look critically at relativistic Kantianism, under the name 'Constructivism', in chapter 13.

What needs emphasizing here is that Kant's position, like that of the foundationalists, starts from an *a priori* epistemology. It is an example of a 'first philosophy', transcending science. But what is the basis for this *a priori* knowledge? Indeed, why suppose there is any such?

In my view, Kant and the foundationalists use the wrong method and proceed in the wrong direction. We should use the *empirical* method, not the *a priori* one, and should set scepticism aside. I shall do this in the next three sections. This will show that we should proceed from the Realism issue to an epistemology, not vice versa (Maxim 3).

5.7 THE ARGUMENT
FOR COMMON-SENSE REALISM

The argument for Common-Sense Realism starts from folk theory and scientific theory. These theories posit many observable physical entities. By and large we are confident of these posits. Nevertheless, we are cautious, allowing for error: we commit ourselves to most of those entities. Our folk theory, including some folk epistemology, gives us a view of those entities: they exist objectively and independently of the mental. That is how we arrive at our Realism.

Suppose we are asked to defend this doctrine. We point out that arguments against it and for anti-Realist alternatives fail (5.3–5.6). There is no plausible worked-out alternative to Realism. In a sense, Realism is the *only* theory in town. Can we do any better than this, giving a positive argument *for* Realism? Why are these posits *necessary* (2.3)?

Donald Williams believes that Realism can be established inductively, as the passage that opened this chapter indicates. He thinks it is confirmed day by day in innumerable ways (1966: 147–8). I agree (once scepticism has been at aside). However, as Putnam points out (1975b: 21–32), the induction in question is very unusual. The induction is supposed to be an explanatory one – an inference to the best explanation, or abduction – yet it is hard to see what it is that Realism explains (more strictly, what it is that the theories, on which Realism is cautiously based, explain). The difficulty is that the very language in which we normally describe the basic phenomena is a 'thing language': it near enough *presupposes* Realism. We seem not to have a language that is neutral between Realism and some alternative theory in which to describe the phenomena. This reflects the fact that there has never been a viable alternative theory.

Intuitively, what we want is a language to describe the facts of *experience*, for if Realism is to explain anything, it must be these facts. And we do have such a language, but it is straightforwardly parasitic on 'thing language'. It is the afore mentioned 'as-if' language (5.3). (The invented 'adverbial' language, mentioned in section (5.3), would also do the trick. But it is just as parasitic on 'thing language'.)

Consider a simple situation in which a Realist would assert the existence of a common-sense object: for example,

(1)   There is a black raven on the lawn.

The Realist would also be prepared to assert the more cautious statement

(2)   It is as if there is a black raven on the lawn.

(2) is more cautious because, unlike (1), it does not posit the existence of a black raven (or lawn). Anyone, apart from a thorough-going sceptic, should be prepared to assert such 'as-if' statements in appropriate circumstances (even if he thought he were a brain in a vat stimulated by Superscientist). It is because of the truth of such statements that people have been tempted to posit sense data. However, (2) does not posit sense data (or indeed any entity at all).

We now raise the questions: What is the explanation of (2)? Why does the world seem the way it does? The obvious answer is that the world seems that way because it *is* that way. It is as if there is a black raven because there is a black raven. The answer has a trivial air to it, but is good none the less. The trivial air arises, first, because we have no way to describe the explanans except in parasitic 'as-if' terms; second, because we do not normally feel any need to explain why it is as if there are *x*'s unless we are seriously contemplating some answer other than the obvious one that there are x's. We are not seriously contemplating such an answer, because there is none with any more plausibility than brain-in-the-vat fantasies. However, if an explanation is insisted on, the Realist one is a good one. And if we actually had an independent, non-parasitic experiential language, which we could *in principle* have, the air of triviality would disappear. Realism is indeed confirmed day by day in innumerable ways. It is confirmed by almost every 'as-if' statement we are inclined to assent to. (This bears on the discussion of success in section 7.3.)

The underlying truth of representative Realism is that we can infer Realism from more epistemically basic statements (5.4). These statements are not 'about our sense data' but they are, in a way to be brought out further in section 6.6, 'close to our experience'.

This is not to say that we do *as a matter of fact* infer the existence of the external world from the way things seem. It seems almost certain that our basic non-inferential beliefs are ones about the external world: we take Realism for granted. Nevertheless, such beliefs, like any others, can be questioned. If they are, they can be justified (though not to sceptical standards).

5.8 NATURALIZED EPISTEMOLOGY

The thoroughgoing sceptic sets the standards of knowledge (or rational belief) too high for them ever to be achieved. Our best science shows us this. It shows us, for example, that if knowledge is to be gathered, we must eliminate implausible hypotheses without being able, ultimately, to justify that elimination. It shows us that there is always an (empirical) possibility of error with any (normal) knowledge claim. Standards that our best science shows cannot be met short of instantaneous solipsism – a doctrine that is literally incredible – should be ignored. Scepticism is simply uninteresting: it throws the baby out with the bath water.

(Though this form of skepticism is uninteresting, an example of Hartry Field brings out that something like it might not always be so. Suppose a person has the following theory. His life is humdrum except for his job. He works as the laboratory assistant for Superscientist, who has nineteen brains in vats. Superscientist stimulates each of these brains to believe that it has a humdrum life except for its job. It believes that it is the laboratory assistant for Superscientist who has nineteen brains in vats, each one being stimulated to believe. . . . In these circumstances a sceptical hypothesis is certainly interesting.)

Having dismissed the quest for certainty, for rock-hard foundations, and for ultimate justification, what then remains for epistemology? It is left with the task of *explaining* our coming to know science (and common sense). There are two parts to this explanation, a descriptive part and a normative part. The descriptive part explains how as a matter of fact we form our opinions. The normative part explains what makes these opinions knowledge (in so far as they are). We seek a scientific explanation of our knowing science. The epistemic relation between humans and the world itself becomes the object of scientific study. Epistemology becomes naturalized.[3]

Naturalized epistemology takes science, and hence its posits pretty much for granted. And an obvious starting assumption is the aforementioned one that these posits exist objectively and independently of the mental. So it approaches epistemology from a Realist standpoint; it is in accord with Maxim 3. However, naturalism does not prevent a reconsideration of Realism. I shall make one in the next section.

In the next chapter I shall consider our entitlement to such notions as belief and truth. Here I shall simply use them. Even if we are not entitled to them, we do not at present have any convenient way of dispensing with them in doing epistemology.

We are born into the world with dispositions to respond selectively to the experiences caused by stimuli at our surfaces: we have innate similarity standards. Furthermore, we are innately disposed to infer in certain ways. The world bombards us with stimuli. The innate machinery is activated, 'ordering' the resulting experience. We are theorizing. We presume that even these first steps take us 'beyond experience', positing an external world, however primitive. In these first steps we arrive at beliefs (partly) *as a result of* experience. We do not, however, *infer them from* experience (cf. representative Realism: 5.4) for, inference being a relation between beliefs, that would require that our first beliefs were about experience, which is contrary to our presumption and highly implausible. After a few years of this process, during which we have gained a language, we find ourselves the possessors of a complex and sweeping theory positing the existence of tables, trees, cats, and so forth. We have come up with the folk theory of the external world.

At this point we are way 'beyond experience'. (1) We believe singular statements about observed physical objects. (2) Further, we believe singular statements about unobserved, but observable, physical objects. (3) Further still, we believe general statements covering many unobserved, but observable, physical objects.

We do not stop at this point. Folk theory grows into science as it goes self-critical and systematic. This move may seem even more daring: we talk of such entities as electrons, muons, and curved space-time; we generalize about entities that are not simply un-observed, but unobservable.

The first task of naturalized epistemology is to discover the nature of this belief-forming process. What methods of inference do we employ? Presumably they include simple induction at least; but they will certainly include others. In my view they include abduction. What is the precise nature of these methods? When is one employed, when another? In what circumstances do we abandon a theory?

It is well known that questions like these are not easy to answer. For example, we have learnt from Duhem and Quine that our theory of the world (better, set of theories) is tested against experience as a whole. There are many ways in which we react in the face of recalci-trant experience, apart from abandoning the particular theory that may seem threatened by that experience. We can adjust our theory of the instruments involved or an auxiliary theory or a low-level statement of conditions. We can decide not to accept the ob-servation statement which the experience tempts us to make (perhaps we are hallucinating). We can accept the problematic observation statement and hope that the future will bring a means of accom-modating it (as Newtonians did with their observations of the peri-helion of Mercury).

The first task of naturalized epistemology is a *psychological* task (which is not to say that it should be done only in psychology departments). It is simply descriptive of how people *do* infer and form beliefs. This leaves untouched the question of how they *should* infer and form beliefs. Some belief-forming procedures may be good, others bad. We have good reason *a priori* to suspect that some belief-forming procedures that humans actually use will be bad. The empirical evidence that some are bad is impressive (see, e.g., Kahneman and Tversky 1973). People are sometimes irrational (cf. 10.5). Some procedures we use will be better than others. And it may be that there are procedures which we don't use which are better than those we do. This task of finding good rules of inference is not psychological. In tackling it, naturalized epistemology becomes normative: a good procedure is one we ought to follow. (This norma-tive part of the task seems to be a departure from Quine, who thinks that all epistemology is psychology.[4])

A good belief-forming procedure leads to justified beliefs. Goodness consists, roughly, in tending to lead to truth, in being reliable.

Relative goodness is partly indeterminate, as Hartry Field has helped to bring home to me. There are at least these three considerations to balance off against each other: power, degree of probability, and degree of truth. Power is important because we want procedures that yield significant truths, truths with a lot of content. Degree of probability is important because we want procedures that give high probability to conclusions. Degree of truth is important because we went procedures that yield conclusions with high degrees of truth. Balancing these considerations is difficult. For example, how do we compare a procedure according to which it is 0.5-probable that a proposition with a lot of content is 0.5-true with one according to which it is 0.7-probable that a proposition with much less content is 0.7-true? Despite this indeterminacy, I see no reason to doubt that most questions of the goodness of procedures are concerned with objective matters of fact.

Though this normative task is outside psychology (outside 'narrow' psychology, at least: 6.5), it is not outside science. We do not follow the foundationalist in seeking an *a priori* solution. It is an empirical question which procedures are good. Our theories about which ones are good must be tested against the ongoing history of science. Good procedures should tend to yield good scientific theories. This depends, of course, on our prior judgements of which scientific theories are good, and so is very much within science. These prior judgements are nevertheless in principle revisable: it is conceivable that our confidence in an epistemological theory could lead us to revise a judgement about a scientific theory. However, at this time such revision is unlikely, because we are so far from an epistemological theory in which we could have that degree of confidence.

Hilary Putnam has often remarked on our *a priori* preference for some theories over others. Thus we eliminate out of hand the theory that our experiences are simply the result of a Deceitful Demon. This *a priori* preference reflects our innate disposition to favour some belief-forming procedures over others. So this *a priority* should be no more worrying to the empirically minded than the innateness. Is the innateness worrying?

It is not, because it is explicable along Darwinian lines. If a belief-forming procedure *is* a good one, then it is not surprising that it should be innate. Good procedures lead to truths which are conducive to survival. Thus natural selection will favour organisms with good procedures.

Appeals to Darwin cannot of course *establish* that a procedure is a good one against thoroughgoing scepticism. All that is required for a procedure to be naturally selected is that it yields theories that are adequate at the level of experience. This adequacy does not require that the theories be true. But the naturalized epistemologist is not trying to answer the sceptic. His appeal to Darwin is simply to show that the innateness of certain procedures, which as a matter of scientific fact are good, is scientifically explicable.

The naturalized epistemologist agrees with Kant (5.6) that there are two elements to knowledge and that one is experiential. In describing the other element, he prefers talk of innate predispositions to the Kantian talk of *a priori* concepts. Where he differs sharply from Kant is that he does not move from this view of the knowledge process to a veiw of what is known. The move is in the reverse direction: we use our view of what is known to arrive at our view of the knowledge process. In this way metaphysics is put before epistemology, and the latter becomes, like everything else, empirical (Maxim 3)'.

5.9 EPISTEMOLOGY NATURALIZED AND ANTI-REALISM

I have rejected foundationalist and Kantian arguments for anti-Realism (5.3, 5.5, and 5.6). If there is a good argument against Realism, it must be from the perspective of epistemology naturalized.

From this perspective, science and common sense *for the most part* supply knowledge. There is no question of discarding them altogether, for they constitute the boat on which we must stay afloat. However, it is always appropriate to use some parts to look critically at others. Perhaps some parts of the boat should be rebuilt. An anti-Realist argument would show that the boat will float best without any Realist planks.

I set aside until section 5.10 the question of whether Scientific Realism shows Common-Sense Realism to be mistaken. Our concern here is with the task of resurrecting traditional anti-Realism – particularly of the sense-datum variety – from the naturalized perspective. The task seems hopeless.

The first difficulty is that our ordinary scientific theory, as it stands, is thoroughly Realist: the whole boat is built of Realist planks. We talk of stones, trees, and cats, not of sense data. Naturalized epistemology confirms that these objects have the independence and objectivity that is definitive of Common-Sense Realism. If anti-Realism is to get started, our theory must be revised.

What reason is there for positing sense data at all? From the naturalized perspective, the Argument from Illusion (5.3) can hardly be taken seriously. Its premise (2) is completely implausible. When Macbeth thinks that there is a dagger before him, he is simply wrong: there is nothing there. And we have (as did Shakespeare) an outline of the explanation of this hallucination. In the favourite case of illusion, the person sees a straight stick that looks bent because of the refractive properties of water. Arguments from the relativity of perception fare no better.

Of course, the scientific theories of cognition and perception may supply good reasons for positing mental representations and images. These differ from sense data in not being objects that we perceive. More seriously for the anti-Realist case, they are posited in thoroughly Realist sciences committed, for example, to the independent existence of people.

Whether the 'mental facts' are described in terms of representations or images or simply in the 'adverbial' or 'as-if' form mentioned earlier (5.4), it is hard to see how a naturalistic argument for anti-Realism can be built on these facts. For example, an anti-Realist argument along the lines of the one in section 5.5 clearly fails: it is not the case that we have non-inferential (immediate, direct) knowledge only of these facts; even if it were, why could we not gain inferential knowledge of a reality beyond these facts, now that we have left scepticism behind? Indeed, in so far as we need an argument *for* Realism, it can be built on these facts (5.7).

In sum, once the sceptical problematic is abandoned in favour of a naturalized epistemology, arguments against Realism lack all cogency. (See also 12.6.)

Finally, consider the alternative to Realism. Given the failure of the phenomenalist's translation programme, any anti-Realist alternative will have to be revisionist in a strong sense: there is no way to revive even our singular knowledge of the physical world by reconstruing it as about sense data (5.5). It would take a very strong argument against Realism to make this alternative seem the best explanation of the phenomena we are presented with.

Realism alone explains 'the regularities in our experiences' (5.7). It lends itself to a plausible epistemology (5.8). We shall see in chapter 6 that it is part of a good explanation of language. It has no rivals that can be taken seriously. No theory could have better credentials.

5.10 COMMON-SENSE REALISM AND SCIENCE

My argument for Common-Sense Realism, based on epistemology naturalized, gives primacy to science. Yet it is often thought that the scientific viewpoint undermines the common-sense one. It is necessary, therefore, to show that science in fact throws no doubt on my defence of Common-Sense Realism.

The area of common sense that seems most threatened by science is that concerned with the secondary properties ('qualities'), especially that concerned with colours. It cannot be claimed that science as a whole does not countenance these properties: biology and psychology countenance them. The problem is that *physics* seems not to countenance them; 'the world of physics is a colourless, soundless, odourless, and tasteless world' (Smart 1963: 64). So it is only from the physicalist standpoint that science threatens the common-sense view of the secondary properties. Further, it is only from the *Scientific Realist* standpoint that science threatens common sense. If we were to take an anti-Realist view of physics, construing talk of electrons, muons, and curved space-time as a mere instrument for dealing with the observable world, then clearly physics would pose no problem for the secondary properties. I favour physicalism (2.5), and will argue for Scientific Realism (chapter 7). Even so, I do not think that science throws doubt on Common-Sense Realism.

There are three basic positions on the secondary properties. Objectivism is the view that these properties are 'in physical entities'. Subjectivism is the view that they are 'in perceiving minds'. Eliminativism is the view that they are not 'in anything' at all. Common-Sense Realism requires the existence of such entities as stones, trees, and cats. At worst, science, viewed physicalistically and Realistically, shows that these objects lack secondary properties: objectivism must be abandoned in favour of either subjectivism or eliminativism. To show this is not to show that these objects do not exist; it is simply to show that the common-sense view of them is error-ridden. To reach the anti-Realist conclusion, we need the further premise that any common-sense physical object *must* have secondary properties. But there seems to be no good reason for anyone who, on scientific grounds, is anti-objectivist to adopt this essentialist premise. Rather she should view a common-sense physical object as a system of unobservable particles that is wrongly thought to have secondary properties.

It is not necessary, therefore, to take a stand on the vexed issue of the secondary properties to defend Common-Sense Realism.

Nevertheless, there is no denying the sense of loss which the Realist would feel if the objects he believed in did lack secondary properties. So I shall later offer an objectivist account based on Locke (13.6). We shall see then that accounts of this sort have significance for the Realism debate: they throw light on constructivism and on the independence of Realist entities (13.7).

NOTES

1 The sceptic is not entitled to the view that his own ego is all there is: he has no basis for ruling out richer worlds. So, strictly, he should not embrace solipsism. The point is that the most he is justified in accepting is the solipsist's world. He remains agnostic about the rest. (Thanks to Hartry Field and Brad Petrie.)

2 It is tempting to think that scepticism can be answered along the following lines: 'Scepticism involves a commitment to a sceptical standard of justification. What is the basis of this commitment? It is a piece of *a priori* epistemology that we need not accept.' This answer is another example of saddling the sceptic with a knowledge claim which he has no need to make. He should not commit himself to the sceptical standard of justification. He should insist that the Realist needs a justification that the Realist does not have for *rejecting* that standard. In other words, the sceptic should follow the above-mentioned strategy of avoiding assumptions even at the epistemological level. (Thanks to David Linzer.)

3 Quine has been the most influential philosopher in establishing naturalized epistemology; see particularly 'The Scope and Language of Science' (Quine 1966: 215–32), 'Epistemology Naturalized' (Quine 1969: 69–90, repr. in Kornblith 1985b), and Quine 1975. See also Goldman 1978 and Kornblith 1980 and 1985a for some very helpful discussions.

4 But perhaps not: see Quine 1966: 220. Kornblith 1985a nicely distinguishes the normative from the descriptive.

6

Why do we Need Truth?

6.1 SCEPTICISM ABOUT TRUTH

It is difficult to take seriously the question 'Why do we need truth?'
It seems obvious that we need it. For example, 'semantically ascend-
ing' to talk of the truth of sentences from talk about the way the
world is seems, particularly to the Realist, as familiar and natural as
day. Truth seems so useful and ubiquitous.

The Moorean complacency that this engenders should no survive
the discovery of the notions of truth that I have lumped together
under the term 'deflationary' (3.4). For, as Grover, Camp, and
Belnap (1975) and Leeds (1978) bring out, a great deal of the utility
of truth can be accounted for by taking it as one of these anaemic
notions. Yet our question concerns a much more robust notion, a
notion that explains something about the world; our question is
concerned with truth as a genuine property of sentences. Why do we
need a 'causal-explanatory' (Putnam 1978: 18) notion of truth? The
Realist is interested, particularly, in what a correspondence notion of
truth explains. Is Correspondence Truth (physical) correct (3.3)?

We can come up with many different reference schemes for a
language, each such scheme determining a truth scheme (in the
Tarski way). The problem for correspondence truth is showing
that the reference scheme we call 'reference', determining the truth
scheme we call 'truth', is the 'important' relation between words and
the world; we need to show that truth 'plays a distinguished role in
our traffic with the world' (Leeds 1978: 113). We should not take
truth for granted (Maxim 4).

Leeds has made the problem seem particularly difficult by sketching an eliminativist physicalist theory, derived from Quine,[1] which is
thoroughly sceptical about the semantic realm. My version of such a
theory is as follows.

First, the theory is thoroughly Realist: commitment to the independent objective existence of the likes of trees and electrons is unequivocal. Part of the world that the theory is committed to consists of linguistic phenomena. Structured collections of microscopic particles, people, interact among themselves and the world by producing sounds and inscriptions. These sounds are part of the behavioural output of people, causally related in certain complicated ways by the central nervous system to physical stimulation of the sense organs. We don't need to talk of beliefs, but simply of parts of the central nervous system that are causally efficacious in certain ways between input and output.[2] We don't need to talk of the sounds produced as being true of, or referring to, the world of trees and electrons. We talk of their complicated relationship to stimuli and behaviour. We don't need to talk of meanings being communicated from one person to another by these sounds. We talk of the physical effects of the stimuli which these sounds produce on people who have been through a certain learning process. And so on. People and their utterances are treated simply as parts of the physical world having no 'intentional' properties. If we knew enough physics, we could explain everything that is going on with people.

This bleak picture poses a deep problem for any friend of Correspondence Truth with physicalist leanings. I have such leanings (2.5). The picture purports to offer a physicalistically acceptable explanation of 'how our language enables us . . . to get along in the world' which does not make 'essential reference to a particular interpretation of that language' (Leeds 1978: 116).

The common practice of combining the issue of Realism with the issue of truth leads people to think that there is something incoherent about this Leeds–Quine view. But this practice is mistaken (chapter 4; Maxim 2).

Suppose the Leeds–Quine view is correct. In what respect do we not 'need' truth? We do not need it in that we can explain all phenomena without recourse to it. In considering such questions of need, we must not be too demanding, on pain of concluding, for example, that we do not need chemistry because, we are told, it can be 'reduced' to physics.

Related to questions of need are questions of entitlement. Consider the case of the gene. We have a clear need to posit genes to explain inherited characteristics. But what are genes? Only if there is a scientifically acceptable answer to this question are we entitled to talk of genes, however great our need to talk of them. With the advance of chemistry, such an answer has, of course, been discovered.

So even if we can show a need for truth, we must still show that we are entitled to it. In virtue of what is a sentence or belief true? Though the questions of need and entitlement are distinct, we can expect answers to the one to throw light on answers to the other. And the stronger the answer to one question, the less pressing is the other question.

The Leeds–Quine, negative answers to the questions about truth stem from physicalism and Realism. So also does my attempt to offer positive answers. The task (which accords with Maxim 3) is to show that Realism, together with some observations about the world the Realist believes in, leads by abduction to Correspondence Truth (physical). The observations with which we will be particularly concerned are about people; for if truth has an explanatory role, it must be in our theory of the higher animals and their languages.

I have argued for Common-Sense Realism in the last chapter. What I shall be arguing for here is Correspondence Truth (*common-sense* physical), and I shall be concerned only with the question of need. On the question of entitlement, I shall not add to my earlier brief remarks and references elsewhere (3.3). I shall consider the broader doctrine, Correspondence Truth (physical), after arguing for Scientific Realism in the next chapter (7.5).

It is not hard to enrich the Leeds–Quine picture; but going all the way to truth is hard. I regard my attempted justification as much more programmatic than complete.

6.2 WHY WORRY ABOUT NEED?

Many philosophers are dismissive of worries about the need for truth. One can detect two strains of thought in these dismissals.

First, if truth has a place, it is because truth *conditions* have: sentences have truth-conditional meaning, and/or beliefs have truth-conditional content. The Leeds–Quine eliminativist about truth denies that anything has such meaning or content. In response to this, a certain 'transcendental' style of argument is surprisingly popular. Some philosophers argue that the denial of truth-conditional content is not simply false, as a matter of empirical fact, but that in some sense it *must* be false; it is 'incoherent', 'self-refuting', 'pragmatically inconsistent', and so on. We can put their view in Kantian terms: it is 'a condition on the possibility of theorizing at all' that there be items having truth-conditional content. To deny this is, in Lynne Rudder Baker's vivid phrase, to commit 'cognitive suicide'

(1987: 148). The transcendental argument establishes *a priori* that we need truth. Any further matter of its explanatory role lapses.

Suppose we go along with the common assumption that something would not be a belief if it did not have truth-conditional content, if it were not in that respect intentional.[3] Then, to establish that there must be beliefs is to establish that something does have such content. A naïve transcendental argument to this effect runs as follows:

(1)   The eliminativist sincerely utters, 'There are no beliefs.'
(2)   So the eliminativist believes that there are no beliefs.
(3)   So eliminativism about beliefs involves realism about beliefs.
(4)   So eliminativism is incoherent.[4]

Why is this argument so footling? *Because it starts by ignoring what the eliminativist actually says.* Since she *is* an eliminativist, she rejects the established intentional way of talking. So she will not describe any mental state, *including her own in stating eliminativism*, as a belief. So (2), which saddles her with precisely what she is denying, is blatantly question-begging.

To say this is not to deny that the eliminativist has a problem. She owes us an alternative description to that in (2). This debt is part of a quite general one. The eliminativist must provide an alternative way of talking, including an alternative to truth-conditional semantics, that will enable us to describe, explain, and predict mental and linguistic phenomena in other terms. It is reasonable to think that the hand-waving remarks of the last section fall far short of what is required. So it is reasonable to think that eliminativism has not been made plausible. But this does not show that eliminativism *could not be* right. At most, it shows that eliminativism *probably is not* right. The slide from charging that eliminativism is implausible to charging that it is incoherent is totally unwarranted.

A certain myopia afflicts transcendentalists: they do not see that the theory that the eliminativist must provide, *transcendental argument or no transcendental argument*, would supply alternative ways of talking that could be used quite generally, including to describe eliminativism and the eliminativist. The eliminativist's theory, or lack of it, is open to criticism, but there is no room for a transcendental 'first strike' against her. The onus on the eliminativist to provide a theory without truth does not remove the onus on the rest of us to provide a theory with truth.

Some also seem to think that the eliminativist denies herself the right to talk. For, according to her, talking 'does not really say anything; it is mere gibberish'. This simple confusion is an indication of the entrenchment of folk theory. Talking is one thing, the folk theory of talking another. So you can talk without holding the theory. The eliminativist does not recommend silence. She recommends different talk about talk. The eliminativist is not committed to the view that all talk is 'mere gibberish'. A plausible eliminativist theory would surely distinguish, in non-intentional terms, between genuine utterances and gibberish.

Finally, it is futile to keep emphasizing how shocking eliminativism is and how difficult it would be to live with. The eliminativist is thoroughly aware of this. She is fond of pointing out how often in the history of science the truth has been shocking. This is a very good point. What eliminativism calls for in response is neither transcendentalism nor cries of horror, but arguments aimed at what the eliminativist actually says.

Transcendental arguments against eliminativism may take many forms, and may involve any of the intentional notions.[5] However, they all share the question-begging strategy with the naïve argument. The strategy is to start the argument by applying notions to the eliminativist that are laden with precisely the theory that she thinks should be abandoned and to overlook that she would think that notions from a replacement theory were the appropriate ones to apply.[6]

The second strain of thought leading to dismissal of worries about need is quite different.[7] It can be captured in the question 'Since we *have* truth, why should we worry about whether we need it?'

But in what sense *do* we have truth? There is no doubt that we have *some* notion of truth, but *which* notion? We are concerned with the need for a robust correspondence notion. Perhaps all that we have is a deflationary notion. To show that we have the robust notion, it is not sufficient to point to the ubiquity of truth talk and to the way in which this talk apparently pairs sentences with situations; for these phenomena can be explained by deflationary truth (3.4). Some account must be given of robust truth in order to show that we are entitled to it. In the absence of such an account, the claim that we have robust truth not only threatens an unacceptable 'semanticalism' (3.4), but also seems rather implausible.

I have already claimed that we should look for such an account in terms of reference, and then seek to explain reference causally. However, I also indicated that there are difficulties in explaining reference (3.3).

The more impressed one is with these difficulties, the less one should be confident that we do have robust truth. The need question then becomes particularly pressing. If we also have difficulties showing that we need robust truth for some explanatory purposes – if we have difficulties with the need question as well as the entitlement question – it begins to look as if we do not have robust truth after all.

On the other hand, if one is unimpressed with the difficulties for reference, then the need question is less pressing. However, the question does not go away. It is *possible* that we could have robust truth without needing it: that there could be a robust property of truth that explained nothing, that was 'epiphenomenal' (3.4). Nevertheless, it seems unlikely that robust truth would actually be like this. In any case, what we are interested in is a property that does in fact play an explanatory role. If we could show that we were entitled to robust truth by explaining reference causally, we might equally well be able to show that we were entitled to many other truth schemes by explaining other reference schemes causally; there are so many causal relations between people and the world. We want reference, and hence truth, to be not only explicable, but explanatorily special.

In sum, wherever one stands on the entitlement question, one should be worried by the need question.

6.3   FUNCTIONALISM

It is common to approach these questions from a view of the mind. That is how I shall start. However, in the end, I prefer a different approach, one from a view of language (6.7). The theory of the mind I shall sketch is a functionalist one which draws on the ideas of many, including Jerry Fodor (1975, 1981), Daniel Dennett (1978), Hartry Field (1978), and William Lycan (1981a, b, and c).

The cognitive areas (at least) of objects that have minds are 'intentional systems'.[8] The behaviour of these objects is to be explained by their thoughts, especially by their *beliefs* and *desires*. A person is a very complicated intentional system. This system is an institution, or corporate entity, consisting of a whole lot of sub-personal agencies (homunculi) which co-operate with one another to perform psychological functions. These agencies would be represented on a flow-chart of the person as black boxes. It is in virtue of this institutional arrangement and its relationship to the external world that the person has the beliefs and desires that mediate between his input and output. Each of these sub-personal agencies is also an intentional system, to be explained in turn in terms of sub-sub-personal agencies.

And so on all the way down to the lowest-level homunculus, the last rung on the intelligence ladder. The 'beliefs' and 'desires' of this homunculus, mediating between its input and output, are to be explained not by an arrangement of contained intentional systems but by an arrangement of simple input–output functions. The latter are the ultimate black boxes: they have no 'beliefs' and 'desires' mediating between input and output; they are unintelligent; they are behaviourist dispositions. At each level the characterization is functional, not physical; it is irrelevant what physically makes it the case that, given the input, the output is produced.

The precise details of this functionalist theory are not important to the project. One thing that is important is that any theory of this type involves four distinct steps away from the *strictly* physical explanation of the world to be found in the Leeds–Quine theory. The first is the step to behaviourist dispositions. The second is the step to functional organization. The third is the step to a 'narrow' belief–desire functional organization, one lacking intentionality. The fourth is the step to a 'wide' belief–desire functional organization; this is the step to beliefs and desires proper, to ones having intentionality. All these steps are problematic. The first two are the least so. I shall discuss them together now. The third step will be discussed in section 6.4, and the fourth in sections 6.5 and 6.6.

In taking the first two steps, we explain the behaviour of an organism by attributing to it behaviourist dispositions and functional properties and relations. These dispositions, properties, and relations cannot be identified with physical ones, because they can be realized by many different physical properties and relations: type-identity theory of the mind is false. So in talking of these dispositions, properties, and relations, we have already moved beyond the strictly physical. How does this fit into the physicalist picture? Why do we need to talk this way?

Functionalists were the leaders in rejecting type-identity theory. With this went the rejection of classical 'reductionism'. Nevertheless, functionalists are typically very much part of the physicalist tradition in subscribing to token-identity theory and in seeing physics as, in some sense, basic (2.5). The problem then is that, with the rejection of type-identity theory, the sense in which physics is basic is rather unclear. What is the status of psychological properties and relations? What is the status of psychological explanations? What is it for objects to share a psychological property? What sort of fact is that? What does a psychological explanation explain that a physical one cannot?

Consider the first step, for example. We explain why an object broke by saying that it was fragile. I take fragility to be a simple input–output function, a behaviourist disposition like the ultimate unintelligent black boxes in the above theory of the mind. An object will be fragile if it realizes that function; but fragility cannot be identified with any one sort of realization: any physical realization that does the job will do as well as any other for the purposes of this explanation.

A behaviourist disposition is a something-it-matters-not-what that causally intervenes to produce a specified output given a specified input. It does not matter to the explanation what physical structures the object has that disposes it to behave like this. Nor does it matter how the object is internally organized to produce that output given the input. This explanation is the simplest form of functional explanation. (A behaviourist – one sort of behaviourist, at least – must believe that all human behaviour can be adequately explained by behaviourist dispositions.)

Next, consider the second step. Sometimes our explanation of the behaviour of an object depends on attributing to it an inner organization: it has a something-it-matters-not-what with a certain functional organization intervening between input and output; there are 'intervening variables'. Consider, for example, the explanation of a car skidding in terms of accelerator, brake, steering, and so forth. These terms are functional ones. This explanation is good because the car realizes a functional organization linking accelerator, brake, and steering in the appropriate way. Once again a simple identification of the functional with the physical is not possible.

From these two cases we can see that a functional explanation of a physical event is a different sort of explanation from the physical explanation of that event. Why do we need the functional explanation? The correct answer seems to be along the following lines: we get more useful, because more general, explanations by abstracting from the precise physical goings-on. More should be said; but it is hard to believe that the correct account of functional explanations like these will not be one readily assimilated to physicalism.[9] Certainly we should not make the requirement that we show a need for functional explanations too stringent, on pain of rendering all science but physics unnecessary; even chemistry is, in *some* sense, unnecessary. (An example of Putnam's vividly demonstrates the advantages of abstracting from the strictly physical. Why will a l-inch square peg go through a l-inch square hole but not a l-inch round hole? The explanation in terms of the trajectories of elementary particles is almost impossible to produce, and not very helpful; that in terms of the geometry of squares and circles is good and useful; 1978: 42–3).

Perhaps a line suggested by Putnam (1975a: 313–14) and taken up by Field (1975: 389) is sufficient to show the physicalistic respectability of functional properties. The line is that a functional property is a 'second order' physical property: the property of having some 'first order' physical property with a certain causal role.

In sum, I think it is plausible to suppose that we need functional explanations, and that we are entitled to them, while retaining physicalism. I think this is plausible even if the precise place of such explanations within the physicalist world-view is not clear.

6.4 'NARROW' BELIEFS AND DESIRES

The next problem with our theory of the mind is its positing of thoughts. This positing involves two steps (Field 1978: 44), as I have already indicated. These are the third and fourth steps in our move away from strictly physical explanations. They are both difficult to explain and justify. In the third step we posit only 'narrow' beliefs and desires lacking intentionality: they are not 'about' the external world; they are not true or false in virtue (partly) of reference to that world. The fourth step takes us to 'wide' beliefs and desires, ones with intentionality. The distinction will become clearer in section 6.5. In this section, we shall really be considering the third step only, whatever the appearances.

In my sketch of a theory of the mind I spoke of the beliefs and desires of the least intelligent homunculus arising out of an arrangement of simple input–output functions. What sort of an arrangement? Clearly it will have to be a special sort of complicated arrangement. *Some* complicated arrangements certainly do not involve beliefs and desires: think of a car or of a tropistic organism.

At some level on the phylogenetic scale, usually close to humans, we feel confident in attributing beliefs and desires; at other levels, usually close to insects, we feel confident in denying such attributions. Dennett (1978) has described three levels on this scale. At the tropistic level, the organism embodies a series of innate input–output functions. At the Skinnerian level, the organism has an innate capacity to gain input–output functions as a result of reinforcement. At the post-Skinnerian level, the organism has an innate capacity to gain *potential* behaviour control elements of a certain sort: elements that select one of a range of possible outputs given any one of a range of possible inputs, without previous reinforcement. These potential control elements are beliefs and desires, Dennett suggests. He has even shown how the capacity to have such control elements could evolve by natural selection. What is striking about organisms at this third level is the flexibility of their responses to stimuli.

We get reassurance that the attribution of beliefs and desires is both needed (in some sense) and physicalistically acceptable from a consideration of computers. Consider, for example, our explanation of the behaviour of a chess-playing computer. We attribute to it certain desires: most generally, it wants to win; more particularly, at a certain stage of a game, it wants to save its rook. We attribute to it certain beliefs: for example, about how to move the knight and about the likely consequences of a certain move at that stage of the game. It is because of these beliefs and desires that it does what it does.

This reassurance may be short-lived if we discover – as I believe we would with the simpler chess-playing computers – that they play the game more by 'brute force' than by the sort of subtle processes we regard as meriting the title 'thinking'. Nevertheless, it does seem reasonable to suppose that *some* computers have beliefs and desires even if some don't and that we may hope to learn about the distinction from AI research.

In my view, we gain further insight into the sort of internal arrangements constitutive of having beliefs and desires from the writings of Harman (1973), Fodor (1975), and Field (1978). I think we should see beliefs and desires as relations holding between people and sentences in their language of thought. What we look for within, therefore, is a sentential mode of representation which the machine or organism uses in the appropriate way to control its behaviour.

Two points of clarification are called for. First, it is often convenient to write as if the belief and desire relations are between people and sentence *types*. However, this is a mere manner of speaking. We have no need to posit such types here, and get more understanding if we do not do so. The relations are really between people and sentence tokens. A consequence of this is that the standard form of belief and desire attribution ascribes to a person a belief in a token of a certain type.[10] Second, strictly speaking, it is only *core* beliefs and desires that we can see in this way, because most beliefs and desires are never entertained. So beliefs and desires must be seen as dispositions based on core beliefs and desires (Dennett 1978; Field 1978).

This representational idea, together with Dennett's earlier one, suggests that either our object has beliefs and desires or it has not: it is an all-or-nothing matter. This does not of course prevent our making distinctions in intelligence. We can distinguish the contents of beliefs: some sentences in the language of thought employ much richer concepts than others. We can also distinguish the inferential capacities of two objects. Nevertheless, it may be that this all-or-nothing view of beliefs and desires is incorrect. The notions may be vague, so that there is no determinate matter of fact for a certain range of objects as to whether or not the object has beliefs or desires. So far as I can see, this would not have any serious consequences for the view being urged here.

What I have been suggesting is that a realist view of beliefs and desires is compatible with physicalism. I have claimed earlier (6.3) that simpler functional explanations seem compatible with physicalism. I have tried here to make plausible the view that the more advanced functional explanations in terms of beliefs and desires are true (or false) in virtue of some more complicated functional organization within the object. If so, then these explanations will be as physicalistic as the earlier ones. We are a long way from having *shown* that it is so, of course.

6.5   METHODOLOGICAL SOLIPSISM

At the beginning of the last section I said that the step we would be attempting to justify was really only to 'narrow' beliefs and desires. Why is it only this?

I start the answer to this question with more information on the distinction between wide and narrow mental states. Putnam points out that, in a tradition that goes back at least to Descartes, psychological states are thought of as narrow, in that they accord with the assumption of 'methodological solipsism'. Such a state does not presuppose 'the existence of any individual other than the subject to whom that state is ascribed' (1975b: 220). The idea is that a narrow psychological state is entirely supervenient on the intrinsic inner states of the individual; she does not have the state in virtue of its relation to anything else and in particular, not in virtue of its relation to environmental causes or effects of the states. Some familiar psychological states – for example, *being jealous of x* – do not satisfy these constraints, and so are wide.

Having made this distinction, Putnam goes on to argue that no narrow psychological state could determine reference. Consider the

use of the word 'water' by Oscar on Earth and by Twin Oscar on
Twin Earth in 1750, before the chemical composition of water was
known. Twin Earth is exactly like Earth except that the liquid on it,
which has all the superficial properties of water, is not H_2O but
XYZ. Twin Oscar is an exact duplicate of Oscar. Putnam claims
that when Oscar uses 'water', he refers to H_2O – that is, to real water
– but that when Twin Oscar uses 'water', he refers to XYZ – that is,
to what we might call 'Twin water'. Yet Oscar and Twin Oscar are
in the same narrow psychological state, for they are duplicates. So
those states do not determine the extension of 'water'. ' "Meanings"
just ain't in the *head*' (p. 227).[11]

In light of this, what is the status of thoughts? Consider, for
example, Ralph's belief that Malcolm Fraser is arrogant. It is an
intentional state that is *about* Fraser; it determines reference. So
thoughts are not supervenient on what is inside the head; they are
relations to sentences with truth-referential properties that depend on
relations to the environment. Thoughts are wide.

The consequences of this can be brought out by drawing a contrast between thoughts and merely functional states of an object.
Such states are narrow. Let x be an earthly object with the (non-
psychological) functional property of being H_2O-soluble.[12] On the
strength of Putnam's story, we can say that if x were taken to Twin
Earth and plunged into XYZ, it would dissolve. So we *can* truly say
of x, sitting here on Earth, that it is XYZ-soluble. On the strength of
the same story, we can say that if Ralph (while asleep, say) were
taken to Twin Earth and substituted for Twin-Earth Ralph, he
would respond to any Twin-Earth Fraserish stimuli in *exactly* the way
appropriate for someone who had a certain belief about Twin-Earth
Fraser; for he would respond just as Twin-Earth Ralph would. But
we *cannot* truly say of Ralph, sitting here on Earth, that he has that
belief about Twin-Earth Fraser.

Against this background, *the argument from methodological solipsism and
psychological autonomy* has become popular.[13] Its conclusion is that
thoughts, widely construed, have no place in psychology; psychology
should be narrow. The argument runs along the following lines. In
psychology, we are concerned to explain why, given stimuli at her
sense organs, a person evinced certain behaviour. Only something
that is entirely supervenient on what is inside the skin – on the
person's intrinsic internal physical states, particularly those of the
brain – could play the required explanatory role between peripheral
input and output. Environmental causes of stimuli and the effects
of the resulting behaviour are beside the psychological point. The

person and all her physical, even functional, duplicates must be psychologically the same, whatever their environments. Mental states must be individuated according to their role within the individual, without regard to their relations to an environment. How then could thoughts be relevant to psychology, for thoughts have referential properties which are *not* supervenient on what is inside the person's skin? Putnam's Twin-Earth discussion has brought out that dupli-cates may *not* share thoughts.

One can accept this argument without abandoning the idea that a person's relations to mental sentences have a central role in psycho-logical explanation. What has to be abandoned is the idea that the full truth-referential properties of those sentences are psychologically relevant. An influential response has been 'the syntactic theory of mind', according to which only the *syntactic* properties of the sen-tences are relevant (e.g. Field 1978; Schiffer 1981; and Stich 1983). I have set out my own response elsewhere (1989). I summarize.

Burge (1979, 1986) has shown that the argument from method-ological solipsism is much less straightforward than it appears. Nevertheless, I think that the argument is basically correct. It does not, however, establish the syntactic theory of the mind. Rather, it shows that only the 'narrow meaning' of a mental sentence is psychologically relevant. This narrow meaning includes not only the syntactic properties of the sentence, but also the semantic properties of its parts coming from the parts' relations to other words and to sensory inputs – that is, narrow word meanings. Finally, although narrow meaning is not truth-referential, it is *proto*-truth-referential: it abstracts from, 'brackets off', those aspects of the intentional that are outside the skin and irrelevant to an explanation of behaviour; it is intentional *minus a bit*.

Considerations like those in the last section should not be seen as motivating thoughts in the fullest sense, but rather, thoughts with narrow meaning: 'narrow' thoughts. So we still have not found a place for truth conditions, and hence truth; we have not answered our need question. If I am right in thinking that narrow meaning is proto-truth-referential, then, of course, the need question be-comes much less pressing, because such meaning is so close to truth-referential meaning (as Hartry Field pointed out to me). But perhaps I am not right. In any case, we should find an answer to the question.

It is tempting to try to undermine the view that the explanation of behaviour does not require truth, by attending to the special behaviour involved in communication.[14]

We all acquire behaviourally relevant inner states in part from sensory stimuli. We see, hear, smell, touch, and taste many things. So, for example, some of the inner states that guide Ralph's behaviour are the result of stimuli caused by Fraser. However, a lot of Ralph's Fraser-directed behaviour is the result of *linguistic* experience: it is caused not by Fraserish stimuli but by 'Fraser'-ish stimuli. Ralph learns from others. Similarly, others learn from him. How are we to explain this?

Suppose that Ralph gains the belief that Fraser is arrogant (as we ordinarily call it) from reading 'Fraser is arrogant' in the newspaper. How does he do it? An explanation along the following lines is plausible. He assigns to the inscription a certain truth condition: he takes it to be true if and only if Fraser is arrogant. He takes the journalist to be sincere, and so infers that she has a belief that is true if and only if Fraser is arrogant. Finally, he takes the journalist to be reliable in such matters, and so comes to believe that Fraser is arrogant.

In learning from others, we use their beliefs and utterances as guides to reality. Thermometers are instruments we use to tell us about one aspect of reality, temperature. People are instruments we use to tell us about indefinitely many aspects of reality. In both sorts of case we need to correlate states of an instrument with likely states of the world. The correlation requires a relatively simple theory when the instrument is a thermometer. The claim is that it requires a complicated theory involving truth when the instrument is a language-user.

Our attention here has been on the passing on of information, which is typically done by statements. There are other communicative acts: we seek information by asking questions; we attempt to satisfy our desires by uttering imperatives; and so on. The claim is that the explanation of this behaviour must also appeal to truth, though this is not so apparent.

I think that such explanations of communication are along the right lines, but that they do not really motivate truth. The main problem with them is that they beg the question at the crucial point. For Ralph to learn from the inscription, it is certainly the case that he must *understand* the inscription. To do this he has to come to believe (or process the inscription as if he believes) that it *means that* Fraser is arrogant. The above explanation assumes precisely what is at issue: that this understanding and belief involve the belief that the inscription *is true if and only if* Fraser is arrogant. Aside from that, an explanation of behaviour that ascribes to it a belief about truth does not of itself show that truth is an explanatory notion. Consider, for example, the explanation of religious behaviour. The explanation of this may well ascribe to people beliefs that involve the notion of the sacred. But this fails to show that the notion of the sacred is needed in a *good* theory of the world; it fails to show that we need to see anything as sacred. *Belief in* truth might be explanatory without *truth* being so.

I shall now consider the idea that we need truth to explain success.

6.6 INDIVIDUAL AND SPECIES SUCCESS

The view that we need *realism* to explain success has become popular, under the influence particularly of Putnam. Underlying this view are many theses which, so far as I know, have never been clearly distinguished. First, it is common to use the term 'realism' to refer to some combination of an ontological doctrine like Realism and a semantic one like Correspondence Truth: Putnam does so himself (1978: 9, 18–20, 102). I have urged the importance of distinguishing such doctrines (4.1–4.5; Maxim 2). Second, we need to distinguish the many different notions of success that are in question. These are, briefly:

> *Individual success* The success of an individual organism in satisfying its needs and fulfilling its desires.
> *Species success* The success of a species, including success in surviving.
> *Theoretical success* The success of a theory at the observational level: observational success.
> *Scientific progress* The success of scientists in getting better and better theories.

So underlying the view that realism explains success are at least eight different theses.

Putnam certainly thinks that we need truth to explain individual success (1978: 99–103); more strictly, that we need truth values to explain success and failure. His initial proposal is only that we need *some* notion of truth for this purpose, thought he goes on to argue for a correspondence notion in particular. Our concern here is with Correspondence Truth. So my primary concern in this section will be with the thesis that we need Correspondence Truth to explain individual success. I shall also consider the related thesis that we need Correspondence Truth to explain species success.

Putnam may also hold the thesis that we need Realism to explain individual success. In this chapter I am presupposing Realism. However, I shall conclude this section by briefly considering that thesis (and the related one about species success). I shall consider the theses about theoretical success in section 7.3 and about scientific progress in section 7.6.[15]

What is the success that our theory of an individual organism – in particular, a person – needs to explain? What is the phenomenon? One type of success is the satisfaction of needs. We see an organism as having certain needs: for food, drink, and so on. Another type of success is the fulfilment of desires. If the organism is a believer-desirer, then it has certain desires: to oust Fraser, to save Realism, and so forth. These two types of success are presumably related, because desires are causally dependent on needs. Nevertheless, they are different: one could fulfil a desire without satisfying a need, and vice versa. Also, all organisms have needs, but only some have desires.

I have described needs and desires in intentional terms for lack of any other convenient way to describe them. However, in light of our earlier discussion, it is clear that they could be described in non-intentional terms compatible with narrow psychology. Correspondingly, satisfaction and fulfilment would consist in the alleviation (perhaps temporarily) of the appropriate (non-intentionally described) internal state (cf. Schiffer 1981: 217).

These types of success, and the related ones of failure, are the basic ones that need explaining. We will then see behaviour as successful if it leads to success of one of these types and beliefs (perhaps) as successful if they lead to successful behaviour. Moreover, we will see an individual organism as successful if it mostly enjoys these types of success.

So the main suggestion I take from Putnam is that we need to attribute truth values to beliefs to explain such success. Why is that? Further preliminary points need to be made before answering.

First, it is clear that the truth of an organism's beliefs is not always needed to explain the satisfaction of its needs. Some organisms that have no beliefs – for example, insects – satisfy needs. So the explanation of need satisfaction in terms of truth must be restricted to believer-desirers. And the explanation in such cases must, I presume, be via the fulfilment of desires, fulfilment of an 'appropriate' desire satisfies a need.

Second, it is clear that the truth of an organism's beliefs is not always needed to explain the fulfilment of its desires. A desire might be fulfilled independently of anything the organism did or did not do, as a result of its beliefs, to fulfil that desire: aspects of reality right outside its power may be responsible. For example, a person's desire that Fraser be ousted may be fulfilled without that person lifting a finger. So the explanation of desire fulfilment in terms of truth must be restricted to cases where the person's beliefs play a role in that fulfilment.

Third, related to this, beliefs may play a role in desire fulfilment and yet not be the only factor, or even the most important one, that does so. Thus money may be more important to success than wisdom. Reality can intervene in various ways so that a true belief is unsuccessful or a false one successful.

Fourth, where beliefs do play a role, there is a respect in which we obviously do not have to attribute truth values to them to explain success or failure. Consider a particular case of desire fulfilment: an organism evinces behavioural output, *o*, which leads to the fulfilment of desire, *d*. (1) Using our psychology, we can explain why the organism evinced *o*: it has certain narrow beliefs and desires. (2) Using our general theory of the world, we can explain why *o* led to the organism receiving sensory input, *i*. (3) Using our psychology again, we can explain why *i* led to the fulfilment of desire, *d*. So we have given a complete explanation of this instance of success. We can explain similarly an instance of failure.

What then remains to be explained? I take it that what needs explaining is some *pattern* of successes and failures. Some beliefs are conducive to success, and others to failure. What is the difference between these two sorts of belief?

In light of all this, a plausible claim for the role of truth in explaining an organism's success might be as follows. An organism's belief that is true is conducive to the fulfilment of its desires, and one that is false is conducive to their frustration.

Plausible or not, that we *need* truth in our explanation is not obvious. Attributing narrow beliefs and desires to an organism explains its output in that, given those beliefs, it has expectations of the output leading to an input which will fulfil those desires. The role claimed for truth in the above explanation must, therefore, be as follows: the expectations that a belief gives rise to tend not to be disappointed if the belief is true, but tend to be disappointed if it is false. True beliefs tend not to face recalcitrant experience. The problem is that warranted or justified beliefs tend not to either. A belief that is well supported by past experience is likely to be supported also by future experience; so the expectations to which the belief gives rise are unlikely to be disappointed. We can therefore offer the following alternative explanation. A belief of an organism that is warranted is conducive to the fulfilment of its desires, and one whose negation is warranted is conducive to their frustration. This alternative seems as satisfactory as the original in terms of truth. Indeed, if the original is satisfactory, how could this alternative not be? Given that warrantability is conducive to truth, if truth is conducive to success, then warrantability is conducive to success.

A defender of the explanation in terms of truth might well object. Surely a warranted belief would not be conducive to success if it were false. And a true belief would be conducive to success even if it were a guess. These are good points: the epistemic explanation is not satisfactory as it stands. But it seems likely that it can be modified. Its defect is that warrantability depends on the *actual* evidence *so far*. What we need is some notion that takes account of the possible evidence in the long run (which some call 'truth': 3.5).

The Twin-Earth example brings out the unlikelihood that we can make a persuasive case for truth from the explanation of success. Twin-Earth Ralph would be just as successful here as Ralph. The fact that his beliefs are about Twin-Earth Fraser, not Fraser, would be irrelevant to his success in dealing with the latter. What matters to his success is the accuracy of his beliefs at the level of Fraserish experiences. (Think also of a brain-in-the-vat Ralph, which arguably has no beliefs about anything, but is as successful as Ralph.)

In sum, the explanation of an organism's success probably supplies no justification for a move beyond narrow psychology. However, if we can otherwise establish the need for truth, the discussion shows that we can use it to explain success.

Putnam's discussion contains the suggestion that we may need truth to explain another sort of individual success: success in an activity – for example, in bridge-building (see also Field 1986). This success does not depend on a person's attainment of goals, fulfilment of desires, or satisfaction of needs. People may succeed in building bridges whatever their goals, desires, or needs. However, once again, it is hard to see why some sort of epistemic notion would not do the explanatory work as well as truth.

Species success differs from collective individual success only in that the species may survive. But clearly if we can explain individual success, including satisfaction of needs and fulfilment of desires, without truth, we can similarly explain species success (with the help of Darwin).

In bringing out an underlying truth of representative Realism in section 5.7, I mentioned that the 'as-if' level is 'close to experience'. The present talk of beliefs facing recalcitrant experience indicates the respect in which this is so. Suppose a person believes that S. An experience is recalcitrant relative to that belief if it leads him to believe that it is as if not-S. This is not, of course, to say that it leads him to believe that not-S: the experience can be ignored or other beliefs changed (Duhem–Quine). Nevertheless, such an experience must tend to make him believe that not-S.

In this chapter Realism is not in question. However, suppose that it were. Could we justify Realism by claiming that we need it to explain individual (or species) success? It would be fantastic to suppose that this was Realism's main justification. For it to be so, we would have to theorize about an organism without presupposing that it was the Realist environment in which it lived and had that success. But if we were to theorize about the organism in this neutral way, there seems no reason to think that any anti-Realism could not give an adequate explanation of success. It is only because we have *other* reasons for believing in the Realist's world that we suppose that it is an individual organism's interaction with that world that explains its success. Any supposition to the contrary comes, I presume, from confusing individual success with the theoretical success we shall discuss in section 7.3. Our theory of individuals – in particular of people – is entirely the wrong place to start in attempting to justify Realism.

6.7 THE NEED FOR TRUTH

Our approach to the problem of finding a need for truth came from individualistic psychology.[16] We posit thoughts to explain behaviour, the line runs. Truth depends on reference, which is an extra-cranial matter. It is not surprising, then, that we found no pressing need for truth to explain behaviour, even communicative behaviour. For behaviour, it seems plausible to say, is explained by what is intra-cranial. And we have just found the idea that we need truth to explain the success of behaviour unconvincing.

I think that we need a quite different approach. The attempt to motivate truth should not be located in psychology, and its focus should not be behaviour. The attempt should be in semantics, which is not part of psychology, and its focus should be linguistic symbols. To grasp this point, it helps to distinguish sharply between two tasks that are usually, if not always, confused: the explanation of linguistic *behaviour* – communication – and the explanation of linguistic *symbols*.

A piece of linguistic behaviour is a series of bodily movements, usually of vocal cords or hands. A symbol is a datable, placeable part of the physical world *produced by* behaviour with the help of the environment. It is usually a sound or an inscription. The explanation of linguistic behaviour with which we have been concerned in this chapter is a psychological description of its *cause*. Thus it will include an account of the speaker's linguistic competence. The explanation of a linguistic symbol is a description of its *nature*. (In some sign languages, the behaviour is the symbol; but that does not alter the main point. We have a different explanatory interest in it *qua* symbol from *qua* behaviour.) A theory of the production of linguistic symbols is not a theory of the products, the symbols themselves. Of course, given the causal relation between the production and the symbols, we can expect the two theories to be related. But this relationship does not make the two theories identical.

The theory of symbols – semantics – is concerned with the properties of symbols that make them good for certain social purposes. What is it about them that leads people to produce and respond to them as they do? What is it that makes them things we can use to teach, learn from, greet, question, command, joke, abuse, intimidate, and so on?

Analogously, we might be interested in what makes a certain movement of a ball a good tennis shot. The answer would be in terms of such properties as speed, direction, and height. Or we might be interested in what makes a certain chess move good. The answer would be in terms of the myriad possible game continuations; perhaps, in each of these, the move gives white an advantage, and no other move guarantees this. In all these cases we are concerned with objects or events in the physical world 'outside the head'.

However, in each case we might have another concern which is very much with something 'inside the head' (or, at least, 'inside the body'). What is the explanation of the behaviour – certain movements of hand and arm, perhaps – producing good sentences, tennis shots, or chess moves? To answer this, we need a psychological (perhaps physiological) theory, including a theory of competence; we need a theory that explains, for example, how white knew that that particular chess move was good. Such a theory is different from a theory of the objects produced by the behavioural output of a competence, different from a theory of linguistic symbols, tennis shots, or chess moves.

Our talk of symbols has all been about *linguistic* symbols. Earlier I endorsed the view that thoughts are relations to *mental* symbols (6.4). What properties of these symbols make us interested in the thoughts that contain them? Our interest in thoughts is partly, of course, to explain behaviour. To satisfy that interest, we do not need to ascribe full truth-referential properties to the mental symbols (though I do think we need to ascribe proto-truth-referential ones). But we also have social interests in thoughts. We are interested in what way a person believes the world to be, desires the world to be, hopes the world to be, and so on, so that we can adjust our own approach to the world, including that person, accordingly. Semantics should tell us what properties the symbols involved in these thoughts must have for the symbols to satisfy those interests.

So the task for semantics broadens. It is to describe and explain the properties of linguistic *and* mental symbols that enable them to play the variety of social roles in our lives that I have described. It is this task that requires truth and reference.

Having reoriented the question of need, we can see that the ingredients of our earlier discussion of communication (6.5) must be rearranged to motivate truth. Our example was of Ralph learning from a newspaper that Fraser is arrogant. The point is not the role of his *beliefs about* the truth condition of the inscription 'Fraser is arrogant' in explaining his linguistic behaviour. The point is that it is in virtue of the inscription *having* a certain truth condition that it could serve Ralph as a guide to reality. That is the property of the inscription that enables it to serve this role. The task of semantics is to explain the inscription, not the behaviour.

We were in great difficulty trying to show a need for truth while we were looking for something about behaviour that required it. The problem was that whenever we seemed to have an answer, it always seemed likely that we could come up with another explanation – as good, if not better – which did not involve truth. Now that we have focused on explaining symbols, our position is much stronger. Earlier I sketched a theory of truth (3.3). This sort of theory is, I have claimed elsewhere (Devitt and Sterelny 1987), the core of semantics. In general, truth-conditional theories of meaning lack rivals with comparable plausibility. I see no hint of an explanation of symbols sufficient to account for their wide-ranging social use that does not appeal to these sorts of representational properties.

In sum, once we focus on symbols instead of behaviour, we have an easy answer to the need question. We need truth because it is an essential part of the best – perhaps only plausible – theory in town.

To distinguish semantics from psychology is not to make it mysterious. I do think that semantics has a certain autonomy relative to other theories, including psychology. However, given my physicalism, I must see this autonomy as only relative: in some sense, semantics must ultimately be explained in physical terms. But this requirement does not remove the autonomy of semantics any more than it removes that of, say, biology or economics.

Ideally, one would hope to show that semantics was dependent on physics, thus removing all mystery. But that is too much to expect at this time. Meanwhile, there is no reason to be particularly suspicious of the relative autonomy of semantics.

Semantics is a social science. Like all social sciences, it seems to be immediately dependent on psychological facts and facts about the natural environment. The nature of this sort of dependence is complex and hard to describe. Yet each social science proceeds largely undisturbed by the lack of a complete description. And so it should.

Consider some examples. What makes a physical object a pawn or a dollar? What makes a physical event a vote or unlawful? Nothing intrinsic to the objects and events in question; rather, it is the psychological states, within certain environments, of people involved with those objects and events. Exactly what states, what involvement, and what environment is hard to say. Yet people quite properly feel free to theorize about chess, money, elections, and the law. Similarly, we should feel free to theorize about symbols.

A truth-conditional semantics of the sort mentioned can be very much concerned to explain the properties of symbols in terms of psychological states and relations to the environment. While respecting the relative autonomy of semantics, an aim should be to explain it in other terms.

Semantics is like other social sciences in being dependent on psychological facts without being psychology. Just as some objects have an economic nature, some have a linguistic nature. Just as it is the task of economics to explain such properties as price and value, which go to make up the economic nature, it is the task of semantics to explain such properties as truth and reference, which go to make up the linguistic nature. Just as economics is not concerned primarily with the explanation of economic behaviour, so semantics is not concerned primarily with the explanation of linguistic behaviour.

This is not to say that semantics is irrelevant to the explanation of linguistic behaviour, any more than economics is irrelevant to the explanation of economic behaviour. It is because thoughts contain symbols that the latter play a role in the explanation of behaviour.

Furthermore, I think that the explanation of communication sketched above is along the right lines. According to that sketch, people behave as they do linguistically because they have caught onto (which does not necessarily require having beliefs about) the semantic properties of linguistic symbols; they have caught on to the properties revealed by semantics. Explaining behaviour may not motivate truth, but, having otherwise motivated it, we use awareness of it to explain behaviour.

In this chapter I have been considering, from a Realist perspective on the observable world, the role of correspondence truth in the best explanation of various phenomena. Though truth seems natural and appropriate in the explanations of behaviour and its success, it is doubtful whether the full-blown notion is necessary for those tasks. However, as I have argued, truth is necessary for the explanation of the role of mental and linguistic symbols; truth-referential semantics lacks a plausible rival. To complete the justification of Correspondence Truth (common-sense physical), this account of our need for truth must be supplemented by an account of our entitlement – an explanation in terms of reference – along the lines indicated earlier (3.3).

Since this argument is from a Realist perspective, it supplies further evidence for Realism. For, if it is correct, it shows how a wide-ranging set of phenomena associated with language can be accommodated within a thoroughly Realist world-view.

I shall not consider whether and why an anti-Realist needs truth. Arguing from a view of truth to a position on Realism is, I have claimed, a mistake (Maxim 3). However, I have indicated (4.3) that an epistemic notion of truth leads to anti-Realism. Later I shall consider the bearing of verificationism on Realism (14.9).

Finally, I must confess that I have less confidence in the discussion of truth in this chapter than in almost anything else in the book.

NOTES

1 I don't claim that what follows is *all* that Quine's famous scepticism about semantics amounts to. However, it is all that I shall be trying to respond to. I am sympathetic to the following responses to other possible aspects: Leeds 1973; Friedman 1975; Field 1974 and 1975.

2 The naturalized epistemology of section 5.7 talks of beliefs. This talk, like similar talk in the market-place, must be taken as a mere manner of speaking, to be eliminated in the final analysis.

3   It is an interesting feature of eliminativism, as John Bigelow has emphasized to me, that it nearly always involves an essentialist assumption like this: to show that there are no F's, the eliminativist argues that if there were any F's, they would be G, and there are no G's. A possible realist response is then to deny the assumption: F's are not essentially G's; e.g. beliefs are not essentially truth-conditional.

4   Such arguments are common in philosophical conversation. Philip Gasper came close in his review of the first edition of this book: 'We cannot accept eliminativism because it claims that no beliefs have content, and that is something that it would be self-refuting to accept. We cannot give up the idea that we have beliefs about certain things, because to reject that idea would also be to have a belief *about* something' (1986: 447). Baker's discussion (1987: 113–48), in so far as it is offering transcendental arguments, often comes close too. However, much of her discussion can be construed not transcendentally, but as arguments for the *implausibility* of eliminativism. Her discussion exemplifies the unwarranted slide from charging implausibility to charging incoherence; see below.

5   As Baker illustrates (1987: 113–48).

6   This discussion draws on my 1990c. In that paper, I attempt a more thorough exposure of the question-begging strategy of transcendental arguments in the context of a criticism of a sophisticated version proposed recently by Paul Boghossian (1990a). Boghossian (1990b) has responded, accusing me of the 'master confusion' of taking his doctrines of 'irrealism' as distinct from eliminativism rather than as expressions of it. This accusation is a smoke-screen. The irrealist doctrines play the role for him that (2) plays in the naïve argument. By claiming that these allegedly problematic doctrines are expressive of eliminativism, Boghossian gives the impression that they are plausibly attributed to the eliminativist. This is the question-begging strategy once again. In so far as the doctrines are problematic, Boghossian has not produced the slightest reason for thinking that they *are* expressive of eliminativism. He says often that he *intends* them to be so. But this is sadly insufficient to make them so. Devitt and Rey 1991 is a response to Boghossian.

7   The comments of Frank Jackson, David Lewis, Graham Nerlich, and Stephen Stich have helped me to identify and respond to this strain of thought.

8   The term is Dennett's. Dennett uses it (and other mental terms) in an instrumentalist way. I do not: for me it is a matter of objective fact whether an object has beliefs and desires.

9   Churchland (1981) raises some interesting problems for propositional-attitude psychology from a physicalist viewpoint. A reason for thinking that his case against that psychology is not sound is that it would apply equally against *any* functionalist explanation. See Kitcher 1984 and 1985 for some nice criticisms of Churchland.

10   My commitment to this relational view of thought was not as clear as it should have been in my 1981a because of a confused discussion on p. 238. The commitment is clear in my 1984c and 1990b.

11   Searle (1983) rejects Putnam's argument. My 1990a is a criticism of Searle. Putnam's argument played an important role in the rejection of description theories of reference. Historical causal theories are well placed to handle Twin Earth: 'water' refers to water, not Twin water, because the term was, as a matter of historical fact, grounded in water, not Twin water. In contrast, reliable causal theories have a severe problem here: 'water' is as reliably correlated with Twin water as with water. Attempts to solve the problem by limiting the context seem rather *ad hoc*.

12   There is an interesting problem about this property. Though it is narrow, in that an object may have it without anything else existing, there is a respect in which the object's having the property is not entirely supervenient on the object's intrinsic inner state: the object has the property partly in virtue of the nature of H_2O (Devitt 1990a: 94–6).

13   See Field 1978; Stich 1978, 1983; and Fodor 1980a, b. Fodor's views are complicated by the fact that he is also an enthusiast for intentional psychology; see Devitt 1991d.

My own views on methodological solipsism have changed many times since I started struggling with the problem in 1978. Some early results of the struggle are to be found in 1980a and 1981a: 68–9. The discussion in this chapter is very different from that in the first edition (1984a: 80–102). My views up to then were influenced by Hartry Field in two ways: via his writings (1972: 103–4; 1977: 399; 1978: 100–2, 103–4) and through several helpful discussions. They were also influenced by Ken Gemes, Karen Green, Janet Levin, Brian Loar, Michael McDermott, Stephen Schiffer, and Kim Sterelny. For later influences, see my 1989.

14   I was tempted in the first edition (1984a: 91–9).

15   Earlier versions of this discussion of success are to be found in my 1983b, sect. 2, and 1987, sect. 3.

16   The discussion in this section draws on Devitt and Sterelny 1987: 132–3, 161–2, 169–70; 1989: 513–7. Our 1989 article argues against the received, Chomskian view of the linguistic task.

7
Why be a Scientific Realist?

7.1 THE BASIC ARGUMENT FOR SCIENTIFIC REALISM

In chapter 5 I argued for Common-Sense Realism. In chapter 6 and section 3.3 I argued for Correspondence Truth (common-sense physical): those common-sense statements have truth conditions explained in terms of reference to the observable entities of Common-Sense Realism. In this chapter I shall argue for Scientific Realism and Correspondence Truth (scientific physical). I shall argue for the former first (7.1–7.4), in accordance with the maxim that ontological questions should be settled before semantic ones (Maxim 3). The argument for the latter (7.5) will take those scientific statements to have truth conditions explained in terms of reference to the unobservable entities of Scientific Realism. I consider the bearing of success and convergence on the two doctrines (7.3 and 7.6). The discussion then moves into a more critical vein, and considers operationism (7.7) and instrumentalism (7.8). The chapter concludes by discussing the various epistemic attitudes of the Realist toward theories (7.9).

Many of the elements of my argument are familiar (I have found Smart 1963 and 1968 particularly helpful). Much of the novelty in the arrangement of these elements comes from my strict adherence to the maxims set out in section 1.1.

Scientific Realism differs from Common-Sense Realism in asserting the existence of the *unobservable* entities of science, instead of asserting the existence of the *observable* entities of science and common sense. The basic argument for the unobservable entities is simple. By supposing they exist, we can give good explanations of the behaviour and characteristics of observed entities, behaviour and characteristics which would otherwise remain completely inexplicable. Furthermore, such a supposition leads to predictions about observables which are well confirmed; the supposition is 'observationally successful'.

Abduction thus takes us from hypotheses about the observed world to hypotheses about the unobservable one.

Rod Bertolet (1988a, 1988b) has made a nice point in response to this argument. I decided (2.3) to defend a realism committed to the entities posited by science and common sense – Scientific Realism ('entity realism') – but not a realism committed to our theories being right about those entities – Strong Scientific Realism ('theory realism'). This was for tactical reasons: the weaker the realism, the more easy it is to defend. Bertolet has pointed out that the goodness of the above abductive argument for Scientific Realism depends on our theories of unobservables being right (or largely so); observed phenomena are explained not by the mere existence of, say, electrons, but by electrons being the way our theory says they are. This point diminishes the tactical advantage of defending the weaker doctrine. I say 'diminishes', not 'destroys', because I think that it is arguable that when in the past we have been fairly wrong about the nature of entities, hence fairly *wrong in our reasons for* positing them, we have mostly been *right to* posit them (9.4).[1]

Scientific Realism is not committed to all the unobservables of modern science. It does take those commitments, for the most part, at face value: in general they are not to be paraphrased away (4.7). However, in standing back from the totality of commitments, it adopts a more cautious position, allowing for some ontological error in science: it is committed only to most of the unobservables 'confidently' and 'necessarily' posited. Further, it is committed to the independence of those unobservables (2.4). Of course, that independence mostly goes without saying once Common-Sense Realism has been accepted. Scientific Realism is an overarching empirical hypothesis.

The above argument for Scientific Realism is reminiscent of the earlier one for Common-Sense Realism that took us from hypotheses about how things seem to hypotheses about the observable world (5.7). However, there is a difference. Before, we could express what needed to be explained only in an 'as-if' language that was parasitic on the 'thing language' of Common-Sense Realism. This Realism is so ensconced in our thinking that we have only an artificial way of specifying something for it to explain. As a result, the explanation we gave, though good, was somewhat trivial. Here, in contrast, we have a set of entities – the observed ones – with characteristics and behaviour that are describable in a language that is not in any way parasitic on talk of unobservables.

Is this difference significant, so that, while we should accept

Common-Sense Realism, we should reject Scientific Realism? It is hard to see how it could be. The difference simply reflects the extent to which we humans take Common-Sense Realism for granted. Despite this, it is epistemically on a par with Scientific Realism. Both doctrines go 'beyond experience', 'beyond the evidence'; they involve sticking our necks out in similar ways (5.8). In principle, we could construct a non-parasitic experiential language that would make this obvious: the difference between the two abductions would then have disappeared.

The case for the inference to Scientific Realism has further support. Common-Sense Realism concerns not simply observed entities, but rather, observable entities (2.4). Most observable entities have never been observed. Yet in ordinary life and in science it is common to infer the existence of such entities. We observe a footprint in the sand, and infer the existence of a person. We observe the movements of Uranus, and infer the existence of Neptune. What possible ground could there be for someone who accepted such inferences to unobserved observables to reject inferences to unobserved unobservables? None, I suggest.

Could a Common-Sense Realist but an anti-Scientific Realist reject inferences to the existence of *all* unobserved entities, thus maintaining a consistent position? My definition of Common-Sense Realism does seem weak enough to allow this rejection. But what could be its basis? Not *general* scepticism, for that would rule out Common-Sense Realism too. Presumably the basis would be some view along the following lines: we can only know to exist what we observe to exist. Such plausibility as this view has arises, first, from a conflation of observing x with observing *that* x is F. We can observe an x that is in fact an F without observing that it is an F. Common-Sense Realism is not Weak Realism: it is committed to the existence of particular sorts of observables. So Common-Sense Realism requires that we conclude that x is F. The plausibility of the view in question arises, secondly, from overlooking the theory-ladenness of all such conclusions. The assumption that there are F's is a theoretical posit involving epistemic risk whether F's have been observed or not. The relation we have with an observed entity provides us with good evidence of its existence and of what it is like; but that evidence does not differ in kind from what we can have for the existence and nature of unobserved entities (5.8).

I shall return to the idea that our attitude to unobservables should be different from that to observables when discussing van Fraassen (chapter 8).

7.2 ABDUCTION

I have exhibited a fondness for abduction in my arguments for both Common-Sense and Scientific Realism. This fondness is typical of Realists. I shall not attempt any sustained defence of abduction. It is not obvious to me that a basic principle like this calls for such a defence. From the naturalistic stance that I urge, perhaps little more can be said than that abduction is an important part of the best overall theory of the world. Certainly, it can be given no *a priori* defence.[2]

Interestingly, abduction has recently been criticized by two philosophers of a generally realist persuasion, Nancy Cartwright and Ian Hacking. I shall say some words in defence of abduction, as I use it at least, against these criticisms.

Cartwright entitles a section of the introduction to her book 'Against Inference to the Best Explanation' (1983: 4). However, it turns out that her opposition to such inferences is very qualified. Her central and most provocative claim is that 'theoretical laws' are explanatory, but not true; she rejects what I have called 'Strong Scientific Realism' (4.4). It follows from this that she cannot accept abductive inferences *to the truth of a theoretical law*. Nevertheless, she does accept – indeed, she argues forcefully for – abductive inferences *to the most likely cause*. This abduction leads her to a belief in 'theoretical entities', and hence to Scientific Realism (pp. 4–18, 74–99). As far as I can see, the abductive inferences I am relying on are of the sort she accepts.

Cartwright's view of theoretical laws does raise a worry about the position described in the above discussion of Bertolet (7.1). I agreed with Bertolet that my abductive argument depends on our theories being largely right. One way of putting this is that it seems to be necessary that the theoretical laws be by and large true if they are to play their role in the causal story told by science. Cartwright thinks that the laws are not true. Nevertheless, she still thinks that the laws enable us, somehow, to tell the causal story. How can false laws tell true stories? She admits to having no account of how the laws manage this (pp. 161–2). It seems likely that the account she needs will have a lot in common with accounts along the lines of my discussion.

Hacking's position on abduction is puzzling. First, he criticizes abductive arguments for Scientific Realism like mine in ways that seem to miss their point (1983: 53–5). Second, he offers very powerful arguments for Realism that seem to be of exactly the sort cri-

112 *Proposals*

ticized. Indeed, he might be seen as offering an important criterion for a *good* abduction to the existence of unobservables. Third, he gives some brief and totally unconvincing reasons as to why one of his arguments is not of the sort criticized (pp. 201–2). Often in his discussion it seems as if his problem is not with the practice of infer-ring abductively, but with the *term* 'inference to the best explanation'.

Consider, first, Hacking's criticism (pp. 53–4) of the following abductive argument for Realism, which he attributes particularly to J. J. C. Smart: 'It would be an absolute miracle if . . . the photo-electric effect went on working while there were no electrons'; we need to take photons as real in order to understand how, in the case of television, scenes are turned into electronic messages. Hacking's criticism is that 'the *reality* of the photons is no part of the explana-tion.' But this is plainly false: the explanation *quantifies over* photons. Hacking seems to take a response of this sort, mysteriously, as 'beg-ging the question'. Yet, if the explanation is taken literally and seriously and is right, then there are photons; for the explanation is committed to photons (4.6). Of course, the anti-Realist can refuse to take it literally and seriously. But then we are left with no explana-tion: we have no causal story of how the scenes are turned into messages. That is the point of the Realist's argument, and it begs no question. With photons we have a causal explanation; without them we have none.

Consider, next, Hacking's own arguments for Realism:

We shall count as real what we can use to intervene in the world to affect something else, or what the world can use to affect us. (p. 146)

Experimental work provides the strongest evidence for scientific realism . . . because entities that in principle cannot be 'observed' are regularly mani-pulated to produce a new phenomena and to investigate other aspects of nature. (p. 262)

Hacking fills out these general remarks with a detailed discussion of examples. His discussion of microscopes is particularly striking (1983: 186–209; 1981).

Hacking's argument is a very helpful development of just the sorts of considerations in favour of Realism that have moved philosophers like Smart who appeal to abduction. These philosophers point to various observed phenomena P, and seek a causal explanation. Suppose there were an unobservable entity U. This would explain P. Often, the Realist claims, such an explanation is not only good, but the best. So, probably, U exists. Hacking has enriched this view by pointing out that such explanations seem particularly good where P

is *not merely passively observed but actively produced*. (The point is clearly related to the idea that *novel* predictions give us the best reason for believing a theory; see, e.g., Musgrave 1988.) Suppose that U exists. Then, if we do A, that should make U do something leading to P. When we then go ahead, do A, and produce P, we have powerful evidence of the existence of U. Those not afraid of abductive talk would put it this way: the best explanation of P is that we have indeed manipulated U, and so U really does exist. But, however you put it, considerations like this in favour of Realism are what I am referring to in the last section.

Cartwright and Hacking should be seen not as undermining abduction, but rather as saying something about what abductive arguments are and when they are good. (There are further discussions of abduction in sections 8.2 and 8.5.)

7.3   THE ARGUMENT FROM THEORETICAL SUCCESS

Earlier I mentioned the view, made popular by Putnam, that we need realism to explain success. I pointed out that the realism in question is often a combination of a metaphysical doctrine like Realism and a semantic doctrine like Correspondence Truth (cf. Maxim 2). I pointed out further that four different notions of success seem to be in question. So at least eight different theses underlie the view. I argued against four of them: that we needed Correspondence Truth to explain *individual* success; that we needed Realism to explain that success; similarly, that we needed either of them to explain *species* success (6.6). In this section[3] I shall be concerned with a notion of success which is quite different from those two: *theoretical* success.

What *is* theoretical success? It is tempting to talk of truth in answering this question: success consists in leading to true predictions. To begin with, I shall resist this temptation, because I am bent on showing that a robust notion of truth has nothing to do with the explanation of theoretical success.

Suppose a theory says that S. Then it is successful if the world is as if S. The obvious respect in which the world should be as if S is that it should be *observationally* (perhaps even experientially) as if S. So, for example, the theory that there are x's is successful if the observed world is as if there are x's: when we conduct experiments, build bridges, go to the moon, all on the assumption that there are x's, we do not come in for any surprises.

Putnam has the idea that what he calls 'realism', which in this

context is like an amalgam of my *Scientific* Realism with my Correspondence Truth, is needed to explain theoretical success: drop this
explanation, and that success is a 'miracle' (1978: 18–19). So, it is
claimed, this explanation provides a very good argument for realism.

Consider, first, the idea that Scientific Realism explains theoretical
success. This idea is clearly related to my argument in the last
section. But my argument is not that Realism explains the observational success of theories; it is rather that it helps to explain the
behaviour and characteristics of observed entities. For Scientific
Realism, aside from its independence dimension, *is* a more cautious
statement of the ontological claims about unobservables made by
our theories (2.4). This is not to say that observational success is
unimportant to Realism. The test of the above explanation, as of all
others, is that it be successful in practice: the observed world must be
as if there really are the unobservables posited by science. The key
point is that Scientific Realism *is* successful, rather than that it
explains success. We can of course ask for an explanation of that
success: Why is the observed world as if there are unobservable x's?
Realism does indeed give a good answer: it is because *there are*
unobservable x's. The answer has a trivial air to it, because it is only
if we suppose that *there aren't* x's that we feel any need to explain why
it is *as if there are* x's. Explaining theoretical success is a problem for
the anti-Realist. The strength of Scientific Realism is that the anti-
Realist cannot solve that problem. If Scientific Realism, and the
theories it draws on, were not correct, there would be no explanation
of why the observed world is as if they were correct: that fact would
be brute, if not miraculous.

Suppose that a theory posits unobservable x's, but there are in fact
no x's. Why is the observed world as if there are x's? The question is
not disturbing to the Realist. He expects some theories to be wrong.
He seeks an answer in terms of other unobservable entities. Such an
answer is not available to the anti-Realist, because he denies not only
x's but unobservables in general.

In sum, Scientific Realism can be seen as a somewhat trivial
explanation of theoretical success. However, a better view of the
matter is: first, Realism is part of a far from trivial explanation of the
observed world, an explanation which *is* successful; second, its rival,
anti-Realism, can offer no explanation of this success.

This discussion is reminiscent of the argument for Common-Sense
Realism in section 5.7. That argument might be seen as showing that
Common-Sense Realism explains 'experiential' success. After all,
what is it for a theory positing the existence of observable x's to be

successful? It is for it to be experientially *as if* there are *x*'s. So if we explain why it is experientially like that, we have explained the success. And that is what my argument for Common-Sense Realism did. The argument had a trivial air to it because there was not felt need for an explanation. What the argument also brought out was that Common-Sense Realism is confirmed by innumerable 'as-if' statements: it *is* successful. It is better to see success as the test, rather than the explanans, of Common-Sense Realism.

We have at last found something in the idea that what is called 'realism' is needed to explain success. Note, however, that Correspondence Truth has nothing to do with the explanation of theoretical success (*contra* Putnam). Why would anyone suppose otherwise?

First, talk of the 'success of theories', 'scientific success', and so forth may confuse the theoretical success that, we have just been discussing with the earlier individual (or species) success of an organism (6.6; also perhaps with the scientific progress to be discussed in 7.6). Yet the two sorts of success are quite different. Theoretical success is relevant whenever we theorize about anything, not only or particularly when we theorize about organisms. Individual success is relevant only when we theorize about organisms. We can bring out the importance of this difference to the discussion of Correspondence Truth by an example. (1) If there are electrons, and they are the way electron theory says they are, and such and such experimental conditions obtain, then so and so observational result should occur. If it does occur, that is a success of electron theory: in this respect the observable world is as if there are electrons. It is also a success of science and, in some sense, of scientists. However, our theoretical concern here is not with people or their language but with the impersonal world. The success of scientists is not *qua* people but *qua* scientists-in-prediction. There is no need to talk of truth here. (2) We might think electron theory successful in another sense: people who believe and assert 'There are electrons' and so on enjoy success in their interaction with the world (including electrons). The theory helps scientists *qua* people to satisfy their needs and fulfil their desires. Why? What properties do the belief and assertion have that lead them to have this happy effect on our lives? Our theoretical concern here is with people. It is tempting – though, I have argued, probably wrong – to suppose that we need correspondence truth to explain this individual success (6.6).

Second, people may be led to think that we need a correspondence notion of truth to explain theoretical success by confusing that notion with a trivial deflationary notion (3.4). We can certainly find a place for the deflationary notion in our explanation, as we can in any explanation. And it may be more convenient to state the explanation using the notion; for example, we might say that a theory is successful in that its observational predictions are true and that the explanation of this is that the theory is true. However, this semantic ascent is unnecessary. More important, it involves only the deflationary notion. To show this, I have chosen in this section to state the explanation of a theoretical success in a way that makes no mention of truth. Talk of truth is felicitous, but not explanatory.

The point can be emphasized by noting that even talk of theories, the only possible objects of truth here, is unnecessary. This was implicit in the account of what it is to say that the theory that S is successful: it is to say that the observed world is as if S. What we are trying to explain is not something about a theory, but something about the observed world.

The explanation of the success of theories that we have been discussing should be distinguished from two other explanations. First, it should be distinguished from the explanation of why we humans tend to have successful theories. The latter explanation is one in our theory of people. Van Fraassen finds signs of a Realist explanation of this human tendency in a passage in Putnam that he calls 'the Ultimate Argument' (1980: 38–40). (I think the passage is better seen as a version of the argument from the success of theories.) Van Fraassen rejects the claim that we need Realism for the explanation. I agree with him. Given that believing a successful theory is conducive to individual success, the right answer to the question is surely along straightforward Darwinian lines.

Second, the explanation of the success of theories should be distinguished from the explanation of the success of *scientific methodology*. Our methodology is 'instrumentally reliable' in that it leads to theories that make true observational predictions – that is to say, to theories that are successful (in the above sense). Everyone agrees that our methodology does this. But why does it? What is the explanation? Richard Boyd (1973, 1984, 1985) has posed this question, and offered a Realist answer: the methodology is based in a dialectical way on our theories (cf. my 5.8), and those theories are approximately true. He argues ingeniously that anti-Realists of various sorts cannot explain this methodological success satisfactorily, and so his Realist explanation is the best.[4] I think he is probably right (taking his talk of truth as deflationary). But, once again, I do not think that this is the basic argument for Realism.

Scientific Realism is successful at the observational level and, in a trivial way, itself explains that success. Correspondence Truth has no role in that explanation. Putnam has also made popular the idea that realism explains the convergent view of scientific progress in science. I shall consider this in section 7.6.

7.4 EMPIRICISM AND UNDERDETERMINATION

I turn now to an influential empiricist argument against Realism. Boyd, who does not of course agree with its conclusion, has nicely expressed the argument as follows:

Suppose that T is a proposed theory of unobservable phenomena . . . A theory is said to be empirically equivalent to T just in case it makes the same predictions about observable phenomena that T does. Now, it is always possible, given T, to construct arbitrarily many alternative theories that are empirically equivalent to T but which offer contradictory accounts of the nature of unobservable phenomena. . . . T and each of the theories empirically equivalent to it will be equally well confirmed or disconfirmed by any possible observational evidence. . . . scientific evidence can never decide the question between theories of unobservable phenomena and, therefore, knowledge of unobservable phenomena is impossible. (1984: 42–4)

One way of putting this is: we should not believe T, because it is *underdetermined by the evidence*.

It is important to note that the underdetermination in question is not merely by all the evidence we have already gathered. An argument appealing to this underdetermination would be like the one discussed earlier (5.2). If it were good, it would lead to Cartesian scepticism, thus undermining Common-Sense Realism as much as Scientific Realism.

The underdetermination appealed to in the present argument is much stronger: T and its empirically equivalent rival, T', are underdetermined by *all possible evidence*. Not only has no difference, as a matter of fact, *been detected*; no difference *is detectable*. In the face of this, a belief in the unobservable posits of T is alleged to be totally unjustified. Commitment to the existence of those entities, rather than merely to the pragmatic advantages of the theory that speaks of them, makes no evidential difference, and so is surely a piece of misguided metaphysics; it reflects super-empirical values, not hard facts.

Even if this underdetermination thesis were true, it is not obvious that it would support this conclusion. For, once again, if it did, worries about being a brain in a vat might lead to the abandonment of Common-Sense Realism.

Setting that aside, although this underdetermination thesis may be true in *some* sense, it is not true in any *interesting* sense. An interesting sense is one which might plausibly be taken to support the anti-Realist conclusion.

The first step in casting doubt on the underdetermination thesis takes account of the Duhem–Quine thesis: theories face the tribunal of experience in conjunction with auxiliary theories, theories of instruments, assumptions about the background conditions, and so on (5.8). So it is not really *T* that makes predictions, but *T* together with a set of auxiliary assumptions. Perhaps, then, we could vary our auxiliary assumptions until we came up with some that, when conjoined with *T* and *T'* in turn, yielded different predictions. The empiricist will immediately respond by revising the underdetermination thesis. Let *A* be any given set of auxiliary hypotheses. The revised thesis is that *T* & *A* is underdetermined by the possible evidence: we can construct arbitrarily many conjunctions – for example, *T'* & *A'*, – which are empirically equivalent to *T* & *A*. But again, perhaps we could come up with *additional* auxiliary assumptions that, when conjoined with *T* & *A* and *T'* & *A'* in turn, yielded different predictions. There is no end to this procedure. For, according to Duhem–Quine, everything is epistemically related to everything else.

The empiricist does not claim that there are always *actual* theories that fit the evidence as well as *T*, but that there are always *possible* theories. So he relies on our ability to construct *alternative theories* to *T* (or *T* & *A*). But he does not seem equally impressed by our ability to construct *auxiliary hypotheses* to use to test these alternatives against *T* (or *T* & *A*). Yet there is no known limit to our ability to think up such hypotheses. Why then should we believe of any given *T* (or *T* & *A*) that it is underdetermined by the evidence?

The next step in casting doubt on the underdetermination thesis looks critically at its talk of 'possible evidence'. Such talk is open to a variety of interpretations, as we have already noted (3.5). Only if the thesis's talk is given a liberal interpretation does the thesis pose a threat to Scientific Realism. But, on that interpretation, there is not the slightest reason to believe it.

One interpretation of 'possible evidence' is due to Quine: all the observations that would have been made had there been an observer at each point of *actual* space-time (1970a: 179). This is what van Fraassen means by 'the phenomena': all *actual* observable things and events, past, present, and future, whether or not anyone in fact observes them (1980: 12, 60, 64). So this is the notion that features in van Fraassen's talk of empirical adequacy (to be discussed in the next chapter).

The underdetermination thesis involving this very restricted sense of 'possible evidence' may survive the above considerations from Duhem–Quine and so may be true, though I am inclined to doubt it. But that sense of the thesis is too weak for the argument against Realism, as we shall see.

The Quinean sense of 'possible evidence' is restricted, in that it does not cover anything non-actual *except acts of observation*. There are many things that we do not do, but could do, other than merely observe. If we had the time, talent, and money, perhaps we could invent the right instruments and conduct the right experiments to discriminate between the theories. There may be many differences between the theories which we would not have detected had we *passively observed* each point of actual space-time but which we would have detected had we *actively intervened* (Hacking 1983) to change what happened at points of space-time. In this liberal sense that allows for our capacity to *create* phenomena, the class of possible evidence seems totally open.

I remarked earlier that the empiricist is insufficiently impressed with our ability to think up auxiliary hypotheses. This point grows in importance with the present consideration. For many auxiliary hypotheses will concern experimental situations. Every time we invent a new instrument, we add the theory of that instrument as an auxiliary hypothesis. Every time we use the instrument in an experiment, we add assumptions about the circumstances, including ones that make us believe that the instrument is 'working properly'.

In light of this, given any T (or T & A), what possible reason could there be for thinking *a priori* that we *could not* distinguish it empirically from any rival if we were ingenious enough in constructing experiments and auxiliary hypotheses? It is of course *possible* that we should be unable to distinguish two theories: we humans have finite capacities. The point is that we have no good reason for believing it in a particular case. Even less do we have a good reason for believing it of *all* theories; that is to say, for believing that *every* theory faces rivals that are not detectably different.[5]

Behind these Realist doubts about underdetermination lies the following picture. T and T' describe different causal structures alleged to underlie the phenomena. We can manipulate the actual underlying structure to get observable effects. We have no reason to believe that we *could not* organize these manipulations so that, if the structure were as T says, the effects would be of one sort, whereas if the structure were as T' says, the effects would be of a different sort.

In sum, perhaps the underdetermination thesis understood in the restricted way of Quine and van Fraassen is something we should accept. However, there is no reason for believing the thesis understood in the liberal way.

If the liberally interpreted thesis were true, Realism might be in trouble. But why should the Realist be bothered by the restricted thesis? A consequence of that thesis is that we *do not*, as a matter of fact, ever conduct a crucial experiment for deciding between T and T'. This does not show that we *could not* conduct one. And the latter is what needs to be established for the empiricist argument against Realism (Boyd 1984: 50). The restricted empirical equivalence of T and T' does *not* show, *in any epistemologically interesting sense*, that they make 'the same predictions about observable phenomena' or that they 'will be equally well confirmed or disconfirmed by any possible evidence'. It does *not* show that 'scientific evidence can never decide the question between theories of unobservable phenomena and [that], therefore, knowledge of unobservable phenomena is impossible'. It does *not* show that commitment to T rather than T' is super-empirical, and hence a piece of misguided metaphysics.

We have already set aside the Cartesian scepticism occasioned by the thesis that theories are underdetermined by the *actual* evidence to date. No other worry is occasioned by the thesis that theories are underdetermined by the possible evidence, in the restricted sense: by the actual evidence to date *together with* actual observations in the future and actual events that, though observable, are never observed. Consider, first, this example that I heard long ago in a class. 'Here are two theories: first, the laws of current physics hold; second, the laws of current physics hold except when I, Hilary Putnam, stand on this table with a sack over my head and count to 37.' Putnam's point was that these two theories were equally compatible with all the evidence to date, but that this was no reason for scepticism about physics. The theories are also equally compatible with all the possible evidence in the restricted sense (assuming that Putnam never does stand on the table, and so forth). But again, this provides no reason for scepticism. Consider, second, the following possibility: a cosmic calamity destroys humanity tomorrow. Experiments that will, as a matter of fact, be performed would then not be performed. This would reduce the class of possible evidence on the restricted interpretation. Thus, many theories that are not empirically equivalent (in the restricted sense) would be made so by the cosmic calamity. Yet, the calamity is surely irrelevant epistemically. Whether or not such a calamity occurs tomorrow should make no difference to our attitude to T today.

When we construct a bridge, we are interested in whether it will stand up if a certain sort of truck is driven over it, regardless of whether or not such a truck is in fact ever driven over it. Similarly, when we construct a theory, we are interested in whether it will stand up if a certain sort of experiment is performed on it, whether or not such an experiment is in fact ever performed on it. It is in this sense that we want a theory to be compatible with the possible evidence. And we can expect theories that posit different unobservables to be differently related to this sort of possible evidence.

In conclusion, the empiricist argument against Scientific Realism starts from an underdetermination thesis. The restricted thesis of Quine and van Fraassen may be true, but it is too weak for the task of undermining Realism. This task requires the liberally interpreted thesis, which we have no reason to believe.

Is there *any* threat to Scientific Realism? If our approach is guided by my maxims, then we find no powerful argument against Common-Sense Realism. However, we do find one against Scientific Realism. It is a 'meta-induction' arising from the claim that the history of science has been one of ontological *elimination*. We shall strike it first in the next section.

7.5　CORRESPONDENCE TRUTH (SCIENTIFIC PHYSICAL)

So far, discussion of Scientific Realism has not produced any argument in favour of Correspondence Truth (scientific physical). The basic argument for it is simple (and was foreshadowed in section 4.4). Assume that we have established Correspondence Truth (common-sense physical). So our common-sense statements are correspondence-true or false in virtue of reference to observables likes stones, trees, cats, and so on. Next assume that we have established Scientific Realism. So unobservables like electrons, muons, and curved space-time exist. Then the most plausible view is that scientific statements are correspondence-true or false in virtue of reference to those unobservables. There is no motivation for not extending the realm of correspondence truth beyond the common-sense to the scientific. Let us examine this argument a little.

The case for Correspondence Truth (common-sense physical)

requires arguments that we both need and are entitled to correspondence truth. Consider need first. We found a place for correspondence truth in the explanations of behaviour (6.5) and its success (6.6), but no really persuasive evidence that we needed truth for these purposes. I argued that we needed truth to explain the properties of linguistic and mental symbols that enable them to play a variety of social roles, including serving as guides to reality (6.7). This argument for need applies to scientific statements as much as to common-sense ones.

The argument for entitlement envisages an explanation of truth in terms of both structure and reference, together with an explanation of these (3.3). Again, this argument applies equally to scientific statements. However, it may seem to face a special problem with those statements. What theory of reference can we reasonably hope to cover scientific terms?

A description theory is very appealing. On this view, our term 'electron' would refer to electrons in virtue of the fact that our theory associates the term with various descriptions (a weighted most of) which picked out electrons. But then the above-mentioned meta-induction, nicely framed by Putnam (1978: 25), would make it likely that such terms did *not* refer. From our present perspective we can see that, according to the description theory, most of the terms of past theories do not refer, because there is nothing that the associated descriptions pick out; our past theories were mostly wrong. So it would be probable that the terms of our present theories did not refer. Thus Scientific Realism would be false.

I shall return to this argument later, in discussing Kuhn, Feyerabend, and the radical philosophers of science (9.3–9.4). Meanwhile, it is clear that the Realist has good reason to look for some other theory of reference.

We need theories of reference of another sort anyway. The explanation of reference must rest ultimately on a direct causal relation to reality (3.3). Can we hope for a causal theory of those scientific terms which refer to unobservables? Any such theory faces a difficulty over and beyond those that all causal theories face. The relation between a person and an object she perceives seems a promising one on which to build any causal theory. But this relation is not available for scientific terms, because their referents cannot be perceived. What then is the causal relation to these referents that determines reference?[6]

The costs of despair regarding this question are very high. If we hold to Correspondence Truth (scientific physical), then our attempt to explain reference for scientific terms will force us back to a description theory. We have just seen that this threatens Scientific Realism. Yet the arguments for Scientific Realism, independent of anything to do with semantics, are very strong. It should not be given up for semantic reasons, in which we should have much less confidence (Maxim 3). It would be better to abandon Correspondence Truth (scientific physical) than to abandon Scientific Realism. But then we would have lost truth-referential semantics – our only promising semantics – for scientific statements. And it would be hard to stop the rot spreading to common-sense statements. Correspondence truth would have no place in the explanation of language. (I shall consider this idea of preserving Realism at the expense of Correspondence Truth again in 14.9.)

I do not think that we should despair of finding a theory of reference for scientific terms that is compatible with Realism. Perhaps a compromise theory that is part causal and part descriptive will do the trick.

7.6 SCIENTIFIC PROGRESS AND CONVERGENCE

We have already considered six versions of the ambiguous thesis that realism explains success. In this section we shall consider another two, concerned with scientific progress. From time to time scientists replace a theory T with a better one T'. This sort of success is quite different from the individual success and species success considered in section 6.6 and from the theoretical success considered in section 7.3. However, like some of them, it might be referred to by a term like 'scientific success'.

What is the explanation of scientific progress? First, we need an account of its nature. What makes one theory better than another? Second, we need an account of why humans tend to replace a theory by one that is, in that way, better. The explanation we seek will be part of our theory of people and their history, rather than of the largely inanimate world. Talk of theories will be essential to the explanation.

Do we need Realism – in particular, Scientific Realism – or Correspondence Truth (scientific) to explain scientific progress? Manifestly not on a minimal, and fairly neutral, account of the nature of progress. Take T' to be better than T in virtue of its being more *theoretically* successful. T' has more true and fewer false observational predictions than T. Clearly an instrumentalist can explain scientific success understood in this way by building on the Darwinian explanation that concluded section 7.3.

Kuhn and Feyerabend reject this explanation of progress, as they would also the other explanations to be considered in this section. I will consider their views in chapter 9 (see particularly 9.4 and 9.6).

The most popular view of progress, particularly among Realists, is richer than the above one: progress is said to involve *convergence*. This is Putnam's view, for example (1978: 19–23, 123). Convergence in science amounts to the following, *at least*: relative to T', the terms of T typically refer and the laws of T are typically approximately true. Call this doctrine 'Simple Convergence'. More interesting and robust doctrines of convergence are also popular; for example, the doctrine 'Increasing Verisimilitude': T' is typically closer to the truth than T. The doctrines lead to views of the aim of science: thus Increasing Verisimilitude leads to the view that truth is the aim of science. The discussion of the relation between convergence doctrines and realism is a can of worms.

It is sometimes suggested that a doctrine like Simple Convergence or Increasing Verisimilitude is constitutive of scientific realism (e.g. Laudan 1981; S. Blackburn 1980). This is clearly wrong. If there is any relation between realism and convergence, it is an evidential one, which must be distinguished from a constitutive one (Maxim 1).

Suppose that there is no convergence. It does not follow that Scientific Realism must be false: unobservables could exist, whatever the history of science has been like. It does not follow either that Correspondence Truth (scientific) must be false: each sentence in T and T' could be correspondence-true or -false, and yet T and T' not converge.

Nor do the reverse entailments hold. Even idealism is compatible with convergence. And though convergence, as we are understanding it, requires some notion of truth, it does not necessarily require correspondence truth.

Convergence is not constitutive of either Scientific Realism or Correspondence Truth (scientific). It would be uncharitable to take Putnam as claiming that it is (but see 1982: 198–200). He seems to claim, rather, that what he calls 'realism' (see 7.3 above) explains convergence (1978: 20–2, 128). So the claim is an inference to the best explanation. He also raises the thought that were there no convergence, the best explanation of that fact would be anti-realism (pp. 22–5). I shall consider this last thought later.

Let us assume the convergent view of progress. Do we need

Scientific Realism or Correspondence Truth to explain it? Consider the explanation we might give using those doctrines.

First, we need to say more about the nature of convergence from the perspective of these doctrines. This might seem to be easily done along the following lines. The terms of T and T' mostly refer. The set of entities referred to by T is included in the set of those referred to by T'. Now, if we can develop Correspondence Truth to make sense of assigning *degrees* of truth to T and T', we can clearly make sense of Simple Convergence. T' has a higher degree of truth than T about the entities of T, but not vastly higher. So if T' had been true, T would also have a high degree of truth. T is approximately true relative to T'. Making sense of Increasing Verisimilitude is more difficult. Whereas Simple Convergence depends only on increasing truth about a given set of entities, Increasing Verisimilitude requires increasing truth *content* (and decreasing falsity content) in some science. T' could achieve this not only by finding out more about the entities of T, but also by discovering truths about other entities.

Unfortunately, a large and very technical literature shows that assigning degrees of truth and comparing truth (falsity) contents are much more difficult than at first appears. This literature started with criticisms of Popper's notion of verisimilitude by Tichy (1974), Harris (1974), and Miller (1974a and b), and finished (for me) with Niiniluoto (1978). Despite these difficulties, I think we should be optimistic that a doctrine such as Increasing Verisimilitude, which seems so useful in the explanation of progress, can be satisfactorily explained.[7]

Next we need to explain, from our Realist perspective, what makes convergence progressive. We need to tie convergence to other theoretical 'virtues' (Quine and Ullian 1970: 43–53), and in particular, to observational success. Why does convergence lead to such success? If T' is convergent with respect to T, then it gives a more accurate picture than T of the set of entities that constitute the mechanisms underlying part of the observable world. So T' should be more observationally successful than T.

Finally, we need an explanation of why humans tend to adopt theories that are convergent. The aforementioned Darwinian explanation removes any puzzle about our choosing increasingly observationally successful theories. So what remains to be explained is our strategy of achieving this increase by choosing convergent theories. Given that convergent theories (from our Realist perspective) give a more and more accurate picture of the underlying mechanisms, the strategy is clearly a good one. So, presumably, we can look forward to some Darwinian explanation of our catching on to it.

So, technical difficulties aside, Scientific Realism and Correspondence Truth (scientific) can give a good explanation of the convergent view of scientific progress. What seems very doubtful, nevertheless, is that we *need* either doctrine to explain progress. A doctrine of warranted assertability in the ideal limit could allow acceptance of convergence and explain the links with progress. If the Realist can get by in this way without correspondence truth, then the anti-Realist surely can. So the convergence view of progress does not supply a compelling case for Correspondence Truth. Nor does it do so for Scientific Realism. My response here is much the same as it was to the earlier suggestion that we need Realism to explain individual success (6.6). It would be fantastic to suppose that the explanation of progress was the main justification for Realism: the theory of people, in which this explanation belongs, is the wrong place to look for such a justification. And if anti-Realism were otherwise plausible, it would surely not fail for want of an explanation of progress (Goldman 1979: 180).

In sum, I reject the two versions of 'realism explains success' that concern scientific progress. Only one of the eight versions has turned out to be true: we need Realism to explain theoretical success (7.3).

We have been concerned to explain the convergent view of scientific progress, a view that Kuhn and company deny. Suppose they are right, and there is no convergence. Putnam raises the thought that non-convergence threatens the doctrines of Scientific Realism and/or Correspondence Truth (scientific). Consider this thought briefly.

Convergence is explained in terms of a notion of truth. It might be rejected by a Realist because of the above-mentioned technical difficulties with the notion or because of doubts about robust truth in general (e.g. Leeds–Quine, 6.1). Perhaps such a Realist could explain scientific progress in Darwinian terms. However, a Realist who has no general opposition to robust truth, holding to a doctrine like Correspondence Truth, does seem to need convergence to explain progress: he must see progress as some sort of accumulation of truth. I develop this thought more thoroughly in section 9.7.

Discussions of convergence have revealed one other problem for Scientific Realism that is clearly important. Suppose that convergence fails because of ontological elimination. Then Putnam's meta-induction, described in the last section, threatens Scientific Realism directly, without any reference to the explanation of progress. I shall consider it in section 9.4 when discussing Kuhn, Feyerabend, and the radical philosophers of science.

In conclusion, a doctrine of convergence is not constitutive of Scientific Realism or Correspondence Truth (scientific). However, the latter two doctrines together need convergence to explain scientific progress. So the threat of non-convergence to Scientific Realism is only indirect. Convergence is rejected by many because of ontological elimination which directly threatens Scientific Realism via Putnam's meta-induction. Convergence also faces technical difficulties about which I think we should be optimistic. Scientific Realism and Correspondence Truth (scientific) together can explain the convergent view of progress, but this is not their main support: other doctrines could probably do so equally well.

7.7 OPERATIONISM

Common-Sense Realists opposed to Scientific Realism have usually adopted either operationism or instrumentalism. These two doctrines differ not in their ontology but in their semantics. They both, in effect, deny that the unobservables of science exist (or that we have any justification for supposing they do): unobservables are simply 'useful fictions'. The doctrines have very different theories of meaning for theoretical terms.

The main objection to their ontology has already been aired (7.1), and will be discussed further later (8.4); it requires that observability have an epistemic significance which it cannot have. In this section I shall make other objections to operationism; in the next, other objections to instrumentalism.

Both operationism and instrumentalism employ a distinction between 'theoretical' and 'observational' terms. This distinction has usually been based on a view of what we can know. This view gives to observability the same epistemic significance that I have just denied it. However, the distinction could be based on the referential properties of simple terms. Supposing, as we have been, that we can distinguish among putative entities between those that are observable and those that are not, then we can say that a simple observational term is one that purports to refer to an observable entity; a theoretical term is one that does not so purport.

The operationist requires that each meaningful theoretical term be

defined operationally; that is, a specification must be given of the
result of operations or experiments on observable entities that would
justify the application of the term. The term does not refer to unobservables, but is a shorthand for a complex phrase made up of
terms referring to observables. Any theoretical term that cannot be so
translated is meaningless, and should be banished from science.

The operationist's view of theoretical statements is like the
phenomenalist's view of physical-object statements. Just as the
phenomenalist requires that a physical-object statement be translated
into subjunctive conditionals about sense data, so the operationist
requires that theoretical statements be translated into subjunctive
conditionals about observable entities. And operationism fails for
similar reasons (5.5).

First, and most important, the required translations are impossible
for many of the most cherished parts of science. This alone does not
refute operationism: it remains possible to abandon those parts of
science. However, such revisionism makes operationism implausible.

Second, subjunctive conditionals need bases. In virtue of what is it
the case that if we *were* to perform such and such operation we *would*
get so and so observable result? The operationist must leave this,
implausibly, as an inexplicable 'brute fact' of the world.

7.8   INSTRUMENTALISM

According to instrumentalism, a theory is a partially interpreted
formal system. It is a mere computational device or instrument
to take us from observation statement to observation statement.
Whereas the operationist regards theoretical terms as meaningful
because they have definitions that refer to observables, the instrumentalist regards them as largely meaningless because they don't
refer to anything. Hence, for the instrumentalist, theoretical statements are not (correspondence-) true or false. The only meaning
that theoretical statements have is 'inherited' from the observational
language via deductive links. This observational language is referential; it is fully interpreted.

Instrumentalism is a retreat from the thoroughgoing anti-Realism
of phenomenalism, and was favoured by those positivists who found
that doctrine too extreme. It has the great advantage over operationism of not requiring that theoretical language be translated
into observational language. Indeed, the instrumentalist can be as

enthusiastic about theory construction as the Realist. he is a 'quasi-realist' about science (4.8).

In describing the ontology of instrumentalism, I said that the doctrine 'in effect' denied the existence of unobservables. The reason for the qualification is that it is often not obvious what view a particular instrumentalist has on this issue, and some seem to represent themselves as Realists (see discussion in Nagel 1961: 118; Brody 1970a: 184). This appears paradoxical. If electrons exist, why not suppose that the theoretical term 'electron' refers to them, and hence is as meaningful and referential as the observational term 'raven'?

The explanation of the ontological coyness is to be found in the positivists' horror of all things 'metaphysical' and in the 'linguistic turn' in philosophy that resulted (5.4). Pages of instrumentalist writing may go by discussing the *language* of science with hardly a mention of the *ontology* of science (see, e.g., Hempel 1954; cf. Maxim 2). When the ontological issue is mentioned, it is treated as if it were fundamentally unclear. The instrumentalist apparently found talk of language transparent, but talk of existence opaque. Nagel refers to 'the notorious ambiguity if not obscurity of the expression "physical reality" or "physical existence"' (1961: 145-6). A climate of opinion was established in which such a staunch Realist as J. J. C. Smart felt obliged to devote several pages to explaining his use of 'real' (1963: 32-6). (I take it that to say, in this context, that something is real is simply to say that it exists.)

I have already indicated my disagreement with this positivist opinion (4.6). There is nothing particularly obscure or unintelligible about talk of existence or reality, far less indeed than about talk of truth, reference, theories, observational consequences, and so on (on this see Putnam 1971: 57-60). Some help can be given to someone who has difficulty with the talk (see Smart, e.g.), but this cannot pretend to explain the nature of existence. In my view we need no such explanation.

When the constitutive question of whether unobservables exist *is* discussed, it often seems confused with the epistemic question of *how we tell* whether they exist (see, e.g., Nagel 1961: 146-52; Hesse 1967: 407-8). This reflects another tenet of positivism: verificationism. The flight from metaphysics turns the constitutive question into one about the meaning of existence statements. The verificationist theory of meaning turns that into a question of the justification of such statements. (The confusion of the constitutive with the epistemic is often mediated by the word 'criterion', which seems specially designed for that role.) The possibility that an instrumentalist can think that such statements are justified, in some sense, explains the apparent paradox of an instrumentalist representing himself as a Realist.

I shall overlook the coyness and the paradox, taking instrumentalism to be anti-Realist.

If it is granted that the issue of whether unobservables exist is distinct from semantic questions about the language of science (Maxim 2), the question arises, 'Which should we settle first?' My view is that we should settle the ontological one first (Maxim 3). We have very good reasons, quite independent of semantics, for deciding that there are unobservables and which ones there are (7.1). On the other hand, in the absence of a position on the ontological issue, we have little basis for a decision on the semantic one (4.9). Having settled for Realism, we can argue for Correspondence Truth along the lines indicated (7.5). We can also argue against verificationism, as I shall in discussing Dummett (chapter 14).

Let 'S' abbreviate some well-established scientific theory positing the existence of unobservables. The instrumentalist is, of course, in favour of *accepting* 'S'. However, he does not think that we ought to *believe* that S, for he does not believe that there are any unobservables. Rather, he thinks we should believe that 'S' is a good instrument for dealing with the observable world. What, as a matter of empirical fact, *do* scientists believe? Suppose they do believe that S. The instrumentalist then finds himself in apparent opposition to science, and hence on the defensive. He must respond that these beliefs are irrelevant to science. They may make scientists feel better, but they do no scientific work: they are unnecessary ideological baggage. (I make a similar point in section 8.2 against van Fraassen.)

Putnam sometimes writes as if what *constitutes* Realism is scientists having Realist beliefs (1978: 20–2; cf. Devitt 1983b: sect. 2). I think rather that the Realist beliefs of scientists would be *evidence for* Realism. The constitutive question should be kept sharply distinct from the evidential one (Maxim 1).

In these early days, we cannot look to cognitive psychology to tell us definitively what scientists believe. However, we can look for behavioural evidence. Many arguments against instrumentalism can be seen as showing that scientists behave as if they have the beliefs that the Realist says they should have (or are striving to acquire them). Furthermore, those arguments suggest that behaving in that way is important to scientific progress. Thus, (1) if a theory were simply a tool, then its failure to work in a certain area outside its chosen one would show only its restricted range. Yet it is common to seek out remote implications of a theory by conjoining it with others and to regard it as *disconfirmed* if they do not hold (Popper 1963: 111–14). If instrumentalism were right, there would be no significant reason for not having a separate, unrelated theory for each job. Yet what we find is scientists seeking to unify their theories. (2) It is hard not to see much scientific behaviour as a painstaking attempt to discover the nature of underlying mechanisms. (3) If instrumentalism were right, it would be appropriate for the scientist to be complacent about his theory as long as it was working on the surface. Such complacency would have prevented the change from Ptolemaic to Copernican astronomy, as Feyerabend points out (1964). So the evidence of scientific practice suggest that scientists do have the beliefs that Realists think they should have. The success of science indicates the importance of these beliefs, and hence confirms Realism.

Though these considerations of scientific behaviour and belief further undermine instrumentalism, the main argument against it has been given earlier (7.1). It is the simple argument that Scientific Realism helps to explain what we observe, an argument which can be undermined only by attributing to observability an epistemic significance it does not have.

7.9   EPISTEMIC ATTITUDES

The Realist does not recommend to scientists that they should believe strongly in the entities of *all* theories, only in those of the established theories that we have the very best grounds to accept. Toward the entities of other theories, which we in some sense accept, he may recommend a variety of other attitudes, ranging from mild belief to outright disbelief.

Mild belief is the appropriate attitude to the entities of a theory that is doing well but is not yet thoroughly established. Agnosticism is the appropriate attitude to the entities of untried speculations at the frontiers. Outright disbelief is the appropriate attitude to the entities of a theory which we have good reason to think false but which we accept because it is useful. For the Realist does not deny a place to this instrumentalist view of a theory: there is a place for 'mere models' and 'idealizations'. What he insists on is that we should not rest with such a theory. And the more we find a theory to have the usual virtues (coherence, agreement with the evidence, simplicity, etc.), the more we should believe it.

That Realism encourages a variety of epistemic attitudes to theories is important to its plausibility, because we seem to find such a variety among the scientists, as Michael Gardner has pointed out (1979; he urges a view of the factors that lead scientists to move from an instrumentalist to a realist view of a theory; see also McMullin 1984). Further, Realism is able to meet the challenge allegedly posed to it by quantum theory. This theory is certainly useful, but those in the know find it difficult to believe: its 'conceptual peculiarities' (Sklar 1981: 29) cast doubt on its coherence. Controversy rages as to how it should be understood. The Realist should see this as evidence that quantum theory is not to be trusted at this stage as a guide to reality. Perhaps, as Feyerabend has urged (1964), an instrumentalist attitude to it is appropriate.[8]

Scientific Realism does take the posits of science pretty much at face value. However, it is committed only to most of those posited by the theories that we have good reason to believe: it is committed to most of science's 'confident' posits (2.3 and 4.7).

NOTES

1   This paragraph is drawn from my response, 1988a, to Bertolet 1988.
2   For some considerations in support of abduction, see Boyd 1984: 65–75; McMullin 1984: 26–35; and Marinov 1988.
3   Earlier versions of sections 7.3 and 7.6 are to be found in my 1983b and 1987.
4   Van Fraassen is scornful of Boyd's argument (1985: 259–60, 282), but not for any good reason. Boyd is not attempting to stand outside science and *justify* the scientific method, but rather to stand within science and *explain* the success of that method. Similarly, Fine is wrong to see all theories about science as requiring a stance outside science (1986a: 147–8).
5   This is not to deny that we can construct a theory that is empirically equivalent to T (even in the liberal sense). Construction is easy: if T says that S, then the theory that the observable world is as if S is empirically equivalent. However, the latter, 'parasitic' theory does not offer an account of the unobservable world, and so is not a rival to T for the purposes of the empiricist argument we are considering. We shall look at the significance of such parasitic theories when discussing van Fraassen (chapter 8).
    Others who have expressed doubts about underdetermination include Newton-Smith (1978), Ellis (1985), Jardine (1986), and Marinov (1988).
    Boyd thinks that the underdetermination thesis can be saved by reformulating it to apply to 'total sciences', because 'total sciences are self-contained with respect to auxiliary hypotheses' (1984: 50). But they are not self-contained with respect to all the auxiliary hypotheses

relevant to testing a theory. Indeed, even total science, the sum of all total sciences at any time, is not. It is always possible to think up new experiments and hypotheses – ones that are not part of current science – which may be used to test a theory.

6 I have struggled briefly with this problem from the perspective of a historical causal theory (1981a: 201).

7 A satisfactory explanation could allow some indeterminacy in, e.g., a comparison of the truth contents of theories.

  I began working on the explanation of verisimilitude in 1973. My approach was, first, to use a Tarski–Field theory of truth (3.3) and a weighting function for consequence sets to make sense of assigning degrees of truth to a theory. Second, I attempted to compare truth contents of theories. The first draft of this book included an appendix setting out this approach. Those with a better grip than I on the mounting verisimilitude literature advised me against publishing it. I decided to follow this advice. Subsequent comments by Graham Oddie confirmed the wisdom of this decision. For Oddie's views of verisimilitude, see Oddie 1986.

8 Idealizations provide another reason for withholding belief in entities, as Brian Ellis brings out (1985: 54–8).

Part III
Polemics

8

Van Fraassen against Scientific Realism

PART I: Van Fraassen 1980

In this part I shall discuss van Fraassen's *The Scientific Image* (1980). The discussion is a modified version of my discussion of that work in the first edition of this book (1984a: ch. 8). In part II I shall discuss van Fraassen's reply to his critics, 'Empiricism in the Philosophy of Science' (1985).

8.1   INTRODUCTION

Van Fraassen is opposed to scientific realism, which he defines thus: 'Science aims to give us, in its theories, a literally true story of what the world is like; and acceptance of a scientific theory involves the belief that it is true' (1980: 8). Instead, he urges 'constructive empiricism': 'Science aims to give us theories which are empirically adequate: and acceptance of a theory involves as belief only that it is empirically adequate' (p. 12). A theory is 'empirically adequate' if it 'correctly describes what is observable' (p. 4) by 'the human organism' (p. 17). Acceptance of a theory involves not only the above belief, but also 'a commitment to a research programme' (p. 4).[1]

If van Fraassen is concerned with an ontological doctrine which is anything like my Scientific Realism, his definition of realism is a poor one. (1) Talk of truth is beside the point of Realism and quite compatible with anti-Realist positions (4.2–4.5; cf. van Fraassen 1980: 8). (2) The Realist does not think that acceptance of a theory always involves believing it; he thinks that a variety of epistemic attitudes are appropriate to theories (7.7; cf. van Fraassen 1980: 9). (3) Finally, it is a mistake to think that the view that truth is the aim of science is distinctive to Realism.

Minimally construed, it is certainly hard for a Realist to deny this view of the aim. On that construal, the truth in question is deflationary. So, semantically *de*scending, the view is that the aim of science is to discover what entities there are – observables and unobservables – and what they are like. Now any Realist (who is not so radically eliminativist in her epistemology as to eschew talk of discovery) will believe that science *has already* discovered many of the entities there are and approximately what they are like. How then could she plausibly deny that the aim is to discover more? So a basic constraint on a Realist epistemology pushes one strongly toward a view of the aim of science.[2] However, the view is not constitutive of realism, or even peculiar to realism; it could be held by a Kantian idealist, for example.

Of course, it is tempting to go for a more robust construal of the view: to take the aim as correspondence truth. How else are we to make sense of the notion of *discovery*, which seems essential to even the minimal construal? Talk of the aim of science, unlike Realism itself, is concerned with the link between scientists and the world. Ultimately, it demands a semantic theory. Correspondence Truth is an attractive candidate – and one that I favour (ch. 6) – but whether it is the right one is a long way from being determined by Realism. And if it is the right one, it can be adopted by anti-realists as well.

Despite his definition, it is clear that van Fraassen is concerned primarily with an ontological doctrine. Indeed, his approach to realism is refreshingly unsemantic: 'The logical positivists, and their heirs, went much too far in [their] attempt to turn philosophical problems into problems about language' (p. 4). For this reason it does little violence to van Fraassen's position to ignore his definition, taking his arguments to be straightforwardly against Scientific Realism.

Van Fraassen does not agree with instrumentalist semantics. He thinks that electron theory might be true and that, if it were, there would be electrons (pp. 10–11). His disagreement with the Realist is epistemic and ontological. He thinks that the question of whether there are electrons is not one of interest to science. Nor is it one about which we are justified in having an opinion: we should be agnostic.

Van Fraassen thinks that science gives us knowledge only of observables. These are posits of science and common sense; they include familiar objects and events. In my terms, van Fraassen is a Common-Sense Realist. Constructive empiricism is not a doctrine of 'the given'. Our judgements about observables are 'theory-laden' and not indubitable (pp. 14, 56–9, 80–3, 152); in accepting such a judgement 'I am sticking my neck out' (p. 72). So van Fraassen departs from more traditional anti-Scientific-Realists not only in his semantics but in his epistemology. However commendable these departures are, they make both the motivation and the justification for constructive empiricism mysterious.

The key question is: What is epistemically significant about observability? Van Fraassen has surprisingly little to say about this. The reader is left with the impression that van Fraassen sees his view of the significance of observability as *prima facie* acceptable, and that his constructive task is simply to show how this view yields a theory of science that is otherwise plausible. Further, when he does consider the key question, he responds as if it could be pressed only by a sense-datum theorist (pp. 72–3). I think he is wrong on both counts.

Before considering that issue, I shall discuss his arguments against Scientific Realism.

8.2   VAN FRAASSEN'S ARGUMENTS AGAINST SCIENTIFIC REALISM

Van Fraassen notes that Realists typically rely on abduction (cf. 7.2 above). It becomes clear in his reply to critics (1985) that he is totally opposed to abduction. However, in the book (1980) his criticisms of abduction are more limited.

In his first criticism, van Fraassen suggests a modified version of abduction. Let 'S' abbreviate a theory that is the best explanation of some phenomenon. Abduction proper allows us to infer that S. The modification allows us to infer only that the observable world is as if S (pp. 19–21, 71; van Fraassen prefers to put his position metalinguistically, distinguishing the inference that 'S' is true from the inference that 'S' is empirically adequate). So this modified abduction licenses inferences only to the world of the constructive empiricist, not to the world of the Scientific Realist. It is natural to read van Fraassen as endorsing this modified abduction. However, it has since become clear that he does not. His point in suggesting the modification is simply to show 'that we can have no good evidence for the psychological hypothesis that people do in fact follow the rule of inference to the best explanation' (1985: 295n.). His claim is that the evidence of what people in fact do in 'ordinary' cases can give no support to the Realist's hypothesis that they follow abduction over van Fraassen's alternative hypothesis that they follow modified abduction; for the ordinary cases concern observables. The Realist cannot, therefore, gain any comfort from what people do. But van Fraassen is not claiming that they do or should follow modified abduction.

Van Fraassen's example of an ordinary case is the positing of a mouse to explain certain nightly phenomena (scratchings, pattering feet, disappearing cheese). Why does van Fraassen think that the evidence could not decide between the two hypotheses in cases like this? He asks about what it is to follow a rule of inference. He rightly thinks that this cannot require the conscious application of the rule. He goes on to claim that following a rule must consist in a willingness to believe the conclusions the rule allows and an unwillingness to believe the ones at variance with the ones it allows. Since we know that a mouse is observable, our attitudes to possible conclusions cannot distinguish between the two hypotheses about which inferential rule we are following.

Van Fraassen has given an impoverished (and behaviouristic) account of what it is to follow a rule. Following a rule is not a matter of attitudes to conclusions; it is a psychological *process*. Consider the application of the two rules in the case of the mouse. The abductive inference is as follows:

    (1)   certain nightly phenomena;
    (2)   the best explanation of these phenomena is that there is a mouse in the wainscoting;
∴   (C)   there (probably) is a mouse in the wainscoting.

The modified abductive inference includes further steps before C:

    (3)   so the observable world is as if there is a mouse in the wainscoting;
    (4)   a mouse is observable;
∴   (C)   there (probably) is a mouse in the wainscoting.

Inferring in the former way is a different psychological process from inferring in the latter way. On any realistic view of psychological processes, a person following one of these rules will have different things going on in his mind from a person following the other.[3] And such differences are just the sort of thing investigated in cognitive psychology. As far as I know, the rival hypotheses in this case have never been scientifically tested. However, there is no basis for the claim that there is no way to test them. And the claim seems very implausible: note that modified abduction involves more beliefs and more steps. If the hypotheses were tested, I bet that the evidence would favour the Realist's hypothesis. My own informal testing produced no evidence that people entertain *any thoughts at all* about the observability of objects – hence no sign of the likes of (4) – in cases like this.

We can turn the tables on van Fraassen. Though he does not endorse the alternative hypothesis, if people infer as van Fraassen thinks they ought to, they must *somehow or other* give (4) a role in their inference. For, if they did not believe that the mouse was observable, they would not reach the conclusion that there was a mouse. So if psychological investigation shows no sign of (4) playing any role, van Fraassen must accept that people do not infer as he thinks they should. And I bet that investigation would show no sign of (4).

Continuing on in the same critical vein, consider scientists. Suppose that 'S' is a thoroughly well-established theory that posits unobservables and has the best of scientific credentials. What *do* scientists believe? Doubtless, psychology has little to say on this now. However, I bet that the evidence would favour the hypothesis that they believe that S over the hypothesis that they believe that the observable world is as if S. Ernan McMullin agrees: 'The near-invincible belief of scientists is that we come to discover more and more of the entities of which the world is composed through the constructs around which scientific theory is built' (1984: 8–9). If so, scientists are not in accord with constructive empiricism. (See section 7.8 for a similar point against the positivists.)

If I am right in my bets, van Fraassen is in the difficult position of saying that the scientific practice of inferring Realistically is irrelevant to the success of science. For if it leads to success, then we have inductive grounds for it.

Van Fraassen's second criticism is that the Realist's use of abduction depends on the assumption that 'every universal regularity in nature needs an explanation' (p. 21; see also pp. 23, 31). This demand for endless explanation leads to absurdity, and is at odds with contemporary science's acceptance of unexplained regularities in quantum physics (pp. 25–34).

The Realist does have an enthusiasm for explanation: he seeks to push explanation to the limit. However, he agrees with van Fraassen that at any time there must be a limit. More important, he does *not* think that an explanation is not good until everything on which it depends has been explained. That thought would, of course, make good explanation impossible. Explanation must stop somewhere, but it is not obvious at any time where it should stop. Claims, criticized by van Fraassen, that without Realism we would be surrounded by 'cosmic coincidences' and 'miracles' are attempts to bring about a felt need for further explanation.

Properly understood, the Realist's attitude to explanation leads to no absurdity, and supports Realism. Though it is not obvious where explanation should stop, the best evidence that it has not gone far enough is a good explanation that goes further. And that is precisely what a Realist offers. By positing unobservables, he is able to offer good explanations of the behaviour and characteristics of observables that would otherwise be inexplicable. There could be no better argument for Realism.

The Realist can agree with van Fraassen that regularities revealed by quantum physics need no explanation. However, he would be wiser to agree that they might not need one.[4]

I shall return to the issue of abduction in section 8.5, arguing that it is not crucial to the defence of Scientific Realism.

Van Fraassen concludes his criticism of arguments for Realism by discussing what he calls 'the Ultimate Argument' (pp. 38–40), derived from Putnam. This argument finds support for Realism in the explanation of 'why we have successful theories at all' (p. 39). I have already agreed with van Fraassen that it yields no support for Realism, and that the best explanation is a Darwinian one (7.3).

I turn now to the criticism of constructive realism.

8.3 WEAK SCIENTIFIC REALISM

Van Fraassen is agnostic about Scientific Realism, which is committed to the existence of the unobservables of contemporary science. Where does he stand on *Weak* Scientific Realism, which is committed only to the existence of *something* unobservable (2.4)? As far as I can see, he is not explicit about this. However, I take him to be, implicitly, a believer (though p. 24 seems rather agnostic). Certainly he thinks that there *could* be an unobservable world, for he agrees with Maxwell (1962) that observability 'has logically nothing to do with existence' (van Fraassen 1980: 18).

Whatever van Fraassen's view, I claim that Weak Scientific Realism is clearly true. First, the alternative seems wildly implausible given any sort of naturalistic view of humans. The observable world contains entities ranging in size from stars so vast as to be barely conceivable down to specks of dust that are only just visible. It is hard to believe that there are not other objects that are simply too small for us to see. Second, with technological advances, we have come to see more and more objects that are invisible to the naked eye. So we have good inductive grounds for supposing that there exist objects which we cannot now see.[5]

The adoption of Weak Scientific Realism is the first step in rejecting constructive empiricism. For if there are unobservables of some sort, we have *an interest* in discovering which sort there are. These unobservables will constitute the mechanisms underlying the behaviour and characteristics of the entities we observe. So the more we know about the unobservable world, the more we will be able to explain about the observed world.

8.4 THE SIGNIFICANCE OF OBSERVATION

Constructive empiricism must rest, then, not on our lack of interest in unobservables, but on our inability to find out *which* there are. It must rest on the principle that though we are often justified in inferring the existence of a particular (sort of) unobserved observable, we are *never* justified in inferring the existence of a particular (sort of) unobservable.

On the face of it, this principle is strange, for the inferences in the two cases seem to be epistemically the same: they seem to take us beyond the evidence in the same way. And, if my earlier bets are right (8.2), people do not adhere to the principle in their inferential practices. Van Fraassen owes us a powerful argument for his principle. Yet, as I have already remarked (8.1), he gives no such argument.

The strangeness increases when we note that by 'observable', van Fraassen means *observable-to-us* (pp. 17−19). Why is observable-to-*us*, to the human species at this time, epistemically significant, rather than observable-to-*me*? How is it of any help to me what others can observe? Suppose Tom is blind. Because Tom is human, van Fraassen thinks that Tom is justified in believing in the visible world, just like the rest of us. How does he get the epistemic benefit of what we can do and he cannot? Presumably through our testimony. But this amounts to using us as instruments. Why do human instruments make reality epistemically accessible to Tom, while non-human ones do not?

Let us try to construct an argument for van Fraassen's principle on his behalf. The principle assigns special significance to observability. Presumably this must depend on the special significance of observing. How? Here is a suggestion. 'In the past, when we have posited unobserved entities, we have mostly discovered later that we were right if the entities were observable; but have never later discovered this if they were unobservable. For the only way to discover this is to observe the entity.' Why is that? Surely we can discover that we were right simply by getting further evidence, regardless of whether we have observed the entity. And this is as possible for unobservables as for observables. 'But such further evidence is insufficient. The maximum degree of belief in the existence of an entity is justified only if one has observed it; belief in an unobserved entity can never be as justified as belief in an observed one.' It seems that van Fraassen's principle requires a strong claim like this about the significance of observation.

Nobody would want to deny the importance of observation, but surely it cannot have this significance. Note first that mere observation of x, which as a matter of fact is an F, is not an observation *that* it is an F; it will not establish which particular sort of observable object it is. Yet, if we are to be convinced by observation that F's exist, it is the latter that is required. Van Fraassen himself brings out the difference nicely: a Stone Age person could observe a tennis ball without observing that it was a tennis ball (p. 15). What our argument for van Fraassen's principle finds epistemically significant is observing x. So we need an account of the link between observing x and observing that x is an F that makes observing x so significant.

Traditional epistemologies supply such an account. They typically hold that observing x (usually a sense datum) yields incorrigible knowledge of x. However, van Fraassen rightly rejects such traditional views (8.1). Our observational judgements are theory-laden. The entities we come to believe in as a result of observation are theoretical posits. In light of this, how could observation have the significance he requires it to have? He thinks that observation can lead us, with the help of theory, to a justified belief in the existence of observable F's. Why can it not also lead us, again with the help of theory, to a justified belief in the existence of unobservable G's? The contribution of theory seems much the same in both cases. Certainly van Fraassen indicates no difference.

It will help to break down the prejudice against unobservables if we lean hard on the notion of observation. Van Fraassen is aware that the notion is vague. He removes one element of vagueness by making observability relative to a particular species at a particular time, as we have noted. Aside from that, he is not bothered by the vagueness, because he thinks that there are clear cases: seeing with the unaided eye on the one hand, not seeing an electron in a cloud chamber on the other (pp. 16–17). However, even if this is enough to remove the worry about the vagueness of seeing *x*, it does not help with another worry: how is the notion of observability to be applied to senses other than sight? It is noticeable that all van Fraassen's examples of observation are drawn from sight (and he seems to assume that the mouse which he heard he did not observe; pp. 19–20). This is common in discussions of observation. Yet there is usually a suggestion that observability applies to other senses. A quick browse through the relevant entries in three leading dictionaries suggests that the ordinary notion is predominantly, but not exclusively, tied to sight. There seems to be general uncertainty as to whether and how observability applies to the other senses.

Suppose we identified observability with visibility. Then van Fraassen's principle has the highly implausible consequence that if the human race became blind, it would be condemned to total scepticism. For everything would be unobservable.

Clearly then, it is not visibility alone that has epistemic significance. What van Fraassen must require of the 'observable' objects he believes in is that they be visible *or* audible *or* smellable *or* tastable *or* touchable. As soon as other senses come into play, the apparent authority of the information we get from observation begins to wane.

To be observable in this generous sense, an object must be capable of affecting a human sense organ in an appropriately direct way: of emitting or reflecting light of a wavelength that the eye can detect, of emitting a sound of a wavelength that the ear can detect, and so on. When a human does observe an object *x*, he will usually, if not always, arrive at beliefs about *x* as a result of its stimulation of a sense organ in the appropriate way: he judges, say, that *x* is an *F*. If he arrives at his belief without inferring it from another one, we may say that he *observed that x* is an *F*. This non-inferential property of a belief about an observed object is, it seems, what makes a belief observational (but see below).

The fact that a belief is non-inferential does not make it infallible. The belief is not 'given' in the sensory input. It is a result of human processing and 'interpretation'. Doubtless humans are innately programmed to form certain rudimentary beliefs about the external world non-inferentially on the strength of certain input. But all the beliefs that the normal mature adult forms non-inferentially he *learned* so to form in the process of theorizing about the world.

What is special about sight is that it is by this sense, as a result of learning, that the normal person forms the vast majority of his non-inferential beliefs. The blind can, of course, form no such beliefs by sight. They learn, much more effectively than the normal person, to form such beliefs by the other senses (so a blind person in van Fraassen's shoes might have *observed that* there was a mouse in the wainscoting). Even among normal people there are great differences in what can be arrived at non-inferentially by sight, because of great differences in training: a skilled scientist can observe that x is an F where the lay person would need a lengthy process of inference to arrive at that conclusion, as is brought out nicely by Hacking's discussion of microscopes (1981; 1983: 186–209). Whether the belief is one that we are innately programmed to form non-inferentially or one that normal people learn to form non-inferentially or one that blind people form non-inferentially or one that a trained scientist forms non-inferentially does not make it free from epistemic risk. The degree of risk will vary, of course, from belief to belief. Very likely, one of these sorts of belief is, in general, less risky than another. Nevertheless, such a difference does not make all beliefs of the more risky sort unjustified.

It seems possible that many non-inferential beliefs about x are not based on observation of x. An example of a humdrum belief of this sort about an observable object might be the belief that someone has recently crossed a beach, based on observation of footprints. Among scientists there may be beliefs of this sort about unobservables. (Perhaps we would count these non-inferential beliefs about unobserved objects as observational, contrary to what I have so far supposed.) Once again, there would be variation in risk from belief to belief and no basis for ruling all beliefs of this sort unjustified.

Among our inferential beliefs are many about unobserved, but observable, objects. The risk involved in these beliefs does not differ in kind from that involved in the non-inferential beliefs mentioned above. Just like them, some will be justified, and some not.

Finally, some of our inferential beliefs are about unobservables. Perhaps these are in general more risky than any other sort we have considered. But that does not make each one too risky to contemplate. Their risk as a class does not differ in kind from that of the others. Within each sort of belief there will be variations of risk which overlap with that of other sorts. Once we set scepticism aside, there is no basis for ruling out altogether as unjustified any of these sorts.

The epistemic significance of observability required by van Fraassen's principle must arise from the epistemic significance of observing an object. If observation covers the five senses, then it is undoubtedly the only way we humans find out about the world.

However, all the information we get, whether inferential or not, whether about the existence and nature of those observed objects or of other objects, observable and unobservable alike, is theory-laden and risky. We can learn about objects that affect us indirectly, just as we can learn about objects that affect us directly, in the way we call observation. There is no way that observation can have the significance it must have to put unobservables beyond our ken.

PART II: Van Fraassen 1985

I turn now to van Fraassen's reply to his critics.

8.5   ABDUCTION AND THE REALIST STRATEGY

I have used abduction in my arguments for both Common-Sense and Scientific Realism. I do this because I am unconvinced by criticisms of abduction. I have already considered some of van Fraassen's criticisms (8.2; see also 7.2). In his reply to his critics, van Fraassen goes further, claiming that abduction is rejected by 'empiricism'.

It is common to think that abduction is the primary issue in the defence of Scientific Realism (see, e.g., Laudan 1981: 45; Fine 1986a: 114–5; 1986b: 162). This is a mistake: abduction is not the primary issue, unless, perhaps, Common-Sense Realism is also in question. Note, for example, that the argument above against van Fraassen's principle does not rely on abduction at any point. If Common-Sense Realism is not in question, *the primary issue in the defence of Scientific Realism is selective scepticism: epistemic discrimination against unobservables; unobservable rights.*[6]

Where 'S' abbreviates some theory about unobservables, van Fraassen holds that we may be justified in believing that the observable world is as if S, but that we are never justified in believing that S.[7] So Scientific Realism is unjustified. From the Realist perspective, van Fraassen's position amounts to an unprincipled selective scepticism against unobservables. An epistemology that justifies a belief in observables will also justify a belief in unobservables. An argument that undermines Scientific Realism will also undermine Common-Sense Realism.

This leads the Realist to a simple strategy against the anti-Realist. First, she demands from the anti-Realist a justification of the knowledge that he claims to have about observables. Using this, she attempts to show, positively, that the epistemology involved in this justification will also justify knowledge of unobservables. Second, she attempts to show, negatively, that the case for scepticism about unobservables produced by the anti-Realist is no better than the case for scepticism about observables.

The Realist is likely to think that abduction has an honoured place in epistemology. However, it is a strategic error for the Realist to get embroiled in a controversy over abduction or any other form of non-deductive inference when confronting the selective sceptic. What is vital to the defence of Scientific Realism is the success of the above simple strategy, not the defence of any particular form of inference.

Van Fraassen is aware of the Realist strategy, and has responded to it. Yet, strangely enough, his response has always seemed to miss the point. He has not seemed to acknowledge the need to provide any reason for believing constructive empiricism beyond its ability to give a *consistent* view of science. It is as if he believed that a line must be drawn somewhere between entities we can learn about and those we cannot, and that observability is a reasonable place to draw it. But, of course, the Realist sees no reason why a line has to be drawn.

What is the explanation of van Fraassen's response? Part of the answer is that behind van Fraassen's constructive empiricism lies an epistemology that is radically different from the traditional one that has guided my discussion. The details of this new epistemology have only recently begun to emerge, particularly in the book *Laws and Symmetry* (1989; but see also 1984; 1985: pt. I). Van Fraassen aims to leave behind the *defensive* approach of traditional epistemology, reflected in its emphasis on the *justification* of opinion. Instead, inspired by Pascal, he seeks an epistemology which combines probabilism with a certain sort of voluntarism and which emphasizes *change* of opinion (1989: 151–82).[8]

Van Fraassen's discussion of his new epistemology is learned, dense, and very difficult. Perhaps it does supply a justification for selective scepticism against unobservables, but I do not see how. In any case, my defence of Scientific Realism will be from the perspective of the traditional epistemology that van Fraassen rejects. If that defence is a success, it will at least establish that van Fraassen's case against Realism must depend on his new epistemology.

Part of van Fraassen's recent discussion is a severe critique of abduction from his new perspective (1989: 131–50, 160–70). Whatever the merits of this critique, it is worth noting that it is far from obvious that *empiricism alone* counts against abduction.

Empiricism is the thesis 'that experience is the sole legitimate source of information about the world' (1985: 286). As Brian Ellis points out (1985: 48), there is no reason why a Realist should not agree, the alternative being presumably that information is gained *a priori* or by revelation. How does empiricism undermine abduction? Empiricism is quite general, and so should cover epistemology along with everything else. So experience is the sole legitimate source of information about how we should *learn about* the world. Why should we not think that experience shows that abduction is one way of learning about the world? If it does show this, then the 'virtue' of being the best explanation is not in any interesting sense 'super-empirical' after all (cf. McMullin 1984: 29).

Since abduction is not part of my strategy for defending Realism against van Fraassen, I shall say no more about it.

8.6 THE POSITIVE SIDE OF THE STRATEGY

I start with the positive side of the strategy. According to van Fraassen, experience is the only source of information. How do we get from that to the view that 'experience can give us information only about what is . . . observable' (1985: 253)? Why does the latter information exhaust the 'deliverances of experience' (p. 250)? Why is 'fit[ting] the phenomena' (p. 286) equated with empirical adequacy? How do we get from information only *from experience* to information only *about observables*?

We can break van Fraassen's view into three theses:

vF1: Experience yields information about observed entities.

vF2: Information about unobserved observable entities can be inferred from information about observed entities (so experience yields information about unobserved observables).

vF3: Information about unobservable entities cannot be inferred from information about observed entities (so experience does not yield information about unobservables).

To answer our questions, van Fraassen needs a defence of these three theses. His problem is that considerations that support *vF1* and *vF2* undermine *vF3*.

A positivist might start with the following defence of *vF1*: information about observed entities is infallibly 'given' in experience. But van Fraassen does not agree. He thinks that all descriptions of the world in response to experience are fallible, theory-laden, and involve epistemic risk; observation alone does not 'compel' belief in the existence and nature of the entity observed. If the positivist were granted her firm start, it is far from obvious how she could establish *vF2* without falsifying *vF3*. It is even less obvious how van Fraassen can, given his risky start. The inference in *vF2* involves further risk, taking us well beyond the evidence of our fallible descriptions of observed entities. If experience can give us all this risky information, why can it not also inform us of the unobservable world, with the consequence that *vF3* is false? In general, the more risky the information in *vF1* and *vF2*, the less plausible is *vF3*. Ruling out all knowledge of unobservables seems *arbitrary*.

Van Fraassen's treatment of an example of Paul Churchland's is typical of his response to the Realist. Churchland compares our epistemic situation with that of humanoids who can observe much more than us because they are born with electron microscopes over their left eyes. He claims that this massive difference in observability is epistemically irrelevant (1985: 43; see also Gutting 1985: 129 and Musgrave 1985: 205).

Van Fraassen's response is strange (1985: 256–8). He argues that the example poses no challenge to the empiricist's concept of observability-to-us. If we accept the humanoids as people, then 'we have already broadened the extension of *us*, and what is observable to them is observable' (p. 256). If we do not accept them, then our investigation of them has no bearing on observability. But the point is not about the boundaries of observability. It is about the *significance* of those boundaries. If we accept the humanoids, then the boundaries are greatly increased, and so, according to van Fraassen, we know much more about the world. Yet how are we epistemically better off than we are now, without humanoids, using electron microscopes? How does it make any epistemic difference to the rest of us whether the humanoids are or are not human?

8.7   THE NEGATIVE SIDE OF THE STRATEGY

Van Fraassen's disagreement with the scientific realist is over the epistemic significance of observability. He makes three claims in support of his position First, a 'theory's vulnerability to future experience consists *only* in that the claim of its empirical adequacy is thus vulnerable' (p. 254). Second, 'the empirical adequacy of an empirical theory must always be more credible than its truth' (p. 247). Third, he claims that 'it is not an epistemological principle that one may as well hang for a sheep as for a lamb' (p. 254).

'S', positing unobservables, is bolder than the theory that 'S' is empirically adequate, but it takes no further epistemic risk. Van Fraassen's point is that epistemology does not justify believing the bolder 'S'. The extra opinion about unobservables that comes from doing so is a 'display of courage not under fire'; 'it is but empty strutting and posturing' (p. 255).

It is interesting to consider the claim about epistemic risk and vulnerability in the light of the earlier discussion of underdetermination (7.4). What is it for 'S' to be empirically adequate? It is for 'S' to be in accord with all *actual* things and events, past, present, and future, that a person would have observed if present (1980: 12, 60, 64). This involves what I have called a 'restricted' interpretation of the 'possible evidence' for 'S'. But then 'S' and the theory that 'S' is empirically adequate are equally risky only if the interpretation of 'possible evidence' that defines the risk is also restricted. On a 'liberal' interpretation, 'S' is much more risky: there are many experiments that we could perform, phenomena that we might create, none of which is actual, that would place 'S' at epistemic risk, but could not bear on the empirical adequacy of 'S'. 'S' faces the risk of being falsified by things happening that do not in fact happen. Van Fraassen would, of course, favour a restricted interpretation for the risk, and so his claim of equality would be true. Those who favour a liberal interpretation for the risk should also favour one for empirical adequacy, and the claim of equality would still be true. I shall, therefore, prescind from this matter of interpretations in assessing van Fraassen's argument.

We can see that there is something wrong with the argument by following the negative side of the realist's strategy. Let us say, briefly, that 'S' is empirically adequate if it accords with all true statements about the observable world. Introduce the notion of *experiential adequacy*. 'S' is experientially adequate if it accords with all true statements about how the observable world *appears to be*. If 'S' is empirically adequate, it must accord with true statements like 'There is a dagger before me'; but to be experientially adequate, it need only accord with true statements like 'It seems as if there is a dagger before me.' The empirical adequacy of 'S' does not require that it be correct about the unobservable world. The experiential adequacy of 'S' does not require that it be correct about the observable world. Indeed, it does not require that there be an observable world.

Note that experiential adequacy does *not* involve commitment to dubious theoretical entities like sense data (cf. van Fraassen 1980: 72). It simply requires the truth of statements of a sort that are utterly familiar from humdrum situations in which we suspect that appearances have come apart from reality.

Everything van Fraassen says in response to the Scientific Realist can be mimicked by the sceptic in response to the Common-Sense Realist. First, 'S's vulnerability to future experience consists *only* in that the claim of its experiential adequacy is thus vulnerable (so van Fraassen's first claim is false). Second, the experiential adequacy of an empirical theory must always be more credible than its empirical adequacy. Third, 'it is not an epistemological principle that one may as well hang for a sheep as for a lamb.' Epistemology does not justify believing that the observable world *is* as if S, but merely the less bold theory that the observable world *appears to be* as if S. The extra opinion about observables that comes from believing the bolder theory 'is but empty strutting and posturing'.

And that is not the end of it. Even the view that the world appears to be as described by science is open to sceptical doubt. If van Fraassen is really bothered by boldness, if he really wants to stay with what is most credible, avoiding all strutting and posturing, he should believe only in his own present existence.

In brief, van Fraassen's argument is an example of Cartesian scepticism. He is right in thinking that the case for Scientific Realism does not meet the epistemic standard of this thoroughgoing scepticism. But neither does the case for Common-Sense Realism (5.7). If van Fraassen were a total sceptic, the Realist would have to deal with him accordingly. But he is not. His combination of scepticism about unobservables and acceptance of observables is like 'the fatal flaw' of the old-fashioned foundationalist: the application of the sceptical standard to most areas of knowledge, together with the refusal, for no apparent reason, to apply it to areas he cherishes (5.3).

Scepticism insists on standards that only the most credible of our beliefs can meet. With scepticism behind us, van Fraassen's doxastic parsimony is out of place. The empirical adequacy of 'S' is more credible than its truth, but so what? *The issue of Scientific Realism is whether the theory (beyond its observable consequences) is credible at all.* Just the same interests in prediction, manipulation, and explanation that lead us to stick our epistemic necks out in theorizing about the observable world lead us to do likewise about the unobservable world. Van Fraassen takes good theories about observables at face value, recommending that we believe them as they stand. The realist takes just the same attitude to good theories about unobservables: we should believe that S.[9] It is arbitrary to go revisionist at this point, believing only that the observable world is as if S. If van Fraassen must pussyfoot, he should start earlier.

Van Fraassen writes as if Common-Sense Realism needs no justification. If it were not for the fact that philosophers keep denying it, I would agree. But if it were not for the fact that philosophers keep denying Scientific Realism, it would need no justification either. Both realisms take the claims of well-established theories at face value. If a justification for them is demanded, I use abduction. Perhaps that is a mistake. What matters is that the realisms are on a par. What justifies Common-Sense Realism will justify Scientific Realism. Van Fraassen disavows positivist epistemology. Yet his discrimination against unobservables could make sense only if he believed that the observed world really was 'given in experience'.

My defence of Realism against van Fraassen presupposes a traditional epistemology that emphasizes justification. Van Fraassen wants to reject that epistemology in favour of a new, probabilistic one. This is not the place to come to terms with this new epistemology. If van Fraassen has good reasons for his constructive empiricism, they must be found in this epistemology. I have not found them.

NOTES

1　This part of the chapter is based on my review (1982) of van Fraassen 1980. In 1980, I attended an informal seminar of faculty from the University of Southern California and the University of California at Los Angeles. The part (and the review) benefitted from those discussions.
2　'The different views about the aim of science lead naturally to different views concerning its theoretical achievements' (Ellis 1985: 48). I think that this is the wrong way round as an account of both the actual and the rational order of thought.
3　For some further thoughts on following a rule, see Devitt and Sterelny 1989.
4　On these matters, see Musgrave 1985: 212–17.
5　Consider also these phenomena, suggested to me by Keith Campbell: chemical reactions which convert visible solids into invisible gases, the permeability of earthenware, and diffusion through liquids.
6　In support of this, see Boyd 1984: 67–8; 1985: 4; Churchland 1985: 35; Glymour 1984: 191; Hooker 1985: 168–70; Musgrave 1985: 199.
7　He insists on a distinction between the acceptance of a theory and the belief that it is true (1985: 276–81). I do not dispute the distinction.

Though a realist will tend to believe the theories she accepts, she should allow that other epistemic attitudes may be appropriate (7.9).

8   A consequence of this epistemology is that although van Fraassen thinks that we should not hold beliefs about unobservables, he does not think that such beliefs are irrational (1985: 252). Rather, he sees them as 'groundless', 'leaps of faith' (p. 286), and not 'rationally compelled' (p. 296).

9   This may need qualification if Cartwright (1983) is right.

9

Kuhn, Feyerabend, and the Radical Philosophers of Science

9.1 INTRODUCTION

In this chapter I am concerned not so much with the historical Kuhn and Feyerabend as with a movement of which they have been prime, but not sole, instigators. This movement has arisen in the history and philosophy of science, and has espoused a radical epistemology. It rejects the views of the positivists and of Popper, emphasizing the theory-ladenness of all our judgements and the revolutionary nature of theory change. I am in broad agreement with this radical epistemology, as the discussion in chapter 5 indicates. However, the radicals have also espoused a number of semantic and vaguely ontological doctrines, partly under the influence of their epistemology. These doctrines seem to me to be largely, if not entirely, mistaken.

It is obvious that this movement is opposed to Correspondence Truth. Kuhn will have nothing to do with the view that one theory is a better representation of 'what is really out there' than another (1962: 206–7). Feyerabend refers slightingly to 'the theological term *true*' (1969: 342n.).[1] Louis Althusser, who has influenced a Marxist wing of the movement, seems to reject any sort of correspondence notion of truth in the course of his critique of 'the empiricist conception of knowledge' (Althusser and Balibar 1968: 34–69; see also Althusser 1969: pt. VI). Certainly some who have been influenced by him have taken that position (Chalmers 1976: ch. 10; Curthoys and Suchting 1977: pt. V).

Where do the radicals stand on Realism? What, according to Kuhn, Feyerabend, and company, is there? No very clear answer emerges. The radicals, like their arch-enemies the positivists, are ontologically coy (7.8). Their discussions focus almost entirely on epistemic and semantic issues and say very little about the reality to which people are epistemically and semantically linked or about the

nature of the links. They offend against Maxim 3. I shall argue that
they are implicitly anti-Realist.

Let T and T' be two competing 'comprehensive' theories in some
area, differing in 'major', or 'fundamental', ways. The non-epistemic
theses that are most prominent among the radicals are as follows:

> *Meaning Change*   No term in the (special) language of T' is
> synonymous with, or expresses the same concept as, a term in
> the (special) language of T.
>
> *Reference Change*   No term in the (special) language of T' is co-
> referential with a term in the (special) language of T.
>
> *Ontological Change*   No part of the (special) ontology of T' is part
> of the (special) ontology of T.
>
> *Incommensurability*   Because of Meaning Change, Reference
> Change, and Ontological Change, T and T' are semantically
> incomparable.

I shall for the most part set Meaning Change aside, because it is
relevant to Realism and Correspondence Truth only to the extent
that it entails Reference Change. Reference Change and Ontological
Change have been left vague enough to allow several interpretations.

Any interpretation of the radicals' position on Realism must take
account of their commitment to these four theses. In the next section
I shall give such an interpretation. Their position, once exposed, can
be seen to be decidedly unattractive. I shall mostly postpone my
criticisms of it until chapter 13. Any appeal it has arises from alleged
difficulties with Realism. I consider such a difficulty, implied by the
radicals, in sections 9.3 and 9.4. In sections 9.5, 9.6, and 9.7 I turn
to Incommensurability and the opposition to truth. I conclude in
section 9.8 by considering some radical objections to my views.

9.2   REALISM AND THE RADICALS

There is a great deal of realist rhetoric throughout the writings of the
radicals. They talk of an implicitly non-mental, theory-independent
'world', 'nature', or 'reality', made up of 'real objects', which constrains theories and which 'theoretical objects' must, in some sense,
fit (Kuhn 1962: 206; 1970a: 16, 20; 1970b: 235, 263, 267; Feyerabend
1965b: 242, 246; 1969: 303; 1970b: 227; 1978: 169–71; Althusser and
Balibar 1968: 34–69). Despite this, the radicals are commonly, and I

think rightly, taken to be profoundly anti-realist. Their position is a relativistic Kantianism sometimes called 'Constructivism'.

Constructivism has three elements. We have come across the first two already in Kant (5.6):

(1) The only independent reality is beyond the reach of our knowledge and language; it is the noumenal world of things-in-themselves.

(2) The known world is partly our construction; it is the phenomenal world of appearances, created by the imposition of our concepts on things-in-themselves.

Because of (1), Kant is a Weak Realist. Because of (2), he is an anti-Realist (for the known world is the world of physical entities like stones, trees, and cats). The third element is relativism, which is not found in Kant:

(3) The concepts used to construct a known world differ from (linguistic, social, scientific, etc.) group to group, and hence the worlds of groups differ. Each such world exists only relative to an imposition of concepts.

Whereas Kant thinks that all humankind wield the one set of cookie cutters on the dough, the Constructivist thinks that different groups – sometimes linguistic, sometimes social, sometimes scientific, and so forth, depending on the Constructivist – wield different sets.

Combining these three elements yields the following doctrine:

Constructivism The only independent reality is beyond the reach of our knowledge and language. A known world is partly constructed by the imposition of concepts. These concepts differ from (linguistic, social, scientific, etc.) group to group, and hence the worlds of groups differ. Each such world exists only relative to an imposition of concepts.

Constructivism is widespread, as we shall see (13.1). In the scientific form that concerns us here, electrons, muons, and curved space-time are said to exist relative to contemporary theories, but not to past theories; and phlogiston, witches, and the four bodily humours exist relative to various past theories, but not to contemporary ones. None of these things exists or does not exist 'absolutely'. Neither does the familiar observable world of stones, trees, and cats. Only things-in-themselves, which are for ever beyond our ken, exist absolutely.

Some think that attributing this unlovely metaphysics to the radicals creates a straw man (e.g. Suppe 1977: 196). Why then do I do it? First, the attribution accommodates the realist rhetoric. This is taken to be about things-in-themselves. Second, the attribution is in accord with the frequent talk about theorists creating their worlds and living in different ones. This reason may seem decisive immediately. However, there is a problem. Much of this talk is loose, inexplicit, and open to metaphorical interpretation. I shall explore and reject more charitable interpretations of it in my general discussion of Constructivism (13.2).

What would make charity difficult would be explicit anti-Realist claims. These are hard to find. Indeed, the radicals often write *as if* they were Realists. (They are skilled at 'having it both ways', as David Stove (1982) has demonstrated.) However, third, occasionally one does find straightforward anti-Realism. Consider Alan Chalmers' position (since abandoned): 'radical instrumentalism or pluralistic realism' (1976: 129). It

denies that theories are attempts to explain what the world is really like. Concepts such as 'electron', 'force', etc. are real theoretical concepts, but to describe electrons and forces as existing in the real world is to slip into a common-sense conflation that radical instrumentalism attempts to avoid. From the point of view of radical instrumentalism, even the identification of everyday concepts such as 'chair' and 'swan' with objects in the real world is a mistake. (p. 130)

See also David Papineau (1979: 126–33).

Fourth, perhaps the strongest reason for attributing Constructivism stems from the various Change theses and Incommensurability. There can be no doubt that the radicals subscribe to these. On the one hand, Constructivism accommodates them nicely: if worlds really change when theories change, it is not surprising that the meanings, references, and ontological commitments of theories differ; and theories that talk about different things are likely to be incommensurable. On the other hand, it is hard to see how these theses could be accommodated in any other metaphysics. Certainly, from a Realist perspective, Incommensurability is very implausible, as we shall see (9.6).

The Constructivism of the radicals has made it difficult for them to explain such phenomena of scientific life as conflict, confirmation, disconfirmation, and progress. I doubt whether they can. To take just one example, consider Kuhn's view of progress. It is alleged to consist in increasing success at puzzle solving. But how can Kuhn allow the constancy of puzzles through revolutions that this view seems to require?

Constructivism will reappear in the discussion of Putnam (12.5). My main discussion of it is in chapter 13. Any plausibility it has must come from difficulties for Realism.

9.3 COMMON-SENSE REALISM AND THE META-INDUCTION

What are these difficulties for Realism? The radical discussion that raises them is not aimed directly at Realism. It is the discussion that urges the Change theses and Incommensurability. From it we can abstract an argument against Realism as follows. Suppose that, according to the Realist, x exists. Suppose also that a is some term such that the Realist accepts,

If x exists, then a refers to x.

Then any argument to show that a does not refer is one to show that x does not exist. Many radical discussions can be seen as arguing that, from our present perspective, the terms of past theories do not refer. Putnam has brought out neatly, in a passage I have mentioned before (7.5, 7.6), how this threatens Realism: 'the following meta-induction becomes overwhelmingly compelling: *just as no terms in the science of more than fifty (or whatever) years ago referred, so it will turn out no term used now ... refers*' (1978: 25). The Realist who accepts the above schema must see the radical discussion of reference as supporting the view that the entities apparently posited by past theories really do not exist.

As it stands, the conclusion of this argument is stronger than is needed to refute Realism. That doctrine is committed only to the existence of *most* common-sense and scientific physical entities (2.4). To show that this is false, it is not necessary to show that no such entities exist, just that most don't. So a sufficient premise for the meta-induction seems to be: most of the entities apparently posited by any past theory do not exist (but see 9.4). Call this doctrine 'Ontological Elimination'.

How effective is the radical argument against Common-Sense Realism? In my view it is completely ineffective, because Ontological Elimination (common sense), which is restricted to observables, has nothing to be said for it. It is not the case that most past observables do not exist. Indeed, it is not even the case that a significant proportion do not. Our observable physical ontology has expanded through the ages with the discovery of new species, new planets, and so on, but very little has been abandoned: cases like those of witches and the planet Vulcan are rare. There is nothing in the history of theory change to shake the view that we have, in a steady accumulative way, give or take a mistake or two, discovered more and more of the entities that exist ('absolutely') in the observable world. Of course, we have changed our *theories of* many observables, but that is a different matter. The ancients thought that the Earth was flat and that it was the centre of the universe. We might express the subsequent change of opinion by saying: 'The Earth of the ancients does not exist.' But this is a mere manner of speaking: the Earth of the ancients is the Earth we live on, and so certainly exists.

Why think otherwise? Why is any credence given to Ontological Elimination (common sense)? There are two causes. First, the semantic issue of whether terms refer is given priority over the ontological issue of what exists. Second, in considering the semantic issue, a description theory of reference is used. The argument then runs as follows: *a* refers only if the (weighted most of) descriptions commonly associated with it apply to one and only one object. They don't. So *a* does not refer. So, by the schema, *x* does not exist.

My response to this is that it is a mistake to start with the semantic issue (Maxim 3), and a further mistake to settle that issue using a description theory of reference. We should start with the ontological issue. There is then not the slightest reason to suppose that most observables posited in the past do not exist. With our ontology settled, we confront the semantic issue. The task is to find a theory of the link between human language and belief and that ontology (a task I hope already to have motivated: chapter 6). Any theory that denies appropriate links is, of course, a bad one. Given that *x* exists and is the obvious candidate for the referent of *a*, a good theory is likely to link *x* to *a*. Description theories are for the most part not good theories of the terms that concern us: because of problems of 'ignorance and error', they typically have the consequence that *a* does not refer to *x*.

We have already noted that description theories could not be true of all terms (3.3). The main significance of the radicals' argument at the observable level is to put another nail in the coffin of description theories of reference for many terms. It is not that the historical facts of theory change, together with a description theory, show Realism to be false. Rather, those facts, together with Realism, show the description theory to be false. For we should be more confident of Realism than of any theory of reference.

In sum, the radical argument throws no doubt on Common-Sense

Realism. Indeed, it throws no doubt on a stronger doctrine that is committed to the great majority of observables.

9.4 SCIENTIFIC REALISM AND THE META-INDUCTION

The meta-induction against Common-Sense Realism can be easily dismissed. That against Scientific Realism cannot. It runs roughly as follows: when we have (apparently) posited unobservables in the past, we have mostly been wrong; so we are probably mostly wrong in the unobservables that we now (apparently) posit. (The argument is related to Sklar's worry (1981) about the rights of unborn hypotheses. Were these hypotheses to be born, it is likely that some would replace our present theories and, it might be claimed, show our present posits to be mistaken.) The argument is a powerful one against Scientific Realism, because Ontological Elimination (scientific) has some plausibility. Historians of science like Kuhn and Feyerabend (and Laudan 1981) have produced an impressive list of cases which may seem to support this doctrine. Whether or not history does support it is a matter on which I am not competent to judge. However, I very much doubt that history does, and will give some reasons for my doubt. I shall also criticize other aspects of the meta-induction. The Realist has a number of defences available against it.

(a) The radical writings that may seem to support Ontological Elimination (scientific) are predominantly about reference, and reflect a commitment to some sort of description theory of reference (e.g. Kuhn 1970b: 265; Chalmers 1976: 114–15). Once again (9.3) I object to starting with the semantic issue and using a description theory to settle it. (Note that when Laudan allows his opponent – a Putnamian realist – a liberal view of reference, what he allows is a liberal description view; 1981: 24.) Nevertheless, there is no doubt that the radicals have produced *some* convincing candidates for non-existence; for example, phlogiston. This alone is no problem for the Realist, because he believes that we have made ontological mistakes too. Further, he believes that we are likely to be making some now. That is why he is committed only to *most* current unobservables. So what the radicals need to do, at least, is to argue that *most* unobservables posited at some past time *t* do not exist. And the argument must not rest simply on a description theory of reference.

As far as I know, this has never been done. Even if it were done, the argument would have to be generalized to all, or most, past times if it is going to trouble the Realist. He can accept with equanimity that, for *some* times *t*, not Realism(*t*). This radical task seems very difficult. It is surely plausible to claim for many past *t*'s that we still think many of the unobservables then posited exist. Consider the posits of 1925 science, for example.

(b)   Scientific Realism is committed only to most of the unobservables posited by theories that we have the very best grounds for accepting (7.9). It is committed only to most of what I call 'confident' and 'necessary' posits (2.3). So if the premise of the meta-induction is to be acceptable to the Realist, it must be restricted, implicitly, to such posits. It is clearly harder for the anti-Realist to defend Ontological Elimination when so restricted. Perhaps many of the historical cases of elimination which the radicals produce are of posits which scientists did not really make.[2]

(c)   To assess the inference in the meta-induction, we need to state the latter much more precisely than we have done so far.[3] What I am defending, Scientific Realism(now), asserts a many-part disjunction of many-part conjunctions, each conjunct being an existence statement – for example, 'There exist electrons' (2.3 and 2.4). What has the falsity of Scientific Realism(*t*) at some past *t*, a similar disjunction of conjunctions made up of (allegedly) *different* conjuncts, got to do with that? What has the non-existence of phlogiston, for example, got to do with the existence of electrons? Insofar as Realism(*t*) contains different conjuncts from Realism(now), it is entirely irrelevant to Realism(now). So we cannot argue simply:

> For any past *t*, not Realism(*t*).
> So probably not Realism(now).

The irrelevance is concealed by the fact that we have no *convenient* way of identifying Realism(*t*) except by reference to science at *t*. Nevertheless, we could, at the cost of time and effort, identify the doctrine by specifying the appropriate disjunction of conjunctions. This specification would make no mention of science at *t*.

The bearing of science at *t* on Realism(*t*) is that Realism(*t*) is based on that science: the doctrine asserts the existence of most of the unobservables that that science (apparently) posits in the course of explaining observed phenomena. I take it that what the meta-induction challenges is the inference to Realism(now) from what current science (apparently) posits to explain observed phenomena;

hence it is a *meta*-induction. My best attempt to capture it is as follows:

> At any time *t* in the not too immediate past, it would have been a mistake to infer Scientific Realism(*t*) from what science at *t* (apparently) posited to explain observed phenomena, for it turned out that not Scientific Realism(*t*).

> So it is probably a mistake to infer Scientific Realism(now) from what science now (apparently) posits to explain observed phenomena.

The meta-induction does not pretend to *refute* Realism, but it does aim to undermine the only significant reason for believing Realism. It is a *reductio* of the Realist approach to science. If we adopt that approach, taking the apparent posits seriously and at face value, we discover that Realism is baseless.

As it stands, the inference of the meta-induction must be suspect, for the following view of the past is compatible with the premise, and is likely to yield an argument *for* Realism. Take Realism(now) to be committed to 55 per cent of current unobservables. So we give it another name: '55%-realism(now)'. Suppose that the following doctrines held of the past: 25%-realism (1682); 35%-realism (1782); 45%-realism (1882). These are compatible with the falsity of Realism(*t*) for past *t*'s, and yet would be more likely to support 55%-realism(now) than undermine it.

A view of the past not unlike this is a plausible one for the Realist to take. From our current perspective, informed by a naturalized epistemology based on the best contemporary scientific practices, we can see that scientists in the past were often *wrong* to have confidently accepted theories given the evidence available to them. We have the view that not only are scientists learning more and more about the world, but also that they are learning more and more about how to find out about the world; there is an improvement in methodology. As a result, the success rate of confident posits has tended to improve. Whereas immature science was very unreliable in its posits, contemporary science is very reliable, reliable enough for Realism(now). (So restricting Realism to the times of mature science would not risk 'vacuity'; cf. Laudan on Putnam 1981: 34.)

The anti-Realist might attempt to undermine this defence by proposing a meta-meta-induction along the following lines:

> At any time *t* in the not too immediate past it would have been a mistake to infer a naturalized epistemology on the basis of

the best science at *t*; for the application of that epistemology would have led to the false conclusion that though we had often been wrong in our (apparent) unobservable posits, we were improving our success rate and were at *t* reliable enough for Scientific Realism(*t*).

So it is probably a mistake to infer a naturalized epistemology on the basis of the best current science.

The premise of this induction inherits any weakness of the previous one, and adds a weakness of its own. Who knows what a past naturalized epistemology would have led us to conclude? It is far from obvious that it would have led us so astray. Besides that, the inference is open to the same sort of objection as the previous one. The Realist might see a continuous improvement in the accuracy of our view of past improvement: our applied naturalized epistemology is improving. This improvement might, once again, support Realism(now).

This is not the end of the matter, of course. However, it does show that a lot of work needs to be done to turn the meta-induction into a plausible argument against Realism. The problem of the inference seems only soluble by strengthening the premise (cf. 9.3). For example, if we assumed that *no* past unobservable exists – *Complete Onotlogical Elimination* (scientific) – then defence (3) would be in trouble.[4] But the assumption that *most* past unobservables don't exist is already implausibly strong.

The discussion indicates also that even if a convincing meta-induction could be discovered, the realistically inclined philosopher might have a fall-back position. He could replace Realism with a doctrine committed to the existence of a smaller proportion than most of the unobservables. Provided that history shows, from a realist perspective, some tendency towards greater accuracy in our posits, it seems unlikely that there will not be a weaker realist doctrine that is both immune from the meta-induction and sufficient to support that realist perspective. What the anti-Realist needs to establish is that the history of unobservable posits has been thoroughly *erratic*; for example, T' jettisons most of the ontology of T; T''' jettisons most of that of T', and does not retain what T' saved from T; and so on. It seems to me that the radicals are very far from having established this.

We have been considering the direct bearing of Ontological Elimination on Scientific Realism. It also has an indirect bearing, because it might be the reason for denying convergence which the

Realist uses to explain progress (7.6). We have just seen that it is an insufficient reason. Science might be converging, even though most past unobservables do not exist. I return to convergence in section 9.7.

(d) Finally, the Realist can make use of *partial reference* – a notion introduced by Hartry Field (1973) – and with it a more tolerant view of the existence of past posits. The premise of the meta-induction requires that a past Realist would have been wrong to accept a disjunction of conjunctions including, say, in Newton's time, the sentence

(1) There is such a physical quantity as mass.

The problem for the past Realist is that too many such sentences may seem to have turned out to be false. With the help of partial reference, we are likely to be able to save many of these apparently false ones, including (1). Thus it will be less likely that it would be a mistake to accept Realism(t).

Field has argued that Newton's term 'mass' 'partially refers' to each of two physical quantities posited by contemporary physics – relativistic mass (= total energy/c^2) and proper mass (= non-kinetic energy/c^2) – but does not determinately refer to either. Since both these quantities exist, (1) will come out true: it is true relative to the assignment of either of the two partial referents of 'mass'. Furthermore, Field has claimed that many terms (e.g. past uses of 'gene') may be like Newton's 'mass'.

We have no need in our theory for a term that is synonymous with Newton's term 'mass', but we could of course introduce one: for example, 'Newtonian mass'. Then, on the above view, we should accept that there is such a physical quantity as Newtonian mass (Field seems to suggest the contrary; 1973: 470), for that quantity is either relativistic mass or proper mass (though there is no fact of the matter as to *which* it is). Newton was not wrong in his ontology, but he did not carve up that ontology at all its joints. He did not make all the distinctions among entities that should be made. Einstein's ontology differs from Newton's, but it does not (always) eliminate Newton's.

Earlier I pointed out, parenthetically, that the meta-induction was related to Sklar's worry (1981) about the rights of unborn hypotheses. Our present position makes it less likely that among the unborn hypotheses that we would prefer to our present theories there are some which would eliminate our present ontology.

It is important to note that partial reference is required anyway to deal with problems about observables. Thus, from time to time in biology, two different species are confused under the one name: that name partially refers to each. In ordinary life, two different people are confused under the one name (see Devitt 1981a: 141–3 on 'Liebknecht'). In general, reference is an idealization of partial reference.

It may be thought that the partial-reference defence of Realism is unacceptable because the notion of partial reference is fundamentally suspect. Unlike reference, the notion does not feature prominently in folk theory, and so is certainly unfamiliar. Yet partial reference is, I suggest, *prima facie* no more suspect than reference. True, we lack a worked-out theory of partial reference; but we are hardly better off with reference. We should not give up hope of explaining an intuitively good and useful notion. For example, the historical causal theory is easily adapted to the task of explaining partial reference. Oversimplifying, the basic idea is that a term partially refers to two different (sorts of) objects if the network underlying it is causally grounded in both (Devitt 1981a: 142–50, 193–5). And reference change takes place because of changes in the pattern of groundings over time (ibid.: 150–2, 191–2; cf. Fine 1975: part IV, 'Trouble at Harvard').

In conclusion, though the meta-induction constitutes a powerful argument against Scientific Realism, I think it could be met with the aid of the defences I have described. Indeed, I wonder whether the defences would not enable us to defend a stronger doctrine committed to the great majority of current (confident and necessary) posits.

9.5 CONTEMPT FOR TRUTH

The opposition of Kuhn, Feyerabend, and the radicals to Realism is only implicit. Their opposition to Correspondence Truth and such related notions as convergence and verisimilitude is quite explicit (9.1). The basis for their opposition is Incommensurability.

Incommensurability, which I shall consider in the next section, undoubtedly supports an opposition to Correspondence Truth. Nevertheless, there seems to be more behind the radicals' opposition, amounting often to contempt, than a belief in Incommensurability. I offer the following three suggestions as a tentative diagnosis (see also Field 1972: 365–7).

(1)   Entitlement to truth depends on entitlement to reference, for reference is the key notion in the explanation of truth. We are entitled to reference only if we can hope for satisfactory theories of reference. Now the model for theories of truth, urged with enthusiasm by Popper, for example, is Tarski's. Tarski's theory is commonly represented as a complete explanation of truth for certain sorts of languages; yet, as Field (1972) shows, the only explanation of reference Tarski offers is completely trivial (3.3 and 3.4). Philosophers who are dubious about the role of truth are likely to have their doubts confirmed by a theory of truth that offers only a trivial account of the links between language and reality (see, e.g., Chalmers 1976: 121–2).

(2)   Supplement Tarski with scientifically respectable theories of reference, and we get a satisfactory correspondence theory of truth (3.3). One wonders, however, whether memories of older, unsatisfactory correspondence theories linger on to discredit truth (see, e.g., Althusser and Balibar 1968: 46–8; Bhaskar 1975: 167). According to these theories, language 'mirrored' or 'pictured' reality, so that the very structure of the one was identical to the structure of the other (3.2).

(3)   The radical philosophers of science are all opposed to a central feature of traditional epistemology: the desire for *guarantees*, the quest for *certainty*. In recent times a solution has usually been sought in indubitable perception, whether of a sense datum or a raven: 'the given'. Often this perception was also thought to be basic in a theory of meaning. Here we had a link to reality of such immediacy and transparency that it needed no explanation (e.g. in Russell). With the rejection of the idea of the given must go a rejection of this somewhat mystical view of the links between language and reality, and hence of this particular correspondence theory. Perhaps all correspondence theories were thought to be tied in some such way to the given (cf. Maxim 5). Certainly, Rorty seems to think they are (11.4).

To conclude this tentative diagnosis, I wonder whether truth and reference have not become discredited in radical eyes as a result of their being explained in either trivial or scientifically unacceptable ways. Perhaps they also suffer from keeping company with bad epistemology.

Prima facie we need *some* theory of the links between language and reality. Intuitively, truth and reference are central to that explanation. My discussion in chapter 6 supports this intuition. Perhaps the links can be explained otherwise, but the radicals do next to nothing

to show that they can. For the most part, the radicals write as if they
have not been struck by the question. Or else they pose it, and say
not a word to answer it (e.g. Althusser and Balibar 1968: 51–69).

9.6 INCOMMENSURABILITY

Incommensurability is the thesis that because of Meaning, Reference,
and Ontological Change, theories T and T' in the one area are not,
semantically comparable (9.1).[5] Some closely related ways in which
T and T' are not comparable are (see note 1 for references):

(1)   A comparison of their content is impossible.
(2)   They are not comparable by the usual means of examining
      consequence classes.
(3)   The one theory cannot criticize or refute the other.

I have phrased my statement of Incommensurability carefully, to
make it clear that it is fundamentally a *semantic* thesis. Given that T
and T' cannot stand in a contradictory relation to each other (for
example), then of course there can be no question of judging whether
they stand in that relation; but that epistemic point is quite evidently
derivative.

The semantic relations that have often been thought to hold
between T and T' have been *strictly logical* ones. However, I have left
it open whether or not the usual comparisons can be made with less
strict ones. I shall introduce the term 'quasi-logical' to describe
relations that I claim will do the trick.

That radicals like Kuhn and Feyerabend urge a semantic thesis as
well as epistemic theses is obvious from the passages cited in note 1.
Yet it seems necessary to emphasize this constantly. My experience in discussion has been that those sympathetic to Kuhn and
Feyerabend almost invariably confuse semantic and epistemic positions (cf. Maxim 5).[6]

The confusion is encouraged by some unclarity of language.
Consider, for example, the claim that observation statements are
theory-laden. This can mean the semantic thesis (false, in my view)
that the meaning of an observation statement is determined by the
theory from which it is derived. It can also mean the epistemic thesis
(true, in my view) that one's judgement about the truth value of an
observation statement is partly dependent on one's belief in various
theories which may turn out to be wrong.

The confusion that particularly concerns us is that between the semantic thesis that T and T' are not semantically comparable – Incommensurability – and the epistemic thesis that there is no theory–neutral way of making that comparison. The latter seems to me to be true, but unexciting, given that there is no theory-neutral way of judging anything (5.8). The harmlessness of the epistemic truth and its irrelevance to Incommensurability can be brought out by considering a case in which even the radicals would regard comparison as possible: a comparison of statements that arise out of a single theoretical framework or paradigm, and hence 'share meanings'.

Suppose that our aim is to establish an inconsistency using the logical fact that the schemata

(1) Fa
(2) $\sim Fa$

are inconsistent. How can this fact be applied to show that two statement tokens like

(3)   Oscar is a raven
(4)   Oscar is not a raven

are inconsistent? (3) must be a substitution instance of (1) and (4) of (2): the two tokens of 'Oscar' must be of the same semantic type (Devitt 1981a: 10); similarly the two tokens of 'raven'. What is required for tokens to be of the same semantic type? In the present case it is necessary, *at least*, for them to be co-referential. So the inconsistency of (3) and (4) depends partly on facts about reference. These facts are as empirical as any.

Consider a statement about the reference of 'raven' in (3) or (4). It is an 'observation statement' about reference. The general dictum of the radicals applies: we are inclined to accept such a statement partly because we believe the theories (perhaps only folk theories) relevant to it. Our judgement rests ultimately on a range of theories, including a theory of reference and one in biology (Devitt 1979: 36–7). Yet (3) and (4) are themselves (low-level) biological statements. Judgements about the reference of terms in a theory are laden with theories including one in the same science as that very theory. So judgements about the logical relations between statements in a theory are similarly theory-laden. This is a significant epistemic truth underlying Incommensurability; but it no more establishes Incommensurability than it establishes that (3) and (4) are not inconsistent.

Once Incommensurability has been sharply distinguished from any epistemic doctrine, we can see the path to refuting it.

The crucial doctrine for Incommensurability is Reference Change (as Scheffler (1967) pointed out.) Now Michael Martin showed, with an example of overlapping referents, that Reference Change alone is not sufficient for non-comparability (1971). Given certain empirical facts about references, we can use logic to show that two statements chosen from T and T' cannot both be true, even though no term of one statement is co-referential with any term of the other. Our judgement of those facts about reference will be laden with theories, including perhaps T and T', but, as we have seen, that is irrelevant to Incommensurability. The relation between the two statements differs from a strictly logical one only in depending on reference relations other than identity – in Martin's example, on relations of inclusion. I call such relations between statements 'quasi-logical'. Quasi-logical relations are sufficient for theory comparison (Devitt 1979: 38–9).

However, Martin's example is not sufficient to remove the worry of Incommensurability, because most of the cases which the radicals discuss cannot plausibly be seen as ones of overlapping referents. These cases suggest reference *failure* because of Ontological Elimination. I have argued that Ontological Elimination (common sense) is certainly false (9.3), and have given reasons for thinking that Ontological Elimination (scientific) is false too (9.4). If this is right, then we are in a position to reject Incommensurability completely.

Suppose the worst: we have to use partial reference to compare T and T'. Even so, we can establish quasi-logical relations between the two theories. Given certain empirical facts about partial reference, we can use logic – a revision of referential semantics (Field 1973) – to show that a statement in T and a statement in T' cannot both be true (Devitt 1979: 43, 45).

Consider each of the closely related ways in which T and T' are said to be non-comparable. First, Incommensurability claims that a comparison of the content of the two theories is impossible. But comparison *is* possible, despite mistakes in received views of how it is. It is an objective fact that the theories have certain contents. Further, we have ways of finding out what those contents are. Suppose we have a theory of partial reference and certain other theories. With their help we can determine the contents of both T and T'; that is, we can determine precisely what each theory says about the world. We can then compare the contents. One of the theories on which we call will be in the *domain* of T and T', and may *be* T or T'.

Thus, in comparing Newton's theory with Einstein's, we make use of Einstein's to determine that Newton's use of 'mass' partially referred to both relativistic and proper mass. However, the theory in the domain that we call on *need* not be T or T'. Suppose T were Aristotelian mechanics, T' Newtonian mechanics, and T'' Einsteinian. We would then use T'' in comparing T and T'. Of course, theory comparison must always involve *some* point of view about the domain in question. But this is just to say that theory comparison is theory-laden, which is true even when the most commensurable theories are being compared.

Second, Incommensurability claims that T and T' are not comparable by the usual means of examining consequence classes. It was thought that among the statements in the consequence class of a theory, there would be some also in the consequence class of its rival and some others that were the negation of statements in that rival class; in particular, many observation statements of the theory would be of these sorts. Thus the theories could be compared. Whatever the defects of this conception, we can still compare theories by examining consequence classes. Once again, we must first settle partial reference. The situation which Kuhn and Feyerabend have primarily in mind is one in which T and T' are two theories fighting for supremacy in an area (rather than two superseded theories). In that situation, either T or T' must play a crucial role in determining partial reference for *both* T and T'. And the view we have of partial reference if we assume T may differ from that if we assume T'. However, whichever we assume, we can compare the two theories. Having settled partial reference, we determine what follows logically about the truth values of the predictions and observation statements (the members of the consequence class) of each theory from the other. Very likely it will follow from each theory that many such statements of the other theory are false. It may follow, however, that some are true: Field points out that from a relativistic viewpoint most of Newton's experimental claims are true (1973: 468). Whichever theory we choose to settle partial reference, we are comparing theories by examining consequence classes. And the most thorough-going comparison would come from choosing each theory in turn.

Objection: 'The discussion seems to presuppose that the predictions of a theory are derived from that theory alone. This is seldom the case: all sorts of initial conditions, auxiliary and background theories, have to be assumed as well.' These other factors have been ignored to simplify the discussion. We can take account of them if necessary. Where these other factors are not in dispute, we use them, first, to help settle partial reference, and then see what follows from conjoining them to T and T' in turn about the truth values of members of the other's consequence class. Should there be rival views of the relevant other factors, the effect of using each rival can be considered. Comparison becomes more complex in these circumstances, but it is not different in principle from that in the simple circumstances allegedly presupposed.

Third, according to Incommensurability, T and T' cannot criticize or refute each other. This is the crucial respect in which theories are said not to be comparable. The claim is mistaken. A relation of quasi-logical inconsistency can exist between a statement of T and a statement of T'. This relation is as real and objective as the strictly logical relation between (3) and (4), and does not differ greatly from that. With both relations it is a fact of logic that if the extra-logical facts, including those about partial reference, are of a certain sort, then both members of the pair of statements cannot be true.

To conclude, theory comparison is possible even where there is radical reference change. Incommensurability is false. The only worry that remains is one about the extent to which competing theories share partial referents. The radicals have given us no reason for being pessimistic about this. There is, of course, still the problem of judging the relation between theories. However, this epistemic problem is one we have everywhere; moreover, it has nothing to do with Incommensurability and meaning change: we have it even where meanings don't change. We can hope to find out as much about the relation between theories as we can about the rest of reality.

I shall consider some objections to this view of theory comparison in section 9.8.

9.7   CONVERGENCE AND VERISIMILITUDE

It is common to think that scientific theories in a chronological series converge and/or increase in verisimilitude (7.6). Kuhn, Feyerabend, and the radicals are opposed to this common view. The only argument they have for this opposition, along with their opposition to truth in general, is based on Ontological Elimination and Incommensurability, both of which we have rejected.

Nevertheless, the radical argument does seem sufficient to undermine Popper's *theory* of verisimilitude: Reference Change makes comparisons of the sort that Popper describes impossible. Quite apart from that, Popper's theory has the technical difficulties we mentioned earlier (7.6).

Let T' be the successor of T in some science. Then Simple Convergence holds if and only if, relative to T', the terms of T typically refer and the laws of T are typically approximately true (7.6). In light of considerations in this chapter, we can define a doctrine of Complex Convergence by replacing the above talk of reference by talk of partial reference. Suppose we can overcome the technical difficulties and use Scientific Realism and Correspondence Truth to make sense of Simple Convergence, then we can also make sense of Complex Convergence: we replace the explanation of truth in terms of reference by Field's explanation in terms of partial reference.

From our Realist perspective, Complex Convergence implies that science is getting a more and more accurate picture of a set of partial referents. This misses some of the intuitive idea of science converging. According to the doctrine Increasing Verisimilitude, T' is typically closer to the truth than T. This requires increasing truth content (and decreasing falsity content), which can be achieved not only by finding out more about the one set of entities, but by discovering truths about other entities (7.6).

Why worry about Complex Convergence or Increasing Verisimilitude? Scientific Realism does not stand or fall by them. Nevertheless, Realists, like everyone else, have to explain scientific progress. From time to time scientists replace one theory by another which they think better. Further, they continually *aim* for better theories. What makes them better? A Realist who is opposed to any explanatory notion of truth (e.g. a Leeds–Quine Realist: 6.1) might attempt to explain progress in Darwinian terms, without any appeal to a doctrine of convergence. However, I have argued that a Realist should accept Correspondence Truth (chapter 6). If he does so, it seems that he *must* give pride of place in the explanation of progress to convergence doctrines. Progress must involve, in some sense, getting more truth. Indeed, suppose a doctrine of convergence does not hold, because we are actually getting less truth (rather than because of the unintelligibility of the doctrine's key notions). It is hard to see how this would not amount to the implausible denial that there has been progress: science has been regressive or simply erratic. In sum, abduction leads from Realism, Correspondence Truth, and the fact of scientific progress to a doctrine like Increasing Verisimilitude.

Finally convergence is important because its denial is so central to the world-view of the radicals. Without convergence, the radicals have been able to give only thin and unconvincing accounts of scientific progress. With it, Realists can give a good account. Convergence supplies, therefore, a good reason for preferring the Realist view to the radical view. (I do *not* claim, however, that anti-Realists of a different stamp from the radicals might not also be able to use these doctrines to account for progress. So they supply no strong reason for Realism: 7.6).

9.8 RADICAL OBJECTIONS

In this section I shall consider some likely objections to my views from radical philosophers of science. Some of these objections can be anticipated from reading the literature. Others have been put to me in discussion.

Objection (1): These views are 'irrelevant', 'useless', or 'empty', for they give no guidance to the working scientist (or person in the street); thus we are no wiser than before about how to choose between theories. They are no help with our epistemic problems.

Answer: This objection reflects a certain vulgarity of mind, a blindness toward any philosophical problem outside epistemology. Perhaps no radical would put the objection so starkly, yet I have often heard remarks that suggest it.

The truth behind the objection is that Realism, Correspondence Truth, and related doctrines are not *primarily* epistemic. However, Realism does have an epistemic component: its claim about the objectivity of common-sense and scientific entities (2.2). Apart from that, what could be more important to our general attempt to understand the world than a view of what, when the chips are down, there really is? A change in our view of this affects all our views. Further, though Correspondence Truth and related doctrines are semantic (Maxim 5), we need them to explain facts that are clearly epistemic: for example, how science progresses.

The irrelevance of Correspondence Truth and related doctrines to the working scientist should not be exaggerated. (a) If theories have been convergent so far, for example, then scientists have good inductive grounds for favouring a new theory which converges over one which does not (a point derived from Putnam 1978: 21–2). (b) To take another example, my view of the semantic relationship between theories (9.6) has consequences for the comparative testing of theories.

Suppose we are testing T against T'. If T were true, its consequence class would contain only true members. The truth values of the members of T''s consequence class, in these circumstances, would be likely to vary: some might come out true, some false, and some neither. Next, consider the situation if T' were true. We would have to reassign truth values to the statements in both classes: 'true' to those in T''s and varying ones to those in T's. So, considering the union of the two classes, we have one assignment to its members when we assume T and another when we assume T'. Now our choice between T and T' can be guided by seeing which assignment corresponds best with what we are prompted to say when we test the members of the union against reality. Putting this another way, when we confront the world in the frame of mind of T', do we have more or less recalcitrant experience than when we confront it in the frame of mind of T? If less, then we have a reason for choosing T'. Finally, 'a crucial experiment' will have the following characteristics. Suppose O_i is the consequence predicted by T in the experiment, O'_i that predicted by T'. On the one hand, if T is true, the experiment will make O_i seem true and O'_i false; on the other hand, if T' is true, the experiment will make O_i seem false and O'_i true.

In saying this, I am not, of course, offering an algorithm for theory choice, but merely suggesting one (important) factor that guides it. So a 'crucial experiment' will not be crucial in that its results will establish that one theory is to be preferred to another. It will be crucial in that its results will supply both a reason for one theory and a reason against the other at the same time.

Feyerabend, in his discussion of crucial experiments (1970b: 226; 1970a: 88), sees difficulties in saying that it is the same experiment that confirms one theory and refutes the other, because the two theories will have very different views of the experiment. This is a mistake. A term can be used in the language of each theory to refer to the experiment, and the referent of the two terms will be the same. Feyerabend's difficulties arise from a description theory of reference.

Objection (2): Suppose that T' has recently replaced T in some science. Then, according to the views in section 9.6, we would do best to use T' to compare T and T'. So the comparison is not objective.

Answer: That depends on what is meant by 'objective'. It is a matter of fact, independent of any theory and of what anyone thinks, that T' and T are or are not, say, quasi-logically inconsistent. In that sense the comparison is objective. It is true that we cannot have opinions on the relation between T' and T without using theories that may be wrong; but if this shows a lack of objectivity, then objectivity is not to be found anywhere. It is true also that our opinions here require a theory of the very area of reality that is the concern of T and T'. However, that is true also of our opinion in section 9.6 that (3) is logically inconsistent with (4).

The objection arises, of course, because the theory we use is T'. Why should this be a problem? It may be felt that if we are to compare T and T', we should stand on neutral ground: the lack of objectivity is a lack of neutrality. I suspect that this feeling arises from the following misconception: that T and T' are in competition, and that I am using T' to choose between them. I am not choosing between them, but judging what semantic relation holds between them; that is I am judging a fact that is quite independent of the question as to which theory is better. That semantic relation, whatever it is, will hold in virtue of the links between each theory and an area of reality. Naturally, then, we shall use our best theory of that area of reality, along with other theories, to judge that relation. The best theory may be T' (though it need not be). The use of T' to judge this bit of semantic reality no more reflects on the objectivity of the judgement than does our use of best theories anywhere. What we face here is not lack of objectivity but, once again, theory-ladenness. Finally, the likely consequences of changing our view of the area of reality that concerns T and T' should not be exaggerated. Though it is possible that two statements which we judge to be quasi-logically inconsistent using T' to fix partial reference would not seem so using T'', it may well be the case that, where T, T', and T'' are any actual series of scientific theories, such judgements mostly remain unchanged.

Objection (3): Truth is not *the* aim of science. There are many aims. Some who are involved are interested in winning wars, some in making profits, some in academic advancement, some in power, some in money, and so on.

Answer: This objection confuses a claim about the aim or purpose of an activity, its *telos*, with the motives of those who practice and commission that activity. The objection is right about motives; yet the aim of science is still truth. Similarly, we can distinguish the aims of, say, literature, education, or auditing from the motives of their practitioners.

Objection (4): The view that truth is the aim of science prescribes a mindless search after knowledge for knowledge's sake.[7]

Answer: It does not. It prescribes only that *if* you want to do science, you should seek the truth. It says nothing on the advisability of doing science. Feyerabend has raised the question of the relationship between science and the furthering of the happiness and full development of individual human beings. He urges that the latter must be the ultimate touchstone (1970b: sect. 7). I agree, and suggest that it would yield no general justification for science. We need to apply it to each part of our present science, taking a long-sighted view of the likely consequence of that part. If we do, it seems to me, then we shall get many different answers: some science will seem justified, some futile, some wicked, and so on.

Feyerabend writes (1970b: sect. 7) as if any science that proceeds in accordance with his principles of tenacity and proliferation will be compatible with a 'humanitarian outlook'. This is surely not so. We can imagine, for example, that Hitler's researchers were guided by those principles as they went about their study of human extermination.

Objection (5): All this talk of truth is idle and 'metaphysical', for we are only entitled to claim that something is true if we know it with absolute certainty, and we do not know this of anything (Chalmers 1976: 124–7; Bhaskar 1975: 248–50).

Answer: This old[8] and surprisingly common objection involves a simple mistake. Claims of truth do not imply any claim of certainty or unrevisability (Maxim 5). 'Snow is white' is true if and only if snow is white. Whatever evidence or lack of it we have for snow being white is evidence or lack of it for the truth of 'Snow is white'. So to assert that a scientific statement is true involves no greater epistemological commitment than simply asserting the statement itself, something which even the radicals do. Indeed, to assert that a statement is only approximately true involves less epistemological commitment than to assert it. Friends of the truth-related notions can be as fallibilist as anyone.

Objection (6): The view is of no interest unless it is accompanied by some instructions on how to tell the degree to which a theory is true, how to tell whether one theory is closer to the truth than another, how to tell whether we are achieving our aim of approaching the truth. In the absence of criteria, such talk is meaningless (Chalmers 1976: 124–7; Bhaskar 1975: 248–50; Laudan 1981: 32).

Answer: As it stands the objection is too extreme; for it depends on a verificationist theory of meaning. However, it raises an important matter. Something needs to be said on the epistemic problems it stimulates. What needs emphasizing is that those problems exist in much the same form whether we talk of truth or not. How does the enemy of truth tell whether to accept a theory? How does he tell whether one theory is better than another? How does he tell whether science is progressing? These are very difficult questions; but there is not reason in principle why the friend of truth could not simply adopt whatever the enemy of truth said in answer to them, saying, for example, 'Yes, that is how I tell whether one theory is closer to the truth than another.' If the enemy of truth is a fallibilist, the friend can go along with him, further adding, 'Of course I may be wrong in my judgement, just as you may be.'

There is one final objection which I will mention now, but set aside until later. It is claimed that such doctrines as Realism and Correspondence Truth require the impossible: that we have 'direct access' to independent reality, without the medium of theory (Bhaskar 1975: 248–50). The doctrines are alleged to commit the empiricist sin of confusing the 'object of knowledge' with the 'real object' (Althusser and Balibar 1968: 51–69). This objection strikes me as completely misguided. I shall answer it when discussing Putnam, who puts it vividly (12.6).

I conclude that there is nothing 'metaphysical', 'theological', or otherwise wicked about Realism, Correspondence Truth, and related doctrines. Indeed, despite the arguments of the radical philosophers of science, we have good reason to believe these doctrines.

NOTES

1 For more along these lines from Kuhn and Feyerabend and for support for the theses attributed to the radicals in the next paragraph but one, see particularly Kuhn 1962: 110–34, 143–58, 198–207; 1970b: 263–77; 1977: 300–6; Feyerabend 1962; 1965b: 230–5; 1965a; 1970a: 81–90; 1970b: 214–29; 1975: 223–85.

2 For some critical remarks on Laudan's examples along these lines, see McMullin 1984: 17–18.

3 Perhaps I should emphasize that no meta-induction to the probable falsity of our current theories about unobservables is sufficient to cast doubt on Realism(now). For Realism(now) is concerned with the *existence* of those unobservables. They may exist even though our current theories of them are false.

4 Though Realism might be saved by arguing that contemporary science

represents a *radical* improvement in our methodology. (Thanks to Elliott Sober and Kim Sterelny.)

5 This section is a modified and shortened version of Devitt 1979. My main disagreement with that article is that it does not abide strictly enough by Maxim 3: it tends to discuss the semantic issue of Incommensurability without sufficient prior attention to the metaphysical issue of what there is.

6 The discussion of Popper's doctrine of verisimilitude supplies another example of this confusion. He has stated often enough that the doctrine is not epistemological (e.g. Popper 1963: 234), and has even supplied some of the history of the confusion of semantics with epistemology (1963: 236–7, 399–404). Yet he is 'grossly misunderstood' on this score (1972: 58). Two examples of misunderstandings are Robinson 1971 and Swinburne 1971. (I do not claim that there is *no* basis for misunderstanding.)

7 Lakatos (1974: 253) thinks that '*Logik der Forschung* is consistent with the game of science being pursued for its own sake.'

8 According to Putnam, 'a minor pragmatist called Felix Kaufmann' made much the same objection, to which Carnap made much the same reply as I make here (1978: 2–3).

10

Davidsonians against Reference

10.1 INTRODUCTION

I have argued that we need an explanatory correspondence notion of truth (chapter 6) and that we hope to have one explained in terms of genuine, objective reference relations. These relations in turn require explanation. For this explanation, we look ultimately to causal theories of reference (3.3 and 7.5).

Donald Davidson also sees the need for an explanatory correspondence notion of truth; but in 'Reality without Reference' (1984: 215–25), a response to Field (1972) among others, he denies the need for and possibility of a theory of reference.[1] John McDowell (1978) has been strongly influenced by Davidson, and has responded similarly to Field.[2] Many other philosophers have adopted what are recognizably Davidsonian lines in theorizing about people and their languages (e.g. Rorty 1979, 1982; Dennett 1978; Wallace 1979; Platts 1979).

Taski seemed to claim that his theory of truth made that notion physicalistically respectable. Field (1972) argued that this was not so. What Tarski really showed was that truth was explicable in terms of reference. To make truth physicalistically respectable, a theory of reference has to be added to Tarski's theory.

McDowell agrees with Field's criticism of Tarski's claim about truth and physicalism: 'I believe Field is right about Tarski's view of the relation between physicalism and his work on truth. I believe also that, given the physicalism he espouses (which is probably, Tarski's doctrine too), Field is right to regard Tarski's claim as overblown' (McDowell 1978: 111; see also p. 116). However, McDowell goes on: 'What I want to dispute is [a view about] how semantics and physics are, related, which Field aims to motivate by these considerations about Tarski' (p. 131).

This disputed view is the one that underlies my discussion of, and commitment to, theories of reference. In place of it, McDowell offers his Davidsonian view that has no place for such theories.

A striking problem about semantics is that different theories within it often seem to arise from quite different perspectives of the task and of how to go about accomplishing it. Many disagreements over particular issues reflect these deep differences. This seems to be the case in my disagreement with the Davidsonians over reference.

This was not sufficiently apparent to me at the time of the first edition of this book or of an earlier discussion (1981a: 118–124). I tended then to approach the Davidsonian rejection of reference from the sort of perspective set out in chapters 3 and 6. Semantic theories that talked of truth were to be seen as attempts to explain, in the normal scientific way, the meanings of symbols and the contents of thoughts. The theories were scientific investigations of an area of reality like any other, in this case the area of semantic facts. From this 'factual' perspective, Davidsonian arguments against reference were difficult to discern, and their conclusions implausible. However, the Davidsonians seem to have a different, *a*scientific perspective on semantics, depending on principles of 'charity' and 'rationality', which puts them close to Quine. I shall call this perspective 'interpretative'. From the interpretative perspective, the Davidsonian view of reference is easier – though I do not say easy – to understand.

Nevertheless, I shall start my discussion along the lines of the first edition (1984a: 164–70), criticizing Davidsonian semantics, particularly McDowell's version, without placing it in the interpretative perspective (10.2–10.3). I do this for three reasons. First, Davidson is notoriously difficult to understand. It is natural and common to take many of Davidson's writings, particularly those in the late 1960s, as reflecting the factual perspective. This way of taking those writings inspired, for example, Bill Lycan's book *Logical Form in Natural Language* (1984), a thorough working-out of a truth-conditional semantics. Second, my criticisms from the factual perspective bring out the extent to which the Davidsonian rejection of reference needs another perspective. Third, I shall argue (10.4–10.5) that the interpretative perspective is unsupportable.

The primary concern of this chapter is with the Davidsonian rejection of reference. However, I shall conclude by assessing Davidson's position on Realism, with particular attention to his view that there is no sense to the idea of a conceptual scheme (10.6).

10.2 ELIMINATIVISM AND SEMANTICALISM

What are we to make of the Davidsonian view of truth and reference as contributions to the normal, scientific explanation of meaning? Do Davidsonian arguments, taken independently of the interpretative perspective, cast doubt on theories of reference?

To answer these questions, it helps to compare the Davidsonian view with three relatively clear positions. The first two of these are:

(1) *Leeds–Quine eliminative physicalism*   Our theory of the world is strictly and austerely physical, having no need of any explanatory semantic notion (6.1).

(2) *Semanticalism*   Our theory of the world has need of explanatory semantic notions which are basic and inexplicable in non-semantic terms – for example, in physical terms.

('Semanticalism' is Field's term for the analogue in semantics of dualism in psychology and of vitalism in biology; Field 1972; 92).

The eliminativist position is clear and powerful, though difficult to believe. I have argued against it in chapter 6. According to it, there are no semantic facts to be explained. The only notion of truth which it countenances is the trivial deflationary notion. (3.4). This notion requires no theory of reference.

There are certainly signs of this position in Davidsonian writings; see, for example, Davidson's many approving references to Quine's indeterminacy thesis, which is an eliminativist view. However, the Davidsonian cannot go all the way with the eliminativist. He agrees that reference should be abandoned, but he must save truth. 'Truth is a crucially important explanatory concept' (Davidson 1990: 313) in the theory of people and their languages: that is what the Davidsonian theory of meaning is all about. Further, McDowell talks of sketching a view of 'the point of contact between semantical facts and the underlying physical facts' (1978: 118–19). So he thinks that there are such semantical facts. (I go along with McDowell in hoping that talk of facts is 'only a *façon de parler*'; p. 129n.). He emphasizes the importance of Convention T in testing whether a truth theory 'is correct' (pp. 119–20; see also Davidson 1984: 222–3). It seems as if McDowell thinks that there are good explanations of behaviour which make reference to semantic facts (pp. 121–2).

What sort of facts are these ones about truth? The notion of truth involved seems not to be explained, reduced, or defined by the Davidsonians; it is 'primitive' (Davidson 1990: 299; 1984: 221–3;

Wallace 1979: 324). It seems as if the facts are non-physical: the Davidsonian position is (2), an anti-physicalist semanticalism.

This reading of the Davidsonians does not sit well with the many signs of their sympathy for physicalism (e.g. McDowell 1978: 126–8). To reconcile the two, we need the interpretative perspective, which we are setting aside until later (10.4).

What is the bearing of physicalism on the issues of truth and reference from the factual perspective? It is common for people to think that physicalistic theories of reference require an implausibly strong physicalism. Thus McDowell supposes (p. 127) that Field *identifies* reference with a (first-order) physical relation.[3] Such a requirement is indeed hopeless, for the same reason that the type-identity theory of the mind is hopeless (6.3). Reference relations, like mental relations, are ('wide') functional relations which can have many different physical realizations. Field is explicit about this (1975, 1978).

There is room for argument about the physicalistic status of functional theories in general (6.3) and of functional theories of reference in particular. However, most functionalists claim that all tokens are physical, and that the mental and semantic supervenes on the physical in that there are law-like conditionals from the physical to the psychological (which Davidson denies; 1980: 209, 224). If this sort of functionalism can be made good, it is hard to see how it could be incompatible with any reasonable physicalism (2.5; see also McDowell 1978: 126).

Nevertheless, suppose that we conclude that we cannot give a physicalistically acceptable theory of reference along these functionalist lines or any other lines. We then face a dilemma: give up reference or give up physicalism. Suppose that we choose the first horn. How can we hold onto truth as the Davidsonian does? It too needs to be explained in a physicalistically acceptable manner. Perhaps this could be done in terms other than reference, but how? The Davidsonians seem to make no such suggestion. Their position seems to be semanticalist. Further, from the factual perspective, Davidsonian semanticalism seems especially bad. If we are prepared to be semanticalist about truth, why not also about reference? Why not choose the second horn of our dilemma and save reference? And that surely is what we ought to do. Truth needs explaining, whether our semantic theory is physicalistic or not. Why should it not be explained in terms of reference, which is in turn explained functionally? Even the semanticalist of position (2) should reject the Davidsonian view.

If physicalism makes us dubious of reference, it should make us equally dubious of truth: we should accept the eliminativist position (1). On the other hand, if we accept truth, then we should seek an explanation of it in terms of reference, whether physicalistic or not. Physicalism in irrelevant to the Davidsonian discrimination against reference.

Wallace (1979) has offered an argument that might be considered to count against a *functionalist* theory of reference. The argument rests on the possibility of 'transforming a scheme of reference by permutations of the universe' (p. 314). If the argument were sound, then it would provide a case for discrimination against reference, and hence for Davidsonian semanticalism. However, the argument is not sound, as Field (1975) has shown (partly in response to an earlier, unpublished version of Wallace's paper).

Eliminativism dispenses with truth as well as reference. A semanticalism that has truth should also have reference. Neither position justifies Davidsonian discrimination against reference in favour of truth. No more does a third position, which I shall now consider.

10.3 INSTRUMENTALISM

(3) *Instrumentalism* Only the observable world exists (or is known to exist). 'Theoretical' terms do not refer. The statements containing them are mere instruments for prediction etc. (7.7 and 7.8).

Semantic Instrumentalism is obvious in McDowell, but is to be found also in Davidson and other Davidsonians (e.g. Wallace 1979: Platts 1979: 64–7). According to McDowell, Field seeks to reveal 'the adherence of semantics to the physical facts' at 'the level of the *axioms* of a truth-characterization' (1978: 118). These axioms are the referential ones, for example:

'Socrates' designates Socrates.
'Wise' applies to wise things.

McDowell's approach is to invert 'the point of contact between semantic theories and the physical facts' (p. 121): 'it is at the level of its *theorems* that a truth characterization ... makes a contact with those hard physical facts' (p. 122; see also Davidson 1984: 219–20). These theorems are 'T-sentences; for example:

'Socrates is wise' is true if and only if Socrates is wise.

McDowell's discussion of this inversion is instrumentalistic.

Referential axioms of the above sort are part of the deductive apparatus used to derive T-sentences as theorems. That apparatus, according to McDowell, 'needs no anchoring in the physical facts, independently of the overall acceptability of the derived assignments of truth-conditions' (p. 123; see also Davidson 1984: 222–3). Not only does the apparatus not need any independent anchoring in the physical facts, it does not have any: 'there is nothing to the specific primitive-denotation concepts over and above those distinctive deductive powers' (p. 123; see also Davidson 1984: 224).

Two further points will help to bring out the instrumentalistic nature of McDowell's view. First, it is his appreciation of the test of material adequacy that leads him to this inversion (pp. 119–20; see also Davidson 1990: 300). The test is, of course, Convention T, which requires that the theory yield T-sentences that are, like the one above, correct.[4] We judge whether the theory is correct by seeing whether or not this is so. Analogously, we judge (partly at least) whether our physical theory, with its talk of microscopic entities like electrons, is correct by seeing whether it is correct at the macroscopic level. The path from this epistemic point to the view that there aren't really any microscopic entities is precisely the path trodden by the instrumentalists.

Second, consider the view that McDowell has of the 'physical facts' that the theory must make contact with. Implicitly these are only what he later calls 'the hard' physical facts (p. 122): facts about the structural properties of utterances, behavioural facts, and environmental facts. What he is talking about here is not the physical *facts*, but the physical *evidence*. To suppose that the only facts a theory must make contact with are the evidential ones is instrumentalistic.

A Realist with the factual perspective will suppose, by contrast, that there is a factual realm underlying the evidential one with which he is trying to make contact. Thus a Realist who adopts a physicalistic semantic theory of the sort I have urged will hold that there is a realm of physical things, which really have functional properties like being a one-place predication and which really stand in functional relations to objects of referring. It is the task of (applied) semantic theory to describe this realm, to make contact with these facts.

I have already rejected the general instrumentalism of position (3) (7.8). The weight of evidence and argument in recent years has gone heavily against it.

Suppose nevertheless, that we were to adopt position (3). It would not support Davidsonian semantic instrumentalism. A problem for any instrumentalism is to justify the sharp distinction it requires between the 'observational' sentences which are factual and the 'theoretical' ones which are mere instruments. The Davidsonians would need T-sentences, unlike referential axioms, to be 'observational'. This would be an extraordinary claim. A vast amount of theory goes into judging whether a T-sentence is true. We need a theory of the society of organisms (or whatever) which we take to be speakers of the language and of all individuals whose behaviour we use as evidence; we need a view of their needs, desires, beliefs, emotions, sensations, characters, and history. Further, we need a theory of the environment in which they live (Devitt 1981a:110–13). There should be no temptation to suppose that, looking at the world with an innocent eye, we can simply *observe* whether a T-sentence is correct or not (Devitt 1981a: 121). If position (3) were correct, it would yield not the Davidsonian view, but the view that T-sentences also were mere instruments: they are no more factual than the referential axioms (a Quinean conclusion reached by a different route). Position (3) does not justify discrimination against reference in favour of truth.

The Davidsonians are of course right to emphasize that the evidence for a semantic explanation is at the level of sentences. But this does not support the view that truth, but not reference, is a place of 'direct contact between linguistic theory and events, actions or objects described in nonlinguistic terms' (Davidson 1984: 219). The whole semantic theory including talk of truth and reference is tested at once by the evidence, and rather indirectly tested at that, for there are many other theories involved as well.

In sum, from the factual perspective, the Davidsonians combine an unacceptable semanticalism about truth with an unacceptable instrumentalism about reference. However, it seems as if the Davidsonians have a different perspective on semantics, to which I now turn.

10.4 THE INTERPRETATIVE PERSPECTIVE

Davidson begins the introduction to *Inquiries into Truth and Interpretation* (1984) as follows:

What is it for words to mean what they do? In the essays collected here I explore the idea that we would have an answer to this question if we knew how to construct a theory satisfying two demands: it would provide an interpretation of all utterances, actual and potential, of a speaker or group of speakers; and it would be verifiable without knowledge of the detailed propositional attitudes of the speaker. (p. xiii)

This should not be taken as suggesting that the semantic task is to give theories of interpretation for particular languages; for English, Swahili, and so on. Rather, it is suggesting that the task is to say how to construct such theories. We need *a theory of* theories of interpretation. That is what Davidson thinks would throw light on the nature of meaning, on 'what it is for words to mean what they do'.

I have argued against this suggestion elsewhere (1981a: 90–2).[5] *Prima facie* a theory of interpretation for L is simply a method of translating that language into ours (Harman 1974). It *gives* the meaning of a symbol of L by using a symbol in our language. Why suppose that a theory of such theories would *explain* the meaning that the alien symbol and ours share? Why suppose that it would tell us about the properties in virtue of which a symbol, whether alien or not, is able to play its striking role?

Davidsonians do not offer an explicit argument for this view of the semantic task, but I think the implicit argument arises from a behaviouristic Quinean scepticism about meaning. That scepticism leads to the view that there can be no *explanatory* notion of meaning; symbols do not have meaning properties that explain their roles and are awaiting discovery. So all that remains of meaning are our *practices* of interpreting each other, practices which our scepticism does not allow us to see as describing an independent semantic reality. This argument has no force, of course, for those who do not share the scepticism.

In sum, from the factual perspective, the task is the description and explanation of semantic properties that play roles in explanatory theories of language and mind. This perspective is supported by the considerations in chapters 3 and 6. From the interpretative perspective, the task is to say how to construct theories of interpretation. The interpretative perspective implicitly rejects the factual task, but the factual perspective does not reject the interpretative task. However, the two perspectives differ radically in their views of how to accomplish that task.

From the factual perspective, the interpretative task is not central to semantics. Nevertheless, we can consider this task from that perspective, and it will be helpful to do so before further discussion of Davidson.

We have already noted that deflationary truth can play a role in interpretation (3.4). A person who has caught onto deflationary truth has caught onto the fact that all *appropriate* instances of Schema T,

   s is true if and only if *p*,

are true. An appropriate instance is one obtained by substituting for '*p*' a sentence which has the same meaning as the sentence referred to by the term substituted for '*s*' (setting aside problems arising from indexicals). So an appropriate instance provides an interpretation. Suppose now that the person is confronted by a sentence – call it 'Harry' – which she does not know how to interpret. Since she does not understand Harry, she has no easy route to the appropriate instance of T that is about Harry; she does not know which sentence in her own language means the same as Harry and should be substituted for '*p*'. However, suppose that she has evidence for

   Harry is true if and only if snow is white.

This is evidence that the biconditional is an appropriate instance of T, and hence that Harry means that snow is white. Of course, even if the evidence for the biconditional were conclusive, it would not *establish* that the bioconditional was an appropriate instance; the biconditional might be true for some reason other than that Harry means that snow is white. Nevertheless, evidence for the biconditional *is* evidence for the interpretation, and if the evidence were that the biconditional was law-like, it would be very good evidence.

   So if we knew a law-like biconditional of the above sort for *every* sentence in L, we would probably know the interpretation of L. But that knowledge cannot be given by any finite list of biconditionals because, if L is a natural language, it will contain an infinite number of sentences. However, a Tarski-style truth theory yields an infinite set of biconditionals as theorems. So if we knew such a truth theory for L, we would probably know the interpretation of L.

   From the factual perspective, this truth theory could also tells us *something* about meaning. For the structure it reveals in showing how the truth condition of a sentence depends on the reference of its parts is likely to be just the structure that a theory of meaning will have to appeal to in explaining how the meaning of a sentence depends on the meaning of its parts. To this extent, the above 'theory of interpretation' is, after all, a contribution to a theory of meaning. However, it could not *be* a theory of meaning, because it rests on a deflationary, and hence non-explanatory, notion of truth. Indeed, that notion *is explained in terms of meaning*, as is made evident by the above account of what it is to be an appropriate instance of Schema T.

Finally, we should note that, *for the purpose of providing evidence for an interpretation*, the truth theory does not need to be supplemented by theories of reference. All that matters for that purpose is the law-like truth of the biconditional theorems. Theories of reference might well provide useful *evidence* for the truth of the theorems, but they would not be essential. By contrast, if a truth theory is *for the purpose of explaining a correspondence notion of truth* as part of a scientific account of meaning (or whatever), then the theory needs to be supplemented by theories of reference. That was Field's point.

The interpretative task looks very different from Davidson's interpretative perspective. First, Davidson does not think of the notion of truth in his theories of interpretation as deflationary. He thinks that a deflationary notion must be captured totally by a Tarskian definition, and his notion is not so captured (1990: 288). Why must a deflationary notion be so strictly Tarskian? I have followed many others in explaining a notion that is not so and that seems to deserve the name 'deflationary'. However, this is largely a verbal point.

My deflationary notion is not part of a theory of meaning. It is explained in terms of semantic notions that will themselves require explanation in a theory of meaning. What about Davidson's notion of truth? Early on, in 'Truth and Meaning' (1984: 17–36), Davidson seemed to have the idea that a Tarski-style truth theory for L not only supplied an interpretation of L but also explained truth. However, he soon came to recognize that the truth theory could not do both jobs (1990: 286n.). Typically, he then seemed to present truth as an unexplained primitive, as I have indicated (10.2). This gives rise to the charge of semanticalism. Davidson has in mind a complicated way out of this charge.

In the passage quoted, Davidson mentions two demands on a theory of interpretation. The first is to be met by a Tarski-style truth theory. The second is to be met by his view of how to tell whether a particular truth theory fits a particular speaker; it is to be met by epistemic considerations. (This way of meeting these demands is, therefore, his theory of theories of interpretation.) At first sight, the epistemic considerations seem no help with the worry about semanticalism. They seem to be telling us how to get an interpretation by applying a truth theory containing an already understood, unexplained notion of truth. They do not seem to be telling us anything about that notion. However, Davidson seems to have in mind that the combination of these epistemic considerations with truth theories can do *both* jobs. Since his notion of truth is not deflationary (see above), a Tarskian definition could not tell us all about it. What such a definition misses is the generality that

Davidson's notion, like the ordinary notion, must have. Tarski showed how to define truth predicates for many languages but did not tell us what all these predicates have in common (Davidson 1990: 285–8). Nevertheless, Tarski did tell part of the story: he revealed the 'pattern or structure' of truth. The story is completed by the epistemic considerations: saying 'how to identify the presence of such a pattern or structure in the behavior of people' (p. 295). What the combination tells us about truth does not amount to a *reduction*, and so in that respect truth is primitive (pp. 314–6). Truth, it seems, is explained 'in use': truth theories, together with the circumstances in which they apply, tell us all there is to know about truth.

In brief, with the help of the epistemic considerations, Davidson hopes to *both* explain truth (cf. Maxim 5) *and* use it to yield interpretations, and hence explain meaning. The considerations are *constitutive* of correct interpretation and of truth.

Davidson proposes two epistemic considerations. The first starts from a very narrow view of the evidence: 'meaning is entirely determined by observable behavior, even readily observable behavior' (p. 314). We must tie the truth theory to the speaker by such evidence. Furthermore, we cannot tell whether a truth theory applies to a speaker without a view of her beliefs, desires, and other attitudes. And we cannot assume that we have such a view in advance of interpreting her. 'What is wanted, then, is an approach that yields an interpretation of a speaker's words at the same time that it provides a basis for attributing beliefs and desires to the speaker' (p. 316).

We might anticipate that readily observable behaviour is far too thin a basis to do all this work: to determine interpretations, to determine attitudes, *and*, let us not forget, *to explain truth*. And so it proves. Davidson adds a second epistemic consideration: principles of 'rationality' and 'charity'. These principles yield a way of accomplishing the semantic task that is different from the normal way of empirical science.

I think that the resort to these principles is motivated by the same behaviouristically inspired scepticism about meaning that led to the interpretative perspective on the semantic task. The thin behavioural base seems appropriate to Davidson because he is implicitly rejecting the factual perspective on the semantic task. From that perspective, the semantic properties of symbols are explanatory in theories of mind and language. Thus, on the one hand, their existence is supported by a wide spectrum of evidence, and, on the other hand, their nature is not determined by that evidence. For Davidson, by contrast, there is no such nature independent of the enterprise of interpreting the symbols. Without the principles of charity and rationality, the thin behavioural base would leave Davidsonian semantics with an unwelcome dilemma. The physicalist horn is a radical eliminativism: the thin behavioural base is all there really is to meaning and truth. The semanticalist horn accepts that meaning is explained in terms of a largely unexplained notion of truth.

In its adoption of the principles of charity and rationality, the interpretative perspective is an attempt to avoid this dilemma. The Davidsonian hopes to have substantive semantic facts without being a semanticalist by treating the facts as being, in some sense, outside science. McDowell has been most explicit. He agrees with Field that Cartesianism is unscientific; for it holds

that there are questions of the sort physics purports to be able to handle, to which the answers are stubbornly non-physical. . . . But it is a different matter to refuse to accept that all questions fall within the province of science so understood. We can agree that semantics, on the view here taken, is not in that sense scientific (though there is plenty to justify its claim to be scientific in some more relaxed sense) without thereby agreeing that it is *un*scientific. (1978: 128).

In semantics we do not seek explanations as we do in physics and chemistry; rather, we seek to *rationalize* people's behaviour; we *impose* an interpretation on them. This yields a special sort of non-physical understanding (pp. 121–6). The interpretative perspective is an attempt to have irreducible semantic facts while maintaining physicalistic respectability.

The Davidsonian interpretative perspective is interestingly reminicent of the European *Verstehen* tradition, according to which the social sciences differ from the natural ones in requiring a sort of empathetic understanding. Indeed, Graham MacDonald and Philip Pettit (1981) have derived a *Verstehen* view from an explicitly Davidsonian perspective. They have also claimed that this is the only good route to *Verstehen*.

I must conclude this section by considering the consequences of the interpretative perspective for theories of reference. From this perspective, the only 'reality' determined by the behavioural evidence and the principles of charity and rationality consists of T-sentences. A truth theory that yields the right T-sentences as theorems will have captured all the semantic 'reality' there is to capture. Talk of reference in that theory is a mere instrument for yielding the T-sentences. If this perspective were right, there would indeed be no place for theories of reference.

10.5 THE PRINCIPLES OF CHARITY
AND RATIONALITY

The principles of charity and rationality are essential aspects of the solution to the interpretative – hence semantic – task, according to the interpretative perspective. To what extent, if any, are they sound? Inevitably my discussion of this question shows signs of my factual perspective, for I know no other. Nevertheless, I think the discussion demonstrates that the principles lack any *intuitive* support.

Davidson's discussion of charity and rationality (1980, 1984) interweaves several different principles. I start by dividing his commitment in two. First, he is committed to a principle I call 'charity': it is constitutive of a person's having beliefs and expressing meaningful utterances that his beliefs and utterances be, as far as possible, true according to one's own lights, and allowing for some explicable error. An important consequence of this principle is that we must be mostly right in our own beliefs. Second, he is committed to a principle I call 'rationality': it is constitutive of having beliefs and expressing meaningful utterances that the person be rational, or more or less so.[6]

These two principles yield the special way of accomplishing the semantic task that is partly definitive of the interpretative perspective: we seek understanding by imposing an interpretation.

I have argued against the principles of charity and rationality before (1981a: 115–18). Our task in attributing beliefs and meanings to a person is an explanatory one. The canons of good explanation we use here are just the same as those (largely unknown) ones we use everywhere else. A good explanation is likely to see the person as often agreeing with us, but it is likely also to see him as often disagreeing. Thus our best explanation of many of our fellows may take an uncharitable view of their opinions on religion, semantics, politics, the weather, and so forth. I could find no good reason for introducing the special constraint of charity on an explanation simply because its subject is a person.

My reaction to the principle of rationality was more complicated, because a person can be rational or irrational in various, quite different ways. And it seems clear that there is a constitutive principle about one of those ways: the rationality of behaviour, given beliefs and desires. But this sort of rationality is quite different from either that of beliefs, given experience, or that of beliefs, given other beliefs, which is itself a complex form of rationality. I might also have added that it is quite different from that of desires, given needs. (A heart patient who desires to eat saturated fats has an irrational desire, given that what he needs is poly-unsaturated fats.) I could find no good reason, once again, for introducing a special constraint of rationality, of any of these latter sorts, on an explanation of a person.

My brief discussion of the correct constitutive principle of rationality (1981a: 116) was not satisfactory. I take behaviour to be simply bodily movement. It is certainly *not* the case that a person's behaviour, in this sense, must be rational, given his beliefs and desires. A lot of his behaviour does not stem from his beliefs and desires. Such behaviour as does stem from them – his actions – must of course be rational, given those beliefs and desires: that is what it is for behaviour to be an action. In attributing beliefs and desires, we are aiming to explain behaviour in a way that makes it rational (in this respect).[7] Nevertheless, it is possible, though unlikely, that none of a believer-desirer's actual behaviour is rational (in this respect): his beliefs and desires give him a tendency to act in certain ways that circumstances prevent him from doing. It is an entirely empirical question as to how much of his behaviour is rational., and hence correctly described as his actions. However, it is constitutive of having beliefs and desires that they make some *possible* behaviour rational.

My dismissal of the principle of charity still strikes me as sound. It is an entirely empirical question as to how true a person's beliefs are. Davidson's frequently stated claim (e.g. 1984: 199–200) that the possibility of error and disagreement depends on general correctness and agreement seems to me to be without force. Davidson agrees that some error is possible. Why does disaster suddenly strike our explanation if we suppose that error goes beyond the Davidsonian limit? I have heard the suggestion that although we can ascribe error in a few areas, we cannot in most. But what difference does it make to my attempt to explain a person uncharitably in, say, semantics that I have already explained him uncharitably in, say, religion and politics? Why does accumulation of error make a difference?

My dismissal of the other constitutive principles of rationality was, I think, too swift. I does seem plausible to suppose that *some* requirement of the rationality of beliefs, given beliefs (the complexities of which I shall explore below), is constitutive of being a believer-desirer: the beliefs must cohere in some sort of way, though that way should allow for a good deal of inconsistency. At the present stage of cognitive psychology, it is hard to be more precise. (It is noteworthy that Davidson tends to include qualifications like 'by and large' and 'more or less' in his statement of the principle of rationality.) Perhaps there is also something in the idea that beliefs must be rational, given experience, and desires, given needs, but this seems much more dubious.

The principle of rationality that I have committed myself to – that of behaviour, given beliefs and desires – is clearly present in Davidson (1980: 233). Yet it is irrelevant to the support of Davidson's interpretive perspective. Indeed, the principle is implicit in my quite un-Davidsonian discussion in chapter 6. What is more prominent in Davidson's discussion is a concern for consistency. This suggests the vaguely stated requirement of the rationality of beliefs, given beliefs, that I have just found plausible. However, once again, any such principle that comes out of future psychology is as compatible with Fieldian as with Davidsonian semantics. It is not clear whether Davidson has any requirement of the rationality of beliefs, given experience, or of desires, given needs. What is absolutely dominant in Davidson's discussion is the principle of charity. It is this principle that must save Davidsonian semantics if anything can. I reject in totally.

In my earlier, critical treatment of the principles, I was careful not to deny certain related epistemic, methodological, and pragmatic claims that might be made (1981a: 117). I assume that it must be the plausibility of these claims that accounts for much of the popularity of the principles. Yet these claims are quite distinct from the principles. They give charity no support at all, and support only harmless rationality.

I start with some epistemic claims. Good, though certainly not conclusive, evidence for thinking that an alien's beliefs are more or less true and that his beliefs and desires are more or less rational is that he is still around to be speculated about. Truth and rationality are conducive to success (6.6). An alien who is prone to massive error and irrationality is unlikely to last long. If he does last, further explanation is called for.

This talk of success is too general. An alien is likely to suffer some failure, as well as to enjoy success. It matters to our attributions of correctness and rationality in which respects he is a success and in which a failure. In the light of such information, it may be plausible to attribute to him true beliefs in some areas and false ones in others, rationality in certain respects and irrationality in others.

Suppose our best theory of ourselves is that our beliefs are more or less true and our beliefs and desires more or less rational. Then any evidence we have that an alien is like us in design is evidence that he is in these respects like us. Thus, if we have evidence that he is a 'normal' member of our species, then we have evidence that he is about as correct and rational as we are.

Any evidence we have that an object is the member of a species that has *evolved* is evidence of some sort of goodness of design. So, if we have reason to believe also that the object is a believer-desirer (and not, for example, an insect), then we have reason to believe that it is in this respect well-designed, and hence correct and rational.

We may have other evidence of the alien's design. We may have very good reason for thinking him *different* from us in various respects. Pehaps he is a robot we built. Perhaps he has evolved in quite different ways to suit quite different circumstances (on another planet). In such cases, we would expect him to differ from us in correctness and rationality.

The constitutive principle about the rationality of behaviour, given beliefs and desires, supplies an important constraint on the beliefs and desires that we can plausibly attribute to the alien, a constraint that has nothing to do with the truth of his beliefs or of his success. In so far as we see a piece of behaviour as an action, we must attribute to him a belief and desire that explains it.

Other constraints arise from our need to have a plausible theory of how an alien's beliefs relate to the experiences he has been through, and of how his desires relate to his needs, on the one hand, and to his beliefs on the other. Thus we might be prepared to attribute to him a bizarre religious belief because we have a theory of human need for religion, a reactionary political belief because we have a theory of ideology, or a false physical belief because we have a theory of education.

Faced with this variety of evidence and this background theory, we seek *the best explanation* of the alien. We 'impose' on him only in the trivial sense that we 'impose' any theory on nature: we come up with a theory of him that is underdetermined by the evidence. The theory is likely to judge him correct here, incorrect there, rational in this respect, irrational in that. And as we move from alien to alien, our judgements are likely to vary. I will illustrate this variation with two alien chess-players, one a computer, the other a human, and one complicated area of rationality, that of beliefs, given beliefs.

We can divide this area of rationality into four, possibly five, parts. First, there is the question of the goodness of the rules of deductive and inductive inference that the alien uses when he reasons from belief to belief. Second, there is the question of the variety of the rules of inference that he uses. One alien can be more rational than another through using a wider variety of good rules. (Note that the question of what rules of logic an alien uses is quite different from the question of what laws of logic he believes: an analogous point is made about linguistic competence in my 1981a: 101–10). Third, there is the question of whether he reasons where he should and for as long as he should. An alien may be wanting in rationality by not applying his rules where it would pay off to do so. Fourth, there is the question of coherence and consistency. In so far as this is additional to the above, it is the question of whether the alien unifies his beliefs or allows them to remain 'in compartments'. Fifth, there may be a question of how fast the alien reasons. Perhaps this would not count as a question of rationality according to our ordinary concept, but it would appear to count as a question of intelligence. And it is certainly a relevant consideration in assessing the other parts of an alien's rationality.

Now compare the computer and the human chess-player in these respects. (I shall assume that this computer, though certainly not all computers, is a believer-desirer.) It is very likely that we will rate the computer higher than the human in the last two respects. A modern computer is likely to reason vary fast and to avoid inconsistencies. The typical chess computer changes its rationality in the third respect with changes in the 'level of difficulty' setting; in part, such changes alter the time the computer can reason before making its moves. A computer is less rational on a low setting than it is on a high one for that reason alone. Comparison with a human will vary accordingly, but seems likely to favour the computer. The computer is likely to come out on top also in the first respect, because it is likely that every rule of inference it uses is good, whereas that is not likely to be true of the human. It is in the second respect, of course, that the human will almost certainly be far superior: he will use a much greater variety of good inference rules than the computer, leading to a much greater flexibility in behaviour. We can be confident of this, because we know that we don't know enough about the good rules of inductive inference used by humans to be able to build a computer that uses them.

Earlier I allowed that the rationality of beliefs, given beliefs, may be in some way constitutive of having them. In what way? I take it that we can rule out the fifth of respect, above: speed of inference does not seem in any way constitutive. Failures in the fourth respect lead to compartmentalization. To some degree, such failures are present in all of us. In an extreme form, they lead to 'split personal-ities'. In principle, there seems to be no limit to such failures. If anything is to be constitutive, it must be found in the first three respects. It seems that the believer-desirer must use at least one rule of inference (second respect) to some degree (third respect). Must it be good (first respect)? I don't know. Certainly we do not want to require that all the rules used must be good, on pain of concluding that humans are not believer-desirers (see, e.g. Kahneman and Tversky 1973). And it is not clear that we should require that more than one rule be used (second respect) or to what extent any rule must be used (third respect). We simply do not know enough about the nature of belief to solve thes problems.

A methodological point that follows from our epistemic ones is that it is not advisable to assume *a priori* that an alien is perfectly correct and rational ('optimally designed'; Dennett 1978: 17–19), and to qualify this assumption only as we are forced to by the alien's behaviour. We may have good *a priori* reasons for thinking that the alien is limited in various respects. These reasons might come, for example, from knowledge of computer technology or of the psychology of gamblers or of people with certain accents. Since aliens are not always in all respects correct and rational, it is not a good strategy to start explaining them by assuming they are.

If an alien fails miserably to be correct and/or rational in some respect, this may have pragmatic consequences for us. It may make it very difficult – perhaps even impossible – for us to construct plausible belief–desire explanations of his behaviour. It may make it inadvisable to try; we would do better to seek a physical explanation by examining his hardware. But these consequences in no way establish that the alien does not have beliefs and desires; nor do they even show that in other respects the alien is not correct and rational. (The consequences might hold if the alien reasoned extremely slowly but was otherwise super-rational.)

I shall conclude with a thought on why it is difficult to imagine an alien who is mostly mistaken or irrational. I suggest this is difficult because it is difficult to imagine how such an alien could survive. However, if we could throw off the shackles of Earthly background assumptions, exercising a science-fiction imagination, perhaps we could imagine this. Suppose we had complete knowledge of the psychological processes of an alien who is neither perceptive nor smart. We could imagine it being mostly wrong in the following way. We have designed the environment in which it lives so that the environment has the following two properties: (1) it systematically misleads the alien (causes the alien to have false beliefs); (2) it saves the alien from the unfortunate consequences of those false beliefs.

(In imagining Superscientist manipulating a brain in a vat, we are imagining an extreme case of this sort.) With a bit more effort, I suspect that we could imagine a mostly irrational alien surviving. If not, so much the worse for our imaginations. We need more than such failings to support the principles of charity and rationality.

No doubt my discussion of these principles reflects my factual perspective. But this perspective, which treats semantics like any other science, is independently plausible. We need a powerful reason if we are going to treat semantics in a special way. Aside from this, I think that the discussion demonstrates how hard it is to see these principles as *descriptive* of reality from any perspective. Why bother to adopt them then? It seems as if the Davidsonian adopts them simply because without them no interpretation would be possible: 'What makes interpretation possible ... is the fact that we can dismiss *a priori* the chance of massive error, (Davidson 1984: 168–9). But if the principles were necessary for interpretation, why should we bother with interpretation? What is the point of attaching a meaning to a person's words if they don't *really* have that meaning? Of course, it may seem obvious that they really do have a meaning. But in that case, principles that have no basis in reality can have no part in a theory that explains the meaning.

Davidson makes many approving references to Quine's argument for the indeterminacy of translation. Quine also embraces a principle of charity (1960: 59n., 69n.; 1969: 46). So it is interesting to compare Quine's position with Davidson's. I take it that any Quinean principle must be a purely pragmatic one, because it follows from the indeterminacy thesis that there are near enough no psychological or semantic facts to be constituted by anything. People do not have beliefs; nor are their utterances meaningful in any strong sense. This physicalistic eliminativism seems inconsistent with the interpretative perspective, which allows semantic facts outside science. Of course, there is a puzzle about Quine. If this is his view, why does *he* bother with interpretation?

In conclusion, Davidsonians give truth the central role in semantics, but deny any place to theories of reference. From a factual perspective, taking semantics to be a normal empirical science concerned with explanatory properties, the Davidsonian view combines an unacceptable semanticalism about truth with an unacceptable instrumentalism about reference. The Davidsonians have a different perspective which, if sound, would justify their view of reference. However, this interpretative perspective is doubly mistaken. The semantic task is not that of saying how to construct theories of interpretation. Principles of charity and rationality have far too little basis in reality to play the role assigned to them.

10.6 REALISM AND CONCEPTUAL SCHEMES

Where does Davidson stand on Realism? It is tempting to think that his commitment to the principle of charity is sufficient to convict him of anti-Realism. Realism's independence dimension makes it possible that we could be completely wrong about the world. The principle of charity denies that we could: for the most part, if we believe that p, then p.

However, before we give in to this temptation,[8] we need to examine the direction of dependency (cf. the discussion of the bizarre theory of truth in section 4.3). Realism is threatened only if the world is dependent on the believer. This seems not to be the Davidsonian view. The view seems rather to be that beliefs are somehow dependent on the world. Given that the world is a certain way, Davidson claims, we cannot interpret anyone as believing that it is any other way. I have argued that this claim is quite false; nevertheless, it is not anti-Realist.

This is an illustration of the importance of Maxim 2. Semantic theories may lead a person into anti-Realism (4.3); but such theories do not, on their own, amount to anti-Realism. This is as true of the Davidsonian theory of interpretation as it is of the rejection of correspondence truth.

One paper, 'On the Very Idea of a Conceptual Scheme' (Davidson 1984: 183–98), does seem to cast doubt on Davidson's Realism. The main conclusion of that paper is closely linked to the principle of charity, and is something of a *reductio* of Davidsonianism: the 'very idea' makes no sense. As a result, no sense can be made of the idea that people differ in their conceptual schemes: for example, that Ptolemy's astronomy is a different scheme from Galileo's; that a Buddhist's scheme is different from a physicalist's; that ours is different from the ancients'.

Davidson's argument starts by associating conceptual schemes with languages and assuming that schemes are identical if their associated languages are intertranslatable. He goes on to argue for the controversial premise that something is a language only if it can be translated into our language. So something could be a conceptual scheme only if its language could be translated into ours. But such a language could not express an *alternative* scheme. The argument has been ably criticized by Nicholas Rescher: 'the key category in this area is surely not *translation* but *interpretation*' (1980: 326). I would prefer to say that the key category is explanation.

A realist about reference is in a good position to defend a common-sense view of what it is like to discover someone with a different conceptual scheme. Armed with our theory of reference and best theory of the world, we set about explaining the person. (1) We discover that the person's language divides up the world differently: he is committed to the same entities, but groups them differently or makes distinctions that we do not make (e.g. the Eskimos *vis-á-vis* snow), with the result that his words are not co-referential with ours. (2) We discover that he has a term for entities which we have not previously noticed: perhaps his environment contains a species that we have not discovered. As a result of our investigation of him we change our view of the world, and introduce a new term into our language. (3) We discover that he has a term for an entity we know not to exist. We may introduce that term into our language to express this fact and to describe his beliefs. In all these cases we discover that a person whose language we could not (to a degree) translate has a different conceptual scheme.

The significance of translation is perhaps even less than this suggests. It is surely part of the atheist's conceptual scheme that there are no gods. Yet, to express this central difference between him and the theist, he uses the very same language that the theist uses. One can have concepts, and yet think them empty. People can differ in their conceptual schemes by holding true different sentences in one language.[9]

In the course of his argument for the controversial premise that something is a language only if it can be translated into our language, Davidson says a number of things that cast doubt on his Realism. Kuhn's and Whorf's acceptance of the idea of a conceptual scheme depends, Davidson claims, on a certain 'dualism': 'I want to urge that this . . . dualism of scheme and content, of organizing system and something waiting to be organized, cannot be made intelligible and defensible' (1984: 189). The dualism requires that 'there be something neutral and common that lies outside all schemes' (p. 190). He rightly sees that for Kuhn this neutral something ('nature') is a mere thing-in-itself (9.2). Davidson certainly rejects this world. And it is the world that Rorty applauds Davidson for losing (Rorty 1982: 14–16).[10] However, Davidson seems to go further: he gives up 'dependence on the concept of an uninterpreted reality, something outside all schemes and science' (1984: 198). I so doing, he claims not to 'give up the world'; but one wonders. In what sense is there, for him, *any* reality independent of theory?

Davidson's later comments should remove doubts about his Realism. Thus, referring to the above paper, he remarks that giving up the dualism 'does not mean that we must give up the idea of an objective world independent of our knowledge of it, (1984: xviii). Very recently, in talking about his discussions of truth, he says that he 'was concerned to reject the doctrine that either reality or truth depends on our epistemic powers' (1990: 304–5).

In any case, the realist about reference need not accept Davidson's controversial premise or his principle of charity. Without them, Davidsonianism could be no threat to Realism.

NOTES

1   The denial was implicit, as least, in his earlier writings on semantics; e.g. 'Truth and Meaning' (1984: 17–36). Davidson no longer calls his notion of truth a 'correspondence' one; see ch. 3, n. 4, above.

2   McDowell obtained 'aid and comfort from Hilary Putnam's 1976 John Locke Lectures' (1978: 111n.), pt I of Putnam 1978. This is not surprising, since the lectures have a Davidsonian ring to them. That they should have this is surprising, however, given Putnam's earlier decisive refutation of Davidsonian semantics: '*this* is a *theory* of . . . *meaning?*' (1975b: 261).

3   Putnam (1978) may also make this mistake about Field (Devitt 1980b: 402). This would be ironic, since Field takes his view that reference is a 'second order' physical relation from Putnam's suggestions about the mind (1975a: 313–14).

4   McDowell finds Field's treatment of Convention T 'contumelious', no less (McDowell 1978: 119).

5   I also criticized Davidson's view that the sort of theory we want is, in some sense, a theory of the speaker's understanding (1981a: 92–110; see also 14.4–14.6 below).

6   Among the many others who subscribe to some version of these principles are Putnam (1978: 38–41; 1981: 117–19) and Dennett (1978: 17–22). Schiffer (1981) subscribes to a related principle, a principle of 'reliability'.

7   Janet Levin's very persuasive critique of principles of rationality casts doubt even on this (1988).

8   As I did in the first edition (1984a: 180) and as Papineau (1987) does (cf. my 1991b).

9 For more along these lines, see the critique of linguistic relativism in Devitt and Sterelny 1987: 172–84. See Aune 1987 for another criticism of Davidson's view of conceptual schemes.

10 In the first edition, I took Davidson's lost world to be Realism's world of physical entities (1984a: 180). Roberto Salinas (1988) criticizes this mistake and has interesting suggestions about the relation between Davidson's discussion of conceptual schemes and Realism.

11

Rorty's Mirrorless World

11.1 INTRODUCTION

In his book *Philosophy and the Mirror of Nature* (1979), Richard Rorty rejects the view that our thoughts or our sentences 'mirror', or in any other way 'correspond to', nature. Why? The main reason is clear. The view is part of the sceptical problematic which has dominated modern philosophy and which Rorty thinks should be set aside.[1]

That problematic starts from the assumption that we have mental representations (thoughts) or linguistic representations (sentences) of reality. The sceptic doubts the accuracy of these representations. The non-sceptic affirms their accuracy: they correspond to reality, and so are true. Rorty wants no part of this. He urges a view of truth derived from Davidson. There is no (non-trivial) question of representations corresponding or failing to correspond to reality; hence the problem of scepticism dissolves. Philosophy cannot 'underwrite or debunk claims to knowledge' (1979: 3). *A priori* foundationalism – indeed, epistemology as a whole – is dead. The philosopher should 'give up the desire for confrontation and constraint', replacing this role of 'cultural overseer' with that of the 'informed dilettante'. We should take up hermeneutics; we should engage in 'conversation' (pp. 315–18), be 'edifying without being constructive' (p. 360).

In brief, Rorty thinks that philosophers are obsessed with scepticism. His message to us is: stop it, or you will go blind.

There is no doubt that the correspondence theory of truth has been part of the sceptical problematic. And, as a naturalistic philosopher, I agree with Rorty that we should free ourselves from that problematic and the *a priori* view of philosophy (5.8). Philosophy is indeed not an 'all-encompassing discipline which legitimizes or grounds the others' (p. 6). I welcome Rorty's historical discussion in support of this view. However, I have two objections to Rorty's position and one worry about it.

First objection: Rorty clearly thinks that we *need* to reject the correspondence theory in order to free ourselves from the sceptical problematic. Yet surely there is no such necessary connection between semantics and epistemology (Maxim 5). We can abandon the sceptical problematic because we see 'the quest for certainty' as essentially hopeless and because we think that there is no place in a scientific world-view for the *a priori* epistemology implicit in such a search. Furthermore, once we are free of the problematic, it is an open, empirical question whether a correspondence theory of truth has a place in the total world-view. I think that it has (chapter 6).

Second objection: Why should the rejection of scepticism and *a priori* philosophy lead us into hermeneutics? Naturalistic philosophers see a systematic and constructive role for philosophy in conjunction with science.

The worry: There is an aura of anti-realism about Rorty's discussion. Rorty is aware of this and tries to allay it. A central part of his meta-philosophy is that we should move, as he puts it in the title of a recent paper, 'Beyond Realism and Anti-Realism' (1986a), for that issue is at the centre of the discredited problematic (1979: 139–40). I sympathize. However, the issue must be settled firmly the realist way before we leave it behind. It is not obvious that Rorty has so settled it. Indeed, Rorty is usually regarded as an anti-realist.

I shall start by removing the worry about realism. I shall then go on to sustain the two objections.

11.2 RORTY ON REALISM

The aura of anti-realism in Rorty arises mainly from his rejection of the correspondence theory of truth and from his enthusiasm for Kuhn. I shall argue that Rorty is, nevertheless, a realist.

Just as Rorty thinks that the correspondence theory played an important role in the sceptical problematic, so also he thinks that it played an important role in the development of the realism issue. And, of course, he is right (4.5). Nevertheless, as I have argued, a metaphysical doctrine like Realism is quite distinct from the correspondence theory of truth (4.1–4.4). So his rejection of that theory does not show that he is opposed to Realism.

Nor can we draw any anti-Realist conclusions from Rorty's occasional approving references to the pragmatists' approach to language (e.g. 1979: 265–6). In so far as Rorty is committed to a 'pragmatic theory of truth', his commitment is only to the deflationary strand in pragmatist thinking about truth (1986b: 333–8). Robert Brandom (1988), whom Rorty cites approvingly (p. 335n.), has emphasized this strand, distinguishing it from the much more radical 'stereotypical' strand that leads to acceptance of appropriate instances of a schema like '*s* is useful if and only if *p*'. The deflationary strand is metaphysically neutral. The stereotypical strand is not; though an argument would still be needed to get from it to anti-Realism (4.3).

Of course, *relativism* about truth leads straightforwardly to anti-Realism via the equivalence thesis: *s* is not true 'absolutely', but only relative to *x*; so it is not the case that *p* 'absolutely', but only relative to *x* (4.3). There are certainly plenty of signs of *epistemic* relativism in Rorty: *s* is justified only relative to *x*. Epistemic relativism is often confused with relativism about truth (13.1), although they are in fact very different (Field 1982: 562–7; Maxim 5). I see no sign that Rorty confuses them.

Where, then, does Rorty stand on Realism? He has been quite explicit. He refers to it as a 'banal anti-idealist thesis' and 'as no more than out-dated rhetoric' (1986b: 354).[2] What are we to make of this dismissal? The mistaken linking of the realism issue to issues about truth is at the centre of the answer.[3] But we can say more.

Rorty clearly regards the existence dimension of Realism as too obvious to be worth stating (see, e.g., 1982: 14). The interpretative problem is over the independence dimension. I detect three strands in Rorty's thought about independence, and hence about Realism. Strand 1 is that the independence dimension is true, but boring. Strand 2 is that in so far as the dimension is clear, it is trivial. Strand 3, which is related to this, is that the controversy is not really over this clear but trivial doctrine, but over an unclear and misguided doctrine about other sorts of entities altogether.

Strand 1 arises simply out of the abandonment of the sceptical problematic, and so is congenial (chapter 5). However, I think that the naturalistic philosopher should resist the suggestion that the Realism issue is *completely* boring. It *ought* to be boring; but as long as anti-Realism is alive, well, and living in Britain, France, America, the East, and even in some areas of Australia, the issue retains some interest. Realism is like atheism.[4]

The rejection of the sceptical problematic is, of course, central to Rorty's philosophy, and so it is not hard to see signs of strand 1 in his work. Signs are also to be found, interestingly enough, in his discussion of Kuhn.

Rorty is enthusiastic about Kuhn, but his enthusiasm is qualified. What he really likes is Kuhn's epistemology: the rejection of the 'given' and the emphasis on theory-ladenness. He does not accept the two elements of Kuhn's philosophy that suggest anti-Realism. First, Rorty distances himself from Kuhn's ' "idealistic"-sounding' view that the proponents of different theories ' "see different things" or "live in different worlds" ' (1979: 324).[5] Indeed, he thinks it absurd to say 'that we make objects by using words' (p. 276).[6] Second, he does not subscribe to the incommensurability thesis that pushes Kuhn into his idealistic metaphysics. Kuhn's incommensurability thesis is fundamentally semantic: the languages of different paradigms do not share meanings; so the theories of different paradigms cannot stand in the logical relations required for theory comparison (9.6). Rorty has an incommensurability thesis, but it is epistemic.

By 'commensurable' I mean able to be brought under a set of rules which will tell us how rational agreement can be reached on what would settle the issue on every point where statements seem to conflict. (p. 316)

He distinguishes this sense of 'commensurable' from the semantic one (p. 316 n.). His incommensurability thesis is: there is no 'algorithm for theory choice' (p. 324). This thesis is quite congenial to a naturalistic Realism.

The signs of strand 1 in Rorty are not clear, because his discussion of realism is influenced as much by his Davidsonian view of the mind and language as by his rejection of the sceptical problematic. Indeed, he writes – quite falsely, I shall argue (11.4) – as if the Davidsonian view is part and parcel of that rejection.

Strand 2 arises out of that Davidsonian view. More generally, it arises out of Rorty's opposition to the correspondence theory. He does not think that there is 'a clear and non-trivial sense to be given' to the notion of ' "facts" and "objective relations" independent of the mind' (1976: 327). For him, the independence in question is to be made clear by giving a Davidsonian construal of the view that 'it is the *world* that determines the truth' of beliefs and utterances (1982: 12). And this construal makes the view trivial.[7]

The triviality comes from the principle of charity: 'Most of our beliefs . . . simply *must* be true.' For 'what could count as evidence that the vast majority of them were not' (p. 12)? As a result, 'we shall automatically be "in touch with the world" ' (p. 13); 'truth as correspondence' becomes an 'uncontroversial triviality' (p. 15).

Since the independence of the known world of common sense and science is trivial, Rorty thinks that the realist must be insisting on the independence of some other world. This introduces strand 3. What the realist wants is the notion of a world *so* 'independent of our knowledge' that it might, for all we know, prove to contain none of the things we have always thought we were talking about.... [This] must be the notion of something *completely* unspecified and unspecifiable – the thing-in-itself, in fact. (p. 14)

The controversy has been over a world 'which could vary independently of the antics of the familiar objects; ... something rather like the thing-in-itself' (1986b: 354n.); 'the purely vacuous notion of the ineffable cause of sense and goal of intellect' (1982: 15).

According to strand 3, therefore, the traditional disagreement between realists and idealists has *never* been over the familiar world mentioned in my doctrine Realism. It is not just that that doctrine loses its interest once the sceptical problematic is set aside, as in strand 1; the doctrine is trivial, hence banal, even within that problematic.

Rorty's attitude to the mysterious thing-in-itself is brought out nicely in the title of a paper I have quoted frequently above, 'The World Well Lost' (1982: 3–18). The claim that there is such an independent world is certainly not trivial, but it is unclear and uncalled for.

Strands 2 and 3 come from Rorty's Davidsonian semantics. In the next section I shall consider the bearing of this semantics on Realism. But first I shall briefly assess strand 3.

We can certainly do without the world that Rorty wants to lose, a Kantian thing-in-itself for ever beyond our ken (12.5, 13.2). And there is no doubt that disputes about it have played a part in the realism issue. Nevertheless, I shall be so bold as to disagree with Rorty about the history. I think that the central issue in the realism dispute has been over the existence and independent nature of the *known* world; it has been over Realism.

Consider one of the greatest anti-realists, Kant. His view of the noumenal world of things-in-themselves has been important. However, his view of the phenomenal world of appearances has surely been more so. This world is the known one of stones, trees, cats, and the objects of science. Kant's idea that this world is partly our construction – for how else could it be known? – has dominated two centuries of anti-realism.

Passmore has this to say about the last century: 'The main tendency of nineteenth-century thought was towards the conclusion that both 'things' and facts about things are dependent for their existence and their nature upon the operations of a mind' (1966: 174). It is clear that the things in question are the known ones, not the ineffable

Polemics

ones. The popularity of the Kantian idea has not diminished in this
century (13.1).

11.3 DAVIDSONIAN SEMANTICS AND REALISM

According to Rorty's strand 2, we need Davidsonian semantics to
make any sense of the independence talked of in Realism. And then,
he thinks, Realism becomes trivial.

I think Realism is clear enough without Davidsonian semantics.
This is not to say that the mind-dependency claims made by *anti*-
Realists are always clear. However, Realists reject all mind dependencies, whether clear or not, except for the familiar causal relations
between minds and the external world; we throw stones, plant trees,
see cats, and so on (2.2). More can certainly be said to clarify the
independence dimension. I shall do so in chapter 13 (see also section
14.3).

Rorty's distaste for traditional epistemological and metaphysical
issues like Realism is so great that he hankers after a language in
which they cannot be formulated (1986b: 351). And in a recent paper
(1986a) he writes as if he has already found such a language. I can
see no justification for this rather romantic attempt to break with the
past.

Before considering whether Davidsonian semantics makes Realism
trivial, we should mention the more disturbing question: Does that
semantics make Realism *false*?

The reason for thinking that it does is the principle of charity.
As Rorty puts it, 'we know perfectly well what the world is like
and could not possibly be wrong about it (1982: 14). (It was the
Realists' insistence on a level of independence unobtainable from
the Davidsonian perspective that encouraged Rorty's strand 3 identification of the Realist's world with a thing-in-itself.) However, our
discussion of Davidson showed that the principle of charity alone is
insufficient to establish anti-Realism. And it is otherwise clear that
Davidson is not an anti-Realist (10.6).

Rorty's comforting view that we cannot be wrong about the world
reflects not anti-Realism, but a false theory of people and their
language.

Davidsonian semantics does not undermine Realism; but does it
make Realism trivial? The semantics does trivialize the view that 'it
is the *world* that determines the truth'. However, this view is not
essential to Realism. Furthermore, anti-Realists think of the world as

dependent on us in various ways, and it is not trivial to reject these dependencies. Davidsonian semantics alone will certainly not suffice for that rejection.

In sum, strand 1 of Rorty's thought about Realism is near enough correct: Realism is true, and ought to be boring. Strand 2 is mistaken: we do not need Davidsonian semantics to make Realism clear; and that semantics does not make Realism trivial. Strand 3 is wrong in claiming that the traditional dispute was over things-in-themselves, but right in wanting to have nothing to do with such dim entities.

Having set to rest the worry about Realism, I shall move on to the first objection and the issue of correspondence truth.

11.4 THE CORRESPONDENCE THEORY, THE SCEPTICAL PROBLEMATIC, AND DAVIDSONIAN SEMANTICS

Rorty's rejection of any correspondence theory of truth (other than his trivial Davidsonian one) is total. We must discard 'the notion of the mind as Mirror of Nature' (1979: 170). 'We have to drop the notion of correspondence for sentences as well as for thoughts, and see sentences as connected with other sentences rather than with the world' (pp. 371–2). 'Truth' does 'not name a relation between utterances on the one hand and "the world" on the other' (1976: 322). What mainly distinguishes contemporary correspondence theories from the pragmatic view that Rorty takes from Davidson is their commitment to 'word–world relationships for individual statements'. There are no such relationships (pp. 322). Rather, the language as a whole relates to reality. 'Nothing will explicate "theory-independent truth"' (1979: 281). In particular, reference does not do so. We have no need of a theory of reference.

What has Rorty got against the correspondence theory? Once again, Davidsonian semantics plays a large role.

The major thing that Rorty has against the correspondence theory is its guilt by association with the sceptical problematic (a view we have come across before: 9.5, 9.8). Indeed, he sees that problematic under every correspondence theorist's bed.[8] On the one hand, an interest in a notion of reference that makes 'language safe for "truth-as-correspondence-with-reality"' is taken to be an epistemological interest (1976: 331). On the other hand, rejection of Rorty's Davidsonian view of truth is taken to involve the belief 'that we have, deep down inside us, a criterion for telling whether we are in touch with reality or not, when we are in the Truth' (1982: xxxviii). Both these elements are to be found in Rorty's distinction between 'pure' and 'impure' philosophy of language. The impure is 'explicitly epistemological' (1979: 257), and is 'roughly coextensive with' the theory of reference (p. 270). The impure is 'burdened with the task of blocking scepticism' (p. 288). The 'de-epistemologized' (p. 259), pure philosophy of language is near enough identified with Davidsonian semantics (p. 299). The pure is not concerned 'to explain the relationship between words and the world' (p. 262) or with ' "how language hooks onto the world" ' (p. 265).

In brief, Rorty thinks that to resist Davidson is to hanker after an answer to the sceptic. It seems as if Davidsonian semantics is not to be judged simply on its merits as a theory of language, but rather, borrowing the words of one of Rorty's heroes, that semantics is needed 'to shew the fly the way out of the fly bottle' (Wittgenstein 1953: §309).

Doubtless the interest of some philosophers in non-Davidsonian semantics has been epistemological. It is plausible to suppose this of verificationists like Michael Dummett, for example. However, there is no basis for supposing it of many others, particularly those associated with causal theories of reference.[9] There is no necessary connection between purity and Davidson.

This reaction to Rorty reflects my commitment to Maxim 5: Distinguish the issue of correspondence truth from any epistemic issue.

The correspondence theory of truth and the theory of reference are parts of a theory of language and mind, not attempts to justify knowledge (chapter 6). In my view, sentence meaning is to be explained largely in terms of truth conditions; those conditions are to be explained in terms of syntactic structure and the reference of words;[10] reference must then be explained in part causally, in part descriptively. I have called the doctrine of truth involved in this explanation 'Correspondence Truth', even though it lacks the obscure mirroring metaphor of the traditional correspondence theory, because it is sufficiently like the traditional theory (chapter 3). Scepticism has nothing to do with Correspondence Truth, and is set aside anyway (chapter 5).

Rorty claims that my correspondence theory succumbs to 'the pre-Wittgensteinian urge' 'to coalesce the justificatory story and the causal story' (1986b: 353–4). An example will help to show that this is not so. Consider the sentence 'Amanda is a cuscus.' It has a simple structure, in virtue of which its truth value depends on reference in the following way: it is true if and only if there is an object designated by 'Amanda' and that object is among the ones that 'cuscus' applies to. Structure, reference, and reality are the way they are, independently of our opinions. Thus, if the sentence is true, it objectively corresponds to objective reality. This does absolutely nothing to show that it *is* true. The question of justification is left untouched by the theory.

The choice between such contemporary correspondence theories and Davidsonian semantics is an empirical one. The choice should not be influenced by the fact that the ancestors of correspondence theories kept company with bad epistemology.

Rorty has a response to this line of thought. He raises a very good question: 'what data [must] the philosophy of language explain' (1982: xxiv)? In particular, what do correspondence notions of truth and reference explain? He dismisses the answer, the success of science (pp. xxiv–xxv), rightly in my view (6.6, 7.3). In the next section we shall consider his dismissal of another answer. Since he can find no satisfactory answer, he suspects the worst: in denying a concern for scepticism, correspondence theorists are trying to conceal something; they are closet foundationalists:

semantics has *not* become completely disjoined from epistemology, despite advertisements to that effect. Most philosophers of language want ... an account of our representations of the world which guarantees that we have not lost touch with it, an answer to the sceptic which flows from a general account of the nature of representation. (1982: 128)

I see no basis for Rorty's worst fears. Nevertheless, he has hit on the weakest point of the correspondence theory: the lack of a convincing and agreed account of why we need such a theory in the first place. It is certainly very difficult to say why we do need it. My best attempt is in chapter 6.

Perhaps this solution is wrong, and another one right. Perhaps there is no solution, and correspondence truth should be abandoned. Whatever the truth of the matter, sceptical concerns play no role in the debate. In insisting that those concerns are central to correspondence truth, Rorty shows all the zeal of a convert: having rejected sin, he sees it everywhere.

Finally, Rorty's view is a little paradoxical. *Prima facie*, it is Davidsonian semantics, not the theory of reference, that attempts to answer the sceptic. Davidson claims to establish the aforementioned principle of charity, according to which most of our beliefs must be true. What could be a more complete answer to the sceptic? Davidson himself thinks that he has answered the sceptic (1983: 309–10).[11] Rorty deals with this embarrassment ingeniously and at some length, arguing that what Davidson really does is not answer the sceptic, but repudiate his question (1986b: 342–4). I am not convinced.

Rorty's views on the relation between scepticism and Davidsonian semantics undoubtedly provide the principal reason for his rejection of correspondence truth. However, there are other reasons. In the rest of this section I shall briefly consider some other things he says in support of Davidsonian semantics and against the correspondence theory. In the next section I shall consider a reason that is relatively independent of that semantics.

(1) As already indicated, Rorty subscribes to the principle of charity. He acknowledges that Davidson's argument for the principle seems open to the charge of verificationism (1982: 5–6). He makes a valiant attempt to save the argument despite this, by claiming that the charge depends on taking the notion of truth in question as the correspondence one, whereas it is no more than the 'homely and shopworn' notion (1979: 306–11). I don't think that it does depend on this. In any case, I have argued that the principle is false (10.5).

(2) Rorty attributes to Davidson the view that the only philosophy of language that we need is that of the 'field linguist' (1986b: 339). We need only what is required for that 'linguist's translation-manual-cum-ethnographic-report' (p. 341). This view – stemming from what I have called 'the interpretative perspective – is alleged to show that we do not need the correspondence notion of truth (p. 342).

The only argument that Rorty detects in Davidson for this limited view of the philosophy of language is that the 'various "confrontationalist" metaphors [that Rorty associates with correspondence] are more trouble than they are worth' (p. 345). This argument is surely inadequate. Why is Davidson's view any more plausible than the following: the only monetary economics we need is that of the 'field economist' interested in preparing an exchange–manual? The philosopher's interest in language, like the economist's in money, is in *explaining* a social phenomenon. Restriction to the impoverished theoretical machinery of the field-worker seems completely inappropriate in both cases.

I do not suppose that the field linguist needs a worked-out correspondence *theory* of language, including a theory of reference (10.4). However, it seems to me likely that he does need correspondence *notions* of truth and reference in preparing his manual; good translation will require that he has caught on to these notions, even though he is unlikely to have a theory of them.

(3)   Davidsonian semantics seems to be 'semanticalist', as we have seen (10.2). Rorty resists this criticism, describing Davidson as a 'non-reductive physicalist' (p. 345), by claiming that the notion of truth used by Davidson is not itself explanatory, but merely 'disquotational' (pp. 345–8; cf. Davidson 1990: 282–95). But how can the certral notion in a theory of meaning not be explanatory (3.4)?

(4)   Finally, apparently under the influence of Davidson (but see Davidson 1990: 302–3), Rorty seems to think that the correspondence theory seeks the impossible; for the attempt to 'see language-as-a-whole in relation to something else to which it applies' (1982: xix) demands 'some transcendental standpoint outside our present set of representations from which we can inspect the relations between those representations and their object' (1979: 293; see also Fine 1986a: 131–2; 1986b: 151–2). 'It is the impossible attempt to step out of our skins' (1982: xix). This is the same as the final objection of the radical philosophers of science to Realism and Correspondence Truth (9.8). I shall consider it when discussing Putnam on 'the God's Eye View' (12.6).

11.5   RORTY AGAINST REFERENCE

Rorty's final objection to the correspondence theory is that it requires a philosophically significant theory of reference, which cannot be had.

Rorty contemplates one task for a theory of reference, and hence for a correspondence theory, that is free of epistemology. It is the task of helping with the problem of 'ancestral error' (1976: 324); we would like an account of our superiority to our ancestors which sees the history of theories as being one of gradual progress (p. 321). The theory of reference – in particular, the historical causal theory – is thought to help, because it implies that our ancestors were mostly referring, despite their many false beliefs. Progress can then be seen as a steady increase in the number of true beliefs that we have about the referents. We are always in touch with reality, and are gradually finding out more and more about it.

Rorty's response to this idea is dismissive. It is also extremely complicated (1976: 324–31; 1979: 288–93). He draws a distinction between three notions of reference: the ordinary notion of 'talking about', which is opaque, and hence allows 'reference to the non-existent'; the philosophical notion featured in the causal theory, which is transparent, and concerned with word–world connections;

and a bridging notion between the two. He alleges that the argument for the causal theory has come from confusing these notions in considering our intuitions. These intuitions mostly concern the ordinary notion of talking about, and partly concern the bridging notion. They show that a description theory of the 'cluster' sort proposed by Strawson and Searle applies to the ordinary notion, except in a few 'special cases' (Rorty 1976: 327). The philosophical notion 'is just not something that anybody has intuitions about' (p. 329), and should be dispensed with.

The above task for the theory of reference remains; but fulfilling it 'is too slight to merit the title of "theory"' (1979: 288); it simply requires

a decision-procedure for solving difficult cases in historiography, anthropological description and the like – cases where nothing save tact and imagination will serve ... [It] is a question about the best procedure for comparing large coherent sets of false beliefs (other epochs, cultures, etc.) with ours. (p. 293)

The procedure is constrained only by our interest in finding a description of the situation which 'avoids paradox and maximizes coherence' (p. 291).

I have three comments. First, helping with ancestral error is certainly something that we should hope for from a theory of reference, but it is not the main task for the theory. That task is helping to explain language (chapter 6).

Second, if my view of the task for reference is correct, the case for causal theories goes beyond appeals to intuitions. Description theories cannot account for the reference of all words, because they simply pass the referential buck to other words. Causal theories offer the only prospects for the ultimate explanation of reference required by the correspondence theory – the explanation of the links between language and the world (3.3).

Third, with the help of his three notions of reference, Rorty does seem able to explain away the difficulties for his view raised by causal theorists. However, if the complexities he introduces into the account of reference are not to be *ad hoc*, they need a justification that is independent of these difficulties. In particular, why suppose that there are the three notions of reference? Rorty thinks that the transparent/opaque distinction supplies a justification. I disagree.

It is plausible to claim that, in ordinary usage, sentences of the form '*x* refers to *y*' are often opaque. If they are, then 'refers' is like many other verbs in English. Examples that Quine uses in his classic discussion 'Opacity in Certain Verbs' (1960: 151–6) include 'looking for', 'hunt', and 'want'. The problem for Rorty is that, if 'refers' is indeed one of these verbs, it will *also* be the case that some sentences of the above form will be transparent. Sentences containing such intentional verbs can be construed either transparently or opaquely, as Quine points out. This is not to say that the *verbs* are ambiguous. The ambiguity lies in the *constructions*; the sentences are syntactically ambiguous.[12]

It follows from this that a philosophical notion of reference cannot be distinguished from the ordinary one on the ground that the former is transparent whereas the latter is opaque. Furthermore, the ordinary notion *is* concerned with word–world connections, most strikingly so in transparent constructions. This is not to say that philosophical notions of reference do not differ from the ordinary one. The ordinary notion is very vague. Philosophers tend to make it more precise in various ways and to use it only in transparent constructions.

Since the sharp distinction which Rorty draws between the ordinary and the philosophical notion of reference is spurious, the motivation for supposing that there is a bridging notion disappears.

The collapse of Rorty's sharp distinction prevents the isolation of the philosophical notion of reference, concerned with word–world connections, from the intuitions that Kripke and others relied on in arguing for the causal theory. Our intuitions must involve the ordinary notion; but if that notion is simply a vaguer version of a philosophical one, then those intuitions are directly relevant to any theory containing the philosophical one. What Kripke and others did was to compare our intuitions about the truth value of ordinary transparent sentences using 'refer' with philosophical theories of reference. They claimed that the intuitions decisively favoured the causal theory for names and natural-kind terms. (Of course, comparison with such intuitions should not settle the fate of a theory. The intuitions simply reflect folk wisdom, and the folk may not be wise, as Rorty would be among the first to insist; 1982: xxix–xxx. However, that said, it is an undoubted plus for a theory to be in accord with the folk.)

The failure of Rorty's attempt to isolate the philosophical notion means that the full weight of his case against the causal theory's account of word–world connections must be borne by his response to the causal theory of the ordinary notion.

We accommodate his mistaken view that the ordinary notion is opaque by considering the notion only in opaque sentences. We then have sentences about which Rorty has intuitions. He claims that, normally, a person opaquely refers to whatever he *thinks* he is referring to (1976: 324); he is 'the sole judge' (p. 325); he refers to the object that most of his associated beliefs are true of; that object is the 'intentional object' of his thought (1979: 289; 1986b: 340–1). In brief, Rorty rejects the claims of causal theorists, and assumes a description theory for the ordinary notion of reference and for determining intentional objects. If he is right, this will count against the causal theory's account of the philosophical notion of reference (though, of course, Rorty does not think so, because he mistakenly thinks that he has isolated that notion).

How does Rorty deal with all the Kripkean cases which seem to show that the description theory is wrong? He treats them as special cases. They are special in that 'we know something [the subjects] don't' (1979: 289); they are what I call cases of 'ignorance and error'. In such cases, he agrees, the causal theory applies; but in general the description theory is correct. This manoeuvre is as *ad hoc* as can be. Any theory can be saved by excluding all counter-examples from its domain. Causal theorists claim to have a theory that applies to all cases. According to this theory, people are never the sole judge of the referent of the names and natural-kind terms they use. A person may have the knowledge required by the description theory, but that knowledge is irrelevant to reference. If the causal theory works generally, it is clearly to be preferred to Rorty's *ad hoc* modification of the description theory.

What reasons does Rorty have for thinking that the causal theory does not work generally? One reason is implicit. He thinks that the causal theory cannot handle 'reference to the non-existent', which is allowed by the ordinary notion. This sort of reference is undoubtedly a problem for the causal theory. I think that it can be handled (1981a: ch. 6). As far as reference to existents is concerned, Rorty assumes, in what seems a blatantly question-begging way, that a description theory normally applies. He does not respond to the evidence that the causal theory always applies.[13]

11.6 NO EXCUSE FOR HERMENEUTICS

This chapter began by laying to rest the worry about Realism occasioned by Rorty. I have now finished my discussion of the first objection to Rorty. The various reasons he has for rejecting the correspondence theory of truth, including its alleged association with the sceptical problematic, are not persuasive. I finish by considering the second objection.

Rorty not only rejects our past, with its interest in scepticism and correspondence; he offers a vision of the future. Philosophers should emulate 'the three most important philosophers of our century: Wittgenstein, Heidegger, and Dewey'. What Rorty likes about these philosophers is that 'their later work is therapeutic rather than constructive, edifying rather than systematic, designed to make the reader question his own motives for philosophizing rather than to supply him with a new philosophical program' (1979: 5–6). He calls what we should practice 'hermeneutics', while distancing himself from some of the views, particularly idealist ones, that have been associated with that term.

The basis that Rorty gives for this prescription is inadequate. I agree that we should set the sceptical problematic aside. However, we should move not into hermeneutics, but into systematic and constructive naturalistic philosophy.

One example of this philosophy is the dispute that has occupied the last two sections of this paper. Do we need a correspondence notion of truth to explain language? Rorty does not – certainly, should not – suppose that his Davidsonian view that we do not need it can be established *a priori*. The question is a crucial empirical one for a systematic, constructive theory of language. Of course, the question is not a *low-level* empirical one; but then neither are many empirical questions in, say, physics. The fact that we try to answer the question from an armchair does not prevent it from being empirical; we bring with us to the chair memories and books recording the relevant evidence.

Occasionally Rorty writes as if a philosophy that has gone naturalistic is no longer philosophy (1979: 188, 384–5). This seems like a boring question about what to call 'philosophy'. What matters is that some empirical sciences, like the study of language, have high-level conceptual problems, including some about the relation of those sciences to others, which philosophers are by training particularly suited to tackle.

Just as there is a place for a naturalistic philosophy of language, so there is one for a naturalistic epistemology. Rorty rejects the possibility of such an epistemology because, following Quine, he assumes that it will simply be psychology: it will describe our ways of learning about the world, but will not say how we ought to learn about the world (pp. 221–30). Rorty thinks that such a study does not merit the title 'epistemology'. Perhaps not, but that is not all there is to naturalized epistemology. Such epistemology does tackle the normative question. Using the evidence of our epistemic successes and failures in science and in ordinary life, we theorize about how best to learn about the world. Learning about learning is an empirical activity, just like learning about anything else (5.8).[14]

The study of language and knowledge comes within cognitive science. That science generates many problems to which philosophy can make a systematic and constructive contribution. So also do physics, mathematics, and biology. And what about moral, aesthetic, political, and social theories?

In conclusion, philosophy can abandon the sceptical problematic without abandoning correspondence truth and without limiting itself to the edifying practices of the informed dilettante. Rorty has not shown us that it should abandon that truth and limit itself to those practices. The aura of anti-Realism in Rorty's discussion is misleading: Rorty is a Realist.

NOTES

1 This chapter is based on my 1988b.
2 These comments are on a statement of realism in my critique of Dummett (1983a: 76), which is the basis for chapter 14 below.
3 Arthur Fine also dismisses the realism issue for this reason (1986a, 1986b).
4 Hence Rorty's claim that I regard Realism as 'an interesting and controversial thesis' (1986b: 354) is a bit misleading.
5 See also 1982: xlvi n,. in which he distances himself from Berkeley, and p. xlvii n., in which he distances himself from Goodman.
6 Rorty's reaction to such talk in Kuhn and Goodman is nevertheless sympathetic. He construes it metaphorically. I think that it is intended to be taken literally (9.2, 13.3).
7 The views of Davidson that have most influenced Rorty are found in the 1973 paper 'On the Very Idea of a Conceptual Scheme' (Davidson 1984: 183–98). Rorty was also influenced by Stroud 1968. For some comments on Rorty's interpretation of Davidson, see Davidson 1990: 279–88.
8 So too does Fine. And like Rorty, Fine favours a Davidsonian view of truth, and finds reason in this combination of opinions for setting the realism issue aside (1986a, 1986b).
9 In their criticisms of Rorty, Chris Murphy (1981: 342–3) and Michael Losonsky (1985) also argue that the theory of reference is not linked to the sceptical problematic.

10 This does *not* entail that word meanings either are *learnt* before (cf. Rorty 1979: 303 4) or are the *evidence* for (cf. Rorty 1986b: 343) sentence meanings. Word meanings are prior in the order of explanation, not necessarily in the orders of understanding and evidence.

11 Charlie Martin describes Davidson's position as 'the New Cartesianism' (1984b: 240).

12 I have used the causal theory to explain the semantics of such constructions in 1981a: 263–7.

13 I think there are reasons, arising out of Donnellan's discussion of definite descriptions (1966), for restricting the generality of the causal theory (1981a: 40–1); but these are beside the present point.

14 On this, see Chris Murphy's excellent critical notice of Rorty 1979 (1981: 343–5).

12

The Renegade Putnam

12.1 INTRODUCTION

Hilary Putnam's views have already played an important role in this book. Early Putnam (1971, 1975a, and 1975b) was a major influence on my views. My struggle with middle Putnam (1978: pt I–III) led me to a much clearer view of what the doctrines of Realism and Correspondence Truth were (chapters 2–4 above) and of the bearing of certain arguments to do with success and convergence (6.6, 7.3 and 7.6) on those doctrines. Middle Putnam has a Davidsonian argument against reference (1978: 38–41) which I hope is rebutted by the argument in chapter 10.

One concern of this chapter will be another argument from middle Putnam against reference: the argument from the alleged interest-relativity of explanation. However, my main concern will be with the anti-Realism of late Putnam (1978: pt IV; 1981; 1983; 1987); in particular with his model-theoretic argument about reference. After years at the vanguard of Realism, Putnam abandoned the cause. He finds his former position 'incoherent' (1978: 124).

Putnam's new world-view comes out most clearly in, *Reason, Truth and History* (1981). Briefly, his aim is to 'break the strangle hold' of a number of dichotomies, particularly that between 'objective and subjective views of truth and reason'. The former he associates with those committed to a 'copy' or 'correspondence' theory of truth; the latter with philosophers like Kuhn, Feyerabend, and Foucault (p. ix). He offers a neo-Kantian alternative, 'the metaphor' for which is: 'The mind and the world jointly make up the mind and the world' (p. xi). Truth is identified with idealized rational acceptability (p. 55) just as it was by Peirce. He rejects the 'God's Eye View' (p. 74) of 'metaphysical realism'; that 'externalist perspective' is replaced by an 'internalist' one (p. 49). Next, 'being rational involves having criteria of *relevance*,' and 'all our values' are involved in those criteria. 'A being with no values would have no facts either' (p. 201). This dissolution of the fact–value dichotomy leads to a 'non-alienated' view of truth (p. xii).

He earlier described the metaphysical realism he opposes as follows. It requires that

there *be* a determinate relation between terms in L and pieces (or sets of pieces) of THE WORLD . . . THE WORLD is *independent* of any particular representation we have of it . . . *truth* is . . . *radically non-epistemic*. (1978: 125)

Metaphysical realism also 'transcends . . . any one theory' (ibid.). Setting that aside, an example of metaphysical realism would be the combination of the main two doctrines I have been urging: Realism and Correspondence Truth.

He has two basic arguments against metaphysical realism and for his internalist alternative: one, the model-theoretic argument from reference; the other, the argument from values. I shall consider only the former.

However, I start with an argument that is aimed only at reference. This is an argument of middle Putnam, before he adopted an explicitly anti-Realist stance. (The argument does not appear in late Putnam; though perhaps we should see the argument from values in 1981 as a massive development of that argument.)

12.2   INTEREST-RELATIVITY OF EXPLANATION

Putnam argues that explanation is interest-relative and that, as a result, there is indeterminacy of reference (1978: 41–60).[1] He concludes that 'Field's program [for a physicalistic explanation of reference] is a species of *scientific utopianism*' (p. 58).

One problem about Putnam's doctrine of the interest-relativity of explanation is its unclarity. What counts as an 'interest'? Set that aside for a moment. Another problem is that the argument for the doctrine is brief and unpersuasive.

The argument starts with three heterogeneous examples, the first of which is as follows: 'Professor X is found stark naked in the girls' dormitory at 12 midnight.' Putnam points out that the following would be a terrible explanation:

He was stark naked in the girls' dormitory at midnight – ϵ and he could neither leave the dormitory nor put on his clothes by midnight without exceeding the speed of light. But (covering law): nothing (no professor, anyhow) can travel faster than light. (p. 42)

Why is it terrible? According to Putnam, because we want an explanation addressed to our interests in prevention or control. And if we had other interests, I take Putnam to be suggesting, we would want a different explanation. There is no absolutely good explanation, only good ones relative to this or that interest.

Why should we be pushed into this relativity of explanation? Why not explain the phenomena by the elliptical nature of requests for explanation leaving explanation as absolute as ever? In asking 'Why was Professor X stark naked in the girls' dormitory at 12 midnight?' we are asking what caused him to be in that situation, and we presuppose a whole lot of background knowledge which is obvious under the circumstances. Of course we *have* interests that make us ask *that* question; but a good answer to it is good absolutely, given the presupposed background knowledge. Much more certainly needs to be said to establish this absolutist response, but, given the familiar discussions of related problems to do with causation, we surely need a substantial argument before plunging into interest-relativity. Putnam does not provide such an argument.

Another of Putnam's examples to illustrate the interest-relativity of explanation is as follows:

> Willie Sutton (the famous bank robber) is supposed to have been asked 'Why do you rob banks?' His reply was 'That's where the money is.' Now (this example is due to Alan Garfinkel) imagine:
> (a)   a priest asked the question;
> (b)   a robber asked the question. (p. 42)

Once again, Putnam's own comments do not seem to support his relativism:

> The priest's question means: 'Why do you rob banks – *as opposed to not robbing at all?*' The robber's question means: 'Why do you rob banks – as opposed to, say, gas stations?' (pp. 43–4)

In other words, the questions are elliptical. Interests are irrelevant to what counts as a good answer to either question.

The third of Putnam's examples is much more interesting: Why does a 1-inch square peg go through a 1-inch square hole and not through a 1-inch round hole? (p. 42) An explanation in terms of the trajectories of elementary particles is not good; one based on the geometry of squares and circles is. Putnam claims that the latter explanation is good relative to certain methodological interests (p. 43).

Putnam has used this example before in discussing the mind (1975b: 295–8). It seems to raise a problem similar to those raised by functionalist explanations in general, as I have already pointed out (6.3). These explanations seem to be better ones than those that talk of the underlying physical mechanisms; certainly they have more general application. How then do the two sorts of explanation relate to each other? This is an interesting question for physicalism. Perhaps Putnam's point about methodological interests has some bearing on the answer. More needs to be said in order for us to tell. And much more needs to be said before we should accept a general doctrine that explanation is interest-relative.

The doctrine of the interest-relativity of explanation would be clear enough if it referred only to basic interests like food, shelter, and sex. However, Putnam's examples suggest that 'interest' is to be understood differently from this. It may seem at first that anything that a person might be truly said to be interested in will do, but that view is later rejected (1978: 47). This rejection is welcome; but it leaves me mystified about Putnam's doctrine. It seems as if the only appropriate interests for Putnam are those which might be described as interests in understanding and controlling nature. But then how is his position different (except verbally) from an absolutist one?

What has the alleged interest-relativity of explanation to do with reference? Putnam now thinks that Quine's doctrine of the indeterminacy of reference is true (to some considerable extent), and that this is explained by the interest-relativity of explanation. He claims this in at least three places (pp. 41, 45, 46). Yet there seems to be no argument for this claim at all! What he clearly does argue for is the claim that indeterminacy seems implausible because we overlook the interest-relativity of explanation (pp. 44–5). In overlooking this, we confuse the naturalness of a translation relative to our interests with its objective correctness. He is offering a diagnosis of our resistance to indeterminacy. Such arguments as there are here for indeterminacy itself, for the thesis that there can be several 'equivalent' manuals for translating from one language to another and that there is no fact of the matter which is right, seem to have nothing to do with the interest-relativity of explanation (pp. 44, 48–51). Our interest in rabbits will lead us to prefer a manual that translates the alien's 'gavagai' into our word for rabbit. The Martians' interest in undetached rabbit-parts will lead them to prefer one that translates it into their word for undetached rabbit-part. That does not show that each preference can be equally well met. Not does it show that there is no fact of the matter as to whether the alien is like us or like the Martians. (Compare this with the confusion of the principle of charity with epistemic claims, discussed in section 10.5).

I move on now to consider Putnam's argumant against metaphysical realism.

12.3 THE INTELLIGIBILITY OF REALISM

Suppose that T_1 is a theory at the limit of scientific investigation, 'an ideal theory'.[2] Then T_1 meets all 'operational constraints', correctly predicts 'all observational sentences (as far as we can tell)', is 'complete', 'consistent', 'beautiful', 'simple', 'plausible', and so forth (1978: 125). According to Putnam, T_1 must be true, because truth is nothing but idealized rational acceptability (1981: 55). It is here that Putnam sees a sharp difference between the internalist and the metaphysical realist. For the realist is said to hold that T_1 'might really be false', a supposition that 'appears to collapse into unintelligibility' (1978: 126).

Before considering Putnam's argument, we should see why the supposition is quite intelligible from the perspective of the metaphysical realism I have defended: Realism together with Correspondence Truth.

Consider the ideal theory T_1. Its key features are that it is a correct predictor and that it meets all operational constraints; it fits all the possible observational evidence that we could gather. From my metaphysical realist perspective, to say T_1 is ideal is therefore to say something about the relations between T_1, us, and independent reality: our sense organs, our experimental capacities (7.4), and reality are such that we could never observe anything about that reality inconsistent with T_1. Being ideal is species-relative. To suppose that T_1 might be false is simply to suppose that there might be features of reality which could not affect us at all, or could not affect us in such a way that we come to the right view about them. What we can observe about the world depends not only on the world, but also on us and our relations to that world.

Imagine an intelligent organism like a human but with inferior sense organs and capacities. We have no difficulty in understanding how a theory might be ideal for that organism and yet, from our superior perspective, be clearly false. What the realist believes is that this might be so for any organism, including a human being; for the realist believes that reality is altogether independent of experience.

Nothing that I have said here commits me to the supposition that T_1 might be false, simply to the view that, so far as Realism and Correspondence Truth are concerned, T_1 might be false: there is no inconsistency between that supposition and the two doctrines; the supposition is perfectly intelligible.

What view should we take of the supposition? Since truth for us is correspondence truth, what we need to settle is our attitude to instances of the schema

> If s is rationally acceptable in the ideal limit, then s is correspondence-true.

Now we are certainly committed to appropriate instances of

> If s is correspondence-true, then p

which is one half of Schema T for correspondence truth. So what we need to settle is our attitude to instances of

> If s is rationally acceptable in the ideal limit, then p.

Our attitude to this depends on two matters, as has already been discussed (3.5, 4.3, and 7.4): first, on how it is interpreted; second, on our epistemology.

In what sense are the circumstances 'ideal'? What is it to meet all operational constraints? T_1 fits all possible observational evidence in what sense of 'possible'? There is a range of answers to these questions, depending on how the observer is specified, where he is observing, whether he is using instruments and if so which, and whether he is performing experiments and if so which.

However the questions are answered, we can form no judgement on the schema without an opinion on the circumstances in which it is rational to accept sentences. This requires an epistemology. Realism constrains our epistemology (through its requirement that existence be objective: 2.2); but it does not determine it. Assuming, as we are, that 'possible evidence' in this case is limited by human capacities, it seems unlikely that any Realist epistemology could accept all instances of the schema. So the Realist is likely to agree that T_1 might be false.

12.4 THE MODEL-THEORETIC ARGUMENT

Putnam's model-theoretic argument (1978: 125–7; 1983: 11–18; see also 1981: 29–48) is aimed at metaphysical realism. If the argument were good, the view I have urged – Realism together with Correspondence Truth – would have to be abandoned. The argument leads Putnam himself into a form of anti-Realism to be discussed in the next section.

I summarize the argument. Pick a model for T_1, M. Relative to the interpretation of 'reference' for L that yields M, T_1 must come out true. How could it not then *be* true? This interpretation must meet all operational (and theoretical) constraints on reference, because T_1 is ideal. There can be no further constraints that would rule out M as the 'intended' model. So T_1 is true in any 'intended' model, and so must be true. The idea that T_1 might be false is unintelligible.

Putnam anticipates a response: according to a 'causal' theory of reference, the intended referent of a term is whatever stands in the appropriate causal relation to the term; the model we want, the world, is the totality of such referents, and T_1 may not be true in that model. The problem with this response, according to Putnam, is that all it does is add another theory to T_1: 'How "causes" can uniquely refer is as much of a puzzle as how "cat" can on the metaphysical realist picture' (1978: 126); it is not 'glued to one definite relation with metaphysical glue' (1983: 18). To suppose otherwise is to have 'a magical theory of reference' (1981: 47).[3]

There are some obvious truths which may partly underlie Putnam's position. We can't say anything about the relationship between language and the world without saying something – that is, without using language. One is imprisoned in language in theorizing about anything. The denial of these truths would indeed be unintelligible; but the metaphysical realist is not committed to denying them. I shall return to this in section 12.6.

What the realist needs to say is that at any point in our theorizing, even at the point of the ideal theory T_1, we can stand back from our theory and raise epistemic and semantic questions. The answer to these questions will be further theory from which we can also stand back. Putnam is not, of course, in any position to object to this procedure, because the above anti-realist argument is an example of it: it is a theory about T_1. The realist answer to these questions at any point will see belief in the object theory arising out of a causal interaction between the believers and a reality independent of those beliefs. Related to this, it will always seem intelligible to the realist to suppose that the theory might not be true. The realist will also see the reference of the terms in that theory as determined ultimately by these causal interactions; at least, he will if he uses a causal theory of reference to explain Correspondence Truth (as I have claimed he ought: 3.3). So his answer may include a sentence roughly like

Term *x* is causally related in way A to object *y* and to nothing else

as an explanation of another sentence

x refers to *y* and to nothing else.

In such circumstances he will regard the reference of *x* as determinate. The realist thinks that such circumstances are common. Of course a critic can then stand back and ask about that answer (as Putnam does): 'What determines the reference of "causally related"?' The realist gives him the same sort of answer (setting aside any nominalist scruples):

'Causally related' is causally related in way B to causal relations and to nothing else.

'Causally related' is 'glued to one definite relation' by causal relations, not by 'metaphysical glue'.

Small children soon learn to their delight that there is no end to questions: whatever answer is given to a question can be the subject of another question. A species of this fact, usually discovered later, is that whatever answer is given to a question, another question can be asked about the meaning of that answer. Unfortunately there is no general rule to tell us how long we should tolerate either line of questioning (explanation must stop somewhere.) However, one thing we should insist on: that an answer can be questioned in this way does not show that it was not a good answer to its question.

Putnam asks about the reference of 'cat', 'cow', and so on. We answer in terms of causal relations. Putnam then asks about the reference of 'causally related'. That such a question can be asked does not show that our answer to the first question was not a perfectly good one; it does not show that we have failed to explain how one model among many is the 'intended' one. To show this, it would be necessary to show that there is something about our first answer that needs explanation and that we can't explain. Putnam has not shown this. In particular, he has not shown that our second answer, the explanation of reference for 'causally related', does not explain, so far as explanation is necessary, how 'causally related' uniquely refers. He would want to claim that it does not, of course, because the words 'causally related' that are used in the second answer do not uniquely refer. But that is what he is supposed to be showing us. He is simply begging the question against the realist. However long he continues his questioning, the realist has an answer along the above lines to pick out the desired unique referent.

The question-begging is most striking in the following response to the idea of a causal theory of reference. Putnam claims that 'if reference is only determined by operational and theoretical constraints', then the reference of terms in that theory of reference will be indeterminate (1981: 45–6). Maybe so; but if reference is determined causally, as the theory says it is, then the reference of those terms will be determinate. He is not entitled to assume that the theory is false in order to show that it is false.

This account does not make metaphysical realism 'transcendent' in any interesting sense (cf. the remark quoted in section 12.1 and so far ignored). The semantic theory applies to all theories, even itself. Such self-reference need not be problematic (e.g. a constitutional law can specify the way in which all constitutional laws can be changed). Indeed, should we reach T_1, self-reference is inevitable. The laws of an ideal theory must be both the best available and complete. So of course we would apply those laws in theorizing about T_1 as in theorizing about anything else. There is no problem, despite the semantic paradoxes in epistemic and semantic theories, of the appropriate level of abstraction (Devitt 1981a: 90–2) being part of the object theory so that, when we ask our questions about that theory, we have to apply them to themselves. For example, if our semantic theory says that any term of a certain type refers to whatever is causally related in way B to it, and if that semantic theory itself contains such a term (e.g. 'causally related'), then the theory will apply to that term.

Putnam, in effect, accuses the metaphysical realist of begging the question in appealing to a theory to determine reference for a theory. I have accused him of begging the question in claiming that the reference of 'causally related' is not determinate. These mutual accusations may be confusing, and so I shall repeat the basis for mine.

Putnam claims to be offering an argument against metaphysical realism. At no point is he entitled to *assume* that this doctrine is false. If the doctrine is true, then there will be determinate referential relations between the words of any theory and pieces of the world. This will be true also of the words of any theory of reference used to explain these relations. If such a theory is comprehensive, it will of course apply to its own words. Putnam's anti-realist argument depends on there being no answer to the question about what determines reference for T_1. Using a theory of reference, there is an answer: reference is determined by causal relations of a certain sort. That answer works for 'causally related' just as it does for 'cat'.

Putnam begs the question by simply assuming that 'causally related' lacks determinate reference. Doubtless he is encouraged in this by the apparent triviality of the answer given for 'causally related'. But the triviality of the answer as an explanation does not show that it is not correct; nor does it show that what it is explaining is not real. If you push explanation of any realm far enough, you inevitably reach triviality, for explanation must stop somewhere.[4] In section 12.6 I shall offer a diagnosis of this question-begging.

Suppose that I am wrong and that Putnam's argument is effective against metaphysical realism. That doctrine, as I have pointed out, is a hybrid of a metaphysical doctrine like Realism and a semantic doctrine like Correspondence Truth. Which of the latter doctrines is threatened by Putnam's argument? Only Correspondence Truth. The argument is to do with reference, and has no bearing on Realism.[5] Indeed, the challenge of Putnam's argument can be posed – and often seems to be posed – in a way that presupposes Realism: a representation is related causally to one mind-independent entity but causally* to another; which relation determines reference?

Putnam's famous critique of metaphysical realism is largely beside the point. The critique proceeds by surrounding the metaphysical core of the doctrine, Realism, with a variety of other doctrines, none of which is essential to the core, and attacking those. The model-theoretic argument against Correspondence Truth is one example. Here, briefly, are two others.

First, Putnam commits the metaphysical realist to the doctrine that there is exactly one true and complete description of the world (1981: 49). Further, that doctrine, together with Correspondence Truth, is alleged to require 'a *ready made* world . . . : the world itself has to have a "built-in" structure' (1983: 211). I set this requirement aside until later (13.4). What is it to be a 'true and complete' description of the world? Whatever it is, there is no reason why a Realist has to be committed to there being just one.

Second, Putnam commits the metaphysical realist to a form of essentialism (1983: 205–28). The realist's belief in independent objects of various kinds is alleged to require that those objects be essentially members of those kinds. Putnam's criticism of this essentialism is 'bluff and parody', as Nicholas Wolterstorff points out (1987: 251). More important, it is irrelevant to Realism. The Realist need not accept this sort of individual essentialism; and even if he does accept it, he will surely want to be committed to the independent existence of objects of kinds that are *accidental* to the objects (p. 252).

Even if Putnam's criticisms of these surrounding doctrines were correct, they would leave the Realist core largely untouched.

12.5 PUTNAM'S ANTI-REALISM

Putnam's solution to the problem posed by his model-theoretic argument is to give up the idea that reference is to a mind-independent world.[6] He adopts 'internal realism'. Just as Kant closed the epistemic gap by bringing the world into the mind in some sense, so, likewise, Putnam closes the referential gap. In what sense? How is the metaphor 'The mind and world jointly make up the mind and the world' (1981: xi) to be cashed?[7] ' "Objects" do not exist independently of conceptual schemes. *We* cut up the world into objects when we introduce one or another scheme of description' (p. 52). This construction of objects is not from conceptually uncontaminated experiential inputs, for those inputs are 'themselves to some extent shaped by our concepts' (p. 54).

Is there anything that is uncontaminated? Presumably there must be, to account for the constraints other than coherence on construction; that is, to account for the extent that inputs are *not* shaped by our concepts. Putnam does talk, in a Kantian way, of the noumenal world and of things-in-themselves, thus implying that he is what I call a Weak Realist (2.4). However, he seems ultimately to regard this talk as 'nonsense', even if perhaps psychologically irresistible (pp. 61–2, 83). If the talk is nonsense, then there is nothing that Putnam can say about the constraints (except coherence). This avoids the 'facile relativism' of 'anything goes' (p. 54) by fiat: we simply are constrained, and that's that. Even if the talk is not nonsense, it lacks any explanatory power. To say that our construction is constrained by something beyond reach of knowledge or reference is whistling in the dark. We might as well settle for the dogmatic anti-relativism.

Putnam's position is reminiscent of the relativistic Kantianism which I attributed to Kuhn, Feyerabend, and the radical philosophers of science (9.2):

> *Constructivism* The only independent reality is beyond the reach of our knowledge and language. A known world is partly constructed by the imposition of concepts. These concepts differ from (linguistic, social, scientific, etc.) group to group, and hence the worlds of groups differ. Each such world exists only relative to an imposition of concepts.

In the light of his doubts about the noumenal world, perhaps Putnam's position is what I shall call 'Modified Constructivism': Constructivism without any independent reality. Like the radicals, Putnam thinks that the known world is our own handiwork. He is like them also in being an ontological relativist (despite the above rejection of epistemological relativism): existence of the known world is only existence relative to a theory. However, Putnam's relativism is much more conservative than that of the radicals. He subscribes to some version of the principle of charity (1978: 38–41; 1981: 117–19), which enables him to reject Ontological Change, a central doctrine of the radicals (9.1): though our theories change, our ontology remains much the same. I shall consider Constructivism in more detail in the next chapter.

We have noted that Putnam has encouraged, even if he has not committed, a breach of Maxim 1: taking Convergence to be constitutive of Realism rather than evidence for it (7.6). He has certainly breached Maxim 2: he conflates the metaphysical issue of Realism and the semantic issue of truth (6.6, 7.3 and 12.1). His present argument against Realism is a breach of Maxim 3: he is led to anti-Realism by his attempt to settle the problem of reference. This procedure runs the wrong way: we should settle the Realism issue first, and then let our view of that guide us to a solution of the problem of reference. The mistaken procedure is related to a standard objection to Realism which I shall now consider. That objection breaches Maxim 5.

12.6 REALISM AND THE GOD'S EYE VIEW

Putnam mentions the idea, allegedly held by some realist friends 'in places like Princeton and Australia', that we can compare theories with 'unconceptualized reality' (1983: 163; see also 1981: 130). He suggests that realism requires 'a transcendental match between our representation and the world in itself' (1981: 134). It requires a 'God's Eye View' (p. 74; see also pp. 49, 73), 'direct access to a ready made world' (p. 146), the capacity to say *how* THE WORLD is 'theory-independently' (1978: 133; see also 1981: 49). Similar remarks are made about the realist's view of reference. 'To pick out just *one* correspondence between words or mental signs and mind-independent things we would have already to have referential access to the mind-independent things' (1981: 73; see also pp. 46–7, 51, 66,

211). There is 'a puzzle how we could *learn to express*' what the realist wants to say (p. 46).

Putnam's view is that realism requires our knowing the unknowable and speaking the unspeakable (cf. Maxim 5). Much the same view of realism can be found in many other places. It is the 'final objection' to my position by radical philosophers of science (9.8). It is one of the things that Rorty and Fine have against the correspondence theory of truth (11.4). See also Hauptli's response (1979: 208) to Field (1973) and Rosenberg's discussion (1980: 87–90).

But, of course, this view of realism is a caricature.[8] No sane realist believes any of it. What realists believe is that we can judge whether theories are true of reality, *the nature of which* does not depend on any theories or concepts.

Foundationalist epistemology would not allow any talk of our relations to a mind-independent world in the explanation of knowledge. For how do we know of such relations? Such a world is not immediately accessible to the mind. Similarly, Putnam will not allow talk of these relations to explain reference. For how do we refer to such relations? There can be nothing more to reference than is immediately accessible (internal) to the mind.

It is because Putnam thinks that operational and theoretical constraints are thus accessible to the mind, whereas causal relations to a mind-independent world are not, that he begs the question in his model-theoretic argument against reference (12.4).

The picture that lies behind the caricature of realism is thus one of our theorizing *from scratch*, locked within our minds. But we are not starting from scratch in epistemology and semantics: that is the point of Maxim 3. We can use well-established theories in physics, biology, and so forth, we already have the entities, divided into kinds, and relations which those theories posit. And if we *were* starting from scratch, sceptical doubts would condemn us to instantaneous solipsism (5.5). Putnam puts the epistemic and semantic carts before the ontological horse.

To put the carts back where they belong, we take a naturalistic approach to epistemology and semantics. Reflection on our best science has committed us to the many entities of the largely impersonal and inanimate world (5.7 and 7.1). We go on, naturalistically, to seek an explanation of that small part of the world in which there are problems of knowledge and reference: people and language (5.8). The resulting theory has no special authority: it is just one theory among many of the world we live in. It is possible that this theory should lead us to change the view of what exists that we have obtained from other theories. But great changes are unlikely. It is particularly unlikely that the theory will lead us to question the independence of what exists from theories and theorists, which is the obvious starting place for an epistemology. All the judgements of our theory will be theory-laden, of course. But that is no worry, for it is part of the theory that the judgements of *all* theories are theory-laden. Finally, epistemic and semantic relations are no more inaccessible than other relations. Theorizing about the relation between a thought or expression and an object no more requires a God's Eye View than does theorizing about the relation between, say, David Frost and Richard Nixon. We may wonder whether any relation is reference, but that is an empirical question. Do we need, and are we entitled to, a notion of reference in our explanation of people and language? Among the indefinitely many causal relations between a person and the world, is there a relation to Reagan that plays a special role in our explanation of that person's behaviour involving 'Reagan'? I do not take such questions lightly (e.g. in chapter 6 and in 1981a). Positive answers to them are difficult; but they are not to be dismissed by appeals to transcendental philosophy.

NOTES

1 This section is based on my 1980a: 399–401.
2 The remaining sections of this chapter draw extensively on my 1983b and 1984b and a little on my 1991a.
3 Putnam's argument has generated a storm of responses. Lewis 1984 is a particularly helpful one.
4 For Putnam's response to arguments along these lines, see his 1983: xi–xii, 295–6.
5 Cf., e.g., three recent responses to Putnam: Heller 1988, Fales 1988, and LePore and Loewer 1988. See also T. Blackburn 1988: 179.
6 It is not clear how this helps, as Curtis Brown points out (1988: 152).
7 LePore and Loewer (1988) claim that the metaphor is to be cashed in Putnam's identification of truth with ideal justification. The basis for rejecting this claim is to be found in section 4.3 above. An *argument* is needed to get from any theory of truth to anti-Realism. Putnam's theory of truth has as a consequence all instances of

If *s* is rationally acceptable in the ideal limit, then *p*.

The anti-Realist must give some account of the dependency of reality on our minds that explains this. If we had this account, we would have exactly what we needed to cash the metaphor. The excursion into truth has brought us right back to where we started. In sum, if we cannot cash the metaphor non-semantically, talk of truth cannot be brought to bear on the Realism issue. If we can cash the metaphor non-semantically, we do not need talk of truth to cash it. See also Devitt 1991a: 54–5.

8   Bill Lycan has nicely mocked the caricature with his name 'Turtle Realism': anti-realists should go all the way and accuse realists of believing that the earth sits on the back of a giant turtle (1988: 191). Australian realists believe that the turtle sits on the back of a giant crocodile: 'Crocodile Realism'.

13

Worldmaking

In the beginning was the Word.
Jn 1 : 1

13.1 INTRODUCTION

The view to be discussed in this chapter starts with two ideas from
Kant: the idea of an unknowable, noumenal world independent of us;
and the idea of the known, phenomenal world as partly our creation
through the imposition of concepts (5.6). The third idea that makes
up the view is alien to Kant: relativism. I expressed the view that
combines these three ideas as follows:

> *Constructivism* The only independent reality is beyond the
> reach of our knowledge and language. A known world is partly
> constructed by the imposition of concepts. These concepts differ
> from (linguistic, social, scientific, etc.) group to group, and
> hence the worlds of groups differ. Each such world exists only
> relative to an imposition of concepts.

People in different groups literally live in different worlds. As a
result, the world-views of the different groups are incommensurable.

In earlier sections I have discussed versions of this relativistic
Kantianism found in the radical philosophers of science (9.2) and
in Putnam (12.5). Those versions are just the tip of the iceberg.
Goodman urges the view clearly and provocatively (1978; though, it
will be remembered, he thinks the noumenal world 'not worth fighting for': p. 20). Benjamin Lee Whorf urges the view with mystical
fervour (1956). Particularly obscure versions of it pervade structuralism, post-structuralism, and French thought in general.[1] It is
common in literature departments around the world.[2] It is to be

found in all the social sciences[3] and in 'the sociology of knowledge'.[4] It is the underlying metaphysics of various political movements, including that in the universities against the 'canon' and for 'PC' ('political correctness').[5] Not even feminism has been left untouched.[6]

We have noted that Kant's idea that we make the known world was dominant in the nineteenth century (11.2). In its relativistic form the idea is ubiquitous in the twentieth century. It has some claim to being the most influential bad idea in philosophy.

What reasons are given, or implied, for Constructivism? Primarily, alleged problems for Realism. I have already rejected two sorts. The first is a set of Cartesian worries that have been the main concern of this book; for example, if the Realist's view of stones, trees, and cats were correct, then we could not know them or refer to them. The second comes from approaching the historical facts of theory change with a description theory of reference (9.3–9.4). Elsewhere I have criticized the apparent reason of structuralists and post-structuralists: their denial of reference altogether (Devitt and Sterelny 1987: 215–20). All these reasons offend against Maxim 3 by attempting to settle semantic and epistemic issues before metaphysical ones.

Goodman finds another difficulty for Realism. He claims that there are incompatible true 'versions' of the world. The Realist cannot accept this, but the Constructivist can: each version is true relative to its world. This theme is echoed by Putnam (1978: 130–3; 1981: 72–3). Goodman argues for his claim with a number of examples: from art, of different conceptions of points in geometry, of the movement of the Earth and of spots on a screen. Putnam adds an example about particles and fields. None of these is convincing. To each example the Realist has a response that is vastly preferable to relativism. Most often, the incompatibility can be shown to be only apparent: the differences are matters of emphasis; or there are implicit references to different frameworks; or the statements are about different things. Sometimes the Realist can withhold belief in each of the allegedly true statements. Sometimes he can reject one. These sort of points have been well argued by others (e.g. Wilson 1981, Wolterstorff 1987, and McMichael 1988). As Nicholas Wolterstorff points out: 'The remarkable fact is that Goodman gives no compelling, or even plausible, examples of true statements which say conflicting things about the same thing'. (1987: 257). Quite apart from this, a bizarre metaphysics like Constructivism needs to be based on much more than a small range of examples.

Finally, something that we have glimpsed in the radical philosophers of science is taken by some to count against Realism and for

Constructivism (9.5–9.6, 9.8). It is not so much an argument as a confusion. It is endemic to the sociology of knowledge.[7]

The first step is clear enough. It is claimed that none of our beliefs is indubitable; all are theory-laden and fallible. Furthermore, emphasis is given to the diversity of opinion. The remaining steps must be abstracted from a hopeless confusion of epistemic, semantic, and metaphysical issues. The second step is that theory-ladenness and diversity of opinion imply *epistemic* relativism: beliefs are not justified absolutely, but only relative to something. The third is that epistemic relativism implies *semantic* relativism: beliefs are not true absolutely, but only relative to something. The fourth is that semantic relativism implies *ontological* relativism (of which Constructivism is an example): reality exists only relative to something. This last step is licensed by the equivalence thesis, as we have noted (4.3). Steps two and three are the objectionable ones. Perhaps a case can be made for epistemic relativism; but it will need much more than claims about theory-ladenness and diversity. Those claims are quite compatible with an absolutist epistemology (5.8). And the move from epistemic to semantic, and hence to ontological, relativity has nothing to be said for it (Field 1982: 562–7). Certainly the move needs an argument which it does not get from those apparently unaware that they are making it (Maxims 2 and 5).

In sum, the Constructivist case against Realism is very weak. We shall now consider the case against Constructivism, which is very strong.

13.2 CRITICISM OF CONSTRUCTIVISM

Wolterstorff's initial reaction to Constructivism is as follows:

The anti-realist is of course speaking in metaphor. If we took him to be speaking literally, what he says would be wildly false – so much so that we would question his sanity. (Wolterstorff 1987: 233)[8]

Statements of Constructivism, taken literally, do indeed seem so *prima facie* absurd as to prompt a search for a non-literal, charitable way of interpreting them.

To start with, the idea of noumenal things-in-themselves is explanatorily useless (12.5), and probably incoherent. Constructivists are attracted to things-in-themselves to provide an external constraint on theorizing. The plausibility of the view that there is *some* external constraint is, of course, overwhelming. However, things-in-themselves provide the appearance of constraint without the reality. Since we can, *ex hypothesi*, know nothing about things-in-themselves, we can know nothing about the mechanisms by which they exercise their constraint; nor can we explain or predict any particular constraint. For Kant himself, the very idea of *causal* constraint by the noumenal world is incoherent, because CAUSALITY is one of the concepts imposed by us. So causality is part of the phenomenal world, and cannot hold between the noumenal and phenomenal worlds. If this is not the position of Constructivists, it surely ought to be. Why should causality be the exception to the rule of creation by imposition? If it is not an exception, the Constructivists face the same problem that has baffled Kant scholars for years: the nature of the non-causal constraint exercised by things-in-themselves.

Constructivists often show sensitivity to the mysteriousness of the noumenal world. It is 'a formless chaos of which one cannot even speak in the first place' (Jameson 1972: 109–10). It is hardly ever mentioned without the protection of scare quotes or capital letters.

The noumenal world adds only an invisible fig-leaf to the naked idealism of Constructivism. If the leaf is dropped, we are left with 'Modified Constructivism', which seems to be Putnam's preferred view (12.5). On this view, no account of constraints on our theorizing can be given. The Modified Constructivist might deny that there are any constraints: we can think anything we like. That is not plausible (to put it delicately). Alternatively, he might claim that there are constraints, but that we can, in principle, say nothing about them: it is just an inexplicable brute fact that we cannot think anything we like. This replaces the earlier incoherence with silence. It is hardly an appealing position.

Worse still, if that is possible, is the idea that we make the known world of stones, trees, cats, and the like with our concepts. I indicated the main mystery when introducing Kant (5.6). How could cookie cutters in the head literally carve out cookies in dough that is outside the head? How could dinosaurs and stars be dependent on the activities of our minds? It would be crazy to claim that there were no dinosaurs or stars before there were people to think about them. Constructivists do not seem to claim this. But it is hardly any less crazy to claim that there *would not have been* dinosaurs or stars if there *had been not been* people (or similar thinkers). And this claim seems essential to Constructivism: unless it were so, dinosaurs and stars could not be dependent on us and our minds.

Finally, there is an old problem for relativism which is like the fatal flaw of foundationalism (5.3): arbitrarily excluding from the scope of the theory something dear to the theorist's heart. In this case, why do the languages, concepts, cultures, and so forth that do the worldmaking not themselves exist only relative to. . . ? Relative to what? Themselves?[9] The 'texts' themselves start to shimmer and lose their reality.

These problems provide ample motivation for a charitable metaphorical interpretation of Constructivist talk.

13.3 CHARITY?

A metaphorical interpretation of much of this talk is easy to find. (1) Our *theories* of the world really are our constructions. So we can take talk of world construction as a colourful way of talking of theory construction. (2) It is plausible to think of the mind as imposing theories on our *experiences* of the world. So we can take talk of imposition on the world as a colourful way of talking of imposition on experience. (3) Talk of *x* existing relative to a theory (or whatever) can be taken as a colourful way of saying that there is a *concept* of *x* within the theory.

This charity is encouraged by the careless way in which some Constructivists vacillate between talk of theories and talk of the world. Thus, following a discussion of duck–rabbit Gestalt switches, Kuhn has this to say about the discovery of the planet Uranus:

a number of astronomers . . . had seen a star in positions that we now suppose must have been occupied at the time by Uranus. . . . [Herschel's] scrutiny disclosed Uranus' motion among the stars, and Herschel therefore announced that he had seen a new comet! Only several months later, after fruitless attempts to fit the observed motion to a cometary orbit, did Lexell suggest that the orbit was probably planetary. When that suggestion was accepted, there were several fewer stars and one more planet in the world of the professional astronomer. (1962: 114)

The change from seeing something as a star to seeing it as a planet is striking, just as is the change from seeing a figure as a duck to seeing it as a rabbit. One often says of such changes that 'it's as though the world changes' or of people on different sides of such changes that 'they live in different worlds'. But it would be absurd to take such dramatic and essentially metaphorical statements literally. So surely, one is inclined to think, we should not take Kuhn as claiming that the acceptance of a suggestion by a few astronomers literally destroyed stars and created a planet. (Whorf's vacillations prompt similar charity; 1956: 55, 162, 213, 253.)

One problem with such charity is that Constructivists often recognize the distinction between theories and the world yet *still* press on with the objectionable claims about the world. Consider the following from Kuhn's account of the discovery of oxygen:

At the very least, as a result of discovering oxygen, Lavoisier saw nature differently. And in the absence of some recourse to that hypothetical fixed nature that he 'saw differently', the principle of economy will urge us to say that after discovering oxygen Lavoisier worked in a different world. (1962: 117; see also Feyerabend 1978: 70).

Here the difference between claiming that things *look* different as a result of a theory change and claiming that they *are* different as a result of the change is acknowledged; yet the latter claim is still made. And it is made for a very Kantian reason: 'fixed nature' is beyond our ken; it is the other side of 'the gap'; it is a mere thing-in-itself. Consider also the following from the sociology of knowledge:

the thing and the statement correspond for the simple reason that they come from the same source. Their separation is the *final stage in the process of their construction*. (Latour and Woolgar 1986: 183)

Finally, consider this from an account of structuralism:

since *language* . . . constitutes our characteristic means of encountering and of coping with the world beyond ourselves, then perhaps we can say that it constitutes the characteristic human structure. From there, it is only a small step to the argument that perhaps it also constitutes the characteristic structure of human reality. (Hawkes 1977: 28)

A small step indeed![10]

A charitable interpretation of the Constructivists has an obvious further problem: we must take them as agnostic on metaphysics; for their only remarks that appear to be metaphysical are just the ones that we are charitably interpreting as metaphorical. That leaves them with no metaphysics at all. It is very hard indeed to see them as so unpretentious. To see them this way misses so much of the flavour of their rhetoric, *the aura of significance* with which their views are usually presented and received.

Perhaps the most decisive reason against charity is that the Constructivists must be taken literally to accommodate their most famous and distinctive theses, particularly that of Incommensurability. In brief, if rival theories were not creating their worlds but were about the one world, they would be comparable (9.2, 9.6).

Finally, some Constructivists are too clear and too explicit to make charity an option. That is surely the case with Putnam (12.5). It is notoriously so with Goodman. An exchange with Israel Scheffler is particularly revealing. Scheffler (1980) carefully and sympathetically documents the vacillation in Goodman between talk of versions of the world and talk of the world. He gives sound and sensible reasons for accepting the former talk and rejecting the latter. At one point he expresses his view as follows: 'the claim that it is we who made the stars by making the word "star" I consider absurd, taking this claim in its plain and literal sense' (p. 205). The title of Goodman's response (1980) nails the Constructivist flag to the masthead: 'On Starmaking'. He is unabashed. Indeed, he is rather amused by Scheffler's stuffiness. He challenges Scheffler to show 'which features of the stars we did not make'. He goes on:

we do not make stars as we make bricks; not all making is a matter of moulding mud. The worldmaking mainly in question here is making not with hands but with minds, or rather with languages or other symbol systems. Yet when I say that worlds are made, I mean it literally; and what I mean should be clear from what I have already said. (p. 213)

Making bricks by moulding mud we all understand. Making stars with language strikes Scheffler and, one hopes, many others as absurd. What Goodman says he means does nothing to remove the absurdity. That's the problem.

We have noted that Constructivists blur the crucial distinction between theories of the world and the world itself. This is no accident: such plausibility as Constructivism has depends on the blurring. If Constructivist talk that is apparently about the world is metaphorically about theories, it is true. But then it will not be able to sustain Incommensurability and other theses distinctive of Constructivism. To sustain what is distinctive, the talk must be taken literally. But then it is false. By blurring the distinction, the truth about theories can appear to do the job of the falsehood about the world.

13.4 TENTATIVE DIAGNOSES

The evidence is clear that people are easily beguiled into blurring the crucial distinction between theories and the world. Why? I do not pretend to have an adequate explanation, but I have some tentative suggestions in the direction of one.[11]

The distinction is closely related to the use–mention distinction. Consider the following story (which I owe to Lloyd Reinhardt):

'Sir, how many legs does this donkey have?'
'Four, Mr Lincoln.'
'And how many tails does it have?'
'One, Mr Lincoln.'
'Now, sir, what if we were to call the tail a leg; how many
    legs would the donkey then have?'
'Five, Mr Lincoln.'
'No, sir, for you cannot make a tail into a leg by calling
    it one.'

Mr Lincoln is accusing his respondent of confusing use and mention: confusing what they did with *the word* 'leg' with leg-making. There is a more generous view of the respondent. He is misled into thinking that Mr Lincoln is, first, proposing a new conventional meaning for 'leg' that includes tails and then, second, using the word with that meaning. Only if he *goes on* to conclude that this procedure makes legs will he be confusing use and mention.

There is no doubt that use–mention confusion is strangely appealing. Perhaps it is the root cause of our problem. But then, of course, we wonder why that confusion is so appealing. Furthermore, it is very implausible to suppose that this confusion could have a role in the thinking of philosophers as clever and sophisticated as Goodman (despite the encouragement of passages like 'The English language makes [objects] white just by applying the term "white" to them'; 1979: 347).

I think that the following passage, taken from Frederick Suppe's response (1977) to Scheffler's critique of Constructivism (1967), provides further insight into the problem:

Suppose I adopt a category system containing the category *rose* and I observe an item, call it '*b*'.... what it is to belong to the category *rose* is more or less my free decision; for example, I may decide that a necessary condition for belonging to category *rose* will be that it belongs to categories $c_1, \ldots c_n$. Now if the hypothesis 'Item *b* is a rose' is true, it in effect says that item *b* belongs to categories $c_1, \ldots c_n$. But the 'independent objective control' over hypothesis 'Item *b* is a rose' requires that the truth of the hypothesis depends on whether item *b* has the property of being a rose, where being a rose does not depend in any way upon how I choose to conceptualize or categorize my experience. But then Scheffler's account leads to a set of demands which are *prima facie* contradictory: the truth of 'Item *b* is a rose' requires that item *b* actually belong to category *rose*, where what it is to belong to category *rose* is within my control, but where what it is to be a rose is totally beyond my control. (Suppe 1977: 194–5)

There does indeed seem to be a contradiction. What has gone wrong?

Two features of the passage are interesting. First, Suppe is surely onto something in his emphasis on *freedom*. Constructivists take whatever he is onto and convert it into the freedom to make the world. Second, the use of the term 'category' should sound a warning bell. 'Category' is a term that might have been designed for concealing use–mention confusions[12]: sometimes it refers to *worldly kinds*; sometimes it refers to *mental words or concepts* ('concept' has a similar ambiguity).

The ambiguity of 'category *rose*' affects 'the anti-Realist side' of the alleged contradiction: 'what it is to belong to category *rose* is within my control.' We should interpret this each way in turn, comparing the result with 'the Realist side': 'what it is to be a rose is totally beyond my control.'

First, interpret 'category *rose*' as referring to the kind *rose*. So we understand the anti-Realist side as saying: 'What it is to be a member of the kind *rose* is within my control.' This straightforwardly contradicts the Realist side. Whatever it is to be a member of the kind *rose* simply *is* whatever it is to be a rose. That is something that *the world* has control over, not any of us. The anti-Realist side is false: no freedom here.

If we are to find a place for freedom, it must come from interpreting 'category *rose*' as referring to the word 'rose'. It is a truism that language is arbitrary: we are free to take any sound and make it mean anything we like. And what it does come to mean depends on what we have freely done with it. So it is what English speakers freely did that gave 'rose' its meaning. We must examine the alleged contradiction in the light of this interpretation and this freedom.

On this second interpretation, 'belong to' has to express, infelicitously, the reference relation between a word and objects. The anti-Realist side becomes: 'What it is to be referred to by the word "rose" is within my control.' This is hardly perspicuous. Its truth depends on whether it concerns the word's *condition of reference* or its *reference*.

When English speakers created the meaning of 'rose', they determined its condition of reference:

(1) 'rose' refers (in English) to something in virtue of its being R

(where, of course, 'R' expresses whatever property something must have to be referred to by 'rose'). But it is vital to note that speakers did not fully determine reference. The meaning of 'rose' does not alone determine, for example, that

(2)   'rose' refers to *b*.

To establish (2), we need not only (1) but also

(3)   *b* is *R*.

And (3) is something that is right outside our control. This becomes obvious when we note that something could not be *R*, and hence referred to by 'rose', *unless it were a rose*.

Where does this leave the alleged contradiction? The anti-Realist side claims that what it is to be referred to by the word 'rose' is within my control. If this amounts to the claim that I and my fellow speakers determine (1), then it is true, but there is no contradiction: making the word 'rose' refer in certain conditions is not making those conditions obtain, and hence is not making roses. If the anti-Realist side amounts to the claim that we determine the likes of (2), then it does contradict the Realist side. For, given the truth of (1), if we did thus determine reference, we would determine the likes of (3), and hence determine whether something was a rose: *Something has to be a rose to be referred to by 'rose'*. But we need not worry about this contradiction because, interpreted in this way, the anti-Realist side is false: being referred to by 'rose' is not fully within our control. (1) is controlled by us, the likes of (3) by the world, and the likes of (2) by both.

It may well be the case that we determine *some* sentences like (2). According to the historical causal theory, for example, 'rose' refers to something in virtue of it being of the same kind as the objects in which the term was grounded. Suppose that *b* was a grounding object. (2) is then the result of one of the groundings that established the reference condition of 'rose' reported in (1). Groundings are certainly within our control, and therefore so is (2). But this alone will not determine that anything else is referred to by 'rose', and so could not show that what it is to be referred to by 'rose' is within my control. Nor does it undermine a totally Realist attitude to the fact that *b* is a rose. Calling something a rose does not make it a rose, as Mr Lincoln would insist.

In sum, the Realist side of the alleged contradiction claims that being a rose is not within our control, which is true. The anti-Realist side might be the simple denial of this, which would be false. Or it might be the claim that (1) is within our control, which would be true, but would not contradict the Realist side. Or, finally, it might be the claim that the likes of (2) are within our control, which would yield a contradiction, but would be false. None of this. may be obvious for two reasons: first, the ambiguity of 'category' encourages use–mention confusion; second, the distinction between a condition of reference, which is fully within our control, and reference, which is not, is subtle.

Suppe's discussion concerns the *familiar* kind *rose*. The Realist commits himself to independent objects of such familiar kinds, picked out by words in common sense and science, because these are the ones about which he can be precise. He should allow that there are objects of indefinitely many other kinds, equally independent, that for one reason or another we have not picked out by words. In this respect, Realism is 'modest', as Curtis Brown nicely puts it: 'when we develop a language we are not imposing an organization on the world, but selecting one of the world's organizations for our own use. On this view the world "in itself"' has *more* objects than we usually talk about, not fewer' (1988: 148). The Realist agrees with Putnam's metaphysical realist that there is 'a *ready made* world' (12.4); but this is not a commitment to the world having *just one* 'built-in structure'.

Consider one of the kinds that we have so far overlooked: the kind of object that strains the credulity of tourists from Peoria. Let us introduce a name for this kind of object: 'peorincred'. Now, as a matter of fact, echidnas are peorincreds. But our linguistic decision did not make them so: they always were peorincreds, and would have been even if people had never introduced the word 'peorincred' or any other word. Peorincreds are part of the ready-made world. My response to Suppe's discussion would work just as well if our example were this totally unfamiliar kind instead of the familiar kind *rose*. Indeed, select any set of three physical objects at random, and name the kind consisting of those objects 'blah'. My response would work just as well for the kind *blah*. That arbitrary kind is as independent of us as anything could be.

Part of the freedom that Suppe is emphasizing is the freedom to choose which kinds we shall pick out with words. We have freely chosen to name stones, trees, and cats, but not peorincreds and blahs. Perhaps some Constructivists make two related mistakes about this freedom: they confuse it with something else, and they take Realism to be denying it.

The freedom we have may be confused with one we do not have: the freedom to choose which kinds objects are members of. We can choose to name stones and not peorincreds, but we cannot choose whether something is a stone or a peorincred.

The Realist may be thought to deny the freedom we have by holding that there is something special about the kinds Realism is committed to. The Realist does not hold this. Clearly, our choices about which kinds to name are guided by our interests: explanatory interests, practical interests, perhaps playful interests. A kind picked out by an explanatory interest may qualify as a 'natural' one. I think that the kinds of objects that Realism is committed to *are* mostly natural ones, and hence in that respect special. However, this opinion is not important, because Realism does not involve any claim to that effect. Realism does not claim any special status for its kinds, except their independence. Whether there are any natural kinds, and if so, which they are, is another matter.[13]

In sum, I have several suggestions to help explain the blurring of the crucial distinction between theories and the world. (1) At bottom, I suspect a use–mention confusion. (2) This may be aided by the use of ambiguous terms like 'category'. (3) It is easy to miss the difference between a condition of reference, which is fully within our control, and reference, which is not. (4) Perhaps our freedom to name whatever kinds we like is confused with the freedom to put objects into any kinds we like.

13.5 ARTIFACTS, TOOLS, AND SOCIAL ENTITIES

Further help with the diagnosis of Constructivism may be provided by examining some kinds that really are dependent on us; we *do*, in some interesting respects, make objects members of these kinds. This examination is worthwhile in two other ways. First, it helps to clarify the independence dimension of Realism (2.2). Second, it provides a route to Constructivism that may make the doctrine seem more rational (although I certainly don't say, plausible).

In this section I shall consider artifacts, tools, and social entities. In the next two I shall consider secondary properties and the implications of their dependence on us.

At one point, Goodman expresses his view that we make the world as follows: 'Everything including individuals is an artifact' (1984: 29). The expression is appropriate, because artifacts are indeed the product of human workmanship. Examples like chairs and hammers spring immediately to mind.

Consider briefly the nature of hammers. Must a hammer be an artifact? Surprisingly, no. Certainly, *one* way for something to be a hammer is for it to have been designed for a certain function, hammering. If something has been so designed, it clearly is an artifact. However, some things could be hammers if we used them to hammer from time to time, wherever they came from. Hammers could grow on trees or be found on beaches; many paperweights do and are.

Intuitively, things like hammers, chairs, and paperweights have something in common. It would be convenient to have a word for these similar things. Given that many of them are not made by us, 'artifact' is unsuitable. 'Tool' is not perfect; but it does catch what is essential to these things: their relation to purposive action.

I shall compare tools first with entities as conceived by Realism and second with entities as conceived by Constructivism.

How do tools differ from paradigm Realist entities like stones, trees, and cats? In characterizing the independence dimension of Realism, I rejected all dependencies except 'the familiar causal ones . . . long noted by folk theory' (2.2). So we are Realist about trees, even though we sometimes plant them. Indeed, some entities that we *always* make – and may even make with functions in mind – seem appropriately grouped with the Realist paradigms; consider plastic or gin, for example. Some artifacts should be among the Realist paradigms! The independence that the Realist cares about is compatible with any amount of causal interference in the world by us. In sum, the Realist paradigms may be made. Tools, we have seen, need not be made. Clearly, we must look for other ways to distinguish tools and paradigms.

Tools differ from the Realist paradigms in that *their natures are functions that involve the purposes of agents* (and not just *human* agents: something can be a nest in virtue of what a bird does with it). A hammer is a hammer in virtue of its function for hammerers. A tree is not a tree and gin is not gin in virtue of their functions.

The contrast between paradigm and tool is brought out nicely by *osage orange (maclura pomifera)*, a thorned tree that was once used extensively to keep livestock away from crops. *Qua* tree it is a Realist paradigm, *qua* fence it is a tool. Whether we planted it or it just grew is not crucial to its being tree or fence.

In this book I have used the word 'physical' to cover the Realist paradigms. The present discussion shows that the word is far from perfect for the job: hammers are as physical as anything. But I can think of no better word. ('Natural' would be very misleading, because plastic is not natural in any sense, and stones may not be natural in the usual special sense of belonging to 'a natural kind'.)[14]

Realism must be committed to physical entities (in this special sense), *at least*. There is little harm in, but also little point to, a further commitment to tools. There is little harm because, as we shall see, the sort of dependence that tools have on agents does not make them like the worlds of the Constructivists. There is little point, because everything that is a tool is also a physical entity (in the special sense), and so is covered by Realism anyway; thus, a fence may also be a row of trees. The motivation for committing Realism to tokens of common-sense and scientific physical types was to distinguish it from Weak Realism, an idle doctrine that is embraced by most anti-Realists (2.3). The Realist needs to be specific about the independent entities he is fighting for, but it is enough to have an entity under one specification. Adding more specifications does not help in the struggle with the anti-Realist.

Many entities are of *social* kinds: bachelors, money, votes, and so forth. There is similarly little harm in, and no point to, a realist commitment to entities of those kinds.

How do tools differ from entities as conceived by Constructivists? Tools are dependent for their natures on their relations to agents; if there had been no agents, there would have been no tools. Constructivist entities are dependent for their natures on their relations to people (or other thinkers); if there had been no people, there would have been no entities (one supposes; 13.2). Both sorts of entities are, to this extent, dependent on minds. However, they differ in two crucial respects.

First, they differ in their dependence on us. According to the Constructivist, an entity gets its nature from the way we *think* about it. No amount of thinking about something as, say, a hammer is enough to make it a hammer. To be a hammer, it has to have been designed or used to hammer. The way we make tools is not the way Constructivists make worlds.

Second, the two sorts of entities differ in their dependence on the independent world. Tools have both a direct and an indirect dependence. (1) Neither designing something to hammer nor using it to hammer is *sufficient* to make it a hammer. Something like a feather duster could not be a hammer; nor could a hammer be a duster, whatever we intended. No more could either be a chair. It is obvious that only things of certain physical types could be pens, telephones, or airplanes. In this way tools are directly dependent on the world. (2) The independent world influences what we *do* design and what we *do* use as a tool. It is no accident that we do not, as a matter of fact, try to use feather dusters as hammers, or vice versa. Tools are indirectly dependent on the world via the dependency of our intentions on the world. This twofold dependency may be difficult to describe precisely. To be precise for a particular tool would require a precise account of its function, which may not be easy to give. And we would have to take account of the fact that something can be a tool even if it does not work; think of public telephones, for example. There may even be some indeterminacy about the dependency. The important point, however, is that this dependency is a matter of actual and potential causal relations and roles which are open to any amount of scientific investigation.

The contrast with Constructivism is sharp. According to Constructivism, the known world is determined by our thought, which is constrained by a noumenal world in ways that are in principle unknowable. This is mysterious to the point of incoherence. Modified Constructivism is no better; since it either denies any constraint or refuses to say anything about it (13.2). Why do we think that these things are trees and those things are cats, hence making them trees and cats? Why could we not make the known world in any way we liked? Neither version of Constructivism can give satisfactory answers.

Some Constructivists like to talk of 'the social construction of reality'. The talk is appropriate enough if we consider the classification of entities into social kinds. Something is a bachelor, money, or a vote largely in virtue of its complicated relations with us and our intentions, as Marxists and others have emphasized. In a sense, we really do make these entities. However, these entities, like tools, differ from Constructivist entities. First, our contribution to their 'construction' consists in elaborate social practices, not mere thinking or labelling. Second, the world has a perfectly explicable role in determining what could be such an entity and what social practices we adopt.

The world that the Realist is primarily interested in defending is independent of us except in one uninteresting respect. Tools and social entities are dependent on us in interesting ways, but these dependencies are still very different from that of Constructivist worlds. And tools and social entities are dependent on the world in ways that are explicable, not ineffable. Both our role and the independent world's role in the making of these entities differ from those roles in the making of Constructivist entities.

13.6 SECONDARY PROPERTIES

There are three basic positions on the secondary properties: objectivism, subjectivism, and eliminativism. Earlier (5.10), I claimed that the Realist need not take a stand on the vexed question of which is right. Nevertheless, I promised an objectivist account based on Locke. Such accounts have a special interest in the present context because of an ingenious suggestion of Putnam's (1981: 60–4) about how to understand Kant: take Kant as claiming that *all* properties are like Lockean secondary properties. (This was a claim that Berkeley *did* make, of course.) I shall consider that suggestion in the next section.

Locke thought that secondary properties were 'powers to produce various sensations in us' (*Essay Concerning Human Understanding*, bk II, ch. XXX, sect. 2). I think this is very much along the right lines.[15] However, Locke combined this view with one about 'powers' that led him to anti-objectivism about secondary properties: they 'do not really exist in' objects (bk II, ch. VII, sect. 16–22). Others also seem to think that there is something essentially anti-objectivist in the Lockean view (e.g. Armstrong 1968b). This is surely not so: we can hold that the object really does have whatever property it is that causes the appropriate sensation.

Talk of causing sensations should be construed adverbially (5.3). So the secondary property of redness is the power to make us 'sense redly'. Powers are dispositions, which should be treated functionally (6.3). So redness is not identified with one particular arrangement of particles, but *realized by* (possibly) many.

This objectivist account of the secondary properties leaves a problem in the philosophy of mind. What is it, for example, to sense redly? This must be explained without appeal to redness. I favour a functionalist theory of mental properties. There is some controversy about whether such a theory can deal satisfactorily with phenomenological properties like sensing redly. I am not convinced by the arguments – mostly, in fact, mere intuitions – to show that it cannot.[16] If it cannot, I suspect that a retreat from a strictly functional to a partly biological theory of such properties will do the job. This is not the place to argue the matter.

According to my account, an object is red in virtue of its power to have a certain effect on (normal) *humans*. Nevertheless, this account does not involve an improperly anthropocentric view of external reality. Let S be any species other than humans. We can define a property of redness-for-S: it is the power to make members of S sense redly. We should be as objectivist about redness-for-S as about redness. And we need not be apologetic about our special interest in redness-for-humans, an interest that leads us to refer to it with the simple term 'redness'. This interest does not make redness-for-humans any more 'in the object' than redness-for-S.

Relativity is even more pervasive with the secondary properties than my account indicates. An object is red in virtue of its power to make (normal) humans sense redly *in normal conditions*. Let C be any condition. We can define redness-for-S-in-C. We should be objectivist about this for any C, just as for any S. Once again, we need not apologize for our special interest in one condition, the normal condition of human life.

I think that a Lockean account of secondary properties along these lines is promising. It is as well, however, that such an account is not essential to Realism, because the account undoubtedly has problems (as far as colours are concerned at least). Hardin (1988) has shown that there are several features of the way colours appear that are due to the workings of our visual system and cannot be accounted for in an objectivist account. For this to be *decisive* against an objectivist account, these features would have to be *essential* to colours. So what the objectivist must do is, first, deny that there is a basis for this essentialism and, second, claim that, as far as those features are concerned, our ordinary view of colours is simply wrong. The right theory of colour would be largely Lockean, but partly eliminativist.

13.7 SECONDARY PROPERTIES AND CONSTRUCTIVISM

Realism is committed to the independence of entities classified under physical types (in my special sense). This independence is very thoroughgoing. We should also be committed to the independence of entities classified socially or as tools, but in this case the independence must be more qualified (13.5). What about the independence of entities classified under types of secondary properties? How independent are entities *qua* red things, for example?

I have emphasized that Realism does not require a stance on the secondary properties. This new question is different. The old one was concerned with the bearing of the secondary properties dispute on the independent existence of entities classified under physical types. The new one is concerned with the independent existence of entities classified under types of secondary properties.

In itself this new question has little interest. Just as everything that is a tool is a physical entity, so also is everything that has a

secondary property. So all such things are covered by Realism anyway. The interest in the question comes from the further light it
throws on Realism's independence dimension and on Constructivism.

Suppose that objects classified by secondary properties did *not* have
the independence that Realism demands. Suppose, next, that all
properties were like the secondary ones. As Putnam puts it:

everything we say about an object is of the form: it is such as to affect *us* in
such-and-such a way. *Nothing at all* we say about any object describes the
object as it is 'in itself', independently of its effect on *us*. (1981: 61)

This is the path to anti-Realism of Putnam's suggestion about Kant.
It is also a path to the relativistic Kantianism of Constructivism.[17]

Consider red things as our example of entities classified by a
secondary property. On my Lockean account, they have their natures
as red things in virtue of causing us to sense redly; their effect on
us is what makes them red. In this important respect they are not
independent of us. Nevertheless, like tools, they differ from Constructivist entities in two respects: the way they depend on us and the
way they depend on the independent world.

Concerning the first, things are red in virtue of how we *sense* them;
Constructivist entities have their natures in virtue of how we *think
about* them. There is a further difference. According to the Constructivist, we are assuming, if there had been no people, there would
have been no stars or dinosaurs. According to the Lockean, if there
had been no people, there would still have been red things; there
would still have been things that would cause people to sense redly.
Concerning the second, there is no limit in principle to what we can
say about how the world independent of us determines that things
are red. We simply have to discover what it is that causes us to sense
redly. By contrast, for the Constructivist, the role of the independent
world is ineffable; like God, it works in mysterious ways. And we
need not rehearse the problems of Modified Constructivism.

I gestured toward a non-cognitive functionalist explanation of
sensing redly. Suppose, however, we were to give a cognitive explanation: to sense redly is to *judge* that something is red or that it is as if
it were red, or to be *disposed to judge* that something is red or that it
is as if it were red. An explanation along these lines may be hard
to motivate, and it certainly has problems; for example, that of
explaining the concept RED without appeal to redness and that
of accommodating the great differences in colour concepts among
people with the same colour discriminations. But, setting motivation

and problems aside, consider the bearing of this sort of cognitive explanation on the above contrast with Constructivism.

The explanation largely removes the first of the two differences between red things and Constructivist entities: things *are* red in virtue of how we think of them. We do seem to make them the way Constructivists think we make worlds. Despite this, it remains the case that there would have been red things but not Constructivist entities if there had been no people.

The explanation leaves the second difference untouched. Something is red in virtue of causing a certain judgement in us. We can hope to find a scientific account of the mechanisms by which the thing – with a nature quite independent of our judgements – has that effect. By contrast, the Constructivist can give no account of what, outside the realm of thought, influences and constrains the thoughts that construct the known world. The independent world has a real role in making red things, not its pseudo-role in making Constructivist entities.

In sum, even on a cognitive version of our Lockean account of the secondary properties, red things differ from Constructivist entities. Suppose, however, that we followed Putnam's suggestion and gave a Lockean account along those lines for *all* properties, primary as well as secondary. Then we would lose our only differences with Constructivist entities.

The generalized Lockean account makes the nature of everything depend on our judgements: for any x and for any F, x is F in virtue of the fact that x causes us to judge that it is F (or be disposed to, etc.). So we can no longer tell the scientific story of an *independent* world's causal influence on our judging that something is red, or whatever. We cannot explain that influence by appeal to the properties of objects that have natures that are independent of our judgements of their natures. There is no longer any basis for claiming that red things (or whatever) would have existed if there had been no people. The situation is worse. If the Lockean account is generalized to all properties, then surely it should be generalized to all relations. So it should cover causality. So not only have we lost the independent world that influences our judgements, we have lost the independent influence (as Kant did; 13.2). The known world is all the result of our imposition. The generalized Lockean account is Constructivism.

Putnam would agree. Philip Pettit, it seems, would not.[18] So let us say more.

I have demonstrated earlier that red things, though partly dependent for their redness on us, are not Constructivist. Why then does this not carry over when we generalize? *Because that demonstration was against a Realist background*, a world of stones, trees, cats, and so on that was quite independent of our judgements.[19] The background supplied the crucial contrast between the way red things and Constructivist entities depended *on an independent world*. The way red things depended on that world for their redness was a causal relation open to any amount of scientific investigation. So talk of this dependence yielded a genuine explanation of constraints on our thinking and hence on our worldmaking. The generalized Lockean account removes the Realist background. It leaves the dependence of red things (and everything else) on an independent world mysterious. Talk of this dependence yields only the empty facade of an explanation of constraints on our thinking and worldmaking. The contrast with Constructivist entities is lost.

The generalized account can, of course, talk of causal relations between objects. However, the relations and objects talked of are both created by our judgings. Set aside worries occasioned by our creating the relations, and consider those occasioned by our creating the objects. Given that what causes our judgings are objects created by those very judgings, what is left of the idea that our judgings are constrained by an independent world? The problem for the generalized account is with the causation of judgements by an independent world, not causation in general.

The natures of objects referred to in explanations of judgement may themselves depend on judgements without leading to Constructivism, provided that, *in the end*, we get explanations that refer to natures that are not so dependent. Consider, for example, the following explanation: x made me think that it was like the sound of a trumpet because x was red. According to our earlier account, x's being red is dependent on a judgement. Despite this, we can use the fact that x is red to explain another judgement without collapsing into Constructivism, because the judgement involved in that fact can itself be explained by reference to a judgement-independent nature; we can explain it in terms of the reflective properties of x's surface, for example. On the generalized account, however, this explanatory procedure never reaches a judgement-independent nature: the explanation of the judgement that is constitutive of x's being red refers to another judgement-dependent nature; and so on. Unless we finally get to natures independent of our judgings, all these explanations of our judgements in terms of objects with certain natures collapse into explanations of one judgement by another. For the nature of every object collapses into a judgement.

So Putnam is right in thinking that generalizing Locke is a route to Constructivism. The route starts with a plausible Lockean account of the secondary properties, and takes two steps. The first step is dubious, but not so large: take the effect on us that determines the nature of a secondary property to be cognitive. The second step is a giant one: generalize this account to all properties.

There are two objections to the giant step. First, as I pointed out earlier (13.1) and have argued throughout this book, the very plausible alternative doctrine, Realism, does not face any problems that could motivate this move to anti-Realism. Second, the resulting anti-Realism is highly objectionable. The plausibility of the Lockean account of the secondary properties rests heavily on its commitment to the independent nature of the world that is responsible for the relevant effects on us. There is no puzzle about typing objects by their effects on us provided that we can appeal to typings that are not dependent on us to explain those effects. A little bit of worldmaking is alright against a background of a world that we did not make and that influences our little effort. The generalization of the Lockean account removes what is essential to the plausibility of the account.

Putnam's route to Constructivism does not make Constructivism plausible; but it does come much closer than any other to making it seem rational. So the route may help with the diagnosis of Constructivism. The route presumably plays a role in Putnam's thinking. Perhaps it underlies Goodman's challenge to Scheffler to show 'which features of the stars we did not make'. But could such a philosophically subtle route explain the enormous popularity of Constructivism? Could something like it be deep in the unconscious behind the following typical Constructivist response to a realist?

> *Realist* (pointing to a cat): Surely you don't deny that this cat would exist whatever we thought.

> *Constructivist*: Of course it would, but not as a cat. We make it a cat.

Could it underlie such passages as the following?

We do not wish to say that facts do not exist nor that there is no such thing as reality. In this simple sense our position is not relativist. Our point is that 'out-there-ness' is the *consequence* of scientific work rather than its *cause*. (Latour and Woolgar 1986: 180–2)

Who knows.

Finally, the discussion of the secondary properties has shown that entities are red, just as they are hammers or bachelors partly in virtue of their relations to us and partly in virtue of the independent world. However, their dependencies on us and the independent world are not like those of Constructivist entities.[20]

NOTES

1 Passmore refers nicely to 'the French intellectual's dream . . . of a world which exists only in so far as it enters into a book' (1985: 32).

2 The following is from a leading literary theorist: 'The France you are talking about will always be the product of the talk about it and will *never* be independently available. What the example of France shows is that all facts are discourse specific (since no fact is available apart from some dimension of assessment or other)' (Fish 1980: 199; my thanks to Alex Byrne).

3 In the theory of the media, e.g., it is common to find views like the following: reality is not 'out there'; it is 'a vast production, a staged creation – something humanly produced and humanly maintained' (Carey 1989: 26; my thanks to Judith Lichtenberg).

4 Consider this typical statement: 'Despite the fact that our scientists held the belief that the inscriptions could be representations or indicators of some entity with an independent existence "out there", we have argued that such entities were constituted solely through the use of these inscriptions. . . . objects . . . are constituted through the artful creativity of scientists' (Latour and Woolgar 1986: 128–9; my thanks to Fiona Cowie).

5 See Searle 1990 for an excellent discussion of this.

6 Consider the following from a feminist theorist: 'The notion of *a* feminist standpoint that is truer than previous (male) ones seems to rest upon many problematic and unexamined assumptions. . . . There is no force or reality "outside" our social relations and activity . . . that will rescue us from partiality and difference' (Flax 1987: 642; my thanks to Tamar Gendler).

7 See Barnes and Bloor 1982, e.g.

8 This is a fairly typical 'outsider's' response to Constructivism. Thus David Stove has this to say in his chapter 'Philosophy and Lunacy: Nelson Goodman and the Omnipotence of Words' (1991: 27–42): 'the statement that worlds can be made with words: a statement which, as Hume said of the doctrine of the real presence, "is so absurd that it eludes the force of all argument"' (p. 31). David Papineau takes Constructivism to be so absurd that he ignores it altogether in his discussion of realism (1987; cf. Devitt 1991b). See also Rorty's view, section 11.2 above.

9 On this, see Elder 1986.

10 Note the inference in the following passage also: 'What Austin discovers at the end of *How To Do Things With Words* is that all utterances are

performatives – produced and understood within the assumption of some socially conceived dimension of assessment – and that therefore all facts are institutional, are facts only by virtue of the prior institution of some such dimension' (Fish 1980: 198).

11 My suggestions are for a *rational* explanation. For some learned, and very entertaining, suggestions of a different sort, see Stove 1991. Stove thinks that anti-Realism, like religion, stems from our need to have a *congenial* world.

Georges Rey has made several suggestions to me along similar lines to explain the popularity of Constructivism among people who perceive themselves as oppressed or who identify with those they perceive as oppressed. In opposing the illegitimate imposition of the views of, say, one culture or class upon another, they come to oppose the imposition of *any* authority whatsoever, even the legitimate authority that might come from actually *knowing* something about an independent world. Their sense of self-worth becomes so tied to the worth of their views that it must not be *possible* for anyone – racist, sexist, or scientist – to undermine those views. The only way such absolute safety can be obtained, of course, is to deny that there is any world independent of one's views.

12 The psychological literature on concepts and categories gives ample testimony to this; see, e.g., Markman 1989: 6–12.

13 Throughout this discussion, I have talked in an ontologically robust way about kinds. Nominalists might well object. I sympathize, for I have nominalist leanings. However, the talk is just a very convenient manner of speaking. The Realist insists against the Constructivist that whether or not something is a stone, a rose, or a peorincred is not a matter of our linguistic doing. Whether or not there are kinds *stone, rose,* and *peorincred* is another matter.

14 This discussion has semantic consequences: 'artifactual kind term' and 'natural kind term' are not semantically interesting descriptions; Devitt and Sterelny 1987: 75–8.

15 My account is a modified version of one that appeared in section 5.10 of the first edition (1984a: 70–1).

16 See Rey 1991 for a functionalist theory of phenomenological properties.

17 Putnam's idea of generalizing a Lockean account of secondary properties to all properties is discussed by Field (1982: 557–62).

18 Pettit proposes a generalized Lockean account in attempting to solve the problem of rule-following (1990). He has followed up with a very interesting paper (1991), partly stimulated by Mark Johnston (1987a, 1987b, 1989), in which he examines the relation between the generalized Lockean account and realism. He divides realism into three theses, the second of which is near enough my Realism. Surprisingly, he thinks that the generalized account is compatible with this thesis.

19 Frederick Kroon has rightly described something like the generalized Lockean account as a realism 'not worth fighting for'. He wrongly takes

my Realism as such a realism because of its lack of commitment to our being right about the properties of things (1988: 147–9). He overlooks that Realism is committed to our being right about one property of, say, tigers: that they are tigers (2.3). This is what commits me to more than merely noumenal entities; it distinguishes Realism from Weak Realism.

20 I am indebted to Alex Byrne, Keith Campbell, Peter Godfrey-Smith, Geoffrey Hellman, Frank Jackson, Michael Slote, David Stove, and, enormously, Georges Rey for comments on a draft of this chapter.

14

Dummett's Anti-Realism

14.1   INTRODUCTION

Michael Dummett argues against realism.[1] In the philosophical circle centred on Oxford, the influence of this argument is already great.[2] Elsewhere its influence is growing.[3] Crispin Wright, an able and vigorous defender of Dummett, claims that Dummett has 'set up what promises to be one of the most fruitful philosophical research programmes of this century' (1981: 67). On the other hand, many philosophers are sceptical about Dummett's argument: it smacks too much of positivism and Wittgensteinianism.[4] I sympathize with the sceptics, and disagree with Wright.

Dummett's argument has a general form that is claimed to cover various 'realisms' – for example, about common-sense physical entities, about scientific entities, about mathematical entities, and about the past. My concern in this book has been only with the first two of these, which I have lumped together under the name 'Realism' (2.4). That is what I need to defend from Dummett's argument. However, I shall focus entirely on defending Common-Sense Realism (but will follow my usual practice of abbreviating its name to 'Realism'). I take it as obvious that if this defence is good, it will carry over to Scientific Realism (which gets very little special attention from Dummett).

The twentieth century has seen a 'linguistic turn' in philosophy. I have already noted this turn in the positivists (7.8). Dummett's argument against Realism exemplifies a strong commitment to the turn: 'The whole point of my approach to [the various disputes concerning realism] has been to show that the theory of meaning underlies metaphysics. If I have made any worthwhile contribution to philosophy, I think it must lie in having raised this issue in these terms' (1978; xl). For Dummett, 'the goal of philosophy is the analysis of the structure of *thought*.' He justifies the pre-eminence he assigns to the philosophy of language by its bearing

on that analysis (1978: 458).[5] Dummett thus stands opposed to two of
the maxims that have guided this book: according to Maxim 2, the
metaphysical issue of Realism should be distinguished from any issue in
the theory of meaning; according to Maxim 3, the metaphysical issue is
pre-eminent.

There are three premises in Dummett's argument for anti-Realism:

> A   The Realism dispute is the dispute about whether statements
>   have realist (evidence-transcendent) or only verificationist truth
>   conditions.

The statements we are concerned with here are, of course, ones containing words like 'stone', 'tree', and 'cat': 'common-sense physical
statements'. An example of a doctrine claiming that these statements
have realist truth conditions of the Dummettian sort is my Correspondence Truth (common-sense physical) (3.3 and 3.4). According to
that doctrine, these statements have truth conditions that are not in
any way constrained by our epistemic capacities (Maxim 5). So it is
possible that a statement might be true and yet that we might not be
able to detect this (which is not to say that the truth of any true
statement is *actually* undetectable: 3.5, 7.4). In this respect, statements
have 'evidence-transcendent' truth conditions, in Dummett's sense.
Since Correspondence Truth has already been (partly) explained I shall
allow it to stand in for all such doctrines. So, for Dummett, abbreviating,
Realism *is* Correspondence Truth.

> B   The dispute about truth conditions is the dispute about whether
>   the competent speaker's understanding is realist (evidence-
>   transcendent) or only verificationist.

It follows from B that if the understanding is only verificationist, then
Correspondence Truth is false. With A, this leads to anti-Realism.

> C   The competent speaker's understanding is only verificationist.

(A consequence of B and C is that verification is a more basic semantic
notion than truth.)

There is general agreement on only one thing about Dummett's
philosophy: it is difficult. So it may seem improbable that it could
be made 'as simple as A-B-C' (as John Bigelow nicely remarked to
me). In fact, B and C conceal complications: each has two distinct
versions. With those complications taken into account, I do indeed
claim that the above three premises, together with their supporting
arguments, constitute Dummett's argument against Realism.[6]

Dummett focuses his discussion of Realism on verificationism and premise C. The discussion of A and B is slight. Yet these two premises are crucial to Dummett's case against Realism. My focus will be on them.

I have already argued, in effect, against A. I shall start by arguing that Dummett subscribes to A (14.2), and that his argument for it is inadequate (14.3). I distinguish two versions of B, hence two of C, which Dummett conflates. B_1 and C_1 are based on the assumption that linguistic competence involves propositional knowledge of truth conditions. B_2 and C_2 see competence as merely a practical ability (14.4). I argue that Dummett gives the 'propositional assumption' about competence no adequate support (14.5), and that it is false (14.6). So B_1 and C_1 are false. Verificationist arguments to show that speakers do not *know* realist truth conditions are irrelevant to Correspondence Truth. I go on to consider competence as a practical ability. Interest then centres on C_2, the view that the sentences understood by the competent speaker have only verificationist truth conditions. I set out Dummett's argument for this (14.7) and reject it (14.8). I argue that, in any case, verificationism has little bearing on Realism. Theories of language and understanding should not determine theories of the world (14.9).

14.2 DUMMETT'S COMMITMENT TO A

I have argued (chapter 4) that no doctrine of truth is in anyway constitutive of Realism. So premise A is false.

This conclusion does not mean, of course, that the issues of Realism and truth have no bearing on each other. Indeed, I think it is hard find a plausible epistemology for Realism that can be combined with most, if not all, epistemic doctrines of truth (4.3). And I have argued that a Realist should accept Correspondence Truth (chapter 6). These are examples of abductions from one position to another. (I shall say more of such inferences in section 14.9.) However, links of this sort are weak, and should lead to great caution in running the two issues together.

Dummett is not at all cautious. He often straightforwardly identifies the two issues. Thus he says that the realism–anti-realism dispute 'concerns the notion of truth appropriate for statements of the disputed class; and this means that it is a dispute concerning the kind of *meaning* which these statements have' (1978: 146; see also pp. xxx, 22–3, 155, 314, 358–9; 1979b: 3; 1981: 432–4, 441).[7]

On this view, the doctrine of Correspondence Truth is *constitutive* of

Realism: it is the doctrine that common-sense physical statements 'possess an objective truth-value, independently of our means of knowing it'; their meanings 'are not directly tied to the kind of evidence for them we can have' (1978: 146; see also 1973: 466; 1981: 434, 446; 1982: 55). On the other hand, the anti-Realist claims that such a statement

is true only if we have established it as true; or only if we either have done so or shall do so at some future time; or only if we have some procedure which, were we to carry it out, would establish it as true; or, at least, only if there exists something, of the sort that we normally take as a basis for the assertion of a statement of that class, such that, if we knew it, we should treat it as a ground for the truth of the statement. (1981: 443)

Sometimes Dummett urges an apparently weaker view: that the theory of meaning 'underlies' the realism dispute (1978: xxx, xl) or supplies 'the premises' for various positions in the dispute (1977: 382–3; 1978: xxviii, 229). However, Dummett attaches no significance to the difference between these two views: 'Realism rests upon – or better, consists in – an adherence to a truth-conditional semantics for our language' (1979a: 218).

Given that what I have characterized under the term 'Realism' is, *prima facie*, quite different from any semantic doctrine, it is appropriate to wonder whether my disagreement with Dummett over premise A is 'merely verbal'. Perhaps he is using the term 'realism' in connection with common-sense physical statements in such a way that he does not intend it to have any bearing – at least, not any direct bearing – on the traditional metaphysical dispute.

This is certainly not the case. He describes the realism that he identifies with (rests upon) a semantic doctrine in a traditional way: 'on a realistic conception of the physical universe, that universe constitutes an objective reality, independent of our knowledge of it ' (1977: 382; see also 1978: xxv, 228). He sees the realism that is threatened by his discussion as a doctrine about what there really is, an ontological-metaphysical doctrine (1977: 386; 1978: 146–7, 230; 1981: 428–30, 449–52; 1982: 106) opposed to idealism (1973: 671, 681; 1978: 145; 1981: 504–5) and phenomenalism (1978: 147). His problem is old, but the semantic approach is new (1978: xxxi). Indeed, as the passage quoted at the beginning of this chapter shows, Dummett thinks that any worthwhile contribution he has made to philosophy lies in this approach to such metaphysical problems. Finally, Dummett sometimes expresses the anti-realism that his argument inclines him toward in ontological terms, though the expression is brief and obscure. His anti-realism 'appears a more radical repudiation of objective reality than idealism' (1979a: 223); reality comes into existence as we probe, though we do not create it; it is not fully determinate (1978: xxviii–xxix, 18–19, 229–30; 1979a: 221–2).

Others in the British School influenced by Dummett see their semantic discussions as bearing on Realism. They typically start these discussions with a metaphysical statement of the realism issue. This is immediately replaced by a formulation in terms of truth, which is then taken not as deflationary, but as part of a theory of meaning.[8] And Wright maintains that 'the distinguishing mark of the idealist' is his view that 'realism is founded on a misunderstanding of the nature of truth' (1986: 2).

So the difference of opinion over premise A is not merely verbal. Dummett sees his discussion as bearing directly on Realism. He does think that the particular form of his semantic version of Realism may depart somewhat from traditional usage. He thinks that usage has confused two issues: (a) the issue of whether statements of one kind (e.g. physical) can be reduced to those of another (e.g. sense-datum); (b) the issue of whether statements of the one kind are determinately true or false (1978: xxxii, 157–9; 1979b: 1–5). His departure from tradition, he thinks, comes in his setting (a) aside and taking (b) as the basic issue.

Traditionally, as I have pointed out, there have been two dimensions to Realism: the dimension of existence and the dimension of independence from the mental. Now the second of these has often been an issue of reduction: Can physical objects be reduced to ideas or sense data? This issue of ontological reduction is not the same as Dummett's (a), an issue of linguistic reduction (5.4). But overlook that, for Dummett sets (a) aside. My central disagreement concerns (b). What has the ontological issue of what exists to do with (b), the linguistic issue of determinate truth values? On the face of it, nothing at all.[9]

14.3 DUMMETT'S ARGUMENT FOR A

Dummett completely misconceives the Realism issue. Why? The crux of the explanation is that, for Dummett, any metaphysical view is 'a picture which has in itself no substance otherwise than as a representation of the given conception of meaning' (1977: 383; see also 1978: xxviii–xxix). The metaphysical view adds only a 'metaphor' (1978: xxv–xxvi, 229). Such a picture or metaphor is none the less 'natural' (p. xxviii); it will 'force itself' on us (pp. 229–30); it is irresistible' (pp. xxviii, 230). So while Dummett will from time to time use the language of the traditional metaphysical dispute, when the chips are down, he talks only of meaning.

Dummett's belief in this 'Metaphor Thesis' – metaphysics beyond meaning is mere metaphor – is central to the explanation of various puzzling aspects of his discussion that we have noted: first, of his holding premise A; second, of his attaching no significance to the difference between A and the apparently weaker view that the dispute over truth 'underlies' the Realism dispute; third, of the brevity and obscurity of his account of the ontological consequences of his anti-Realist argument.

Why does Dummett believe the Metaphor Thesis? Why does he think that the metaphysical dispute about Realism cannot stand on its own feet? The cause is clear, but it supplies no good reason.

Dummett's view of metaphysics comes from his philosophy of mathematics (1978: xxiv). He thinks (1) that the critical disagreement between platonists and intuitionists is over the appropriate forms of reasoning in mathematics, and that this is a disagreement over the meaning of mathematical statements, over the type of truth conditions those statements have (1977: 380; 1978: xxvii–xxviii). Now this alone does not show, of course, that there is not another, even if less critical, disagreement over the metaphysical issue of the nature of mathematical objects; it does not show that there is not also a substantive disagreement over whether these objects are independently existing, abstract objects or are creations of the human mind. Nevertheless, (2) Dummett wants to claim that there is no such further substantive disagreement. He is impressed by Kreisel's remark that 'the problem is not the existence of mathematical objects, but the objectivity of mathematical statements' (quoted, e.g., at 1978: xxviii). He thinks that the disagreement over objects adds only metaphors to the discussion, one metaphor seeing the mathematician as an astronomer, the other seeing him as an artist (1977: 382–3; 1978: xxv–xxvi, 229). Suppose this is so. It does not show, of course, that *all* metaphysical disagreements about the ontological status of objects have no substance beyond a disagreement over meaning. Perhaps the disagreement between Realists and idealists over physical objects is substantive, even though that between platonists and intuitionists over mathematical objects is metaphorical. Yet (3) Dummett wants to extend his claim about mathematics to all fields (1977: 381–3; 1978: xxix): he arrives at the Metaphor Thesis.

Consider (2). Why does the disagreement over mathematical objects add only metaphors to the disagreement over meaning? As far as I can see, Dummett does little more than claim that it adds only this. For Dummett, it seems, the metaphysical disagreement makes no literal sense on the face of it, and the only way to interpret it is to relate it to the issue of meaning.

A certain argument features prominently in Dummett's discussion of mathematical objects. Take the disagreement over these objects literally. Dummett argues that it does not bear on the disagreement over meaning. Assuming a platonist ontology does not lead to a platonist view of meaning and logic; assuming an intuitionist ontology does not lead to an intuitionist view of meaning and logic (1973: 507–8; 1977: 382–9; 1978: 230–47).

Suppose Dummett were right about this lack of bearing of the ontological dispute on the semantic one. (I don't think he is, for reasons indicated at the beginning of section 14.2 and considered again in section 14.9. Dummett's argument depends on his views about meaning, which I discuss later.) The mere fact that a disagreement does not have any consequence for semantics does not show that it is not a real one, does not show that it is only metaphorical. Most real disagreements are irrelevant to semantics.

Despite the lack of argument for it, Dummett's claim about the metaphorical nature of the disagreement over mathematical objects seems to me to have some plausibility. However, consider how it would strike a hard-core platonist. For him the disagreement does not seem metaphorical; he thinks he has a clear conception of independently existing mathematical objects, a conception that he finds vividly different from a conception of mental constructs. He will think Dummett's view mistaken. Furthermore, Dummett's argument that the platonist's ontology does not settle his semantics gives the platonist no reason to think otherwise.

We see the importance of this when we examine move (3) in Dummett's argument for the Metaphor Thesis: the extension of his view about mathematics to other fields. What reason is there for extending such sympathy as we may have for Dummett's position against the hard-core platonist to his position against the hard-core Realist? As far as I can see, Dummett offers no argument for the extension beyond claiming that the argument about the lack of bearing of ontology on semantics carries over from mathematics to other fields (1977: 381; 1978: xxix). Even if this were so, and the argument were good, it would no more show that the metaphysical dispute about physical objects is metaphorical than it earlier showed that the metaphysical dispute about mathematical objects was metaphorical.

Not only is the extension from mathematics unargued, it is highly implausible. The difference between the mathematical and physical worlds is striking.[10] The platonist's conception of independently existing mathematical objects strikes many people as far-fetched. What are they like? Where do they exist? How could we come to know about them? The intuitionist's conception is no more transparent. How could numbers be mental constructions or free creations of the human mind? These conceptions are so odd, so hard to grasp, that a metaphorical interpretation of the dispute is tempting (though I don't say right). By contrast, the Realist's conception of independently existing physical objects is the very core of common sense. There is certainly some vagueness about it, some room for further explanation of the sort that I have attempted in chapter 2; but it is not in the least bit metaphorical. Indeed, if this talk cannot be taken literally, what talk can? It must be close to a bench-mark of the literal. (See also 4.6.)

Dummett is far from alone in finding the realism issue obscure. I have already mentioned Rorty, who thinks that we need Davidsonian semantics to clarify the issue (11.3). And there are many others.[11] Though these philosophers do little to demonstrate the alleged obscurity, I think we can discern what bothers them. It is indeed hard to know what to make of the usual statements of anti-realism. We have struggled with this problem in discussing Constructivism (chapter 13). However, the problem is about *anti*-realism, not realism.

A first stab at a clear statement of realism denies *any* dependencies of the world on our minds. An intelligible claim of the mind-dependency of the world stands clearly opposed to this realism. An intelligible claim about meaning or truth is beside the metaphysical point. Unintelligible claims can be ignored. Realism does not become unclear because it is sometimes opposed by nonsense.

A qualification to this statement of realism is immediately called for, and was made: realism allows for the familiar causal interactions between minds and the world (2.2). Realism disallows all other dependencies. That is sufficient to characterize realism about objects like stones, trees, and cats. If we wanted to be realist about tools and social entities, we would have to say more (13.5).

The centre of the realism debate has always appeared to be over the nature of reality. The realist position on reality is perfectly clear. The anti-realist position is often not; but what it is unclear about is reality, not something else altogether. The fashionable assumption that anti-realism is not about what it appears to be about is highly implausible. It requires argument, not casual assertion.

In this part of the chapter, I have argued that Dummett subscribes to premise A and that it is false. His reason for adopting A is the Metaphor Thesis. This rests on an unsupported, though possibly plausible, claim about the metaphorical nature of the ontological dispute in the philosophy of mathematics and on an unsupported and highly implausible extension of that claim to the dispute about physical reality.[12]

I should mention a *motive* that Dummett seems to have for adopting A. He is interested in giving an account of realism in general, irrespective of subject-matter. This account cannot be achieved by taking it to be about entities, because 'certain kinds of realism, for instance realism about the future or about ethics, do not seem readily classifiable as doctrines about a realism of entities' (1982: 55). The generality can be achieved by taking realism to be about statements.

I have three comments on this. First, it needs to be shown that a general account can be given. Perhaps the various realisms are unrelated, or only loosely related (family resemblance). Second, if a general account is possible, it needs to be argued that the account should take realism to be about statements. Third, a crucial test case for both arguments would be realism about the physical world. I have argued that this *is* about entities and that Dummett has given no convincing reason for supposing otherwise.

Experience suggests that some people will not accept that Dummett subscribes to A, despite the evidence that he does. Whether he does or not, the falsity of A has two consequences for his position that are worth emphasizing. First, nothing follows simply about Realism from any thesis about the truth conditions of statements. Even if an argument is made against Correspondence Truth, a further argument is needed to establish anti-Realism. So the fate of Realism does not hang on the success of criticisms of Dummett's B and C such as I shall be offering in the next few sections. Second, and more important, there is the possibility of a quite different approach to the defence of both Realism and Correspondence Truth. Guided by Maxim 3, we can reverse the order of argument. We can give a non-semantic argument for Realism, and then use Realism to establish Correspondence Truth. This is the procedure I followed in chapters 5 and 6. We can then argue, as I shall in section 14.9, that this way of proceeding rests on far firmer foundations than Dummett's. This is a more radical critique, rejecting not just the details of Dummett's argument, but the philosophical methodology it exemplifies.

14.4   VERSIONS OF B AND C

Dummett's second premise is:

> B   The dispute about truth conditions is the dispute about
>   whether the competent speaker's understanding is realist
>   (evidence-transcendent) or only verificationist.

This is a corollary of Dummett's thesis that 'a theory of meaning is a
theory of understanding' (1973: 92; 1975: 99). With A, it yields the
view that if understanding is only verificationist, Realism is false.

On the face of it, B is odd. How could a semantic dispute about
the truth conditions of sentences be a psychological dispute about the
competent speaker's understanding? How could disputes about such
different sorts of property be the same?[13] Yet Dummett does equate
the two disputes (1976: 68–9; 1978: 153–5, 358–9).

In one of his more recent writings, Dummett is much more cautious about the equation. He still believes that it is true, but now
thinks it 'far less clear' (1981: 308) and 'more problematic' (pp. xiii,
74; see also p. 55). However, he does not go into the matter, but sets
it aside for a 'projected volume' (p. 76).

Why should anyone equate the two disputes? We must distinguish
clearly, though Dummett does not, two versions of B, reflecting quite
different assumptions about the nature of speaker competence. The
first, and most prominent, version is based on the assumption that
competence consists (at least in part) in knowledge of truth (falsity)
conditions[14]:

> B₁   The dispute about truth conditions is the dispute about
>   whether the competent speaker *knows* realist (evidence-
>   transcendent) or only verificationist truth conditions.

The knowledge in question here is propositional, or theoretical: it is
knowledge-that and not, for example, mere knowledge-how. So on
this assumption, an L-speaker's understanding of a sentence of L
consists in his knowing that the sentence is true-in-L in such and
such circumstances. Now if he knows this, it must be so. Therefore, a
dispute over whether the truth conditions that a speaker knows are,
as a matter of fact, realist or only verificationist would settle the
question of whether the truth conditions *are* realist or only verificationist. At least, it would settle this if we assume that whatever truth
conditions a sentence has, the speaker will know it to have. This
assumption is probably implicit in the 'propositional assumption'
about competence. So we have established B₁.

With the propositional assumption goes a version of C also:

> C_1 The competent speaker *knows* only verificationist truth conditions.

The rival to this, which the believer in Correspondence Truth is thought to be committed to, is the view that a speaker knows realist (evidence-transcendent) truth conditions.

The propositional assumption about competence is a received wisdom of contemporary semantics. As Herbert Heidelberger has pointed out, it seems to be regarded as uncontroversial, 'perhaps unworthy of serious discussion'. Yet it is not 'obviously true' (1980: 402).[15] In my view, it is false. Hence B_1 and C_1 are false. I think competence is simply a set of grounded skills or abilities. I shall indicate why in section 14.6.

The attribution of the propositional assumption, and hence of B_1, to Dummett is well based, but not certain. Philosophers who make the assumption usually hedge their bets. Dummett is no exception. It is clear that he thinks of competence as 'a practical ability'; but this alone does not count against the attribution, because he mostly writes as if the ability consisted in propositional knowledge of truth conditions. However, rather than straight-forwardly identifying the ability with the knowledge, he seems to prefer to say that it can be 'represented' as that knowledge (1973: 461–2; 1975: 105–9, 121–5; 1976: 69–71; 1977: 373; 1978: 128–9; but compare 1982: 63–4, 85, 105). Further he thinks that part of this knowledge is only 'implicit', or 'tacit' (1976: 70–1, 80; 1977: 373–4; 1978: 129; 1982: 62).[16] This use of weasel words in stating the propositional assumption casts doubt on Dummett's commitment to it. Finally, the aforementioned caution about the relation between meaning and understanding spreads also to the propositional assumption (1981: xiii, 55, 74–7).[17] So I shall not rest my case against Dummett on attributing this assumption to him.

Abandoning the propositional assumption and taking competence as simply a practical ability, we get another version both of B and of C:

> B_2 The dispute about truth conditions is the dispute about whether the sentences understood by the competent speaker *have* realist (evidence-transcendent) or only verificationist truth conditions.

> C_2 The sentences understood by the competent speaker *have* only verificationist truth conditions.

These differ from B_1 and C_1 in making no mention of knowledge. B_2 must be true, given the tautological assumption that the competent speaker understands the sentences of the language. Interest then focuses on C_2. I shall argue in section 14.8 that it is false.[18]

14.5 AN ARGUMENT FOR THE PROPOSITIONAL ASSUMPTION?

Meanwhile, we must consider B_1 and the propositional assumption on which it depends. The dependence requires that we take the assumption strictly and literally: it is no mere manner of speaking; the speaker really does know that the truth conditions are such and such.

At first sight it may seem that Dummett's lengthy arguments for a verificationist and against a realist theory of understanding (e.g. in 1975 and 1976) constitute an argument for the propositional assumption. For the conclusion is always presented as: the speaker knows only verificationist truth conditions that is, as C_1. However, this way of putting the conclusion simply reflects Dummett's conflation of the propositional and non-propositional views of competence. There is nothing in Dummett's argument for verificationism, however sound, that makes it an argument for C_1 rather than C_2.

Despite the popularity of the propositional assumption, I can find nothing in the literature that could seriously be called an argument for it. Apparently it is thought to follow in some obvious way from the claim that speakers 'know the meaning' of sentences in their language and from the slogan that 'the meaning of a sentence is its truth conditions.' Some passages in Dummett hint at this (e.g. 1975: 105–9; 1976: 68–9; 1978: 153–5). Consider also the following summary of Dummett's views by Colin McGinn:

> If [a Tarskian theory of truth] is to serve as a theory of meaning for L, and if speakers are acknowledged to know what sentences of L mean, then there must be a sense in which the theory states, or serves to state, what speakers of L know in knowing what sentences of L mean.[19] (1980: 20; see also Wright 1976: 221)

Remarks like these are common in the literature, and yet they represent not so much an argument as a play on words. Every attempt I have made to construct an argument around such remarks turns into a travesty. The following attempt, suggested by Dummett's discussion of Frege's distinction between sense and reference (1978: 117–26, particularly 124–6),[20] is typical (X is a competent speaker):

(1)　X understands S.

∴　(2)　X knows the meaning of S.

(3)　The meaning of S = the truth conditions of S.

∴　(4)　X knows the truth conditions of S.

∴　(5)　X knows what the truth conditions of S are.

Let TC be the truth conditions of S.

∴　(6)　X knows that the truth conditions of S are TC.

No objection can be taken to (1). And the move to (2) is acceptable enough if (2) is taken as a mere everyday manner of speaking. However, if (2) is to be construed as requiring that there exist some entity – the meaning of S – which X knows in the sense that he is acquainted with it, then we should resist the move. We need a strong argument, not just ordinary talk, before we accept such a requirement on linguistic competence. (2) does have to be construed in this way if (4) is to follow from it and (3). Some entity has to exist which is both the meaning of S and the truth conditions of S, such that if X is acquainted with the one, he is acquainted with the other. Thus the inference will not go through if we construe (2) as just another way of saying that X knows what the meaning of S is and construe (4) likewise (i.e. construe it as (5)): knowing-what contexts are opaque. (And is (2) any more acceptable construed this way than the other way?)

Next, consider (3), the other premise in the inference to (4). It is based on the slogan that the meaning of a sentence is its truth conditions. As slogans go, this is a good one in my view. Nevertheless, it is only a slogan. One way of interpreting it would be as follows: it is because a sentence is true in such and such circumstances, and only in those circumstances, that it plays the special semantic role in our lives that it does play. There is no reason to suppose that a theory guided by this slogan will posit any entity, the meaning of S, or any entity, the truth conditions of S, as (3) requires. Furthermore, even if the theory *were* to posit such an entity, and even if (2), construed as positing an entity, *were* acceptable, there would be no reason to suppose that the former 'theoretical' entity would be the same as the latter 'ordinary' entity. Certainly the mere fact that they were both *called* 'the meaning of S' would not show that they were the same.

These are the worst aspects of the argument, perhaps, but the rest of it is also bad. First, (5) does not follow from (4): a person can be acquainted with an entity without knowing what the entity is. (Of course, as I have noted, we could construe (4) as (5), but then it would not follow from (2) and (3).) Second, the inference from (5) to (6) is dubious, to say the least. The main problem with it is that knowing-what seems to be context-dependent (as Dummett himself notes, but sets aside: 1978: 126).[21] Finally, (6) cannot be inferred directly from (4), ignoring (5): X can be acquainted with an entity without knowing *that* it is anything in particular.

The argument seems like a travesty, because it involves a naïve view, first, of an ordinary use of the word 'meaning'; second, of a theoretical slogan; and third, of the connection between the ordinary use and the slogan. So I don't attribute the argument to Dummett. However, I do claim that if this, or something like it, is not his implicit argument for the assumption that competence requires knowledge of truth conditions, then (aside from some brief remarks considered in the next section) he has offered not even the glimmer of an argument for the assumption. If the assumption is false, so also are B_1 and C_1.[22]

14.6 ARGUMENTS AGAINST THE PROPOSITIONAL ASSUMPTION

In my view, competence in a language does not consist in any semantic propositional knowledge at all. It is a set of grounded skills or abilities. It consists in being able to do things with a language, not in having thoughts about it. Understanding a language no more involves having propositional knowledge of a semantic sort about the language than being able to ride a bicycle involves having propositional knowledge about mechanics or being able to digest food involves having propositional knowledge about digestion.

Gilbert Harman has raised a very good objection to the propositional assumption (1975: 286). The knowledge it attributes to the speaker requires that he have some way of representing to himself the conditions that would make sentences true. But what does competence in the representing language consist in? Either the same problem has reappeared, or we are faced with an equal one.[23]

I have raised a related objection (1981a: 97–100). Briefly, a person could not have semantic propositional knowledge without having the semantic vocabulary of some language. That vocabulary is an isolable part of a language, just as is the biological or economic vocabulary. A person could be competent in the non-semantic part of a language without being competent in its semantic part or in the semantic part of any other language. So competence in the non-semantic part does not consist in semantic propositional knowledge. So competence in the language as a whole does not either.[24]

The propositional assumption about *full semantic* competence apparently made by Dummett and other philosophers is reminiscent of the similar assumption about *syntactic* competence apparently made by Chomsky and other linguists. The latter assumption has been widely criticized and, in my view (Devitt and Sterelny 1989: 501–3), stands totally refuted. Most of that refutation carries over fairly straightforwardly to the former assumption.

This is not the place to attempt the large task of giving a theory of competence and its relation to semantic properties. In the course of offering a historical causal theory of reference, I have elsewhere made some preliminary remarks toward the task (1981a: 101–10, 129–33, 196–9; Devitt and Sterelny 1987: 125–6, 148–50; 1989: 517–19). These indicate how we might view competence as a set of grounded skills or abilities. I summarize.

My causal theory explains the nature of reference in terms of a certain sort of causal chain, a chain with three kinds of link: groundings of word in object; reference-borrowings when a word is passed on or reinforced in a person; and abilities with a word gained and sustained by groundings and reference-borrowings. Implicit in this is a view of competence. Thus, to have the ability we all have with 'cat', to understand the English word 'cat', is to be appropriately linked to the network of causal chains for 'cat', a network involving other people's abilities as well as groundings and reference-borrowings. To have this ability, a person must be able to combine 'cat' appropriately with other words to form sentences. He must be able to have thoughts which those sentences express. Furthermore, these thoughts must be grounded in cats. A Twin-Earthian, who in other respects has the same ability with 'cat' that we have, does not have our understanding of the term, because his ability is grounded not in cats, but in apparently similar, but really quite different, animals, Twin-Earth cats. However, having our ability does not require *knowing that* 'cat' has any particular semantic or syntactic property, nor does it require being able to recognize cats.

Though reference must, ultimately, be explained by a causal theory (3.3), it is plausible to think that some terms are explained by a description theory. Take 'bachelor' as a likely example. Competence with 'bachelor' will then consist in associating it with the appropriate other terms: say, 'adult', 'unmarried', and 'male'. This association may involve certain knowledge of bachelors – that they are unmarried, for example – but it does not involve any knowledge of 'bachelor'; it does not involve any semantic knowledge.

Finally, syntactic competence is the skill of matching sentences of the language with thoughts having appropriate structures. This skill will require the internalization of something like the grammar that linguists are discovering, though not necessarily that very grammar; but it will not require any propositional knowledge of the grammar.

Putting skills of this sort together, the competent speaker has the ability to match sounds and thoughts according to the conventions of the language. Thus an English speaker matches 'The cat is on the mat' with the thought that the cat is on the mat. This does not require *knowing that* the sentence is true in English if and only if the cat is on the mat. It does not require knowing any semantic facts about the sentence at all.

On this view of linguistic competence, any propositional knowledge of a language that a person has is something over and above his competence, something gained from theorizing about the language.

I have mentioned (14.4) that Dummett is more cautious about the propositional assumption in one place (1981). In his brief discussion of the matter, he introduces a consideration which he seems to think favours the assumption. 'The reason why we are impelled to speak of *knowledge* here is that speech must be a conscious activity, since it is *the* rational activity par excellence' (pp. 310–11). Dummett sees this as related to the fact that normally a person knows whether he understands an expression or not (p. 81).

I agree that speech is a conscious activity (setting aside talking in one's sleep), and that normally a person does have the knowledge Dummett mentions; but I do not think that either of these facts supports the propositional assumption. (1) Speech is conscious in that it requires thought. But the required thought need not be about semantics. Only if the speech is about language will the thought be semantic. But then, of course, the speech and the thought will exemplify not the ordinary speaker's understanding, but semantic theorizing. (2) The fact that we normally know whether we understand an expression or not shows that this is a piece of semantic theorizing of which we are mostly capable. Similarly, we mostly know such profundities as that 'Snow is white' is true-in-English if and only if snow is white. However, there is no necessary connection between such knowledge and our ordinary understanding. It is possible for someone to understand expressions of L without having any concept *of* L, and hence without the capacity to have any thoughts about his understanding of L.

To summarize this section and the last: Dummett gives the propositional assumption no adequate support. I have argued that the assumption is false, and have suggested an alternative view of competence. If I am right, then B_1 and C_1 are false.

It is worth highlighting the consequence of this for Dummett's verificationist argument against Realism. If the propositional assumption is false, then a person committed to Correspondence Truth should hold only to the view that the speaker understands sentences that *have* realist truth conditions. So it is quite beside the point to argue against him that speakers do not *know* realist truth conditions. Yet that is the central thrust of Dummett's verificationist argument against Davidson (Dummett 1975 and 1976; see also Wright 1976 and 1979. Davidson is open to the argument, of course, because he accepts the propositional assumption). Establishing merely that speakers do not know realist truth conditions casts no doubt on Correspondence Truth. Even less does it cast doubt on Realism.

14.7 DUMMETT'S ARGUMENT FOR VERIFICATIONISM

Consider now the alternative versions of B and C. B_2 is trivial. Interest settles on C_2:

> C_2 The sentences understood by the competent speaker *have* only verificationist truth conditions.

To establish this, Dummett needs to argue that the speaker could not understand a sentence that as a matter of fact had realist (evidence-transcendent) truth conditions.

In their original form, Dummett's verificationist arguments are permeated by talk of the speaker's knowledge.[25] The present task is to ignore all such talk and abstract an argument that treats competence as simply a practical ability. The task is hard, for the precise argument is elusive. What follows is my best attempt at abstraction (from Dummett 1973: 467–8; 1975: 115–23; 1976: 70–111; 1977: 4–6, 373–80; 1978: xxii–xl, 16–18, 23–4, 132–3, 153–5; 1981: 443–4, 449; 1982: 106; see also Prawitz 1977: 4–7; Wright 1976: 224–8; 1979: 284–6):

(1) The competent speaker's understanding of a sentence S is a practical ability.

(2) This practical ability is an ability to manifest a particular sort of behaviour.

(3) The only sort of behaviour that could manifest the speaker's understanding of S is that behaviour which brings him into the position in which, if the condition obtains that conclusively justifies the assertion of S, he recognizes it as so doing.[26]

∴ (4) The speaker's understanding of S is his ability to manifest behaviour that brings him into the position in which, if the condition obtains which conclusively justifies the assertion of S, he recognizes it as so doing.

(5) The recognizable conditions of S's conclusively justified assertion are its verificationist truth conditions.

Let us put (4) and (5) together and abbreviate by using the phrase 'associates recognitionally'.

∴ (6) The speaker's understanding of S associates S recognitionally with verificationist truth conditions.

This conclusion establishes that all understanding is verificationist, but not that all truth is. The 'only' in C_2 requires that S not have any truth conditions other than verificationist ones: that it not have truth conditions transcending the recognizable conditions of conclusively justified assertion; that it not have realist truth conditions. Dummett has to rule out the possibility that S has realist truth conditions as well as the verificationist ones required for understanding.

(7) S has no truth conditions other than those associated with it recognitionally by the speaker's understanding.

∴ (8) S has only verificationist truth conditions.

S stands here for any sentence understood by the competent speaker, and so C_2 follows immediately.[27]

The three key premises are (2), (3), and (7). The first two of these tie understanding to verificationist truth conditions; the third prevents S from having any truth conditions that are not so tied.

14.8   THE REJECTION OF DUMMETT'S VERIFICATIONISM

My strategy in responding to Dummett's verificationist argument[28] is first to make objections to the argument from the perspective of several contemporary theories, and second, to reject the considerations Dummett offers in support of some of his premises. However, perhaps the most convincing rebuttal of the argument is the strength of the positive case for Correspondence Truth, which I have attempted to demonstrate in chapter 6 and 1981a. I return to this in section 14.9.

Step (4) stands opposed to holism in psychology and epistemology. The stand on psychology comes mainly from premise (2). This requires, for understanding at least, a kind of behaviourism: to have an ability is to manifest a particular sort of behaviour in the appropriate circumstances. In my view, recent work in the philosophy of mind decisively favours functionalism (6.2) over this kind of behaviourism. The difference can be put like this. Behaviourism sees each mental state as a simple input–output function: to be in a mental state is simply to be apt to yield certain behaviour as output given certain stimuli as input. According to functionalism, a mental state is not a simple input–output function: it is related to input and output by causal relations to other mental states, usually complicated relations. Competence with a word or sentence can no more be tied to a particular manifestation than can pain, love, belief, or bravery.[29]

Dummett does argue against a holistic view of understanding, particularly in discussing Davidson and Quine (1973: 592–601; 1975: 115–38; 1978: 134–40, 301–9). However, as far as I can see, the argument depends on accepting the propositional assumption about competence. Furthermore, functionalism differs from the holism of Davidson or Quine.

Dummett's commitment to anti-holist epistemology comes with premise (3). It requires that there *be* a particular recognizable condition in which the belief expressed by S is conclusively justified. In my view, the best recent work in epistemology (on which the naturalized epistemology of section 5.8 is based) and the philosophy of science (particularly by the radicals discussed in chapter 9) shows this to be an impossible requirement. The relation between worldly conditions and a justified belief is much more complicated than is presupposed by the requirement. Many different worldly conditions can produce the same sensory stimulation. Given different past experiences and present beliefs, the same stimulation can produce different experiences. Given different other beliefs, the same experience can lead to different 'observational' beliefs. Given different other beliefs, the same 'observational' belief can lead to different 'theoretical' beliefs. No belief is conclusively justified. Each belief is tied loosely to a range of conditions in which, relative to other beliefs, it is justified in varying degrees. Premise (3) requires an unreconstructed positivist epistemology. If understanding required the capacity to verify conclusively, we would understand nothing.

There are two signs of Dummett's retreating from the epistemic extremism of (3). First, though Dummett usually talks of conclusive justification in presenting his verificationism (e.g. 1973: 148, 467, 514, 586; 1975: 123; 1976: 111, 132; 1977: 375), he now seems to think that this is a mistake (1978: xxxviii; 1982: 95). Second, he is sympathetic to the epistemic holism of Quine's 'Two Dogmas' (1973: 591; 1976: 111; 1978: 297–8). Despite this, he still wants to hold, it seems, that some beliefs – the peripheral ones I have called 'observational' – are conclusively justified in certain specifiable conditions. This is at odds with the theory-ladenness of observation which I have described: the retreat has not gone far enough.[30]

However, the most important point about this retreat is that it threatens the collapse of Dummett's position. How can (3), (4), and (5) be revised? The problem is that there are indefinitely many recognizable conditions that could give a belief *some* degree of support. And the one condition could give some degree of support to indefinitely many beliefs. Are we to modify (3) so that the speaker is to be able to recognize one of these conditions? Or a few? Or many? Or all? Whatever the answer, there seems to be no way to modify (5). We can pick out no condition from S's set of possible confirming conditions and make it the verificationist truth conditions of S in particular.

The retreat leads straight to a holistic verificationism, particularly when it is accompanied, as it should be, by a move to a functionalist theory of the mind. Holistic verificationism is not, of course, any comfort to the believer in Correspondence Truth (14.9). However, it is certainly not what Dummett wants. His 'molecular' verificationism requires a behaviourist psychology and a positivist epistemology.

The distinction between *decidable* and *undecidable* sentences looms large in Dummett's discussion. Undecidable ones, including certain generalizations, subjunctive conditionals, and statements about other minds, are the ones that are thought to be problematic for the view that statements have realist truth conditions. The Duhem–Quine holist epistemology exemplified above makes this distinction look very dubious (outside mathematics perhaps). The discussion of underdetermination showed (7.4) that we may be able to get evidence for or against any sentence. So, in a sense, all sentences may be decidable. But the evidence we have for or against any sentence at any time is not so decisive that no new evidence could change our opinion on the sentence; there is no end to the process of testing. So in that sense no sentence is decidable. This latter fact reflects the way in which the truth of the sentence transcends the evidence: the truth is not explained in terms of, nor is it in any way dependent on, our epistemic capacities; no amount of evidence constitutes that truth (Maxim 5).[31]

The objections so far are free of semantic presuppositions. Not so the one that follows. Apply (3) and (4) to singular and general terms. Someone who is competent with a term must have the ability, roughly, to manifest behaviour leading to recognition of its referent. There seem to be only two ways in which a person might be able to do this. First, he may associate the term with an identifying description, so that the referent is whatever can be recognized as fitting that description. Second, the person may simply be able to recognize the referent. In brief, (3) and (4) require an extended version of a description theory of reference. Causal theories of reference, which form an important part of the theory of understanding summarized above (14.6), were born out of the rejection of description theories for proper names and natural-kind terms. A speaker can use such a term to refer even if he is almost entirely ignorant about its referent. He may not be able to describe, recognize, or know how to track down the referent. Causal theories have a different view according to which reference is fixed by an appropriate causal link to reality. Judging which part of reality is so linked is a job for the experts, not the essence of what every speaker can do. The opinions of experts depend on their theories, and so opinions may differ and change over time, even though reference remains constant. Indeed, there may be no experts.

This is not the place to air this disagreement in detail (but see 9.3). However, the key point is that description theorists of proper names or natural-kind terms have not produced any effective response to the detailed arguments 'from ignorance and error'.[32] And those are the arguments that need to be answered to save verificationism. Though causal theories are a long way from having all the answers for these terms, or any others, they have made very plausible the idea that the reference of some terms, at least, are to be explained by causal links of which the competent speaker may be unaware.

It is worth emphasizing that disagreements over understanding are not settled by whether or not 'we would ordinarily say' that a person has 'fully grasped the meaning' of a term in this and that circumstance. Even if Dummett were right in his claims about such matters (which I think he mostly isn't), that would only show something about our folk theory. What the causal theorist is claiming is that his

more austere concept of understanding is all that is needed to explain
the behaviour of speakers. If folk theory differs, so much the worse
for folk theory (Devitt 1981a: 8, 87–90, 99–100, 198).

Wright misses the significance of the critique of description
theories, seeing no problem in it for the anti-realist. His reasoning is
as follows:

to suppose that the truth conditions of e.g. statements involving singular
terms or natural-kind terms may be determined, in part, by factors of which
someone who understands those statements need not thereby be aware
is . . . quite different from supposing that the truth-conditions so determined
may be realized undetectably. (1986: 34)

But it is not 'quite different' in the respect that matters. If the arguments for the causal and against the description theory are good,
they show that a person, even a whole speech community, may
understand, say, 'Catiline is F' or 'x is an echidna,' without being
able to establish whether those statements are true or false. In that
respect, the truth conditions of the statements 'may be realized
undetectably'. This is not to say, of course, that they *are* undetectable; simply that understanding does not require that they be detectable. For understanding depends not on what people *can do* but on
the causal connections resulting from what they *have done*. So if these
arguments are good, the whole anti-realist case collapses: people *can*
understand statements that have truth conditions transcending their
epistemic capacities.

Alexander George suggests, though he does not endorse, the
view that Dummett's position might be saved if the competent
speaker were required to have only the capacity *in principle* to recognize the verification conditions (1984: 524–6). If the talk of 'in
principle' is construed liberally enough (3.5), this defence would
make Dummett's verificationism indistinguishable from the realist
view it is intended to oppose. It is no part of the realist view that
reference is determined by some aspect of reality that is *essentially*
beyond our ken. So a person, however ignorant of the referent and of
theories of reference and how to apply them, might, in some sense, be
able to discover the referent. But this does not tie competence to any
actual, presently manifestable capacity of the speaker. If the talk of
'in principle' is construed less liberally, the defence will still fall foul
of the arguments from ignorance and error.

Realist theories of understanding, based on causal theories of reference (14.6), reject the idea that understanding must be manifested in

verification behaviour. How then is it manifested? In a multitude of ways, many of them having nothing to do with verification.

Interestingly, Wright has recently accepted the holistic point that there need be no behaviour that is distinctive of understanding a particular sentence. However, he is unabashed; this fact is 'completely irrelevant', because the anti-realist's point was not really about *behavioural* manifestation!

When the anti-realist challenges the realist to indicate a potential manifestation of realist understanding of a statement, he is asking for an account of the *abilities* which would manifest it, not the behaviour. (1986: 23)

First, this interpretation of the anti-realist challenge warrants a protest. That challenge has always appeared to be about the manifestation of understanding in behaviour. And has there been *any* prior statement of a challenge about manifestation in abilities? It begins to look as if Wright aims to present the realist with a moving target. Second, the answer to this new challenge is along the lines already indicated (14.6). Understanding a statement is a complex ability made up of a syntactic ability and various abilities with words. We are only at an early stage in the explanation of any of these component abilities, and so it is hard to say much. Nevertheless, the incompleteness of this realist response does not warrant its dismissal as 'so much hand-waving' (p. 21); nor does it vindicate verificationism. Better a promising new research programme than a discredited old one.

My objections so far have been to (2) and (3). The causal theory is also opposed to (7). It is a consequence of that theory that words have referents, and hence that sentences have truth conditions, which are not associated with them recognitionally by the speaker's understanding.

I have not yet considered Dummett's arguments for (3) and (7). The slogan for these arguments is an appealing one, which Dummett takes from Wittgenstein: 'Meaning is use.' It is important to see that a good deal of this slogan's appeal comes from its suggesting an indubitable fact: it is what people do with words that makes them mean what they do; in particular, taking a central aspect of meaning, it is what people do that makes it the case that a certain object is the referent of a word. Similarly, it is what a person does that makes it the case that a certain object is his child. It no more follows from the first fact that a person must be able to recognize the object in question as the referent (let alone know that it is the referent) than it follows from the second fact that a person must be able to recognize the object in question as his child (know that it is his child). Our actions can relate us to objects and conditions without our having the capacity to recognize the objects and conditions as so related to us (know that they are so related).

The causal theorist can embrace the indubitable fact suggested by the slogan with as much enthusiasm as the verificationist. It alone gives no support to (3) or (7).

Wittgenstein's slogan has to be construed in a Wittgensteinian way to give the required support: 'use' must be taken to mean recognizable conditions of conclusively justified use. That is how Dummett does construe it. The step from the indubitable fact to this construal is a giant one. What justifies it?

It is clear that Dummett thinks that the slogan, and hence (3) and (7), are justified by the nature of communication and by the way language is learned and taught.

A view of communication and a view of understanding are so closely related as to stand or fall together, for communicating successfully with S normally requires speaker and audience to understand S in the same way. Dummett's view, in my terminology, is that they associate S recognitionally with the same verificationist truth conditions. All the objections to his view of understanding apply equally to this view. If communication is to be possible, it must require speaker and audience to associate S with something other than its recognizable conditions of conclusively justified assertion.[33]

Dummett's brief remarks on language learning do not yield a view that is both plausible and supportive of (3) and (7). Often the following argument seems to be suggested (1973: 467–8; 1977: 4–6, 375–80; 1978: 16–18, 188–90; see also Prawitz 1977: 3–6, 10). A person learns to understand S by being taught to associate it with the recognizable condition that in fact conclusively justifies its assertion. He can learn to associate no other semantic property with S. This supports (3). So S can have no other semantic property. This supports (7).

This argument is too crude to be Dummett's actual argument; but it is quite unclear how Dummett would want it modified and how such modifications could remedy its failings.

First, the view of language learning is obviously at odds with the following relatively uncontroversial facts. (1) Most sentences we understand we never hear uttered, for we understand sentences in virtue of understanding words and being able to put words together. (2) We mostly learn a language not from being taught it, but from observing its use. (3) Hardly any of these observations are of sentences in the presence of conditions that are close to being candidates for conclusively justifying the sentences. (4) Many of the observations are of word strings which are not strictly in the language, because they are not grammatically correct. (5) Many of the observations are of false or unjustified assertions which, nevertheless, manifest linguistic competence.[34]

Next, all our earlier objections count against Dummett's view of language learning. Indeed, the perspective of those objections seems much more likely to provide an explanation of the uncontroversial facts of language learning than Dummett's verificationism. So reflection on language learning seems likely to provide a good argument against verificationism. In particular, it suggests that verificationism is too passive. If we are to learn anything in the linguistic situations that we actually experience, we must go way 'beyond the evidence'. I suggest that we learn a language in the course of very active theorizing about the world in general and about people in particular, and that what we primarily learn with sounds is to associate them with the thoughts that are conventionally related to them (1981a: 75–86).

Finally, the support which the crude argument is alleged to give to (7) is spurious. Even if it were the case that speakers recognitionally associate with S only the condition of its conclusively justified assertion, it would not follow that S *had* no semantic property other than association with that condition: the act of association can confer on S properties we don't recognize. See the discussion of parenthood a few paragraphs back.

In this section I have attempted to expose the elements of Dummett's verificationism and indicate their opposition to well-supported contemporary theories in psychology, epistemology, and semantics. If any of those theories is right , Dummett's view is in severe difficultly. I think they are *all* right. Further, there is little in Dummett to cast doubt on them. C_2 is false. Correspondence Truth is unscathed.

14.9 VERIFICATIONISM AND REALISM

Dummett's argument against Realism rests on three premises. I have argued that each of these (except B when construed as the trivial B_2) is false. If I am right, Dummett's argument is bad from beginning to end.

In this section I shall consider the general question of the relation between Realism and verificationism. This is important in order to guard against other verificationist attempts to undermine Realism (and against the inevitable charge that Dummett's *real* argument is other than the one I have attributed to him).

What sort of connection might there be between Realism and verificationism? My argument shows that the issues of Realism, truth, and understanding are distinct. So there will be no entailment relations between a position in one area and a position in the other. What we can expect are abductions holding between positions. With such inferences the case for Realism looks very good.

I think the inference from Realism to Correspondence Truth looks promising, as I have argued in chapter 6. Part of what is needed to fulfil this promise is a causal theory of reference. With that theory goes a non-verificationist doctrine of understanding (14.6 and 14.8). So abduction takes us from Realism to doctrines of realist truth and realist understanding.

Now the striking thing about inference is that it starts from Realism. Those impressed with Dummett will object, claiming that we should start from the theory of understanding and see what we can infer from that about Realism. For example, suppose we can establish a verificationist theory of understanding; then it may be claimed that we can infer from this an epistemic doctrine of truth. Then, given the earlier mentioned difficulty of finding a plausible Realist epistemology to combine with that doctrine of truth (4.3), we can infer anti-Realism. I have three comments on this.

First, the theory of understanding is the wrong place to start. The task is to put together the most plausible comprehensive theory of the phenomena that confront us. Theories of language and understanding are only two among many scientific theories that must be fitted into the comprehensive picture. Realism is an overarching empirical (scientific) theory or principle. It is initially plausible. It is supported by arguments that make no appeal to theories of language or understanding. Its rivals all fail (chapters 5 and 7). What firmer place could there be to stand than Realism, as we theorize in such undeveloped areas as those of language and understanding? In contrast, the poor state of theories in those areas, whether verificationist or not, makes them a bad place from which to start theorizing, particularly in determining overarching principles about the nature of reality. To think otherwise is to put the cart before the horse (Maxim 3).

Second, suppose, however, that a good argument could be produced for a verificationist theory, making us feel inclined to waive our objection in principle to using understanding as a starting place. Suppose, further, that from that theory we could infer anti-Realism in the way suggested. What should not be overlooked is that, however good that inference were, it alone would not undermine the earlier 'promising' inference from Realism to Correspondence Truth. Our choice between these two inferences should be guided by our view of which starting assumption had the greater plausibility. The arguments for Realism are very strong. Those for verificationism are very weak. Indeed, they seem to rest entirely on *a priori* reflections about what meanings we could grasp and what concepts we could have. Why should we believe these claims? What is their *basis*? It would take an argument far stronger than any yet dreamt of to make verificationism the more plausible assumption.

Finally, I doubt that inference to the best explanation from a verificationist theory of understanding would yield anti-Realism. If not, then it does not matter to the Realist how strong a case could be made for verificationism.

Consider the austere physicalism of Leeds–Quine (6.1). This position is unequivocally committed to Realism, but sceptical about semantic notions like truth. It could accommodate a verificationist theory of understanding and meaning and a *deflationary* theory of truth. The threat to Realism would come, via the equivalence thesis, only from an *epistemic* theory of truth (4.3). Given the independent plausibility of Realism, it seems likely that the best explanation of the world for a verificationist would be not that of anti-Realism, but that of Leeds–Quine.

I take theories of language and understanding to be ordinary scientific theories: I take them to be naturalized. I give them no special role in settling our comprehensive world-view. I think we should resist Dummettian attempts to use them as the basis for a 'born-again first philosophy'.

14.10 CONCLUSION

In its more prominent version, Dummett's argument against Realism rests on the theory that linguistic competence consists in knowledge of truth conditions. In general, it rests on a linguistic theory of metaphysics, a behaviourist theory of mind, a positivist epistemology, and a description theory of reference. In my view, all these theories are false. In part I have argued this here; in part I have relied on what has been done elsewhere.

Moving away from Dummett's actual argument to consider the general bearing of verificationism on Realism, I have found little for the Realist to worry about. Realism is too strong a doctrine to be overthrown by current speculations about understanding. Whatever one makes of those speculations, the best theory of the world is Realist. I think the best theory should include Correspondence Truth and a theory of understanding of the sort sketched above (14.6). However, even if I am wrong about this, the Realist should not despair: there is still the Leeds–Quine position. Better to throw all the semantic planks overboard than to abandon the Realist boat.

NOTES

1 This chapter is based on Devitt 1983a.
2 See, e.g., many of the papers in Platts 1980.
3 See, e.g., 'Realism and Reason', in Putnam 1978: 123–38.
4 Wright was once provoked to defend a Dummettian view partly by Peter Strawson's criticisms of that view (1976–7) and partly by 'the grateful reception of [Strawson's] remarks by an audience who seemed, by and large, to think that anti-realism could be nothing other than the Positivism of the Thirties' (1979: 283).
5 Dummett attributes this view of philosophy to Frege, and sees it as definitive of 'analytical philosophy' (1978: 442).
6 A further qualification is necessary: A, B, and C take no account of certain complications that Dummett finds in the Realism dispute, associated with questions of reduction, which Dummett mostly sets aside (but see particularly Dummett 1982). I refer to these questions briefly at the end of section 14.2.

   Richard Kirkham (1989: 207–10) has identified an ambivalence in Dummett. Dummett always argues for a verificationist concept of truth; but sometimes he gives this concept a role in the theory of meaning – though it is not the 'key concept' – and sometimes he gives it no such role at all. My discussion of Dummett's argument presupposes the first of these positions. If we were to presuppose the second, we should, I suppose, replace some of my talk of *verificationist truth conditions* by talk of *verification conditions*. As far as I can see, my argument would be unaffected.
7 I shall often make multiple references to Dummett's work to support an attribution. In so doing, I do not mean to suggest that these are the only places that would supply the support. Sometimes they are only a small sample of such places.
8 Two recent examples of this swift move from metaphysics to semantics are Wright 1988: 25–7 (but cf. 1983: xix–xx) and Luntley 1988: 1–2.

Luntley claims (p. 12) to have 'shown' my criticism of this move to be wrong. He's bluffing. He has simply repeated the move without supplying any justification at all. In a response to my 1983a, George claims that Dummett's linguistic theory of metaphysics is his reason for the move (1984: 518). But what then is the argument for that theory independent of the move? I see no argument in the pages cited by George; simply statements of position.

9 Dummett suggests that the importance of reduction to the Realism dispute has been its role as a step towards (b) (1979b: 5). I suggest that its importance comes from the fact that anti-Realists have typically been conservative. Thus Berkeley did not deny the very existence of the common-sense physical world, but claimed that it could be reduced to something mental. And the phenomenalists liked to give *the impression* that they were saving that world (misleadingly: 5.4). This conservatism was good tactics: abandon it, and the anti-Realist can expect refutation by the kicked stone and the incredulous stare. He may even, like Hume, have difficulty believing what he says (5.5).

10 See the passage from Strawson: 1976–7 quoted by Dummett (1978: xxiv), which makes a similar point.

In a paper from Dummett 1978 not so far cited, 'Platonism' (pp. 202–14), Dummett himself emphasizes the differences between the mathematical and physical worlds, drawing attention particularly to the power of the physical world to affect us through observation. This seems to me to be very much along the right lines. It counts against the extension from mathematics to physics that I have attributed to Dummett, and hence against that attribution. However, without the extension, and the Metaphor Thesis that is supported by it, there would be no argument at all in Dummett for premise A.

11 S. Blackburn (1980) argues for a metaphorical view of the realism dispute; cf. section 4.8 above and my 1983c: 669–74. Luntley (1988) wrings his hands frequently over the unclarity of talk of mind-independent reality.

12 I have not considered the details of Dummett's semantic version of realism: he makes the principle of bivalence the touchstone (1978: xxx–xxxii, 149–50, 155; 1979b: 4). The details are not central to my argument.

13 I don't mean to suggest that psychological properties could not enter into an explanation of semantic properties; I am too much of a Gricean for that (1981a: 80–6). My point is only the trivial one that the semantic and psychological properties in question here are very different (pp. 92–3).

14 Parenthetical additions such as those in this sentence should be taken as read in future. There is a more extreme version of the propositional assumption: competence consists in knowledge of the *axioms of a semantic theory* that yield statements of truth conditions as theorems.

15 He goes on to argue that though knowledge of truth conditions does not

imply competence, competence 'nearly enough' implies the knowledge.
I reject the latter argument (1983c: 674–5).

16 Dummett also makes the mysterious remark that a theory of meaning,
which is for him a theory of understanding, is not 'a psychological
hypothesis', partly on the ground, it seems, that something with
'internal mechanisms' unlike ours – e.g. a Martian or a robot – might
have the required implicit knowledge (1976: 70). This overlooks the
distinction between psychological and physical mechanisms (6.3).
A Martian or a robot that is physically different from us might be
psychologically the same. The remark is mysterious, because if understanding is anything, it is (at least partly) psychological.

17 I know of only one earlier writing in which Dummett does not conflate
the view that understanding is propositional with the view that it is
a practical ability. This is in his 'Comments' (1979a) on Putnam's
'Reference and Understanding' (in Putnam 1978 and Margalit 1979).
He there contemplates dropping the view that a theory of truth is a
theory of understanding, and thus dropping the propositional assumption. In effect, he rests his case on B_2 and C_2.

18 The discussion in this section repeats one in the first edition (1984a:
204–6) that caused Richard Kirkham 'distress' (1989: 213). What
he found particularly distressing was my (partial) interpretation of
Dummett's claim that speakers have implicit knowledge of semantic
propositions as the propositional assumption. According to Kirkham,
what Dummett means by this claim is that speakers do not really
know these semantic propositions at all, but behave *as though* they
did (p. 212). Perhaps so; but if so, one wonders why Dummett never
said so. Indeed, one wonders why Dummett and others, including
Kirkham, persist in talking of implicit knowledge at all, rather than
using Kirkham's interpretation. '*x* behaves as though he believes *p*' is
actually briefer than '*x* manifests implicit knowledge of *p*,' which is the
main locution in which 'implicit knowledge' appears. More to the point,
the interpretation is much clearer and much less misleading than the
original. As Kirkham himself points out, the 'interpretive literature . . .
is nearly unanimous' in ascribing the propositional assumption to
Dummett on the basis of his talk of implicit knowledge (p. 207). Why,
then, persist with such misleading talk? Whatever the answer, the talk
gives many arguments an unearned plausibility arising from the special
'logic' of the propositional knowledge that the talk suggests.

Kirkham goes on to offer a detailed version of a Dummettian argument. He does not comment on my discussion of C_2 (1984a: 211–18;
sections 14.7–14.8 below), which is not based on ascribing the propositional assumption to Dummett. It seems to me that Kirkham's argument, interpreting its talk of 'implicit knowledge' as he intends, is open
to the same objections as the argument for C_2 that I discuss. In
particular, his premise 4 stands or falls with (4) below.

19 McGinn is mostly critical of Dummett. However, he seems to agree

with the view I have quoted. In general, he concedes a great deal to Dummett without question.

20 In this discussion Dummett considers the view that sense is no more than reference. He takes this to be the view that competence is no more than *knowledge* of reference. He goes on to argue that this knowledge consists in propositional knowledge of a certain sort. Roughly, I have constructed the argument I claim to be suggested by this passage by replacing 'reference' by 'truth condition'.

21 See also Boër and Lycan 1975 and Devitt 1981a: 222–4.

22 Wright cites me as an example of a 'curious muddle' among realists about the 'simple point' that if anti-realist doubts about realist truth are correct, 'we – the theorists – have no business involving that "notion" in any sort of theory, whether conceived as descriptive of the content of object-language speaker's understanding or not'. He thinks it worth repeating the point, 'emphasizing the obvious' (1986: 238). The point leads him to describe my argument in the above section (and in 1984a: 206–9) as 'futile if what one is trying to do is to protect realist semantics from anti-realist attack' (p. 238). Well!

    (1)   Why does Wright think we poor realists are in this 'curious muddle'? I suppose because he attributes to us the view that, to save realism from Dummett, it is *sufficient* to criticize his position on the propositional assumption. Could Wright have failed to notice the rest of this chapter (1984a: 209–20)?

    (2)   And, of course, even if one were thus muddled, rejecting any bad argument for anti-realism would be far from futile. The bad arguments must be taken one by one. Rome wasn't built in a day.

23 This objection indicates an important fact about competence in L: this competence might cover many competences, including, e.g., competence in understanding spoken L, competence in writing L, and, most important, competence in thinking in L (Devitt 1981a: 102). In this chapter I mostly follow the usual, rather misleading practice of conflating competence in speaking L with competence in understanding (spoken?) L and of writing as if these competences were the only ones that concerned us.

24 Wright points out 'that it may be perfectly proper to ascribe certain propositional attitudes to a subject even though there is no, as it were, *canonical* specification of the content of those attitudes, no specification of their content which exactly captures their content-for-the-subject' (1986: 224). He gives the case of ascriptions of beliefs to a dog as a persuasive argument for this. One way of making Wright's point is that we may be entitled to ascribe a belief to a person or dog *transparently*, and yet have no correct way of ascribing that belief *opaquely*. However, even for a transparent ascription to be correct, there must be *some* way that the person or dog represents to itself the individuals and properties

in question. So there must be some way that the person in my objection represents to himself semantic properties if he is to have semantic propositional knowledge.

Wright sees problems in ascribing implicit knowledge of the axioms of the semantic *theory* to speakers, but no problem in ascribing the *theorems* of that theory (pp. 237–8). The above two objections apply as much to theorems as to theory.

25 The 'Comments' (1979a) mentioned in n. 17 are an exception. However, the argument there is: (1) very brief; (2) unclear (to me, at least); and (3) aimed specifically at Putnam's theory of truth, which does not make use of an explanatory notion of reference, and hence is not what I have called 'Correspondence Truth' (3.3 and 3.4; 1980a).

26 Dummett makes this claim only of sentences for which he thinks our knowledge of truth conditions is implicit. Where the knowledge is explicit, the manifesting behaviour is the statement of those conditions (1977: 373). He thinks that the basic manifesting behaviour must be for sentences for which we could not state truth conditions.

27 Dummett sometimes leans towards preferring a semantics based on falsification to one based on verification (1976: 127–37). This preference would require obvious adjustments to my version of Dummett's argument. The difference between falsificationism and verificationism can be overlooked for our purposes.

28 For some objections to Dummett related to some of mine, see Millar 1977 and Currie and Eggenberger 1983.

29 Dummett concludes a discussion of the realist view that a person who dies without ever being put in danger either was brave or was not with the following astounding statement: 'It is evident that only a philosophically quite naïve person would adopt [the] realist view' (1978: 150). In my view, he was brave if he realized the appropriate functional state and not brave if he did not. His quiet life is beside the point.

30 Charlie Martin nicely remarks: 'There is a great deal in all of this that is nostalgic – the move from conclusive or "strong" (as it used to be called) to not-conclusive or "weak" verification, the occasional gestures to "in principle" and then the withdrawal to more "effective" or "practical" procedures' (1984a: 8).

31 Compare this with Wright's requirement for understanding a statement: 'the availability to investigation of a state of affairs of the very kind which constitutes the truth-condition of a statement'; mere defeasible evidence is not enough (1986: 14). Later he gives some examples of statements that meet this condition. They concern the tastes of various substances, and are decidable because one has 'the ability to recognize the taste of the samples by placing them in one's mouth, thereby to verify or falsify descriptions of their taste. . . . recognizing the taste of something by tasting it *is* recognizing that in virtue of which the true description of its taste is true' (p. 17). It is as if, with a decidable statement, we have 'direct access' to the truth condition; it is 'given' in experience; here the world forces itself upon us.

32 Responses to Kripkean claims about 'rigid designation' have been
    more effective. But these claims are beside the present point, for the
    arguments from ignorance and error make no appeal to the modal
    intuitions on which the claims depend.

33 Cf. Wright on undecidable statements: 'The inescapable price, it
    appears, of rejecting the Wittgensteinian premise is surrender of any
    possible reason to suppose that there is such a thing as mutual under-
    standing' (1986: 20).

34 Talk of 'correct use' encourages a confusion here. An assertion can be
    correct in the sense of manifesting competence, but incorrect in the
    sense that it expresses a mistaken view of the world. Mistaken views are
    one thing, linguistic incompetence another.

Part IV
Conclusions

15

Conclusions

This book has been concerned with two issues: Realism and truth. Central to my approach is the view that these issues are quite distinct: no doctrine of truth is in any way constitutive of Realism. In this, I stand opposed to many, but most obviously to Dummett (chapters 4 and 14).

Realism is an overarching ontological doctrine about what there is and what it is like. It is committed to most of the physical posits of common sense and science and to the view that these entities are independent of the mental. It has an epistemic aspect: the entities do not depend for their existence or nature on our opinion; they exist objectively. It is a very plausible doctrine, because it takes the posits of science and common sense pretty much at face value (chapter 2 and section 4.7).

If truth is not deflationary – if it is a robust explanatory notion – then it must have a place in the theory of people (believer–desirers) and their language. So its place is in a theory of a small, but important, part of the world which the Realist believes in. If the doctrine of truth is a correspondence one, then it must, *contra* Davidson, explain truth in terms of reference. I call such a doctrine 'Correspondence Truth' (chapters 3 and 10).

Common-Sense Realism has been threatened by scepticism: 'How can we have knowledge of objects that are independent of us?' Foundationalist attempts to answer scepticism typically closed the gap between knower and known by bringing the world, in some sense, into the mind: they were anti-Realist. Foundationalism is a failure, and presents no viable alternative to Common-Sense Realism. In the final analysis, scepticism is unanswerable and is best set aside. We should move to a naturalized epistemology which confirms the Common-Sense Realism that is our natural starting place (chapter 5).

Common-Sense Realism can be argued for, somewhat artificially: it helps to explain the way things seem (or, more accurately, the theories on which it is based help to explain this). This 'inference to the best explanation' or abduction can be represented as follows:

The way things seem → Common-Sense Realism

The artificiality reflects the fact that Common-Sense Realism hardly needs a positive argument (5.7).

There is nothing artificial about the argument for Scientific Realism: that Realism helps to explain the behaviour and characteristics of the observed world (7.1).

Observed behaviour and characteristics → Scientific Realism.

We have no reason to believe an underdetermination thesis that would count against this Realism (7.4).

Scientific Realism is committed to unobservables. To reject it, while accepting Common-Sense Realism and inferences to the existence of unobserved observables, as van Fraassen does, is to attach an epistemic significance to observability which it does not have (chapter 8).

Justifying Correspondence Truth is a very difficult task. Entitlement to truth depends on entitlement to reference. That entitlement depends ultimately on causal theories of reference which are in their infancy. Why do we need truth? We do not seem to need it to explain behaviour, even linguistic behaviour. What we need it for, I suggest, is to describe and explain the properties of symbols that enable them to play a variety of social roles. The argument is another abduction. It starts from Realism, together with some observations about the world the Realist believes in, particularly about people and their language, and infers Correspondence Truth (physical) (chapter 6 and section 7.5):

Realism & the role of human symbols → Correspondence Truth (physical).

It is common to link Correspondence Truth to epistemic doctrines arising out of the sceptical problematic. Rorty, for one, thinks that those who urge Correspondence Truth hanker after certainty. However, Correspondence Truth is part of a theory of language, and need not be tied to any search for epistemic foundations (11.4).

My approach to truth naturalizes semantics, just as we earlier naturalized epistemology. A consequence of this naturalization is that Realism is settled first, epistemology and semantics afterwards.

This is appropriate, for the common-sense and scientific theories on which Realism is based are in far better shape than any theory in epistemology or semantics.

Foundationalists proceeded in the opposite direction: they inferred a position on the Realism issue from their epistemology. A recent trend, encouraged by Dummett and Putnam, has been to infer a position on the Realism issue from semantics. In particular, an epistemic doctrine of truth (e.g. warranted assertability) is likely to lead by inference to the best explanation to anti-Realism. For it is very difficult for a Realist to find a plausible epistemology to accompany an epistemic doctrine of truth:

> Epistemic truth → anti-Realism.

However, inferences of this sort have the wrong starting place (4.3 and 14.9).

It has been common to think that we need realism to explain success. In considering this view, we must distinguish between the ontological doctrine of Realism and a semantic doctrine like Correspondence Truth with which it is often conflated, and between four sorts of success: individual success, species success, theoretical success, and scientific progress. So there are at least eight different theses underlying the popular view (6.6).

Individual success is primarily the success of an organism in satisfying its needs and fulfilling its desires. Species success is concerned particularly with the success of a species in surviving. Abduction does not seem to take us from either sort of success to Correspondence Truth (physical):

> Individual or species success -↛ Correspondence Truth (physical).

Realism is part of the best explanation of these successes; but then it is part of the best explanation of almost anything. It would be fantastic to suppose that Realism's main justification was to be found in the theory of organisms. Other metaphysical positions could surely explain these successes (6.6).

Theoretical success is quite different: the theory that S is successful if the world is as if S. Realism does explain this success:

> Theoretical success → Realism.

However, the explanation is somewhat trivial. It is better to see Realism as part of a far from trivial explanation of the world (as above), an explanation which *is* successful; further, to see anti-

Realism as failing because it can offer no explanation of that success. Correspondence Truth has nothing to do with the explanation (7.3):

Theoretical success -/> Correspondence Truth (physical).

It is common to take scientific progress as consisting in convergence. Realism and Correspondence Truth can give a good explanation of this convergent view of progress if they can solve some technical problems about which I think we should be optimistic. However, there is no reason to think that we need either doctrine for that purpose: once again, other metaphysical positions could surely do as well (7.6).

Only one of the eight theses underlying the view that we need realism to explain success has turned out to be true: Realism explains theoretical success.

Convergence in science has often been linked closely to Scientific Realism. If the doctrine has a place, it is in our theory of people and their struggle to understand the world. It is in no way constitutive of Scientific Realism. Nor is it of Correspondence Truth (scientific) (7.6). Nevertheless, convergence is important to both doctrines.

Non-convergence alone poses no direct threat to Realism. However, non-convergence because of Ontological Elimination does. According to Ontological Elimination, most of the unobservables apparently posited by past theories do not exist. Then it may seem likely that most of the unobservables apparently posited by present science do not exist. This meta-induction is the one powerful argument against Scientific Realism. (There is no such argument against Common-Sense Realism: the premise that most of the observables apparently posited by past theories do not exist is plainly false: 9.3). Though powerful, the argument is dubious on close examination. Its premise seems too strong, gaining such plausibility as it has from a false description theory of reference. And once the inference is carefully set out, it is suspect:

Ontological Elimination -/> anti-Scientific Realism.

The anti-Realist needs to demonstrate that the history of unobservable posits has been thoroughly erratic. This he has not done (9.4).

Convergence is indirectly important to Scientific Realism in the following way. If that Realism is combined with Correspondence Truth (scientific), as it should be, then it needs a doctrine of convergence to explain scientific progress (7.6 and 9.7).

Scientific progress & Scientific Realism & Correspondence Truth (scientific) → convergence.

Indeed, it is difficult to explain progress from any perspective without a doctrine of convergence, as the writings of Kuhn, Feyerabend, and the radical philosophers of science illustrate (9.7):

Scientific progress & non-convergence → ?

The radicals reject Correspondence Truth and convergence largely because of Incommensurability. Indeed, it is plausible to think that Incommensurability *entails* these rejections. Incommensurability is a semantic thesis: the semantic relations necessary for the comparison of theories do not hold between theories. This must be distinguished from the epistemic thesis that there is no theory-neutral way of judging what semantic relations hold between theories. The epistemic thesis is unexciting, because there is no theory-neutral way of judging anything (9.6 and 9.8). Incommensurability itself is exciting, but false. Once Ontological Elimination has been rejected, the semantic relations required for comparison can be based on the theories' referential relations – or, at worst, partial referential relations – to a common ontology (9.6).

The radicals have a lot to say about epistemology and semantics, but little about ontology. Nevertheless, a position can be inferred from their writings: Constructivism, a relativistic Kantianism. According to this doctrine, all that exists independently of us and our theories are things-in-themselves beyond reach of knowledge or reference. On these we are thought to 'impose' a theory to yield an ontology-relative-to-theory. Theorists make the worlds they live in and study; as theories change, so do worlds (9.2). Putnam has a similar view (12.5), as have Goodman and many many others. Constructivism is the metaphysics of our time.

Despite its popularity, the arguments for Constructivism are feeble, and often confused (13.1); and the doctrine itself is absurd (13.2). Indeed, it is *so* absurd that one is inclined to think that Constructivist talk should not be taken literally. However, a metaphorical interpretation proves impossible to sustain (13.3).

Constructivists blur the crucial distinction between theories and the world. Why? I suspect that there are several confusions; for example, that of use with mention and that of the freedom to name whatever kinds we like with the freedom to put objects into any kinds we like (13.4).

There are some entities that, in interesting respects, we do partly 'make'; for example, tools and entities classified by their social

properties or (Lockean) secondary properties. These entities are
dependent on us in ways that Realism's entities – stones, trees, cats,
and the like – are not. However, those dependent entities still differ
from Constructivist entities in the form of their dependence on us.
More important, they differ strikingly in their relationship to the
independent world. They are dependent on that world in causal
ways open to scientific investigation. By contrast, Constructivist
entities are dependent on that world – a mere thing–in–itself for
Constructivists – in ways that are mysterious to the point of incoherence (13.6–13.7).

Putnam has proposed a route to Constructivism: generalize a
Lockean account of secondary properties to all properties. This route
comes closer than any other to making Constructivism seem rational.
However, careful examination of the route helps show why Constructivism is so absurd. The plausibility of the Lockean account of the
secondary properties depends on its Realist background of entities
with natures that are not dependent on us. For that background
enables a genuine explanation of the influences and constraints on
our judgements exercised by an independent world. The generalized
account removes this background: the natures of all entities depend
on our judgements. No account of independent influence and constraint is then possible (13.7).

Putnam and the radicals share a certain common view of the problem for Realism: Realism requires that we can know the unknowable
and speak the unspeakable; it requires a 'God's Eye View'. This view
arises from thinking that we start from scratch in epistemology and
semantics. However, from our naturalistic perspective, we already
have the entities of the physical world when starting our epistemology and semantics. The relations which those sciences require are
no more ineffable than any others (12.6).

Dummett's argument against Realism is perhaps the most influential contemporary one. I have already indicated some objections
to it: it wrongly identifies the ontological issue of Realism with the
semantic issue of truth, and it picks the wrong starting place in
theorizing about Realism. That starting place is with the issues of
linguistic understanding and truth. He argues for a verificationist
theory of this understanding. Often this argument seems to rest on
the unsupported and false view that speakers *know* the truth conditions of sentences in their language. Aside from that, it rests on a
behaviourist psychology, a positivist epistemology, and a description
theory of reference, all of which are false (chapter 14).

If we approach the theory of people and language from a Realist perspective, then, just as we can hope to infer Correspondence Truth (physical), so we can hope to infer a non-verificationist theory of understanding:

Realism & the role of human symbols → non-verificationist understanding.

Dummett favours an inference that starts from verificationist understanding. Even if that view of understanding could be established, I suggest that it would lead not to anti-Realism, but to the austere Leeds–Quine Realism (14.9).

Verificationist understanding -/→ anti-Realism.

I have not considered any inferences from anti-Realism to theories of knowledge, truth, understanding, or anything else, because anti-Realism is an unlikely starting place. What drives people to anti-Realism are theories of knowledge and language. From the naturalistic perspective of this book, there is no good reason to be so driven.

From this naturalistic perspective, also, philosophy has a systematic and constructive task. We should not follow Rorty's advice, engaging only in the edifying conversation of the informed dilettante (11.6).

List of Major Named Maxims and Doctrines

MAXIMS

Maxim 1 In considering realism, distinguish the constitutive and evidential issues.

Maxim 2 Distinguish the metaphysical (ontological) issue of realism from any semantic issue.

Maxim 3 Settle the realism issue before any epistemic or semantic issue.

Maxim 4 In considering the semantic issue, don't take truth for granted.

Maxim 5 Distinguish the issue of correspondence truth from any epistemic issue.

DOCTRINES

Common-Sense Realism Tokens of most current observable common-sense and scientific physical types objectively exist independently of the mental (2.4).

Complex Convergence Relative to T', the successor theory of T in some science, the terms of T typically partially refer, and the laws of T are typically approximately true (9.7).

Constructivism The only independent reality is beyond the reach of our knowledge and language. A known world is partly constructed by the imposition of concepts. These concepts differ from (linguistic, social, scientific, etc.) group to group, and hence the worlds of groups differ. Each such world exists only relative to an imposition of concepts (9.2).

Correspondence Truth (x) Sentences of type x are true or false in virtue of: (1) their structure; (2) the referential relations between their parts and reality; (3) the objective and mind-independent nature of that reality (3.3).

Fig-Leaf Realism See Weak, or Fig-Leaf, Realism.

Incommensurability Because of Meaning Change, Reference Change, and Ontological Change, T and T' are semantically incomparable (9.1).

Increasing Verisimilitude Where T' is the successor theory of T in some science, it typically has a greater truth content (and smaller falsity content) than T' (7.6).

Meaning Change Where T and T' are competing 'comprehensive' theories in some area, differing in 'major' or 'fundamental' ways, no term in the (special) language of T' is synonymous with, or expresses the same concept as, a term in the (special) language of T (9.1).

Ontological Change Where T and T' are competing 'comprehensive' theories in some area, differing in 'major' or 'fundamental' ways, no part of the (special) ontology of T' is part of the (special) ontology of T (9.1).

Ontological Elimination Most of the entities apparently posited by past theories do not exist (9.3).

Physicalism (1) The only entities that exist are physical entities (or those composed only of physical entities); (2) ultimately, physical laws explain everything (in some sense) (2.5).

Realism Tokens of most current common-sense and scientific physical types objectively exist independently of the mental (2.4).

Reference Change Where T and T' are competing 'comprehensive' theories in some area, differing in 'major' or 'fundamental' ways, no term in the (special) language of T' is co-referential with a term in the (special) language of T (9.1).

Scientific Realism Tokens of most current unobservable scientific physical types objectively exist independently of the mental (2.4).

Simple Convergence Relative to T', the successor theory of T in some science, the terms of T typically refer, and the laws of T are typically approximately true (7.4).

Strong Scientific Realism Tokens of most unobservable scientific types objectively exist independently of the mental, and (approximately) obey the laws of science (4.4).

Weak, or Fig-Leaf, Realism Something objectively exists independently of the mental (2.4).

Bibliography

Alston, William P. 1979 'Yes Virginia, there is a Real World'. *Proceedings and Addresses of the American Philosophical Association* 52: 779–808.

Althusser, Louis 1969 *For Marx*. London: Allen Lane, Penguin Press.

Althusser, Louis, and Étienne Balibar 1968 *Reading Capital*. French edn 1968. Trans. Ben Brewster. London: New Left Books, 1970.

Anscombe, G. E. M. 1965 'The Intentionality of Sensation: A Grammatical Feature'. In *Analytical Philosophy*, second series, ed. R. J. Butler. Oxford: Basil Blackwell, 158–80.

Appiah, Anthony 1991 'Representations and Realism'. *Philosophical Studies* 61: 65–74.

Armstrong, D. M. 1961 *Perception and the Physical World*. London: Routledge & Kegan Paul.

Armstrong, D. M. 1968a *A Materialist Theory of the Mind*. London: Routledge & Kegan Paul.

Armstrong, D. M. 1968b 'The Secondary Qualities'. *Australasian Journal of Philosophy* 42: 225–41.

Aune, Bruce 1987 'Conceptual Relativism'. In Tomberlin 1987: 269–85.

Ayer, A. J. 1940 *The Foundations of Empirical Knowledge*. London: Macmillan.

Ayer, A. J., ed. 1959 *Logical Positivism*. New York: Free Press.

Baker, Lynne Rudder 1987 *Saving Belief: A Critique of Physicalism*. Princeton: Princeton University Press.

Barnes, Barry, and David Bloor 1982 'Relativism, Rationalism and the Sociology of Knowledge'. In Hollis and Lukes 1982: 21–47.

Bertolet, Rod 1988a Critical Study of Devitt 1984a. *Dialectica* 42: 59–71.

Bertolet, Rod 1988b 'Realism without Truth'. *Analysis* 48: 195–8.

Bhaskar, Roy 1975 *A Realist Theory of Science*. Leeds: Leeds Books.

Blackburn, Simon 1980 'Truth, Realism, and the Regulation of Theory'. In French, Uehling, and Wettstein 1980: 353–71.

Blackburn, Simon 1984 *Spreading the Word*. Oxford: Clarendon Press.

Blackburn, Thomas 1988 'The Elusiveness of Reference'. In French, Uehling, and Wettstein 1988: 179–94.

Block, Ned 1981 *Readings in Philosophy of Psychology, Volume 2*. Cambridge, MA: Harvard University Press.

Boër, S., and W. G. Lycan 1975 'Knowing Who'. *Philosophical Studies* 28: 299–344.

Boghossian, Paul 1990a 'The Status of Content'. *Philosophical Review* 99: 157–84.

Boghossian, Paul 1990b 'The Status of Content Revisited'. *Pacific Philosophical Quarterly* 71: 264–78.

Boyd, Richard N. 1973 'Realism, Underdetermination and a Causal Theory of Evidence'. *Nous* 7: 1–12.

Boyd, Richard N. 1984 'The Current Status of Scientific Realism'. In Leplin 1984b: 41–82.

Boyd, Richard N. 1985 *'Lex orandi est lex credendi'*. In Churchland and Hooker 1985: 3–34.

Brandom, Robert 1984 'Reference Explained Away'. *Journal of Philosophy* 81: 469–92.

Brandom, Robert 1988 'Pragmatism, Phenomenalism, and Truth Talk'. In French, Uehling, and Wettstein 1988: 75–93.

Brody, Baruch A. 1970a Introduction to Brody 1970b, pt 2, 182–7.

Brody, Baruch A., ed. 1970b *Readings in the Philosophy of Science*. Englewood Cliffs, NJ: Prentice-Hall.

Brown, Curtis 1988 'Internal Realism: Transcendental Idealism?' In French, Uehling, and Wettstein 1988: 145–55.

Bunge, Mario, ed. 1964 *The Critical Approach to Science and Philosophy*. New York: Free Press.

Burge, Tyler 1979 'Individualism and the Mental'. In French, Uehling, and Wettstein 1979b: 73–121.

Burge, Tyler 1986 'Individualism and Psychology'. *Philosophical Review* 95: 3–45.

Carey, James W. 1989 *Communication as Culture: Essays on Media and Society*. Boston: Unwin Hyman.

Cartwright, Nancy 1983 *How the Laws of Physics Lie*. Oxford: Clarendon Press.

Chalmers, A. F. 1976 *What is this Thing Called Science?* St. Lucia, Queensland: University of Queensland Press.

Churchland, Paul M. 1979 *Scientific Realism and the Plasticity of Mind*. Cambridge: Cambridge University Press.

Churchland, Paul M. 1981 'Eliminative Materialism and Propositional Attitudes'. *Journal of Philosophy* 78: 67–90. Repr. in Lycan 1990: 206–23.

Churchland, Paul M. 1985 'The Ontological Status of Observables: In Praise of the Superempirical Virtues'. In Churchland and Hooker 1985: 35–47.

Churchland, Paul M. and Clifford A. Hooker, eds 1985 *Images of Science: Essays on Realism and Empiricism, with a Reply from Bas C. van Fraassen*. Chicago: University of Chicago Press.

Currie, Gregory, and Peter Eggenberger 1983 'Knowledge of Meaning'. *Nous* 17: 267–79.

Curthoys, J., and W. Suchting 1977 'Feyerabend's Discourse Against Method: A Marxist Critique'. *Inquiry* 20: 243–397.

Davidson, Donald 1980 *Essays on Actions and Events*. Oxford: Clarendon Press.

Davidson, Donald 1983 'A Coherence Theory of Truth and Knowledge'. In *Kant oder Hegel?*, ed. Dieter Henrich. Stuttgart: Klett-Cotta. Repr. in LePore 1986: 307–19. (Page references are to LePore.)

Davidson, Donald 1984 *Inquiries into Truth and Interpretation*. Oxford: Clarendon Press.

Davidson, Donald 1990 'The Structure and Content of Truth'. *Journal of Philosophy* 87: 279–328.

Davidson, Donald, and Gilbert Harman, eds 1972 *Semantics of Natural Language*. Dordrecht: D. Reidel.

Dennett, Daniel 1978 *Brainstorms*. Cambridge, MA: Bradford Books.

Devitt, Michael 1979 'Against Incommensurability'. *Australasian Journal of Philosophy* 57: 29–50.

Devitt, Michael 1980a Critical Notice of Putnam 1978. *Australasian Journal of Philosophy* 58: 395–404.

Devitt, Michael 1980b ' "Ostrich Nominalism" or "Mirage Realism"?' *Pacific Philosophical Quarterly* 61: 433–9.

Devitt, Michael 1981a *Designation*. New York: Columbia University Press.

Devitt, Michael 1981b 'Donnellan's Distinction'. In French, Uehling, and Wettstein 1981: 511–24.

Devitt, Michael 1982 Review of van Fraassen 1980. *Australasian Journal of Philosophy* 60: 367–9.

Devitt, Michael 1983a 'Dummett's Anti-Realism'. *Journal of Philosophy* 80: 73–99.

Devitt, Michael 1983b 'Realism and the Renegade Putnam: A Critical Study of Putnam 1978'. *Noûs* 17: 291–301.

Devitt, Michael 1983c 'Realism and Semantics: Part II of a Critical Study of French, Uehling, and Wettstein 1980'. *Noûs* 17: 669–81.

Devitt, Michael 1984a *Realism and Truth*. 1st edn. Oxford: Basil Blackwell.

Devitt, Michael 1984b Review of Putnam 1981. *Philosophical Review* 93: 274–7.

Devitt, Michael 1984c 'Thoughts and their Ascription'. In French, Uehling, and Wettstein 1984: 385–420.

Devitt, Michael 1986 Review of Passmore 1985. *Australasian Journal of Philosophy* 64: 511–14.

Devitt, Michael 1987 'Does Realism Explain Success?' *Revue internationale de philosophie: New Trends in Realism: An Australian Perspective* 41: 29–44.

Devitt, Michael 1988a 'Realism without Truth: A Response to Bertolet'. *Analysis* 48: 198–203.

Devitt, Michael 1988b 'Rorty's Mirrorless World'. In French, Uehling, and Wettstein 1988: 157–77.

Devitt, Michael 1989 'A Narrow Representational Theory of the Mind'. In *Rerepresentation: Readings in the Philosophy of Mental Representation*, ed. Stuart Silvers. Dordrecht: Kluwer Academic Publishers, 369–402. Repr. in Lycan 1990: 371–98.

Devitt, Michael 1990a 'Meanings just ain't in the Head'. In *Method, Reason and Language: Essays in Honour of Hilary Putnam*, ed. George Boolos. Cambridge: Cambridge University Press, 79–104.

Devitt, Michael 1990b 'On Removing Puzzles about Belief Ascription'. *Philosophical Studies* 71: 165–81.

Devitt, Michael 1990c 'Transcendentalism about Content'. *Pacific Philosophical Quarterly* 71: 247–63.

Devitt, Michael 1991a 'Aberrations of the Realism Debate'. *Philosophical Studies* 61: 43–63.

Devitt, Michael 1991b 'Naturalistic Representation: A Review Article of Papineau 1987: *Reality and Representation*'. *British Journal for the Philosophy of Science* 42: in press.

Devitt, Michael 1991c 'Realism without Representation: A Response to Appiah'. *Philosophical Studies* 61: 75–7.

Devitt, Michael, 1991d 'Why Fodor can't have it Both Ways'. In *Meaning in Mind: Fodor and his Critics*, ed. Barry Loewer and Georges Rey. Oxford: Basil Blackwell, 95–118.

Devitt, Michael, and Georges Rey 1991 'Transcending Transcendentalism: A Response to Boghossian'. *Pacific Philosophical Quarterly* 72: in press.

Devitt, Michael, and Kim Sterelny 1987 *Language and Reality: An Introduction to the Philosophy of Language*. Oxford: Basil Blackwell.

Devitt, Michael, and Kim Sterelny 1989 'Linguistics: What's Wrong with "the Right View"'. In *Philosophical Perspectives, 3: Philosophy of Mind and Action Theory*, ed. James E. Tomberlin. Atascadero: Ridgeview Publishing Company, 497–531.

Donnellan, Keith S. 1966 'Reference and Definite Descriptions'. *Philosophical Review* 75: 281–304.

Donnellan, Keith S. 1972 'Proper Names and Identifying Descriptions'. In Davidson and Harman 1972: 356–79.

Dretske, Fred 1981 *Knowledge and the Flow of Information*. Cambridge, MA: MIT Press.

Dummett, Michael 1973 *Frege: Philosophy of Language*. London: Duckworth.

Dummett, Michael 1975 'What Is a Theory of Meaning?' In Guttenplan 1975: 97–138.

Dummett, Michael 1976 'What Is a Theory of Meaning? (II)' In *Truth and Meaning: Essays in Semantics*, ed. Gareth Evans and John McDowell. Oxford: Clarendon Press, 67–137.

Dummett, Michael 1977 *Elements of Intuitionism*. Oxford: Oxford University Press.

Dummett, Michael 1978 *Truth and Other Enigmas*. Cambridge, MA: Harvard University Press.

Dummett, Michael 1979a 'Comments'. In Margalit 1979: 218–25.

Dummett, Michael 1979b 'Common Sense and Physics'. In *Perception and Identity*, ed. G. F. MacDonald. Ithaca, NY: Cornell University Press, 1–40.

Dummett, Michael 1981 *The Interpretation of Frege's Philosophy*. Cambridge, MA: Harvard University Press.

Dummett, Michael 1982 'Realism'. *Synthese* 52: 55–112.

Edwards, Paul, ed. 1967 *The Encylopedia of Philosophy*. New York: Macmillan.

Elder, Crawford L. 1986 'Why the Attacks on the Way the World Is Entail There Is a Way the World Is'. *Philosophia* 16: 191–202.

Ellis, Brian 1979 *Rational Belief Systems*. Oxford: Basil Blackwell.

Ellis, Brian 1985 'What Science Aims to Do'. In Churchland and Hooker 1985: 48–74.

Fales, Evan 1988 'How to be a Metaphysical Realist'. In French, Uehling, and Wettstein 1988: 253–74.

Feigl, H., and G. Maxwell, eds 1962 *Minnesota Studies in the Philosophy of Science, Volume III: Scientific Explanation, Space, and Time*. Minneapolis: University of Minnesota.

Feigl, H., and W. Sellars, eds 1949 *Readings in Philosophical Analysis*. New York: Appleton-Century-Crofts.

Feyerabend, Paul 1962 'Explanation, Reduction and Empiricism'. In Feigl and Maxwell 1962: 28–97.

Feyerabend, Paul 1964 'Realism and Instrumentalism'. In Bunge 1964: 280–308.

Feyerabend, Paul 1965a 'On the "Meaning" of Scientific Terms'. *Journal of Philosophy* 62: 266–74.

Feyerabend, Paul 1965b 'Reply to Criticism'. In *Boston Studies in the Philosophy of Science*, vol. 2, ed. R. S. Cohen and M. Wartofsky. New York: Humanities Press, 223–57.

Feyerabend, Paul 1969 'Problems of Empiricism, Part II'. In *The Nature and Function of Scientific Theory*, ed. R. G. Colodny. Pittsburgh: University of Pittsburgh Press, 275–353.

Feyerabend, Paul 1970a 'Against Method: Outline of an Anarchistic Theory of Knowledge'. In *Minnesota Studies in the Philosophy of Science, Volume IV: Analyses of Theories and Methods of Physics and Psychology*, ed. Michael Radner and Stephen Winokur. Minneapolis: University of Minnesota Press, 17–130.

Feyerabend, Paul 1970b 'Consolations for the Specialist'. In Lakatos and Musgrave 1970: 197–230.

Feyerabend, Paul 1975 *Against Method*. London: New Left Books.

Feyerabend, Paul 1978 *Science in a Free Society*. London: New Left Books.

Field, Hartry 1972 'Tarski's Theory of Truth'. In Platts 1980: 83–110. First publ. in *Journal of Philosophy* 69: 347–75.

Field, Hartry 1973 'Theory Change and the Indeterminacy of Reference'. *Journal of Philosophy* 70: 462–81.

Field, Hartry 1974 'Quine and the Correspondence Theory'. *Philosophical Review* 83: 200–28.

Field, Hartry 1975 'Conventionalism and Instrumentalism in Semantics'. *Noûs* 9: 375–405.

Field, Hartry 1977 'Logic, Meaning, and Conceptual Role'. *Journal of Philosophy* 74: 379–409.

Field, Hartry 1978 'Mental Representation'. In Block 1981: 78–114. First publ. in *Erkenntnis* 13: 9–61.

Field, Hartry 1980 *Science without Numbers: A Defence of Nominalism*. Princeton: Princeton University Press

Field, Hartry 1982 'Realism and Relativism'. *Journal of Philosophy* 79: 553–67.

Field, Hartry 1986 'The Deflationary Conception of Truth.' In *Fact, Science, and Morality: Essays on A. J. Ayer's* Language, Truth, and Logic, ed. Graham MacDonald and Crispin Wright. Oxford: Basil Blackwell, 55–117.

Field, Hartry 1989 *Realism, Mathematics and Modality*. Oxford: Basil Blackwell.

Fine, Arthur 1975 'How to Compare Theories: Reference and Change'. *Noûs* 9: 17–32.

Fine, Arthur 1986a *The Shaky Game: Einstein, Realism, and the Quantum Theory*. Chicago: University of Chicago Press.

Fine, Arthur 1986b 'Unnatural Attitudes: Realist and Instrumentalist Attachments to Science'. *Mind* 95: 149–77.

Fish, Stanley 1980 *Is there a Text in this Class?* Cambridge, MA: Harvard University Press.

Flax, Jane 1987 'Postmodernism and Gender Relations in Feminist Theory'. *Signs* 12: 621–43. Repr. in *Feminist Theory in Practice and Process*, ed. M. Nelson, G. O'Barr, S. Westfall-Wihl, and M. Weir. Chicago: University of Chicago Press, 1989.

Fodor, Jerry A. 1975 *The Language of Thought*. New York: Thomas Y. Crowell.

Fodor, Jerry A. 1980a 'Methodological Solipsism Considered as a Research Strategy in Cognitive Psychology'. *Behavioral and Brain Sciences* 3: 63–73. Repr. in Fodor 1981: 225–53.

Fodor, Jerry A. 1980b 'Methodological Solipsism: Replies to Commentators'. *Behavioral and Brain Sciences* 3: 99–109.

Fodor, Jerry A. 1981 *Representations: Philosophical Essays on the Foundations of Cognitive Science*. Cambridge MA: MIT Press.

French, Peter A., Theodore E. Uehling, Jr., and Howard K. Wettstein, eds 1979a *Contemporary Perspectives in the Philosophy of Language*. Minneapolis: University of Minnesota Press. Rev. enl. edn of *Midwest Studies in Philosophy, Volume II: Studies in Philosophy of Language*, 1977.

French, Peter A., Theodore E. Uehling, Jr., and Howard K. Wettstein, eds 1979b *Midwest Studies in Philosophy, Volume IV: Studies in Metaphysics*. Minneapolis: University of Minnesota Press.

French Peter A., Theodore E. Uehling, Jr., and Howard K. Wettstein, eds 1980 *Midwest Studies in Philosophy, Volume V: Studies in Epistemology*. Minneapolis: University of Minnesota Press.

French Peter A., Theodore E. Uehling, Jr., and Howard K. Wettstein, eds 1981 *Midwest Studies in Philosophy, Volume VI: The Foundations of Analytic Philosophy*. Minneapolis: University of Minnesota Press.

French Peter A., Theodore E. Uehling, Jr., and Howard K. Wettstein, eds 1984 *Midwest Studies in Philosophy, Volume IX: Causation and Causal*

Theories. Minneapolis: University of Minnesota Press.

French Peter A., Theodore E. Uehling, Jr., and Howard K. Wettstein, eds 1988 *Midwest Studies in Philosophy, Volume XII: Realism and Antirealism*. Minneapolis: University of Minnesota Press.

Friedman, Michael 1975 'Physicalism and the Indeterminacy of Translation'. *Nous* 9: 353–74.

Gardner, Michael R. 1979 'Realism and Instrumentalism in 19th-Century Atomism'. *Philosophy of Science* 46: 1–34.

Gasper, Philip 1986 Review of Devitt 1984a. *Philosophical Review* 95: 446–51.

Genova, A. C. 1988 'Ambiguities about Realism and Utterly Distinct Objects'. *Erkenntnis* 28: 87–95.

George, Alexander 1984 'On Devitt on Dummett'. *Journal of Philosophy* 83: 516–27.

Glymour, Clark 1984 'Explanation and Realism'. In Leplin 1984b: 173–92. Repr. in Churchland and Hooker 1985: 99–117.

Goldman, Alan H. 1979 'Realism'. *Southern Journal of Philosophy* 17: 175–92.

Goldman, Alvin 1978 'Epistemics: The Regulative Theory of Cognition'. *Journal of Philosophy* 75: 509–23. Repr. in Kornblith 1985b: 217–30.

Goodman, Nelson 1978. *Ways of Worldmaking*. Indianapolis: Hackett Publishing Company.

Goodman, Nelson 1979 'Predicates without Properties'. In French, Uehling, and Wettstein 1979a: 347–8. Repr. in Goodman 1984: 48–53.

Goodman, Nelson 1980 'On Starmaking'. *Synthese* 45: 211–15. Repr. in Goodman 1984: 39–44.

Goodman, Nelson 1984 *Of Mind and Other Matters*. Cambridge, MA: Harvard University Press.

Grover, Dorothy L. 1990 'On Two Deflationary Truth Theories'. In *Truth and Consequences*, ed. Michael Dunn and Anil Gupta. Dordrecht: Kluwer Academic Publishers, 1–17.

Grover, Dorothy L., Joseph L. Camp, Jr., and Nuel D. Belnap, Jr. 1975 'A Prosentential Theory of Truth'. *Philosophical Studies* 27: 73–125.

Guttenplan, Samuel, ed. 1975 *Mind and Language*. Oxford: Clarendon Press.

Gutting, Gary 1985 'Scientific Realism versus Constructive Empiricism: A Dialogue. In Churchland and Hooker 1985: 118–31.

Haack, Susan 1987 ' "Realism" '. *Synthese* 73: 275–99.

Hacking, Ian 1981 'Do We See through a Microscope?' *Pacific Philosophical Quarterly* 62: 305–22. Repr. in Churchland and Hooker 1985: 132–52.

Hacking, Ian 1983 *Representing and Intervening: Introductory Topics in the Philosophy of Natural Science*. Cambridge: Cambridge University Press.

Hacking, Ian 1984 'Experimentation and Scientific Realism'. In Leplin 1984b: 173–92.

Hardin, C. L. 1988 *Color for Philosophers: Unweaving the Rainbow*. Indianapolis: Hackett Publishing Company.

Harman, Gilbert 1965 'Inference to the Best Explanation'. *Philosophical Review* 74: 88–95.

Harman, Gilbert 1973 *Thought*. Princeton: Princeton University Press.

Harman, Gilbert 1974 'Meaning and Semantics'. In *Semantics and Philosophy*, ed. M. K. Munitz and P. K. Unger. New York: New York University Press, 1–16.

Harman, Gilbert 1975 'Language, Thought, and Communication'. In *Minnesota Studies in the Philosophy of Science, Volume VII: Language, Mind, and Knowledge*, ed. Keith Gunderson. Minneapolis: University of Minnesota Press, 270–98.

Harris, John M. 1974 'Popper's Definitions of "verisimilitude"'. *British Journal for the Philosophy of Science* 25: 160–6.

Hauptli, Bruce W. 1979 'Inscrutability and Correspondence'. *Southern Journal of Philosophy* 17: 199–212.

Hawkes, Terence 1977 *Structuralism and Semiotics*. London: Methuen.

Heidelberger, Herbert 1980 'Understanding and Truth Conditions'. In French, Uehling, and Wettstein 1980: 401–10.

Heil, John 1989 'Recent Work in Realism and Anti-Realism'. *Philosophical Books* 30: 65–73.

Heller, Mark 1988 'Putnam, Reference, and Realism'. In French, Uehling, and Wettstein 1988: 113–27.

Hempel, Carl G. 1954 'A Logical Appraisal of Operationism'. In Brody 1970b: 200–10. First publ. in *Scientific Monthly* 79 (1954): 215–20.

Hesse, Mary 1967 'Laws and Theories'. In Edwards 1967, vol. 4, 404–10.

Hirst, R. J. 1967 'Realism'. In Edwards 1967, vol. 7, 77–83.

Hollis, Martin, and Steven Lukes, eds 1982 *Rationality and Relativism*. Oxford: Basil Blackwell.

Hooker, Clifford A. 1974 'Systematic Realism'. *Synthése* 51: 409–97.

Hooker, Clifford A. 1985 'Surface Dazzle, Ghostly Depths: An Exposition and Critical Evaluation of van Fraassen's Vindication of Empiricism against Realism'. In Churchland and Hooker 1985: 153–96.

Horwich, Paul 1982 'Three Forms of Realism'. *Synthese* 51: 181–202.

Horwich, Paul 1990 *Truth*. Oxford: Basil Blackwell.

Jackson, Frank 1980 'Ontological Commitment and Paraphrase'. *Philosophy* 55: 303–15.

Jackson, Frank 1985 'Review of Devitt 1984a'. *Australasian Journal of Philosophy* 63: 535–8.

Jameson, Frederic 1972 *The Prison–House of Language*. Princeton, NJ: Princeton University Press.

Jardine, N. 1986 *The Fortunes of Inquiry*. Oxford: Clarendon Press.

Jennings, Richard 1989 'Scientific Quasi-Realism'. *Mind* 98: 223–45.

Johnston, Mark 1987a 'Human Beings'. *Journal of Philosophy* 84: 59–83.

Johnston, Mark 1987b 'Is there a Problem about Persistence?' *Proceedings of the Aristotelian Society*, supp. vol. 61: 105–35.

Johnston, Mark 1989 'Dispositional Theories of Value'. *Proceedings of the Aristotelian Society*, supp. vol. 63: 139–74.

Kahneman, D., and A. Tversky 1973 'On the Psychology of Predictions'. *Psychological Review* 80: 237–51.

Kim, Jaegwon 1980 'Rorty on the Possibility of Philosophy'. *Journal of Philosophy* 77: 588–97.

Kirkham, Richard L. 1989 'What Dummett Says about Truth and Linguistic Competence'. *Mind* 98: 207–24.

Kitcher, Patricia 1984 'In Defense of Intentional Psychology'. *Journal of Philosophy* 81: 89–106.

Kitcher, Patricia 1985 'Narrow Taxonomy and Wide Functionalism'. *Philosophy of Science* 52: 78–97.

Kornblith, Hilary 1980 'Beyond Foundationalism and the Coherence Theory'. *Journal of Philosophy* 77: 597–612. Repr. in Kornblith 1985b: 115–28.

Kornblith, Hilary, 1985a 'Introduction: What is Naturalistic Epistemology?' In Kornblith 1985b: 1–13.

Kornblith, Hilary, ed. 1985b *Naturalizing Epistemology*. Cambridge, MA: MIT Press.

Kripke, Saul A. 1972 'Naming and Necessity'. In Davidson and Harman 1972: 253–355, 763–9. A corrected version, together with a new preface, appeared as *Naming and Necessity*. Cambridge, MA: Harvard University Press, 1980.

Kroon, Frederick 1988 'Realism and Descriptivism'. In Nola 1988: 141–67.

Kuhn, Thomas S. 1962 *The Structure of Scientific Revolutions*. Chicago: Chicago University Press. 2nd edn 1970.

Kuhn, Thomas S. 1970a 'Logic of Discovery or Psychology of Research'. In Lakatos and Musgrave 1970: 1–23.

Kuhn, Thomas S. 1970b 'Reflections on My Critics'. In Lakatos and Musgrave 1970: 231–78.

Kuhn, Thomas S. 1977 'Theory Change as Structure-Change: Comments on the Sneed Formalism'. In *Historical and Philosophical Dimensions of Logic, Methodology and Philosophy of Science*, ed. R. E. Butts and J. Hintikka. Dordrecht: D. Reidel, 289–309.

Lakatos, Imre 1974 'Popper on Demarcation and Induction'. In *The Philosophy of Karl Popper*, ed. P. A. Schilpp. La Salle, IL: Open Court, 241–73.

Lakatos, Imre, and Alan Musgrave, eds 1970 *Criticism and the Growth of Knowledge*. Cambridge: Cambridge University Press.

Latour, Bruno, and Steve Woolgar 1986 *Laboratory Life: The Construction of Scientific Facts*, 2nd edn. Princeton: Princeton University Press. 1st edn 1979.

Laudan, Larry 1981 'A Confutation of Convergent Realism'. *Philosophy of Science* 48: 19–49. Repr. in Leplin 1984b: 218–49.

Leeds, Stephen 1973 'How to Think about Reference'. *Journal of Philosophy* 70: 485–503.

Leeds, Stephen 1978 'Theories of Reference and Truth'. *Erkenntnis* 13: 111–29.

Lenin, V. I. 1927 *Materialism and Empirio-Criticism: Critical Comments on a Reactionary Philosophy*. New York: International Publishers.

Leplin, Jarrett 1984a Introduction to Leplin 1984b: 1–7.
Leplin, Jarrett, ed. 1984b *Scientific Realism*. Berkeley: University of California Press.
LePore, Ernest, ed. 1986 *Truth and Interpretation: Perspectives on the Philosophy of Donald Davidson*. Oxford: Basil Blackwell.
LePore, Ernest, and Barry Loewer 1988 'A Putnam's Progress'. In French, Uehling, and Wettstein 1988: 459–73.
Levin, Janet 1988 'Must Reasons be Rational?' *Philosophy of Science* 55: 199–217.
Levin, Michael 1984 'What Kind of Explanation is Truth?' In Leplin 1984b: 124–39.
Lewis, David K. 1984 'Putnam's Paradox'. *Australasian Journal of Philosophy* 62: 221–36.
Loar, Brian 1980 'Ramsey's Theory of Belief and Truth'. In *Prospects for Pragmatism*, ed. D. H. Mellor. Cambridge: Cambridge University Press, 49–70.
Losonsky, Michael 1985 'Reference and Rorty's Veil'. *Philosophical Studies* 47: 291–4.
Luntley, Michael 1988 *Language, Logic and Experience: The Case for Anti-Realism*. La Salle, IL: Open Court.
Luntley, Michael 1991 'Aberrations of a Sledgehammer: Reply to Devitt'. *Philosophical Studies*: in press.
Lycan, William G. 1981a 'Form, Function, and Feel'. *Journal of Philosophy* 78: 24–50.
Lycan, William G. 1981b 'Psychological Laws'. *Philosophical Topics* 12: 9–38.
Lycan, William G. 1981c 'Toward a Homuncular Theory of Believing'. *Cognition and Brain Theory* 4: 139–59.
Lycan, William G. 1984 *Logical Form in Natural Language*. Cambridge, MA: MIT Press.
Lycan, William G. 1988 *Judgement and Justification*. Cambridge: Cambridge University Press.
Lycan, William G., ed. 1990 *Mind and Cognition: A Reader*. Oxford: Basil Blackwell.
MacDonald, G. F., and P. Pettit 1981 *Semantics and Social Science*. London: Routledge & Kegan Paul.
McDowell, John 1978 'Physicalism and Primitive Denotation: Field on Tarski'. In Platts 1980: 111–30. First publ. in *Erkenntnis* 13: 131–52.
McGinn, Colin 1980 'Truth and Use'. In Platts 1980: 19–40.
McMichael, Alan 1988 'Creative Ontology and Absolute Truth'. In French, Uehling, and Wettstein 1988: 51–74.
McMullin, Ernan 1984 'A Case for Scientific Realism'. In Leplin 1984b: 8–40.
Margalit. A., ed. 1979 *Meaning and Use*. Dordrecht: D. Reidel.
Marinov, Marin 1988 'Inference to the Best Explanation: van Fraassen and the Case of the "fifth force" '. *International Studies in the Philosophy of Science* 3: 35–50.

Markman, Ellen M. 1989 *Categorization and Naming in Children: Problems of Induction*. Cambridge, MA: MIT Press.

Martin, C. B. 1984a 'Anti-Realism and World's Undoing'. *Pacific Philosophical Quarterly* 65: 1–18.

Martin, C. B. 1984b 'The New Cartesianism'. *Pacific Philosophical Quarterly* 65: 236–58.

Martin, Michael 1971 'Referential Variance and Scientific Objectivity'. *British Journal for the Philosophy of Science* 22: 17–26.

Matheson, Carl 1989 'Is the Naturalist Really Naturally a Realist?' *Mind* 98: 247–58.

Maxwell, Grover 1962 'The Ontological Status of Theoretical Entities'. In Feigl and Maxwell 1962: 3–27.

Millar, Alan 1977 'Truth and Understanding'. *Mind* 86: 405–16.

Miller, David 1974a 'On the Comparison of False Theories by their Bases'. *British Journal for the Philosophy of Science* 25: 178–88.

Miller, David 1974b 'Popper's Qualitative Theory of Verisimilitude'. *British Journal for the Philosophy of Science* 25: 166–77.

Millikan, R. G. 1984 *Language, Thought and Other Biological Categories: New Foundations for Realism*. Cambridge, MA: MIT Press.

Moore, G. E. 1922 *Philosophical Studies*. London: Routledge & Kegan Paul.

Murphy, Chris 1981 Critical Notice of Rorty 1979. *Australasian Journal of Philosophy* 59: 338–45.

Musgrave, Alan 1985 'Realism versus Constructive Empiricism'. In Churchland and Hooker 1985: 197–221.

Musgrave, Alan 1988 'The Ultimate Argument for Scientific Realism'. In Nola 1988: 229–52.

Nagel, Ernest 1961 *The Structure of Science: Problems in the Logic of Scientific Explanation*. London: Routledge & Kegan Paul.

Newton-Smith, W. H. 1978 'The Underdetermination of Theory by Data'. *Proceedings of the Aristotelian Society*, supp. vol. 52: 71–91.

Niiniluoto, Iikka 1978 'Truthlikeness: Comments on Recent Discussions'. *Synthese* 38: 281–329.

Nola, Robert, ed. 1988 *Relativism and Realism in Science*. Dordrecht: Kluwer Academic Publishers.

Oddie, G. 1986. *Likeness to Truth*. Dordrecht: D. Reidel.

Papineau, David 1979 *Theory and Meaning*. Oxford: Clarendon Press.

Papineau, David 1984 'Representation and Explanation'. *Philosophy of Science* 51: 55–73.

Papineau, David 1987 *Reality and Representation*. Oxford: Basil Blackwell.

Passmore, John 1966 *A Hundred Years of Philosophy*, 2nd edn. London: Penguin Books. 1st edn 1957.

Passmore, John 1985 *Recent Philosophers: A Supplement to a Hundred Years of Philosophy*. London: Duckworth.

Pettit, Philip 1990 'The Reality of Rule-Following'. *Mind* 99: 1–21.

Pettit, Philip 1991 'Realism and Response-Dependence'. *Mind* 100: in press.

Platts, Mark 1979 *Ways of Meaning: An Introduction to a Philosophy of Language*. London: Routledge & Kegan Paul.

Platts, Mark, ed. 1980 *Reference, Truth and Reality: Essays on the Philosophy of Language*. London: Routledge & Kegan Paul.

Popper, Karl R. 1963 *Conjectures and Refutations: The Growth of Scientific Knowledge*. London: Routledge & Kegan Paul.

Popper, Karl R. 1972 *Objective Knowledge*. London: Routledge & Kegan Paul.

Prawitz, Dag 1977 'Meaning and Proofs: On the Conflict between Classical and Intuitionistic Logic'. *Theoria* 43: 2–40.

Putnam, Hilary 1971 *Philosophy of Logic*. New York: Harper & Row.

Putnam, Hilary 1975a *Mathematics, Matter and Method: Philosophical Papers, vol. 1*. Cambridge: Cambridge University Press.

Putnam, Hilary 1975b *Mind, Language and Reality: Philosophical Papers, vol. 2*. Cambridge: Cambridge University Press.

Putnam, Hilary 1978 *Meaning and the Moral Sciences*. London: Routledge & Kegan Paul.

Putnam, Hilary 1981 *Reason, Truth and History*. Cambridge: Cambridge University Press.

Putnam, Hilary 1982 'Three Kinds of Scientific Realism'. *Philosophical Quarterly* 32: 195–200.

Putnam, Hilary 1983 *Realism and Reason: Philosophical Papers, vol. 3*. Cambridge: Cambridge University Press.

Putnam, Hilary 1985 'A Comparison of Something with Something Else'. *New Literary History* 17: 61–79.

Putnam, Hilary 1987 *The Many Faces of Realism*. LaSalle, IL: Open Court.

Quine, W. V. 1953 *From a Logical Point of View*. 1st edn Cambridge, MA: Harvard University Press. 2nd edn rev. 1961.

Quine, W. V. 1960 *Word and Object*. Cambridge, MA: MIT Press.

Quine, W. V. 1966 *The Ways of Paradox and Other Essays*. New York: Random House.

Quine, W. V. 1969 *Ontological Relativity and Other Essays*. New York: Columbia University Press.

Quine, W. V. 1970a 'On the Reasons for Indeterminacy of Translation'. *Journal of Philosophy* 67: 178–83.

Quine, W. V. 1970b *Philosophy of Logic*. Engelwood Cliffs, NJ: Prentice-Hall.

Quine, W. V. 1975 'The Nature of Natural Knowledge'. In Guttenplan 1975: 67–81.

Quine, W. V., and J. S. Ullian 1970 *The Web of Belief*. New York: Random House.

Ramsey, F. P. 1931 *The Foundations of Mathematics*. London: Routledge & Kegan Paul.

Rescher, Nicholas 1980 'Conceptual Schemes'. In French, Uehling, and Wettstein 1980: 323–45.

Rey, Georges 1991 'Sensational Sentences'. In *Consciousness*, ed. Martin Davies and Glyn Humphries. Oxford: Basil Blackwell.

Robinson, G. S. 1971 'Popper's Verisimilitude'. *Analysis* 31: 194–6.

Rorty, Richard 1976 'Realism and Reference'. *Monist* 59: 321–40.

Rorty, Richard 1979 *Philosophy and the Mirror of Nature*. Princeton: Princeton University Press.

Rorty, Richard 1982 *Consequences of Pragmatism (Essays: 1972–1980)*. Minneapolis: University of Minnesota Press.

Rorty, Richard 1986a 'Beyond Realism and Anti-Realism'. In *Weiner Riehe: Themen der Philosophie, Band I: Wo Steht die Sprachanalytische Philosophie Heute?*, ed. Herta Nagl-Docekal, Richard Heinrich, Ludwig Nagl, and Helmut Vetter. Vienna, 103–15.

Rorty, Richard 1986b 'Pragmatism, Davidson and Truth'. In LePore 1986: 333–55.

Rosenberg, Jay F. 1980 *One World and Our Knowledge of It*. Dordrecht: D. Reidel.

Ruben, David-Hillel 1977 *Marxism and Materialism: A Study in Marxist Theory of Knowledge*. 1st edn, Brighton: Harvester Press. 2nd rev. edn, 1979.

Russell, Bertrand 1912 *The Problems of Philosophy*. Repr. London: Oxford Paperbacks, 1967.

Russell, Bertrand 1948 *Human Knowledge: Its Scope and Limits*. London: George Allen & Unwin.

Salinas, Roberto 1988 'Realism and Conceptual Schemes'. *The Southern Journal of Philosophy* 28: 101–23.

Scheffler, I. 1967 *Science and Subjectivity*. Indianapolis: Bobbs–Merrill.

Scheffler, I. 1980 'The Wonderful Worlds of Goodman'. *Synthese* 45: 201–9.

Schiffer, Stephen 1981 'Truth and the Theory of Content'. In *Meaning and Understanding*, ed. Herman Parret and Jacques Bouveresse. Berlin: Walter de Gruyter, 204–22.

Schlick, Moritz 1932–3 'Positivism and Realism'. *Erkenntnis* 3: Repr. in Ayer 1959: 82–107.

Searle, John R. 1983 *Intentionality: An Essay in the Philosophy of Mind*. Cambridge: Cambridge University Press.

Searle, John R. 1990 'The Storm over the University'. *New York Review of Books* 37, no. 19, 34–42.

Sellars, W. 1963 *Science, Perception and Reality*. New York: Humanities Press.

Sklar, Lawrence 1981 'Do Unborn Hypotheses have Rights?' *Pacific Philosophical Quarterly* 62: 17–29.

Smart, J. J. C. 1963 *Philosophy and Scientific Realism*. London: Routledge & Kegan Paul.

Smart, J. J. C. 1968 *Between Science and Philosophy: An Introduction to the Philosophy of Science*. New York: Random House.

Soames, Scott. 1984. 'What Is a Theory of Truth?' *Journal of Philosophy* 81: 411–29.

Stampe, Dennis W. 1979 'Toward a Causal Theory of Linguistic Representation'. In French, Uehling, and Wettstein 1979: 81–102.

Stich, Stephen P. 1978 'Autonomous Psychology and the Belief–Desire Thesis'. *Monist* 61: 573–91. Repr. in Lycan 1990: 345–61.

Stich, Stephen P. 1983 *From Folk Psychology to Cognitive Science: The Case against Belief*. Cambridge, MA: MIT Press.

Stove, D. C. 1982 *Popper and After: Four Modern Irrationalists*. Oxford: Pergamon Press.

Stove, D. C. 1991 *The Plato Cult and Other Philosophical Follies*. Oxford: Basil Blackwell.

Strawson, P. F. 1976–7 'Scruton and Wright on Anti-Realism etc.'. *Proceedings of the Aristotelian Society*, New Series, 77: 15–22.

Stroud, Barry 1968 'Conventionalism and the Indeterminacy of Translation'. *Synthèse* 19: 82–96.

Suppe, Frederick 1977 Introduction. In *The Structure of Scientific Theories*, ed. Frederick Suppe. 2nd edn. Urbana: University of Illinois, 3–241.

Swinburne, R. 1971 'Popper's Account of Acceptability'. *Australasian Journal of Philosophy* 49: 167–76.

Tarski, Alfred 1949 'The Semantic Conception of Truth and the Foundations of Semantics'. In Feigl and Sellars 1949: 52–84.

Tarski, Alfred 1956 *Logic, Semantics, Metamathematics*. Trans. J. H. Woodger. Oxford: Oxford University Press.

Taylor, Barry 1987 'The Truth in Realism'. *Revue internationale de philosophie: New Trends in Realism: An Australian Perspective* 41: 45–63.

Tichy, Pavel 1974 'On Popper's Definitions of Verisimilitude'. *British Journal for the Philosophy of Science* 25: 155–60.

Tomberlin, James T., ed. 1987 *Philosophical Perspectives, 1: Metaphysics, 1987*. Atascadero: Ridgeview Publishing Company.

Trigg, Roger 1980 *Reality at Risk: A Defence of Realism in Philosophy and the Sciences*. Brighton: Harvester Press.

Van Fraassen, Bas C. 1980 *The Scientific Image*. Oxford; Clarendon Press.

Van Fraassen, Bas C. 1984 'Belief and the Will'. *Journal of Philosophy* 81: 235–56.

Van Fraassen, Bas C. 1985 'Empiricism in the Philosophy of Science'. In Churchland and Hooker 1985: 245–308.

Van Fraassen, Bas C. 1989 *Laws and Symmetry*. Oxford: Clarendon Press.

Wallace, John 1979 'Only in the Context of a Sentence do Words have Meaning'. In French, Uehling, and Wettstein 1979a: 305–25.

Whorf, Benjamin Lee 1956 *Language, Thought, and Reality*, ed. and introduced by John B. Carroll. Cambridge, MA: MIT Press.

Williams, D. C. 1966 *Principles of Empirical Realism: Philosophical Essays*. Editorial assistance by Harry Ruja. Springfield. IL: Charles C. Thomas.

Williams, Michael 1986 'Do We (Epistemologists) Need a Theory of Truth?' *Philosophical Topics* 14: 223–42.

Wilson, Mark 1981 'The Double Standard in Ontology'. *Philosophical Studies* 39: 409–27.

Wittgenstein, Ludwig 1953 *Philosophical Investigations*. Trans. G. E. M. Anscombe. Oxford: Basil Blackwell.

Wolterstorff, Nicholas 1987 'Are Concept-Users World-Makers?' In

Tomberlin 1987: 233–67.

Wright, Crispin 1976 'Truth Conditions and Criteria'. *Proceedings of the Aristotelian Society*, supp. vol. 50: 217–45.

Wright, Crispin 1979 'Strawson on Anti-Realism'. *Synthese* 40: 283–99.

Wright, Crispin 1981 'Critical Study: Dummett and Revisionism'. *Philosophical Quarterly* 31: 47–67.

Wright, Crispin 1983 *Frege's Conception of Numbers as Objects*. Aberdeen: Aberdeen University Press.

Wright, Crispin 1986 *Realism, Meaning and Truth*. Oxford: Basil Blackwell.

Wright, Crispin 1988 'Realism, Antirealism, Irrealism, Quasi-Realism'. In French, Uehling, and Wettstein 1988: 25–49.

Index

abduction, ix, 9, 44–7, 68, 74, 77, 80, 85, 108–13, 124, 132 n., 139–49, 153, 173, 261, 267, 284–5, 296–301
abstract entities, 13, 19, 20–2, 54, 58, 227, 257 n., 264–6
aim of science, 19, 124, 137–8, 153 n., 173, 176–8
Alston, William, P., xii
Althusser, Louis, xi, 155, 156, 167–8, 178
Anscombe, G. E. M., 66
anti-realism *see* realism
Appiah, Anthony, viii, 8, 59 n.
Aristotle, 27, 37 n.
Armstrong, D. M., x, xii, 15, 22, 71, 250
artifacts and tools, ix, 8, 17, 246–9, 251–2, 256, 257 n., 266, 299–300
Aune, Bruce, 202
Ayer, A. J., 68–70

Baker, Lynne Rudder, 85, 106 n.
Balibar, Etienne, 155, 156, 167–8, 178
Barnes, Barry, 256 n.
behaviourism, xi, 89–90, 140, 187, 190, 277, 285, 300
beliefs and desires, 16, 76–7, 84–107, 186–99
Belnap, Nuel D. Jr., 30, 83
Berkeley, George, 15, 50, 67, 70–2,

218 n., 250, 287 n.
Bertolet, Rod, vii, 109, 111, 132 n.
Bhaskar, Roy, 167, 177–8
Bigelow, John, xii, 106 n., 260
bivalence, 22, 287 n.
Blackburn, Simon, ix, 55–7, 59 n., 124, 287 n.
Blackburn, Thomas, 233 n.
Bloor, David, 256 n.
Boër, S., 289 n.
Boghossian, Paul, 106 n.
Boyd, Richard N., 58 n., 116, 117, 120, 132 n., 153 n.
Brandom, Robert, 30, 34, 38 n., 205
brain in vat, 63, 64, 74–5, 100, 118, 198
Brody, Baruch A., 129
Brown, Curtis, 233 n., 245
Burge, Tyler, 95
Byrne, Alex, 256 n., 258 n.

Camp, Joseph L. Jr., 30, 83
Campbell, Keith, xii, 25 n., 153 n., 258 n.
Carey, James W., 256 n.
Carnap, Rudolf, 179 n.
Cartwright, Nancy, 111–13, 154 n.
certainty *see* epistemology, sceptical and foundationalist
Chalmers, A. F., 158, 161, 167, 177
charity and rationality, principles of, 7, 181, 190–9, 201, 206, 208, 211–12, 224, 231

147, 213, 218 n., 232
Fish, Stanley, 256 n., 257 n.
Flax, Jane, 256 n.
Fodor, Jerry A., 88, 92, 107 n.
folk theory, 16, 26, 43, 52–3, 64, 73,
    76–7, 87, 166, 169, 215, 247,
    279–80
Forrest, Peter, xii
Foucault, Michel, 220
foundationalism *see* epistemology,
    sceptical and foundationalist
Franklin, Christine Ladd, 64
Franklin, Jim, 37
Frege, Gottlob, 270, 286 n.
Friedman, Michael, 105 n.
functionalism, 88–97, 106 n., 183–5,
    223, 250, 252, 257 n., 277–8,
    290 n.

Gardner, Michael R., 132
Gasper, Philip, 106 n.
Gemes, Kenneth, 59 n., 107 n.
Gendler, Tamar, 256 n.
Genova, A. C., 14
George, Alexander, 58 n., 280, 287 n.
Glymour, Clark, 153 n.
Godfrey-Smith, Peter, 258 n.
God's Eye View, 8, 178, 213, 220,
    231–4, 300
Goldman, Alan H., xii, 21, 126
Goldman, Alvin, 82 n.
Goodman, Nelson, ix, xii, 8, 15, 17,
    218 n., 235–6, 241–2, 246, 255,
    256 n., 299
Green, Karen, 107 n.
Grice, Paul, 287 n.
Grover, Dorothy L., 30, 38 n., 83
Gutting, Gary, 150

Haack, Susan, vii
Hacking, Ian, 111–13, 119, 146
Hardin, C. L., 251
Harman, Gilbert, xii, 44, 92, 187,
    272
Harris, John M., 125

Hauptli, Bruce W., 232
Hawkes, Terence, 240
Heidegger, Martin, 217
Heidelberger, Herbert, 269
Heil, John, vii
Heller, Mark, 233 n.
Hellman, Geoffrey, 258 n.
Hempel, Carl G., 129
Hesse, Mary, 40, 43, 129
Hirst, R. J., 13–15
Hooker, Clifford A., 39, 43, 153 n.
Horwich, Paul, xii, 30–1
Hume, David, 55, 71, 256 n., 287 n.

idealism, 13–17, 25, 44, 124, 138,
    205–7, 217, 238, 262–4; *see also*
    realism
ideas *see* sense data
identity theory, 89–90, 183
illusion, argument from, 65–6, 80
imposition theory of reality *see*
    constructivism
incommensurability, xi, 7, 156, 158,
    166, 168–72, 179 n., 206,
    240–1, 299, 303
indeterminacy of translation, xi, 182,
    198, 221, 223–4
inference to the best explanation *see*
    abduction
instrumentalism, 6, 7, 18, 19, 23, 57,
    69, 106 n., 108, 124, 127–32,
    138, 158, 184–6, 198; *see also*
    realism, scientific
intentionality, 49, 84–9, 91, 94–5,
    98, 107 n., 216; *see also* reference;
    wide psychology
interpretation, 5, 7, 34–5, 50–3,
    181–3, 186–99, 212
intuitionism *see* realism, about
    abstract entities

Jackson, Frank, viii, 54, 59 n., 106 n.,
    258 n.
Jameson, Frederick, 238
Jardine, N., 132 n.
Jennings, Richard, 58 n.

Millikan, R. G., 29
mind, theory or philosophy of *see*
  behaviourism; beliefs and
  desires; dualism; functionalism;
  identity theory
Moore, G. E., 66, 83
Murphy, Chris, 218 n., 219 n.
Musgrave, Alan, 113, 150, 153 n.

Nagel, Ernest, 129
narrow psychology, 78, 89, 91–100,
  107 n.; *see also* wide psychology
naturalism, viii, 3–4, 7, 29, 73, 111,
  142, 203–6, 217–18, 232–3,
  285, 296, 300–1; *see also*
  epistemology, naturalized
Nerlich, Graham, x, 106 n.
Newton-Smith, 132 n.
Niiniluoto, Iikka, 125
nominalism *see* realism, about
  abstract entities
noumenal world *see* things-in-
  themselves

observation and observability, 6, 18,
  109–10, 129, 131, 139–54, 296
Oddie, G., 133 n.
ontological
  change, 19–20, 156, 158–66,
    168–72, 231, 303
  commitment, 5, 18–20, 42–4,
    50–8, 68–9, 109, 158
  elimination, 69, 121, 126–7,
    159–66, 170, 172, 298–9, 303
  see also realism
opaque and transparent contexts,
  66, 213–16, 271–2, 289–90 n.
operationism, 6, 18, 23, 108, 127–8;
  see also realism, scientific

Papineau, David, 29, 40, 43, 158,
  201 n., 256 n.
Pascal, Blaise, 148
Passmore, John, vii, 40, 207, 256 n.
Peirce, C. S., 37, 45, 58 n., 220

Petrie, Brad, 82 n.
Pettit, Philip, 191, 253, 257 n.
phenomenalism, 15, 68–71, 80, 128,
  262, 287 n.
physicalism, viii, xi, 5, 15, 16, 24–5,
  35, 41, 58, 81, 83–5, 89–93,
  104, 106 n., 182–99, 213, 221,
  223, 285, 287 n., 303
Platonism *see* realism, about abstract
  entities
Platts, Mark, 180, 184
Popper, Karl R., 25 n., 61, 131, 155,
  167, 172–3, 179 n.
positivism, 6, 13, 48, 69, 128–31,
  138, 141, 149–50, 153, 155, 259,
  277–8, 285, 286 n., 300
Prawitz, Dag, 275
Putnam, Hilary, vii–xi, 4, 6–8, 15,
  19, 29, 35, 37, 38 n., 42, 43, 49,
  59 n., 70, 73, 74, 78, 83, 90–5,
  97–100, 107 n., 113–17, 120,
  122, 126–7, 129, 142, 159, 161,
  163, 174, 178, 179 n., 201 n.,
  213, 220–34, 235–40, 245, 250,
  252–7, 288 n., 290 n., 297–300

quantum theory, 132, 141–2
quasi-realism, ix, 5, 29, 55–7, 59 n.,
  129
Quine, W. V., x, xi, 5, 30, 41, 44,
  59 n., 64, 66, 77, 82 n., 83–5,
  89, 101, 105 n., 118–21, 125–6,
  173, 181–2, 186–7, 198,
  214–15, 217, 223, 277–8,
  285–6, 301

Ramsey, F. P., 30, 38 n.
rationality, principle of *see* charity
  and rationality, principles of
realism, vii–xii, 3–9, 13–25, 27,
  84–5, 105, 155–9, 178 n.,
  230–4, 303
  about abstract entities, 13, 19,
    20–1, 22, 54, 58, 227, 257 n.,
    264–6

Wolterstorff, Nicholas, 229, 236–7
Woolgar, Steve, 240, 255, 256 n.
worldmaking *see* constructivism

Wright, Crispin, 56, 59 n., 259, 263,
    270, 275, 280–1, 286 n.,
    289–91 n.